Lecture Notes in Computer Sc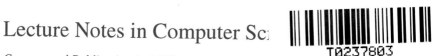

Commenced Publication in 1973
Founding and Former Series Editors:
Gerhard Goos, Juris Hartmanis, and Jan van Leeuwen

Michael Hanus (Ed.)

Practical Aspects of Declarative Languages

9th International Symposium, PADL 2007
Nice, France, January 14-15, 2007
Proceedings

 Springer

Volume Editor

Michael Hanus
Christian-Albrechts-Universität Kiel
Institut für Informatik
24098 Kiel, Germany
E-mail: mh@informatik.uni-kiel.de

Library of Congress Control Number: 2006939136

CR Subject Classification (1998): D.3, D.1, F.3, D.2

LNCS Sublibrary: SL 2 – Programming and Software Engineering

ISSN	0302-9743
ISBN-10	3-540-69608-3 Springer Berlin Heidelberg New York
ISBN-13	978-3-540-69608-7 Springer Berlin Heidelberg New York

Springer is a part of Springer Science+Business Media

springer.com

© Springer-Verlag Berlin Heidelberg 2007
Printed in Germany

Typesetting: Camera-ready by author, data conversion by Scientific Publishing Services, Chennai, India
Printed on acid-free paper   SPIN: 11968177   06/3142   5 4 3 2 1 0

Preface

This volume contains the papers presented at the Ninth International Symposium on Practical Aspects of Declarative Languages (PADL 2007) held on January 14–15, 2007 in Nice, France. Information about the conference can be found at http://www.informatik.uni-kiel.de/~mh/padl07. Following the tradition of previous events, PADL 2007 was co-located with the 34th Annual Symposium on Principles of Programming Languages (POPL 2007) that was held on January 17–19, 2007.

The PADL conference series is a forum for researchers and practioners to present original work emphasizing novel applications and implementation techniques for all forms of declarative concepts, including functional, logic, constraints, etc. Topics of interest include:

- Innovative applications of declarative languages
- Declarative domain-specific languages and applications
- Practical applications of theoretical results
- New language developments and their impact on applications
- Evaluation of implementation techniques on practical applications
- Novel implementation techniques relevant to applications
- Novel uses of declarative languages in the classroom
- Practical experiences

In response to the call for papers, 65 abstracts were initially received. Finally, 58 full papers were submitted. Each submission was reviewed by at least three Program Committee members. The committee decided to accept 19 papers. In addition, the program also included two invited talks by John Hughes (Chalmers University of Technology) and Pedro Barahona (Universidade Nova de Lisboa).

I would like to thank the Program Committee members who worked hard to produce high-quality reviews for the papers with a tight schedule, as well as all the external reviewers involved in the paper selection. I also would like to thank Gopal Gupta for his expert advice in many aspects of the conference and his publicity efforts. Many thanks also to the organizers of POPL 2007 for hosting PADL 2007 as an affiliated event and to Andrei Voronkov for his continuous help with the EasyChair system that automates many of the tasks involved in chairing a conference. Finally, I thank the University of Kiel, the University of Texas at Dallas, and Compulog Americas for supporting PADL 2007.

October 2006   Michael Hanus

Conference Organization

Program Chair

Michael Hanus
Institut für Informatik
Christian-Albrechts-Universität Kiel
24098 Kiel, Germany
E-mail: mh@informatik.uni-kiel.de

General Chair

Gopal Gupta
Department of Computer Science
University of Texas at Dallas
Dallas, Texas, USA
E-mail: gupta@utdallas.edu

Program Committee

Matthias Blume	Toyota Technological Institute at Chicago, USA
Manuel Chakravarty	University of New South Wales, Australia
Marc Feeley	University of Montreal, Canada
Hai-Feng Guo	University of Nebraska at Omaha, USA
Gopal Gupta	University of Texas at Dallas, USA
Michael Hanus	University of Kiel, Germany (Chair)
Michael Leuschel	University of Düsseldorf, Germany
Simon Peyton Jones	Microsoft Research, Cambridge, UK
Enrico Pontelli	New Mexico State University, USA
Germán Puebla	Technical University of Madrid, Spain
Francesca Rossi	University of Padova, Italy
Michel Rueher	University of Nice, France
Christian Schulte	Royal Institute of Technology, Sweden
Zoltan Somogyi	University of Melbourne, Australia
Peter Stuckey	University of Melbourne, Australia
Doaitse Swierstra	Utrecht University, The Netherlands
Simon Thompson	University of Kent, UK
Pascal Van Hentenryck	Brown University, USA
Germán Vidal	Technical University of Valencia, Spain

External Reviewers

Slim Abdennadher
Alex Aiken
Beatriz Alarcon
Jesus Almendros
Puri Arenas
Ajay Bansal
Jens Bendisposto
Gilles Bernot
Gavin Bierman
Stefano Bistarelli
Mireille Blay-Fornarino
Dan Licata
Suhabe Bugrara
Daniel Cabeza
Manuel Carro
John Clements
Jesus Correas
John Dias
Frank Dignum
Greg Duck
Martin Erwig
Marc Feeley
Amy Felty
Matthew Flatt
Matthew Fluet
Marc Fontaine
Arnaud Gotlieb
Dan Grossman
Raul Gutierrez
David Haguenauer
Kevin Hammond
Stefan Holdermans
Jose Iborra
Johan Jeuring
Andrew Kennedy
Andy King
Karl Klose
Srividya Kona
Marco Kuhlmann

Mikael Z. Lagerkvist
Mario Latendresse
Roman Leshchinksiy
Rainer Leupers
Olivier Lhomme
Sylvain Lippi
Andres Loeh
Michael Maher
Ajay Mallya
Massimo Marchiori
Stefan Monnier
Jose Morales
Claudio Ochoa
Ross Paterson
Inna Pivkina
Bernie Pope
Fred Popowich
Norman Ramsey
Francesca Rossi
Michel Rueher
Claudio Russo
Jean-Charles Régin
Kostis Sagonas
Jaime Sanchez-Hernandez
Dietmar Seipel
Manuel Serrano
Luke Simon
Harald Sondergaard
Don Stewart
Martin Sulzmann
Don Syme
Guido Tack
Peter Thiemann
Son Cao Tran
Alicia Villanueva
Qian Wang
Roland Yap
Damiano Zanardini
Neng-Fa Zhou

Table of Contents

QuickCheck Testing for Fun and Profit

John Hughes

Chalmers University of Technology,
S-41296 Gothenburg,
Sweden

1 Introduction

One of the nice things about purely functional languages is that functions often satisfy simple properties, and enjoy simple algebraic relationships. Indeed, if the functions of an API satisfy elegant laws, that in itself is a sign of a good design— the laws not only indicate conceptual simplicity, but are useful in practice for simplifying programs that use the API, by equational reasoning or otherwise. It is a comfort to us all, for example, to know that in Haskell the following law holds:

```
reverse (xs++ys) == reverse xs++reverse ys
```

where `reverse` is the list reversal function, and `++` is list append.

It is productive to formulate such laws about one's code, but there is always the risk of formulating them incorrectly. A stated law which is untrue is worse than no law at all! Ideally, of course, one should prove them, but at the very least, one should try out the law in a few cases—just to avoid stupid mistakes. We can ease that task a little bit by defining a function to test the law, given values for its free variables:

```
prop_revApp xs ys =
  reverse (xs++ys) == reverse xs++reverse ys
```

Now we can test the law just by applying `prop_revApp` to suitable pairs of lists.

Inventing such pairs of lists, and running the tests, is tedious, however. Wouldn't it be fun to have a tool that would perform that task for us? Then we could simply write laws in our programs and automatically check that they are reasonable hypotheses, at least. In 1999, Koen Claessen and I built just such a tool for Haskell, called "QuickCheck" [4,5,7,6]. Given the definition above, we need only pass `prop_revApp` to `quickCheck` to test the property in 100 random cases:

```
> quickCheck prop_revApp
Falsifiable, after 2 tests:
[1,-1]
[0]
```

Doing so exposes at once that the property is not true! The values printed are a counter-example to the claim, `[1,-1]` being the value of `xs`, and `[0]` the value of `ys`. Indeed, inspecting the property more closely, we see that `xs` and `ys` are the

M. Hanus (Ed.): PADL 2007, LNCS 4354, pp. 1–32, 2007.
© Springer-Verlag Berlin Heidelberg 2007

wrong way round in the right hand side of the law. After correcting the mistake, quickChecking the property succeeds:

```
> quickCheck prop_revApp
OK, passed 100 tests.
```

While there is no *guarantee* that the property now holds, we can be very much more confident that we did not make a stupid mistake... particularly after running another few thousand tests, which is the work of a few more seconds.

We wrote QuickCheck for fun, but it has turned out to be much more useful and important than we imagined at the time. This paper will describe some of the uses to which it has since been put.

2   A Simple Example: Skew Heaps

To illustrate the use of QuickCheck in program development, we shall implement *skew heaps* (a representation of priority queues), following Chris Okasaki [15]. A heap is a binary tree with labels in the nodes,

```
data Tree a = Null | Fork a (Tree a) (Tree a)
   deriving (Eq, Show)
empty = Null
```

such that the value in each node is less than any value in its subtrees:

```
invariant Null = True
invariant (Fork x l r) = smaller x l && smaller x r
smaller x Null = True
smaller x (Fork y l r) = x <= y && invariant (Fork y l r)
```

Thanks to the invariant, we can extract the minimum element (i.e. the first element in the queue) very cheaply:

```
minElem (Fork x _ _) = x
```

To make other operations on the heap cheap, we aim to keep it roughly balanced—then the cost of traversing a branch will be logarithmic in the number of elements. This is achieved in a skew heap by inserting elements into the two subtrees alternately. No extra information is needed in nodes to keep track of where to insert next: we *always* insert into the left subtree, but swap the subtrees after each insertion—*skewing* the heap—so that the next insertion chooses the other subtree.

```
insert x Null = Fork x Null Null
insert x (Fork y l r) = Fork (min x y) r (insert (max x y) l)
```

We expect that the two subtrees of a node should be "roughly balanced", but what does this mean precisely? A moment's thought suggests that the left and right subtrees should contain precisely the same number of elements after an *odd* number of insertions, but the right subtree may be one element larger than the left one after an *even* number of insertions. We conjecture that skew heaps are balanced in the following sense:

```
balanced Null = True
balanced (Fork _ l r) = (d==0 || d==1) && balanced l && balanced r
  where d = weight r - weight l

weight Null = 0
weight (Fork _ l r) = 1 + weight l + weight r
```

Now we can use QuickCheck to test our conjecture. To do so we need to generate random skew heaps. Since the only function so far that constructs skew heaps is `insert`, we can construct any reachable skew heap by choosing a random list of elements, and inserting them into the empty heap:

```
make :: [Integer] -> Tree Integer
make ns = foldl (\h n -> insert n h) empty ns
```

We can now formulate the two properties we are interested in as follows:

```
prop_invariant ns = invariant (make ns)
prop_balanced ns = balanced (make ns)
```

We gave `make` a specific type to control the generation of test data: QuickCheck generates property arguments based on the type expected, and constraining the type of `make` is a convenient way to constrain the argument types of both properties at the same time. (If we forget this, then QuickCheck cannot tell what kind of test data to generate, and an "ambiguous overloading" error is reported). Now we can invoke QuickCheck to confirm our conjecture:

```
Skew> quickCheck prop_invariant
OK, passed 100 tests.
Skew> quickCheck prop_balanced
OK, passed 100 tests.
```

We also need an operation to *delete the minimum element* from a heap. Although finding the element is easy (it is always at the root), deleting it is not, because we have to *merge* the two subtrees into one single heap.

```
deleteMin (Fork x l r) = merge l r
```

(In fact, `merge` is usually presented as part of the interface of skew heaps, even if its utility for priority queues is less obvious). If either argument is `Null`, then merge is easy to define, but how should we merge two non-empty heaps? Clearly, the root of the merged heap must contain the lesser of the root elements of l and r, but that leaves us with *three* heaps to fit into the two subtrees of the new Fork—l, r and h below—so two must be merged recursively... *but which two?*

```
merge l Null = l
merge Null r = r
merge l r | minElem l <= minElem r = join l r
          | otherwise              = join r l
```

```
join (Fork x l r) h = Fork x ...
```

The trick is to realize that the two subtrees of a node are not created equal: we ensured during insertion that the left subtree is never larger than the right one. So any recursion should be on the *left* subtree, guaranteeing that the size of the recursive argument at least halves at each call, and that the total number of calls is logarithmic in the size of the heaps. Thus we should merge l with h above, not r, and because merging increases the size of the heap, skew the subtrees again, so that the next merge will choose r instead.

```
join (Fork x l r) h = Fork x r (merge l h)
```

Is this really right? Let us test our properties again! Of course, now skew heaps can be constructed by a combination of insertions and deletions, so our method of generating random reachable heaps is no longer complete. Now we must generate heaps from a random sequence of insertions *and deletions*:

```
data Op = Insert Integer | DeleteMin
  deriving Show
```

```
make ops = foldl op Null ops
  where op h (Insert n)   = insert n h
        op Null DeleteMin = Null
        op h DeleteMin    = deleteMin h
```

One difficulty is that a *random* sequence of insertions and deletions may attempt to delete an element from an empty heap, provoking an error. There are various ways to avoid this: we could arrange not to generate such sequences in the first place, we could generate arbitrary sequences but discard the erroneous ones, or we can simply ignore any deletions that are applied to an empty heap. In the code above we chose the last alternative, because it is the simplest to implement.

Note that make now has a different type—it expects a list of Ops as its argument—and thus so do our two properties. To test them, QuickCheck needs to be able to generate values of the Op type, and to make that possible, we must specify a *generator* for this type.

QuickCheck generators are an abstract data type, with a rich collection of operations for constructing them. Indeed, provision of *first-class generators* is one of the main innovations in QuickCheck. We use the Haskell class system to associate generators with types, by defining instances of

```
class Arbitrary a where
  arbitrary :: Gen a
```

The Gen type is also a *monad*, making available the monad operations

```
return :: a -> Gen a
```

to construct a constant generator, and

```
(>>=) :: Gen a -> (a -> Gen b) -> Gen b
```

to sequence two generators—although we usually use the latter via Haskell's syntactic sugar, the do-notation.

So, we specify how Op values should be generated as follows:

```
instance Arbitrary Op where
  arbitrary =
    frequency [(2,do n <- arbitrary; return (Insert n)),
               (1,return DeleteMin)]
```

The frequency function combines weighted alternatives—here we generate an insertion twice as often as a deletion, since otherwise the resulting heaps would often be very small. In the first alternative, we choose an arbitrary Integer and generate an Insert containing it; in the second alternative we generate a DeleteMin directly.

Now we can check that any sequence of insertions and deletions preserves the heap invariant

```
Skew> quickCheck prop_invariant
OK, passed 100 tests.
```

and that skew heaps remain balanced:

```
Skew> quickCheck prop_balanced
Falsifiable, after 37 tests:
[DeleteMin,Insert (-9),Insert (-18),Insert (-14),Insert 5,
Insert (-13),Insert (-8),Insert 13,DeleteMin,DeleteMin]
```

Oh dear! Clearly, deletion does *not* preserve the balance condition. But maybe the balance condition is too strong? All we really needed above was that the *left subtree is no larger than the right*—so let's call a node "good" if that is the case.

```
good (Fork _ l r) = weight l <= weight r
```

Now, if all the nodes in a heap are good, then insert and merge will still run in logarithmic time. We can define and test the property that all nodes are good:

```
Skew> quickCheck prop_AllGood
Falsifiable, after 55 tests:
[Insert (-7),DeleteMin,Insert (-16),Insert (-14),DeleteMin,
DeleteMin,DeleteMin,Insert (-21),Insert (-8),Insert 3,
Insert (-1),Insert 1,DeleteMin,DeleteMin,Insert (-12),
Insert 17,Insert 13]
```

Oh dear dear! Evidently, skew heaps contain a mixture of good and bad nodes.

Consulting Okasaki, we find the key insight behind the efficiency of skew heaps: *although bad nodes are more costly to process, they are cheaper to construct!* Whenever we construct a bad node with a large left subtree, then *at the same time* we recurse to create an unusually *small* right subtree—so this recursion is cheaper than expected. What we lose on the swings, we regain on the roundabouts, making for logarithmic *amortized* complexity.

To formalise this argument, Okasaki introduces the notion of "credits"—each bad node carries one credit, which must be supplied when it is created, and can be consumed when it is processed.

```
credits Null = 0
credits h@(Fork _ l r) =
   credits l + credits r + if good h then 0 else 1
```

Since we cannot directly observe the cost of insertion and deletion, we define a function `cost_insert h` that returns the number of recursive calls of `insert` made when inserting into `h`, and `cost_deleteMin h`, which returns the number of calls of `join` made when deleting from `h` (definitions omitted). Now, we claim that *on average* each insertion or deletion in a heap of n nodes traverses only `log2 n` nodes, and creates equally many new, possibly bad nodes, so `2*log2 n` credits should suffice for each call. (The first `log2 n` credits pay for the recursion in this call, and the second `log2 n` credits pay for bad nodes in the result).

If we now specify

```
prop_cost_insert n ops =
   cost_insert h <= 2*log2 (weight h) + 1
   where h = make ops
```

then QuickCheck finds a counterexample[1], because this property only holds on average, but when we take credits into account

```
prop_cost_insert n ops =
   cost_insert h + credits (insert n h)
   <=
   2*log2 (weight h) + 1 + credits h
   where h = make ops
```

then the property passes hundreds of thousands of tests. Likewise, the property

```
prop_cost_deleteMin ops =
   h/=Null ==>
      cost_deleteMin h + credits (deleteMin h)
      <=
      2*log2 (weight h) + credits h
   where h = make ops
```

---

[1] Only one test case in around 3,000 is a counterexample. This is because the method we use to generate heaps produces rather few bad nodes. Counterexamples can be found more quickly by generating heaps directly, rather than via `insert` and `deleteMin`, so that the proportion of bad nodes can be increased.

succeeds (where we have used QuickCheck's *implication* operator `==>` to state a precondition that must hold in every test case, to avoid the error that would result by calling `deleteMin` on the empty heap).

Each of these properties states that the credits allocated for the operation, together with the accumulated credits in the heap, suffice both to pay for the operation itself, and for the credits retained in its result. So any sequence of insertions and deletions, starting with the empty heap, will incur only logarithmic cost per operation.

Why bother to test these properties, when Okasaki has already proved them? Well, the proof is informal, and proofs can be wrong. Okasaki's statements are in terms of "big O" notation, rather than the precise formulations above—the "+ 1" in `prop_cost_insert` came as a surprise, for example. Finally, we might have transcribed Okasaki's code incorrectly—or deliberately altered it. Actually, Okasaki uses a different definition of `insert`:

```
insert x h = merge (Fork x Null Null) h
```

This simplifies the proof, because now both insertion and deletion are defined in terms of `merge`, so only `merge` need be considered in the proof. But this definition of `insert` does not preserve balance, even when there are no deletions, which leads me to prefer my own definition above. Also, a specialised insertion function is likely to be more efficient than one using `merge`. But is it safe to replace the definition of `insert` with an optimised one with a different result? Okasaki's proof no longer applies directly, but the property above shows that it is.

We can take this example further. So far, we have tested the heap invariant and complexity properties. But apart from these, do `insert` and `delete` actually implement priority queues? To answer that, we need a *specification* that they should fulfill. One good way to specify them is via an abstract *model* of priority queues—such as ordered lists. Insertion is then modelled by the standard function to insert into an ordered list, and deletion is modelled by the function `tail`. To formalise this, we define a function mapping each skew heap to its model:

```
model :: Tree Integer -> [Integer]
model h = sort (flatten h)

flatten Null = []
flatten (Fork a l r) = a : flatten l ++ flatten r
```

Now, given a function f on ordered lists, and a function g on heaps, we can define a property stating that f correctly models g on a heap h, as follows:

```
(f 'models' g) h =
  f (model h) == model (g h)
```

and formulate the correctness of insertion and deletion like this:

```
prop_insert n ops = ((List.insert n) 'models' insert n) h
  where h = make ops
prop_deleteMin ops = size h>0 ==> (tail 'models' deleteMin) h
  where h = make ops
```

Testing these properties succeeds, and after running many thousands of tests we can be reasonably confident that the stated properties do actually hold.

What this example shows us is that *QuickCheck changes the way we test code*. Instead of focussing on the choice of test cases—trying to guess which cases may reveal errors—we leave that instead to QuickCheck, and focus on the *properties* that the code under test should satisfy. Program development with QuickCheck strongly resembles formal program development, emphasizing formal models, invariants, and so on—but with labour-intensive proofs replaced by instant feedback from testing.

This approach has proved very attractive to the Haskell community, and QuickCheck has become widely used. One of the most impressive applications is in the development of `Data.ByteString`, described elsewhere in this volume. The code contains over 480 QuickCheck properties, all tested every time a new version of the code is checked in. The various `ByteString` types are modelled abstractly by lists of characters—just as we modelled skew heaps by ordered lists above. Many properties test that `ByteString` operations are accurately modelled by their list equivalents, just like our `prop_insert` and `prop_deleteMin`. `Data.ByteString` achieves its high performance in part by programming GHC's optimiser with custom rewrite rules that perform loop fusion and other optimisations. Of course, it's vital that such rewrite rules, which are applied silently to user code by the compiler, preserve the meanings of programs. Around 40 QuickCheck properties are used to test that this is in fact the case.

QuickCheck is also used by Haskell developers in industry. For example, Galois Connections' Cryptol compiler uses 175 QuickCheck properties, tested nightly, to ensure that symbolic functions used by the compiler correspond correctly to their Haskell equivalents.

3   Software Testing

QuickCheck is a novel approach to software testing. But software testing enjoys a somewhat patchy reputation among academics. Dijkstra's influence runs deep: his famous observation that "Program testing can at best show the presence of errors, but never their absence" suggests that mere testing is a waste of time. His comment in the preface to *A Discipline of Programming*, that "None of the programs in this monograph, needless to say, has been tested on a machine", makes us almost ashamed to admit that we do indeed test our own code! We know that even after rigorous testing, countless errors remain in production software—around one every hundred lines on average [13]. Those errors impose a real cost on software users—according to a Congressional report in 2002, $60 billion annually to the US economy alone. That is a lot of money, even in the US—$200 a year for every man, woman and child. Isn't it time to give up on such an inadequate technique, and adopt formal program verification instead?

Before drawing that conclusion, let us put those figures in perspective. The US software industry turns over $200–$240 billion per year. Thus the additional cost imposed by residual errors is around 25–30%. To be economically viable, even a development method that guarantees to eliminate *all* software errors must cost no more than this—otherwise it is more economical simply to live with the errors. How does formal program verification measure up?

An impressive recent case study is Xavier Leroy's construction of the back end of a certified C compiler using Coq [12]. Leroy wrote around 35,000 lines of Coq, of which the compiler itself made up around 4,500 lines, and concluded that the certification was around eight times larger than the code that it applied to. It is reasonable to infer that certification also increased the cost of the code by a similar factor. While such a cost is acceptable in the aerospace domain that Leroy was addressing, it is clearly not acceptable for software development in general. It is not reasonable to expect formal verification to compete with testing unless the cost can be cut by an order of magnitude[2].

Thus we can expect testing to be the main form of program verification for a long time to come—it is the only practical technique in most cases. This does not mean that practitioners are happy with the current state of the art! But while they are concerned with the problem of residual errors, they are really rather more concerned about the *cost* of testing—around half the cost of each software project. This cost is particularly visible since it is concentrated towards the *end* of each project, when the deadline is approaching, sometimes imposing an uncomfortable choice between skimping on testing and meeting the deadline. Current best practice is to automate tests as far as possible, so they can be run nightly, and to derive additional value from automated test cases by interpreting them as *partial specifications*, as Extreme Programming advocates [3].

Yet automated testing of this sort has its problems. It is a dilemma to decide, for each property that the code should satisfy, whether one should write one test case, or many? Writing a single test case makes for concise test code, with a clear relationship between test cases and properties—but it may fail to test the property thoroughly, and it may be hard to infer what the property is from a single example. Writing many test cases is more thorough, but also more expensive, imposes future costs when the test code must be maintained, and may obscure the "partial specification" by its sheer bulk—anyone reading the testing code may fail to see the wood for the trees. As an example of the code volumes involved, Ericsson's AXD301 ATM-switch is controlled by 1.5 million lines of Erlang code, which is tested by a further 700,000 lines of test cases!

A further problem is that nightly regression testing is really testing for errors that have *already been found*—while it protects against the embarrassment of reintroducing a previously fixed error, it is clear that unless the code under test is changed, no new errors can be found. Indeed, 85% of errors are found the *first* time a test case is run [8], so repeating those tests nightly is only a cheap way to

---

[2] This is also the motivation for "lightweight" formal methods such as Microsoft's Static Driver Verifier [2] or ESC/Java [9], which use automated proof techniques to reveal bugs at a very *low* cost in programmer time. But these tools offer no guarantees of correctness—a fact brought home by ESC/Java's use of an unsound theorem prover! They can "at best show the presence of errors, but never their absence" just like testing—although potentially with greater accuracy and at lower cost.

find the remaining 15%. In other words, it can only play a relatively small part in the overall testing process.

QuickCheck has the potential to address all of these problems. QuickCheck properties make much better specifications than automated test cases, because they cover the general case rather than one or more examples. For the same reason, there is no need to write more than one QuickCheck property for each logical property to be tested—a wide variety of cases will be generated anyway. Thus QuickCheck code can be concise and maintainable, without compromising the thoroughness of testing. Moreover, each time QuickCheck is run, there is a chance of *new* test cases being generated, so if QuickCheck is run nightly then, as time passes, we can expect more and more errors to be found. We have demonstrated in practice that the *same* QuickCheck property can reveal widely varying errors, depending on the data which is generated. As a bonus, QuickCheck *adds value to formal specifications* by interpreting them as testing code, making it more worthwhile to construct them in the first place.

We conclude that not only is testing here to stay, but that a tool such as QuickCheck has much to offer software developers in industry today.

4   Shrinking

One of the problems with randomly generated test inputs is that they can contain much that is irrelevant—the "signal", that causes a test to fail, can be hidden among a great deal of "noise", that makes it hard to understand the failure. We saw an example of this above, where the counter-example found to prop_balanced was the long sequence of operations

```
[DeleteMin,Insert (-9),Insert (-18),Insert (-14),Insert 5,
Insert (-13),Insert (-8),Insert 13,DeleteMin,DeleteMin]
```

Clearly, at the very least the first DeleteMin is irrelevant, since it has no effect at all—it is ignored by the make function that converts this list to a skew heap! To address this problem, newer versions of QuickCheck automatically *shrink* failing test cases after they are found, reporting a "minimal" one in some sense. Using one of these new versions instead, testing prop_balanced might yield

```
Skew> quickCheck prop_balanced
Falsifiable, after 22 successful tests (shrunk failing case 10 times):
[Insert (-9),Insert 12,Insert 8,Delete]
```

in which the failing case has been reduced to just four operations. Moreover, we know that removing any of these four would make the test succeed: all four operations are essential to the failure. (There is no guarantee, though, that there is *no* shorter sequence that provokes a failure: just that one cannot be obtained by removing an element from this particular test case. We do still sometimes produce longer failing cases for this property.)

Shrinking failing cases dramatically increases QuickCheck's usefulness. In practice, much time is devoted either to simplifying a failing case by hand, or to debugging and tracing a complex case to understand why it fails. Shrinking failing cases automates the first stage of diagnosis, and makes the step from automated testing to locating a fault very short indeed.

5   Quviq QuickCheck

Although QuickCheck proved popular among Haskell users, the industrial Haskell community is still rather small. However, Erlang supports functional programming, and enjoys a *mainly* industrial community of users. Moreover, that community is growing fast: downloads of the Erlang system were running at 50,000 a month in June 2006, and have been growing quite consistently at 80% a year for the past six years. I therefore decided to develop a version of QuickCheck for Erlang, now called Quviq QuickCheck.

At first sight, adapting QuickCheck for Erlang appears to be rather difficult: Erlang lacks lazy evaluation, and many of the functions in QuickCheck's interface *must* be non-strict; Erlang lacks a static type-checker, and Haskell QuickCheck chooses generators based on the type of argument a property expects; QuickCheck's generator type is a monad, and we make extensive use of Haskell's **do**-notation to define generators. In fact, none of these difficulties proved to be especially problematic.

- QuickCheck functions which must be lazy only use their lazy arguments once, so instead of *call-by-need* it is sufficient to use *call-by-name*—and this is easily simulated by passing 0-ary functions as parameters instead (fortunately, Erlang supports first-class functions). We spare the user the need to pass such functions explicitly by using Erlang *macros* (distinguished by names beginning with a '?') to generate them. Thus Quviq QuickCheck simply provides an interface made up to a large extent of macros which expand to function calls with functions as parameters.
- While Haskell QuickCheck does choose generators for property *arguments* based on their type, it has always provided a way to supply a generator explicitly as well. In Erlang, we must simply always do this. This is a smaller cost than it seems, because in more complex situations, the type of an expected argument is rarely sufficient to determine how it should be generated.
- We can use a monad in Erlang too, in the same way as in Haskell. While we lack Haskell's **do**-notation, we can give a convenient syntax to monadic sequencing even so, via a macro.

The example in the introduction can be rewritten in Erlang like this:

```
prop_revApp() ->
  ?FORALL(Xs,list(int()),
    ?FORALL(Ys,list(int()),
      lists:reverse(Xs++Ys)
      ==
      lists:reverse(Xs)++lists:reverse(Ys))).
```

There are trivial differences: Erlang function definitions use an arrow (->), variables begin with a capital letter (Xs), external function calls name the module as well as the function to be called (lists:reverse). The main difference, though, is the use of the ?FORALL macro, whose arguments are a bound variable, a generator, and the scope of the ∀—the expansion of FORALL(X,Gen,Prop) is just eqc:forall(Gen,fun(X)->Prop end). By using generators which look like types (list(int())), and macro parameters which bind variables, we provide a very natural-looking notation to the user.

Testing this property yields

```
13> eqc:quickcheck(example:prop_revApp()).
..........Failed! After 11 tests.
[1]
[-3,1]
Shrinking.....(5 times)
[0]
[1]
```

in which the counterexample found is displayed both before and after shrinking. In this case, we can see that QuickCheck not only discarded an unnecessary element from one of the lists, but shrank the numbers in them towards zero. The fact that the minimal counterexample consists of [0] and [1] tells us not only that both lists must be non-empty, but gives us the additional information that if the 1 were shrunk further to 0, then this would no longer be a counterexample.

Quviq QuickCheck thus offers a very similar "look and feel" to the original.

6   State Machine Specifications

In early 2006 we began to apply QuickCheck to a product then under development at Ericsson's site in Älvsjö (Stockholm). But real Erlang systems use side-effects extensively, in addition to pure functions. Testing functions with side-effects using "vanilla QuickCheck" is not easy—any more than specifying such functions using nothing but predicate calculus is easy—and we found we needed to develop another library on top of QuickCheck specifically for this kind of testing. That library has gone through four quite different designs: in this section we shall explain our latest design, and how we arrived at it.

As a simple example, we shall show how to use the new library to test the Erlang *process registry*. This is a kind of local name server, which can register Erlang process identifiers under atomic names, so that other processes can find them. The three operations we shall test are

- register(Name,Pid) to register Pid under the name Name,
- unregister(Name) to delete the process registered as Name from the registry, and
- whereis(Name) which returns the Pid registered with that Name, or the atom undefined if there is no such Pid.

Although `register` is supposed to return a boolean, it would clearly be meaningless to test properties such as

```
prop_silly() ->
  ?FORALL(Name,name(),
    ?FORALL(Pid,pid(),
      register(Name,Pid) == true)).
```

The result of `register` depends on what state it is called in—and so we need to ensure that each operation is called in a wide variety of states. We can construct a random state by running a random sequence of operations—so this is what our test cases will consist of. We also need to ensure that each test case leaves the process registry in a "clean" state, so that the side-effects of one test do not affect the outcome of the next. This is a familiar problem to testers.

We made an early decision to represent test cases *symbolically*, by an Erlang term, rather than by, for example, a function which performs the test when called. Thus if a test case should call `unregister(a)`, then this is represented by the Erlang term `{call,erlang,unregister,[a]}`—a 4-tuple containing the atom `call`, the module name and function to call[3], and a list of arguments. The reason we chose a symbolic representation is that this makes it easy to print out test cases, store them in files for later use, analyze them to collect statistics or test properties, or—and this is important—write functions to shrink them.

We can thus think of test cases as small programs, represented as abstract syntax. A natural question is then: how powerful should the *language* of test cases be? Should we allow test cases to contain branching, and multiple execution paths? Should we allow test cases to do pattern matching? For a researcher in programming languages, it is tempting to get carried away at this point, and indeed early versions of our library did all of the above. We found, though, that it was simply not worth the extra complexity, and have now settled for a simple list of commands. We do not regard this is a significant loss of power—after all, when a test fails, we are only interested in *the path to the failure*, not other paths that might conceivably have been taken in other circumstances.

We did find it essential to allow later commands access to the results of earlier commands in the same test case, which presents a slight problem. Remember that *test generation*, when the symbolic test case is created, entirely precedes *test execution*, when it is interpreted. During test generation, the *values* returned by commands are unknown, so they cannot be used directly in further commands—yet we do need to generate commands that refer to them. The solution, of course, is to let symbolic test cases bind and reuse *variables*. We represent variables by Erlang terms of the form `{var,N}`, and bindings by terms of the form `{set,{var,N},{call,Mod,Fun,Args}}`. The test cases we generate are actually lists of such bindings—for example,

```
[{set,{var,1},{call,erlang,whereis,[a]}},
  {set,{var,2},{call,erlang,register,[b,{var,1}]}}]
```

---

[3] `unregister` is a standard function, exported by the module `erlang`.

which represents the Erlang code fragment

```
Var1 = erlang:whereis(a),
Var2 = erlang:register(b,Var1)
```

We refer to Erlang terms of the form {var,...} and {call,...} as *symbolic values*. They represent values that will be known during test execution, but must be treated as "black boxes" during test generation—while it is permissible to embed a symbolic value in a generated command, the actual *value* it represents cannot be used until test execution. Of course, this is an application of *staged programming*, which we know and love.

Now, in order to generate sensible test cases, we need to know what state the system under test is in. Thus we base our test generation on a *state machine*, modelling enough about the actual state to determine which calls make sense, and express the desired properties of their outputs. In this case, we need to know which pids are currently registered. We also need to know which pids are *available* to register: to guarantee that the pids we use don't refer, for example, to crashed processes, we will generate new process identifiers in each test case—and these need to be held in the test case state. Thus we can represent our state using a record with two components:

```
-record(state,{pids,    % list(symbolic(pid()))
               regs}).  % list({name(),symbolic(pid())})

initial_state() -> #state{pids=[], regs=[]}.
```

We have indicated the expected type of each field in a comment: pids should be a list of (symbolic) process identifiers, spawned during test generation, while regs should be a list of pairs of names and (symbolic) pids.

To define such a state machine, the QuickCheck user writes a module exporting a number of callbacks, such as initial_state() above, which tell QuickCheck how the state machine is supposed to behave. This idea is quite familiar to Erlang users, because it is heavily used in the OTP (Open Telecoms Platform) library.

We define how commands are generated in each state via a callback function command(State):

```
command(S) ->
  frequency([{1,stop},
             {10,oneof(
                   [{call,?MODULE,spawn,[]}]++
                    [{call,erlang,register,
                      [name(),elements(S#state.pids)]}
                     || S#state.pids/=[]]++
                    [{call,erlang,unregister,[name()]},
                     {call,erlang,whereis,[name()]}
                   ])}]).
```

Test cases are generated by starting from the initial state, and generating a sequence of commands using this generator, until it generates the atom stop. Thus, on average, the generator above will result in test cases which are 11 commands long. We choose (with equal probability) between generating a call to spawn (a function defined in the current module ?MODULE to spawn a dummy process), register, unregister, and whereis. Generating a call to register chooses one of the elements of the pids field of the state—to guarantee that such a choice is possible, we include this possibility only if this field is non-empty. ([X || Y] is a degenerate list comprehension with no generator, which returns either the empty list if Y is false, or [X] if Y is true).

We also separately define a *precondition* for each command, which returns true if the command is appropriate in the current state. It may seem unnecessary to define *both* a command generator, which is supposed to generate an appropriate command for the current state, and a precondition, which determines whether or not it is. There are two reasons to define preconditions separately:

- We may wish to generate a wider class of commands, then exclude some of them via a more restrictive precondition—for example, after testing reveals that a tighter precondition is needed than we first supposed!
- Shrinking deletes commands from a test case, which means that the following commands in a shrunk test case may appear in a *different* state from the one they were generated in. We need to be able to determine whether they are still appropriate in the *new* state.

In this example, though, we need state no non-trivial preconditions:

```
precondition(S,{call,_,_,_}) -> true.
```

Of course, we also have to define how each command changes the state. This is done by the next_state(S,V,{call,Mod,Fun,Args}) callback, which returns the state after Mod:Fun(Args) is called in state S, with the result V. In this example, spawn adds its result to the list of available pids,

```
next_state(S,V,{call,?MODULE,spawn,_}) ->
  S#state{pids=[V | S#state.pids]};
```

(where [X|Y] means "X cons Y", and S#state{pids=...} is a *record update* that returns a record equal to S except for its pids field). The register operation records its arguments in the regs component of the state,

```
next_state(S,V,{call,erlang,register,[Name,Pid]}) ->
  S#state{regs=[{Name,Pid} | S#state.regs]};
```

unregister removes its argument from that component,

```
next_state(S,V,{call,erlang,unregister,[Name]}) ->
  S#state{regs=[{N,P} || {N,P} <- S#state.regs, N/=Name]};
```

while whereis leaves the state unchanged:

```
next_state(S,V,{call,erlang,whereis,[Name]}) -> S.
```

These clauses make up a simple specification of the intended behaviour of the operations under test. The only tricky point to note is that the result parameter, V, is symbolic during test generation—its value will be {var,1}, {var,2} etc. Thus the states that we build are also partly symbolic—for example, spawning a new process and registering it under the name a results in the state {state,[{var,1}],[{a,{var,1}}]}. We also use the next_state callback during test execution, when it is applied to real values rather than symbolic ones—during execution the state after the same two operations will be something like {state,[<0.51.0>],[{a,<0.51.0>}]}.

Finally, we define a postcondition for each command—if any postcondition fails, then the test case fails. To begin with, let us define a trivial postcondition, so that tests fail only if an exception is raised.

```
postcondition(S,{call,_,_,_},R) -> true.
```

Now, using the state machine library, we define a property to test:

```
prop_registration() ->
  ?FORALL(Cmds,commands(?MODULE),
  begin {H,S,Res} = run_commands(?MODULE,Cmds),
        [catch unregister(N) || {N,_} <- S#state.regs],
        [exit(P,kill) || P <- S#state.pids],
        ?WHENFAIL(io:format("~p\n~p\n", [H,Res]),
                  Res==ok)
  end).
```

Here commands(?MODULE) generates test cases using the callbacks in the current module, and run_commands(?MODULE,Cmds) runs those test cases, returning a history (list of states and results), final state, and "result", which is ok if the test case succeeded. The next two lines clean up after the test case, by unregistering any processes that were left registered, and killing the processes that were spawned. For convenience, we use the ?WHENFAIL macro to add an action that is performed only in failing cases—we print out the history and result.

Testing this property immediately reveals a problem:

```
15> eqc:quickcheck(registration_eqc:prop_registration()).
.Failed! After 2 tests.
[{set,{var,1},{call,registration_eqc,spawn,[]}},
 ...
 {set,{var,41},{call,erlang,register,[a,{var,26}]}}]
 ...
Shrinking.....(5 times)
[{set,{var,4},{call,erlang,unregister,[a]}}]
[]
{exception,
  {'EXIT',{badarg,[{erlang,unregister,[a]},
                {eqc_statem,run_commands,5},...
```

We can see immediately how effective shrinking is: a test case of 41 commands was shrunk to just one! This single call to unregister(a) failed with a badarg exception, and the rest of the output is an uninteresting stack backtrace.

The problem in this case is that unregister raises an exception if there is no registered process with the given name—so if a test case begins with unregister, then it is bound to fail. Our specification does not take this into account. There are two ways to do so:

- *Positive testing*—restrict test cases to avoid the exception, by adding a suitable precondition to unregister (and optionally modifying the command generator to avoid generating such commands in the first place), or
- *Negative testing*—catch the exception in a local version of unregister which we use in test cases instead, and define a postcondition to check that the exception is raised in the correct cases.

Whichever approach we choose, QuickCheck quickly reveals another problem:

```
60> eqc:quickcheck(registration_eqc:prop_registration()).
Failed! After 1 tests.
...
Shrinking.........(9 times)
[{set,{var,5},{call,registration_eqc,spawn,[]}},
 {set,{var,6},{call,erlang,register,[a,{var,5}]}},
 {set,{var,16},{call,erlang,register,[a,{var,5}]}}]
[{{state,[],[]},<0.869.0>},{{state,[<0.869.0>],[]},true}]
{exception,
  {'EXIT',{badarg,[{erlang,register,[a,<0.869.0>]},
                         ...
```

Of course! We tried to register process a twice! If we try to register a process with the same name as an *already registered* process, we would expect registration to fail! Indeed, the Erlang documentation confirms that register should raise an exception if either the name, or the process, is already registered. We define a function to test for this case

```
bad_register(S,Name,Pid) ->
  lists:keymember(Name,1,S#state.regs) orelse
  lists:keymember(Pid,2,S#state.regs)
```

(lists:keymember(Key,I,L) tests whether a Key occurs as the Ith component of any tuple in the list L). We define a local version of register which catches the exception, and add a postcondition to check that the exception is raised exactly when bad_register returns true.

Testing quickly revealed another error, in the case:

```
[{set,{var,4},{call,...,spawn,[]}},
 {set,{var,5},{call,...,register,[c,{var,4}]}},
 {set,{var,12},{call,...,spawn,[]}},
 {set,{var,13},{call,...,register,[c,{var,12}]}},
 {set,{var,21},{call,...,register,[a,{var,12}]}}]
```

The problem here was *not* that the second call to `register` raised an exception—that was expected. The test case failed because the postcondition of the *third* call to `register` was not satisfied—the call *succeeded*, but was specified to fail. The reason was an error in our specification—the definition of `next_state` above takes no account of whether or not `register` raises an exception. As a result, after the first two calls to `register` then our state contained *both* processes {var,4} and {var,12}, registered with the same name c! Then the third call was expected to raise an exception, because the process being registered was already registered as c. Correcting the specification, so that `next_state` returns an unchanged state if `bad_register` is true, fixed the problem. In fairness, the Erlang documentation does not *say* explicitly that the process is not registered if `register` raises an exception, even if that is a fairly obvious interpretation!

A subtlety: note that when we use `bad_register` in `next_state`, then it is applied to a partially symbolic state. So when `bad_register` tests whether the pid is already registered, it compares a *symbolic* pid with those in the state. Fortunately this works: symbolic pids are always variables bound to the result of a spawn, and different calls to spawn return different pids—so two symbolic pids are equal *iff* the pids they are bound to are equal. Care is required here!

We have now seen all of our state machine testing library: to summarize, the user defines callback functions

- `command` and `precondition`, which are used during test generation to generate and shrink test cases that "make sense",
- `postcondition`, which is used during test execution to check that the result of each command satisfies the properties that it should,
- `initial_state` and `next_state`, which are used during both test generation and test execution to keep track of the state of the test case.

Given these callbacks, the user can generate test cases using `commands(Mod)`, and run them using `run_commands(Mod,Cmds)`.

As we saw in the example, the definitions of these callbacks make up a simple and natural specification of the code under test. We quickly found misconceptions in our specification, and enhanced our understanding of the process registry. While most of the information in our specification is also present in the Erlang documentation, we did discover and resolve at least a slight ambiguity—that a process is not actually registered when `register` raises an exception.

As an interesting extension of this example, we decided to test the process registry in the presence of crashing processes. We could easily model process crashes at known points by inserting operations to stop processes explicitly into our test cases[4]. The Erlang documentation says nothing about a relationship between process termination and the registry, but we discovered, by refining our QuickCheck specification, that such a relationship does indeed exist. In brief, dead processes are removed automatically from the registry; attempts to register a dead process apparently succeed (return `true`), but do not change the registry state. This means that sequences such as

---

[4] This doesn't test a process crashing *during* a call to a registry operation.

```
register(a,Pid),
register(a,Pid)
```

can indeed succeed—*if* Pid refers to a dead process. We discovered that stopping a process causes it to be removed from the registry—but *only* after other processes have had a chance to run! To obtain predictable behaviour, we stopped processes using

```
stop(Pid) -> exit(Pid,kill), erlang:yield().
```

where the call to yield() gives up control to the scheduler, allowing time for deregistration. Without such a yield(), a sequence such as

```
register(a,Pid),
stop(Pid),
unregister(a)
```

may or may not succeed, depending on whether or not the scheduler preempts execution after the stop! We were quickly able to develop a formal specification covering this aspect too, despite the absence of documentation—and in the process discovered details that are unknown even to many Erlang experts.

7   Ericsson's Media Proxy

We developed our state machine library in parallel with a project to test Ericsson's Media Proxy, then approaching release. The Media Proxy is one half of a media firewall for multimedia IP-telephony—it opens and closes "media pinholes" to allow media streams corresponding to calls in progress to pass through the firewall, thus preventing other IP packets from travelling through the owner's network for free, and defending equipment behind the firewall from denial of service attacks. The Media Proxy opens and closes media pinholes in response to commands from a Media Gateway Controller, a physically separate device which monitors signalling traffic to detect calls being set up and taken down.

This architecture, of a Media Gateway controlled by a Media Gateway Controller, is standardised by the International Telecommunication Union. The ITU specifies the protocol to be used for communication between the two—the H.248, or "Megaco" protocol [16]. This specification is quite complex: the current version is 212 pages long. The Media Proxy only uses a subset of the full protocol though, which is defined in an internal Ericsson document, the Interwork Description—a further 183 pages. The Media Proxy is controlled by about 150,000 lines of Erlang code, of which perhaps 20,000 lines are concerned with the Megaco protocol.

When we began our project, the Media Proxy had already completed Function Test, and was undergoing System Test in preparation for release. This process takes 3-4 months, during with the development team focus all their efforts on finding and fixing errors. The team follow a disciplined approach to testing, with a high degree of test automation, and have a strong track record for quality and reliability [18]. We worked with Ulf Wiger and Joakim Johansson at Ericsson to test the Megaco interface of the Media Proxy in parallel, by using QuickCheck to generate sequences of Megaco messages to send to the Proxy, and check that its replies were valid.

The biggest part of the work lay in writing generators for Megaco messages. These messages can carry a great deal of information, and the message datatype is correspondingly complex. It is specified in the ITU standard via an ASN.1 grammar, which specifies both the logical structure of messages, and their binary representation on a communications channel, both at the same time. This grammar can be compiled by the Erlang ASN.1 compiler into a collection of Erlang record types, together with encoding and decoding functions for the binary representation. We could thus generate messages as Erlang data structures, and easily encode them and send them to the Proxy—and this test infrastructure was already in place when we began our project.

We did try generating purely random messages conforming to the ASN.1 grammar, and sending them to the Proxy. This was not a successful approach: the messages were all semantic nonsense, and so were simply rejected by the Proxy. This could be an effective form of negative testing, but in this project we were more concerned to test the *positive* behaviour of the Proxy—that it responds correctly to *meaningful* messages.

Thus we had to write QuickCheck generators for complex structures, respecting all the constraints stated in the standard and the Interwork Description. To give a flavour of this, here is a fragment of the ASN.1 grammar in the standard, specifying the structure of a media descriptor:

```
MediaDescriptor ::= SEQUENCE
{ termStateDescr TerminationStateDescriptor OPTIONAL,
  streams CHOICE
  { oneStream   StreamParms,
    multiStream SEQUENCE OF StreamDescriptor
  } OPTIONAL,
  ...
}
```

A media descriptor is a record (sequence), with fields `termStateDescr`, `streams`, etc. Some of the fields can be optional, as in this case, and each field name is followed by its type. In this case the `streams` field is of a union type—it can either be tagged `oneStream` and contain the parameters of a single media stream, or it can be tagged `multiStream` and contain a list (sequence) of stream descriptors. Clearly the protocol designers expect a single media stream to be a common case, and so have included an optimised representation for just this case.

The Interwork Description restricts media descriptors a little, as follows:

```
MediaDescriptor ::= SEQUENCE
{ streams CHOICE
  { oneStream   StreamParms,
    multiStream SEQUENCE OF StreamDescriptor
  }
}
```

When generating media descriptors, we must thus choose between the `oneStream` form and the `multiStream` form, depending on how many streams are to be included. The QuickCheck generator is as follows:

```
mediadescriptor(Streams) when Streams=/=[] ->
  {mediaDescriptor,
    #MediaDescriptor{ streams =
      case Streams of
        [{Id,Mode}] ->
          oneof([{oneStream,streamParms(Mode)},
                 {multiStream,[stream(Id,Mode)]}]);
        _ -> {multiStream,
              [stream(I,M) || {I,M}<-Streams]}
      end}}.
```

Analysing this code, we can distinguish three distinct parts.

- Datastructure construction—the 'MediaDescriptor' record paired with a `mediadescriptor` tag, containing a `streams` field that is either a `oneStream` or a `multiStream`. Very similar code appears in conventional test cases.
- We analyse the streams to be included, distinguishing the cases of one stream and many streams. Here we express part of the logic of the specification.
- At *one* point, we embed a QuickCheck function—`oneof`—to express a choice between alternatives.

Thus the code looks mostly familiar to Ericsson developers—the overhead of turning it in to a QuickCheck generator is very light.

Another example: the standard specifies stream parameters as follows,

```
StreamParms ::= SEQUENCE
{ localControlDescriptor LocalControlDescriptor OPTIONAL,
  localDescriptor         LocalRemoteDescriptor OPTIONAL,
  remoteDescriptor        LocalRemoteDescriptor OPTIONAL,
  ...,
  statisticsDescriptor    StatisticsDescriptor  OPTIONAL
}
```

but the Interwork Description says also that "LocalControl will be included in all cases except when no media (m-line) is defined in the remote SDP", the remote SDP being a part of the remote descriptor appearing among the stream parameters above. Thus we need to know whether or not a remote media will be defined, at the time we decide whether or not to include a local control descriptor. There are quite simply two cases for stream parameters: with, and without, a defined remote media. This is simple enough to express in a QuickCheck generator—we simply decide which case we are in *first*:

```
streamParms(Mode) ->
 ?LET(RemoteMediaDefined, bool(),
```

```
case RemoteMediaDefined of
  true ->
    #StreamParms{ localControlDescriptor =
                    localControl(Mode),
                  localDescriptor =
                  localDescriptor(RemoteMediaDefined),
                  remoteDescriptor =
                  remoteDescriptor(RemoteMediaDefined)};
    false -> ...
  end).
```

We choose a random boolean, `RemoteMediaDefined`, and if it is `true`, we both include a local control descriptor, and pass the boolean inward to `remoteDescriptor`, which then ensures that an m-line is indeed generated. `?LET(X,G1,G2)` binds the variable X to the value generated by G1 in the generator G2—it is syntactic sugar for the 'bind' operator of the generator monad, and corresponds to Haskell's **do**-notation. Of course, this code itself is quite trivial—the interesting thing is that we can only write it thanks to the monadic interface that generators provide.

As soon as our message generators were complete, we began to experience crashes in the Media Proxy. They turned out to be related to the `StreamParms` above. The ASN.1 specification says that all the fields of a `StreamParms` record are optional—which means that it is valid to omit them all, which QuickCheck quickly did. Yet the ITU standard also defines an alternative concrete syntax for messages, as readable ASCII—and we were actually using the ASCII form of messages, to ease debugging. The ASCII form of messages is generated and parsed by a *hand-written* encoder and decoder—obviously, these cannot be generated from the ASN.1 grammar, because they use another syntax. That syntax in turn is defined in the ITU standard by an ABNF grammar... and *this* grammar requires a `StreamParms` record to contain *at least one field*! It doesn't matter which field it is, but at least one must be there. This story illustrates the dangers of giving two formal descriptions of the same thing, with no way to enforce consistency! Now, one would expect the ASCII encoder to reject the messages we generated with empty `StreamParms`, but it turned out that Ericsson's *encoder* followed the ASN.1 specification and permitted an empty record, while the *decoder* followed the ABNF and required at least one field. Thus we could generate and encode a message, that when sent to the Media Proxy, caused its decoder to crash. Clearly, the underlying fault here is in the standard, but Ericsson's encode and decoder should at least be consistent.

Our next step was to generate valid command *sequences*. The Megaco standard defines twelve different commands that the controller can send to the gateway, but we focussed on the three most important, which manipulate the state of a call, or *context* as they are known in Megaco-speak.

– The *Add* command adds a caller (or *termination*) to a context, creating the context if it does not already exist. Terminations are added to a context one-by-one—the Megaco standard permits arbitrarily many callers in a call, while the Media Proxy is designed to handle a maximum of two.

- The *Modify* command modifies the state of a termination, typically activating media streams once both terminations have been added to a context.
- The *Subtract* command is used to remove a termination from a context—when a call is over, both terminations need to be subtracted. When the last termination is subtracted from a context, the context is automatically deleted from the Proxy.

The normal case is that two terminations are added to a context, they are both modified to activate their streams, and then they are both subtracted again.

Contexts and terminations are assigned identifiers when they are first added to the Proxy, which are returned to the controller in the Proxy's reply to the Add message. These identifiers are then used in subsequent messages to refer to already created contexts and terminations. So it was vital that the test cases we generated could use the replies to previous messages, to construct later ones.

We used a predecessor of our state machine testing library to generate and run sequences of Megaco commands. We used a state which just tracked the identifier and state of each termination created by the test case:

```
-record(state,
   termination=[]    % list({symbolic(termid()),termstate()})
).
```

(The empty list is a default field value). For each termination, we kept track of which context it belonged to, and the streams that it contained:

```
-record(termstate,
   context,     % symbolic(contextid())
   streams=[]   % list({streamid(),streammode()})
).
```

Note that since both termination identifiers and context identifiers are allocated by the Proxy, then they are unknown during test generation, and are represented by symbolic components of the state. For example, the identifier of the first termination added might be represented by

```
{call,?MODULE,get_amms_reply_termid,[{var,1}]}
```

where `get_amms_reply_termid` extracts the identifier of a new termination from the reply to an *Add* message. As before, since we know where each termination and context identifier is created, we can refer to them symbolically by *unique* expressions, and compare identifiers by comparing their symbolic form.

We generated *Add*, *Modify*, and *Subtract* commands, being careful to modify and subtract only existing terminations, and to add no more than two terminations at a time to any context. To achieve the latter, we defined functions on the state to extract a list of *singleton contexts* (those with only a single termination), and *pair contexts* (those with two terminations). We could use these functions during test generation, thanks to our unique symbolic representation for context identifiers—we could tell, just from the symbolic state, whether or not two terminations belonged to the same context. Using these functions, we could define, for example, a precondition for *Add*, which ensures that we never try to add a third termination to any context:

```
precondition(S,{call,_,send_add,[Cxt,Streams,Req]}) ->
    lists:member(Cxt,
      [?megaco_choose_context_id
      | singletoncontexts(S)]);
```

(Here `?megaco_choose_context_id` is a "wild card" context identifier, which intructs the Proxy to allocate a new context—so this precondition allows *Adds* which both create new contexts and add a termination to an existing one.)

All of the sequences we generated were valid according to the Interwork Description, and so should have been executed successfully by the Proxy. But they were not—we found a total of four errors by this means. In each case, shrinking produced a minimal command sequence that provoked the error.

- Firstly, adding *one* termination to a context, and then modifying it immediately, led to a crash. This turned out to be because the code for *Modify* assumed that each media stream would have two "ends"—when only one termination was present, this was not the case.
- Secondly, adding a termination to a new context, and then subtracting it immediately, also led to a crash. Interestingly, we found this bug one day, but could not reproduce it on the next. This was because the main development team had also found the bug, and issued a patch in the meantime!
- Thirdly, adding two terminations to a context, and then modifying one of them, led to a crash *if the two terminations had differing numbers of streams*. For example, an attempt to connect a caller with audio and video to a caller with only audio might lead to this failure. The underlying reason was the same as in the first case: *Modify* assumed that every stream has two ends.
- Lastly, adding two terminations to a context, removing the second, adding a third and removing it again, and adding a fourth and removing it again, provoked a crash when the fourth termination was removed! We found this case by shrinking a sequence of over 160 commands, which demonstrates the power of shrinking quite convincingly! It is a test case that a human tester would be very unlikely to try. Of course, it is also unlikely to occur in practice—but the particular test case is just a symptom, not a cause. The underlying cause turned out to be that data-structures were corrupted the *first* time a termination was removed. Even if the corruption was survivable in the normal case, it is obviously undersirable for a system to corrupt its data. If nothing else, this is a trap lying in wait for any future developer modifying the code. It is interesting that QuickCheck could reveal this fault, despite knowing nothing at all about the Proxy's internal data.

One observation we made was that after each bug was found, virtually every run of QuickCheck found the same problem! There seems always to be a "most likely bug", which is more likely to be reported than any other. This is partly because of shrinking: a longer sequence provoking a more subtle bug, such as the fourth one above, is likely also to provoke the most likely one—at least, once some commands have been deleted. So shrinking tends to transform any failing case into one for the most likely bug. We found that, to make progress, we had to add *bug preconditions* to our specification to guarantee that the known bugs would not be provoked. For example, we changed the precondition for *Modify* to

```
precondition(S, {call,_,send_modify,[Cxt,...]}) ->
    lists:member(Cxt, paircontexts(S));
```

to avoid the first bug above. Formulating these bug preconditions is useful in itself: it makes us *formulate a hypothesis* about when the bug appears, *test the hypothesis* by verifying that the precondition does indeed avoid the bug, and *document the bug* in the form of this extra precondition.

This entire study took only around 6 days of work (spread over 3 months), during which we wrote about 500 lines of QuickCheck code (since reduced to 300 by using our latest state machine library). Bearing in mind that the Proxy was already well tested when we started, finding five errors is a very good result.

In a way, it is rather surprising that such simple sequences as the first three cases above were not tested earlier! We believe this is because, while it is quite easy to adapt existing test cases by varying parameters in the messages they contain, it is much harder to construct a sensible sequence of messages from scratch. Indeed, a number of "normal case" sequences are contained in the Interwork Description, and it is likely that these formed a basis for early testing at least. By generating any valid message sequence, we could explore a much wider variety of sequences than could reasonably be tested by manually constructed cases—and so the bugs were there to be found.

We were curious to know how valuable QuickCheck would have been if it had been available earlier in the development process. To find out, we recovered an older version of the Proxy software from Ericsson's source code repository, and tested it using the *same* QuickCheck specification. We found nine errors in six hours, most of the time being spent on formulating appropriate bug preconditions, so that the next bug could be discovered. Ericsson's fault reporting database contained just two reported faults for that version of the software, one of which was among the nine that QuickCheck found, and the other of which was in a lower level part of the software not tested by our specification. This suggests QuickCheck could have helped to find many bugs much earlier. It also demonstrates that the same properties can be used to find many different errors.

It is true that the bugs we found (with the exception of the *Add/Subtract* problem) would not have affected Ericsson's customers—because the Media Proxy is initially sold *only* as part of a larger system, which also contains an *Ericsson* media gateway controller. Ericsson's controller does not send message sequences of the kind that we discovered provoke bugs. On the other hand, we may wonder how the Proxy developers *know* that? After all, the interface between the two is specified by the Interwork Description, which makes no such restrictions. It turns out that the documentation does not tell the whole truth—the teams developing the two products also communicate informally, and indeed, the products have been tested together. So if Ericsson's controller *did* send sequences of this sort, then the bugs would probably have been found sooner. Part of the benefit of QuickCheck testing may thus be to clarify the specification—by making our "bug preconditions" part of the Interwork Description instead. Clarifying the specification is important, not least because the Media Proxy will eventually be used together with controllers from other manufacturers, and at that point it will be important to specify *precisely* what the Proxy supports.

This project was both instructive and sufficiently successful to persuade Ericsson to invest in a larger trial of QuickCheck. We are now in the process of training more users, and helping to introduce QuickCheck testing into several other projects at varying stages of development. We look forward to exciting developments as a result!

8   Concurrency

Concurrent programs are more difficult to test with QuickCheck, because they may exhibit non-deterministic behaviour. Finding a test case which *sometimes* fails is not nearly as useful as finding a test case which always fails. In particular, shrinking is difficult to apply when testing is non-deterministic, because the smaller tests performed while we search for a simplest failing case may succeed or fail by chance, leading to very unpredictable results. Nevertheless, we have had some success in applying QuickCheck to concurrent programs.

In one experiment, we tested a distributed version of the process registry, written by Ulf Wiger to provide a global name server. We constructed an abstract model of the registry, much like that in section 6, and used it to test that sequences of `register`, `whereis` and `unregister` calls returned the expected results. Then we wrote a property stating that for all *pairs* of command sequences, executed in separate processes, each call gave the expected result.

Unfortunately, the "expected result" depends on how the calls in the two processes are interleaved. Observing the actual interleaving is difficult, especially since the registry need not service the calls in the order in which they are made! Indeed, all we can really require is that the results returned by the registry calls in each process correspond to *some* interleaving of the two command sequences—any interleaving will do. We therefore formalised precisely this property in QuickCheck. Potentially we might need to explore *all possible* interleavings of the two sequences, and compare their results to the abstract model, which would be prohibitively expensive. However, we discovered that a simple depth-first search, cut off as soon as the interleaving prefix was inconsistent with the actual results, gave a fast testable property.

Initially, testing succeeded—because the Erlang scheduler allocates quite long time slices, and so although we spawned two parallel processes, each one ran to completion within its first time-slice. But then we instrumented the implementation of the registry with calls to `yield()` between atomic operations, thus ensuring that execution of our two processes would indeed be interleaved. As soon as we did so, we began to find errors. Moreover, they were repeatable, because by calling `yield()` so often, we were effectively using cooperative multi-tasking instead of the pre-emptive variant, and since the Erlang scheduler is actually a deterministic algorithm, it schedules cooperatively multi-tasking programs in a deterministic way. This form of testing proved to be very effective, and ultimately forced a complete redesign of the distributed process registry.

In another experiment, Hans Svensson applied QuickCheck to fault-tolerant distributed leader election algorithms [1]. In such algorithms, a group of nodes elect one to be the "leader", for example to maintain a global state. If the current leader crashes, a new one must be elected, and something sensible must also happen if a crashed leader recovers. Correctness properties include that a leader is eventually elected, and all nodes informed of its identity, and that there are never *two* leaders at the same time.

Svensson used an extension of QuickCheck which records a trace of events, and—by acknowledging events at random—controls the scheduling in ths system under test. The recorded traces then revealed whether or not testing succeeded.

Svensson began by testing an open source implementation by Thomas Arts and Ulf Wiger, already in use in the Erlang community. QuickCheck (and another random testing tool) revealed problems so severe that the code had to be abandoned. Svensson implemented a different algorithm due to Stoller [17], whose proof of correctness supplied many lemmata that could be tested by QuickCheck. Interestingly, QuickCheck revealed an error here too, connected with the way that node crashes are detected in Erlang, but it was easily fixed.

Both algorithms were proven correct in the literature, but their implementations did not work. The underlying reason is interesting: theoretical papers quite rightly make simplifying assumptions about the environment the algorithm will be used in, but real systems do not fulfill them precisely. Practitioners need to adapt the algorithms to the real situation, but then the correctness proofs no longer really apply. In fact, the assumptions are rarely even stated formally, with the result that we cannot really say whether the bug in the second implementation is also present in Stoller's paper—it depends on an aspect of the environment where Stoller's assumptions are not 100% precise.

Thus another way to use QuickCheck is to gain confidence that a formally verified algorithm has been correctly transferred to a real situation!

9   Testing Imperative Code

Can QuickCheck testing be applied to code written in imperative languages? Certainly it can! In fact, we tested the Media Proxy by sending it Megaco commands over TCP/IP—the fact that the Proxy software itself was also written in Erlang was quite irrelevant. In one of our follow-up projects, the system under test is actually written in C++, but this requires no changes at all in the approach. Provided we can conveniently invoke the system under test from Erlang or Haskell, then we can test it using QuickCheck.

But what if we just want to test a C or C++ API, for example, rather than a system that obeys commands sent over a network? Koen Claessen has worked extensively on this. One quite successful approach is just to generate random

C programs that exercise the API, and compile and run them in each test! C compilers are fast enough to make this practical. Another method is to generate an interpreter for API calls from an API specification, link that interpreter with the code under test, and run it in a separate process. QuickCheck can then be used to generate sequences of calls which are sent to the interpreter for execution, and to check the results which are sent back. By using this approach, Claessen has found (and simplified) many bugs in C++ applications.

Would it make more sense to make a *native* version of QuickCheck for C or C++? In fact, Claessen has done this too. The result was certainly fast, but ultimately, not as satisfactory. Remember that QuickCheck code consists not only of random generators, but usually also of a formal *model* of the system under test. QuickCheck is most effective if these models can be built simply and easily, and here, declarative programming languages are playing to their strengths. In comparison, a native imperative version is clumsy to use.

In fact, I believe that testing code is a very promising application area for declarative languages. It is not performance-critical, and since it does not form a part of the final system, the constraints on choice of programming language are much looser than usual. Indeed, it is already quite common to use a separate test scripting language, different from the implementation language of the code under test—so why shouldn't that language be declarative? I believe that the barriers to adopting declarative languages are much lower in this area than for programming in general—particularly if that makes a tool such as QuickCheck more convenient to use. Time will tell if I am correct!

10   Erlang vs. Haskell

It is interesting to compare Erlang and Haskell as host languages for QuickCheck. We initially expected an Erlang version to be a little clumsier to use than the Haskell original, because of the lack of lazy evaluation, Haskell's type system, and monadic syntax (see section 5). Yet the difficulties these caused turned out to be minor. On the other hand, Erlang's *lack* of a type system turned out to bring unexpected benefits. For example, the Haskell QuickCheck generator for times of day, represented as pairs of hours and minutes, is

```
liftM2 (,) (choose 0 23) (choose 0 59)
```

(where (,) is the pairing operator, and liftM2 lifts it to operate on monadic values). The Erlang QuickCheck generator is

```
{choose(0,23), choose(0,59)}
```

(where {X,Y} is Erlang's notation for pairs). The Erlang notation is more concise and intuitive, and definitely easier to sell to customers! In general, Quviq QuickCheck permits any data-structure containing embedded generators to be used as a generator for data-structures of that shape—something which is very convenient for users, but quite impossible in Haskell, where embedding a generator in a data-structure would normally result in a type error. This technique is used throughout the generators written at Ericsson.

Moreover, our approach to state machine testing involved symbolic representations of programs. In Haskell, we would need to define a datatype to represent function calls, with one constructor per function under test, and write an interpreter for those calls—just as we did in section 2 for `insert` and `deleteMin`. In Erlang, we could represent a call just by two atoms and a (heterogenous) argument list, and provide a single generic interpreter `run_commands`, thanks to Erlang's ability to call a function given only its name and arguments. This reduces the programming effort for the library user quite significantly.

Of course, the penalty for using Erlang is that type errors are not found by a type checker! Instead they must be found by testing... but this is easier than usual thanks to QuickCheck. We made many type errors when constructing the complex datatype of messages intended for the Media Proxy—but we found them immediately by testing that all messages we generated could be encoded to ASCII, and decoded again. Far from being second best, we conclude that Erlang is actually a very suitable host language for QuickCheck!

11   Discussion

Random testing is an old technique [10], which is attracting renewed interest—as shown, for example, by the new *International Workshop on Random Testing*, first held this year. It has been very successful for so-called *fuzz testing*, where nonsense inputs are supplied to try to provoke software to crash [14]—"monkey testing" of GUIs is an example of this. Random testing is more difficult to apply for *positive* testing, where meaningful inputs are supplied to the software under test, and its correct behaviour is tested. QuickCheck's flexible control of random generation makes it particularly suitable for this task.

Shrinking failing test cases is a powerful diagnostic technique, due to Hildebrandt and Zeller [11], who used it, for example, to shrink a test case that crashed Mozilla from 95 user actions on a web page consisting of almost 900 lines of HTML, to three user actions on one line of HTML ! Their *delta debugging* method starts from *two* tests, a successful one and a failing one, and uses a generic algorithm to search the space between them for two most-similar tests, one successful, and one failing. QuickCheck searches only from a failed test, towards smaller test cases, but using arbitrary user-defined shrinking methods.

Even though shrinking is powerful, we find it works best when the *original* failing test is not too large. New QuickCheck users are often tempted to generate *large* test cases, probably because doing so by hand is labour intensive, while using QuickCheck it is easy. Yet large test cases run slowly—so fewer tests can be run in a reasonable time—and when they fail, the reason is hard to understand. Shrinking them is at best time consuming (because many tests must be run), and at worst, may not result in as small a failing test as possible. In our experience, it is better to run many, many small tests, rather than a smaller number of large ones. Most errors can be provoked by a small test case, *once the error is understood*—and it is these small test cases which we want QuickCheck to find.

There are, of course, errors that no small test can find, such as errors that occur when a large table overflows. We encountered such an error when testing an implementation of purely function arrays, represented as binary trees with lists of up to ten elements in the leaves. An optimised array construction function failed when constructing a tree more than two levels deep... that is, with more than 40 elements. QuickCheck rarely provoked this case, until we explicitly increased the test size. Yet, in such cases, the software *should* still work if the table were smaller, or if the lists in the leaves were up to three elements, rather than ten—so why not reduce these constants for testing? Doing so makes the boundary cases much more likely to be exercised, and so increases the probability of revealing errors. When looking for a needle in a haystack, nothing helps so much as making the haystack smaller!

We have found that a complete formal specification of the code under test is often unnecessary. Simple properties are often enough to reveal even subtle errors, which is good news for testers. A nice example is our discovery of data-structure corruption in the Media Proxy, using properties which only interact with it via protocol commands. However, more precise specifications may find errors with fewer tests, and find smaller failing cases, because the error is revealed faster. In our example, a single *Add* and *Subtract* would have been sufficient to reveal the corruption, instead of the seven-command sequence we found.

One subtle change that QuickCheck brings about is a change in the *economic value* of failing test cases. Developers tend to pounce on the first failing case, re-run it, turn on debugging and tracing, and generally invest a lot of effort in understanding *that particular case*. When test cases are constructed painfully by hand, or even reported in the field, then this makes sense—test cases are valuable, compared to the developer's time. When a new failing case can be generated in seconds, then this no longer makes sense. Perhaps the next run of QuickCheck will find a smaller case, and save much diagnostic effort! It makes sense to generate several failing cases, and choose the simplest to work with, rather than rush into debugging as soon as the first failure is found. Or, if the cases found are overcomplex, it may be worthwhile to improve the shrinking strategy, and see whether that leads to a simpler case to debug. Improved shrinking may bring benefits in many future tests as well, so the effort is well invested.

We have found that testing with QuickCheck is perceived as quite difficult by developers. It is initially hard to see what to test, and the temptation is to make minor random variation of parameter values, rather than formulate more general properties. Using QuickCheck successfully is close in spirit to finding a good way to formalise a problem—which has occupied plenty of researchers over the years! It is therefore important to develop good "model specifications" that developers can follow, and to *simplify, simplify, simplify* the use of QuickCheck as much as possible. A good example of this is our state machine testing library, which is built entirely on top of the QuickCheck core. In principle, this could have been written by any user—but in practice, if it took me four iterations to get the design right, after seven years experience of QuickCheck, then it is unreasonable to expect new users to develop such toolkits for themselves.

Thomas Arts and I have founded a start-up, Quviq AB, to develop and market Quviq QuickCheck. Interestingly, this is the *second* implementation of QuickCheck for Erlang. The first was presented at the Erlang User Conference in 2003, and made available on the web. Despite enthusiasm at the conference, it was never adopted in industry. *We tried to give away the technology, and it didn't work!* So now we are selling it, with considerably more success. Of course, Quviq QuickCheck is no longer the same product that was offered in 2003—it has been improved in many ways, adapted in the light of customers' experience, extended to be simpler to apply to customers' problems, and is available together with training courses and consultancy. That is, we are putting a great deal of work into helping customers adopt the technology. It was naive to expect that simply putting source code on the web would suffice to make that happen, and it would also be unreasonable to expect funding agencies to pay for all the work involved. In that light, starting a company is a natural way for a researcher to make an impact on industrial practice—and so far, at least, it seems to be succeeding.

Finally, recall that Koen Claessen and I originally developed QuickCheck for fun. Perhaps for that very reason, using QuickCheck *is* fun! We see developers on our courses filled with enthusiasm, raring to test their code. Testing is not always seen to be so alluring—indeed, it is often regarded as something of a chore. QuickCheck really *makes testing fun*—and that, in itself, is a worthwhile achievement.

Acknowledgements

Most of the material in this paper is based on joint work, with my colleagues Koen Claessen and Hans Svensson at Chalmers, Thomas Arts at the IT University in Gothenburg, and Ulf Wiger and Joakim Johansson at Ericsson. Time constraints made it impossible to write this paper together, but their contributions are here nonetheless. Any mistakes are, of course, my own!

References

1. Thomas Arts, Koen Claessen, John Hughes, and Hans Svensson. Testing implementations of formally verified algorithms. In *Proceedings of the 5th Conference on Software Engineering Research and Practice in Sweden*, 2005.
2. T. Ball, E. Bounimova, B. Cook, V. Levin, J. Lichtenberg, C. McGarvey, B. Ondrusek, S. Rajamani, and A. Ustuner. Thorough static analysis of device drivers. In *EuroSys 2006*, 2006.
3. Kent Beck. *Extreme Programming Explained: Embrace Change, Second Edition*. Addison Wesley Professional, second edition, November 2004.
4. Koen Claessen and John Hughes. Quickcheck: a lightweight tool for random testing of haskell programs. In *ICFP '00: Proceedings of the fifth ACM SIGPLAN international conference on Functional programming*, pages 268–279, New York, NY, USA, 2000. ACM Press.
5. Koen Claessen and John Hughes. Testing monadic code with quickcheck. In *Haskell '02: Proceedings of the 2002 ACM SIGPLAN workshop on Haskell*, pages 65–77, New York, NY, USA, 2002. ACM Press.

6. Koen Claessen and John Hughes. Specification-based testing with QuickCheck. In Jeremy Gibbons and Oege de Moor, editors, *Fun of Programming*, Cornerstones of Computing. Palgrave, March 2003.

7. Koen Claessen, Colin Runciman, Olaf Chitil, John Hughes, and Malcolm Wallace. Testing and tracing lazy functional programs using quickcheck and hat. In Johan Jeuring and Simon Peyton Jones, editors, *4th Summer School in Advanced Functional Programming*, volume 2638 of *LNCS*. Springer, 2003.

8. Mark Fewster and Dorothy Graham. *Software test automation: effective use of test execution tools*. ACM Press/Addison-Wesley Publishing Co., New York, NY, USA, 1999.

9. Cormac Flanagan, K. Rustan M. Leino, Mark Lillibridge, Greg Nelson, James B. Saxe, and Raymie Stata. Extended static checking for Java. In *Proceedings of the ACM SIGPLAN 2002 Conference on Programming Language Design and Implementation (PLDI'2002)*, volume 37, pages 234–245, June 2002.

10. Dick Hamlet. Random testing. In J. Marciniak, editor, *Encyclopedia of Software Engineering*, pages 970–978. Wiley, 1994.

11. Ralf Hildebrandt and Andreas Zeller. Simplifying failure-inducing input. In *ISSTA '00: Proceedings of the 2000 ACM SIGSOFT international symposium on Software testing and analysis*, pages 135–145, New York, NY, USA, 2000. ACM Press.

12. Xavier Leroy. Formal certification of a compiler back-end or: programming a compiler with a proof assistant. In *POPL*, pages 42–54, 2006.

13. John Marciniak and Robert Vienneau. Software engineering baselines. Technical report, Data and Analysis Center for Software, 1996. http://www.dacs.dtic.mil/techs/baselines/.

14. Barton P. Miller, Louis Fredriksen, and Bryan So. An empirical study of the reliability of unix utilities. *Commun. ACM*, 33(12):32–44, 1990.

15. Chris Okasaki. Fun with binary heap trees. In Jeremy Gibbons and Oege de Moor, editors, *Fun of Programming*, Cornerstones of Computing, pages 1–16. Palgrave, March 2003.

16. Telecommunication Standardization sector of ITU. ITU-T Rec. H248.1, gateway control protocol. Technical report, International Telecommunication Union, September 2005.

17. S. Stoller. Leader election in distributed systems with crash failures. Technical Report 169, Indiana University, 1997.

18. Ulf Wiger, Gösta Ask, and Kent Boortz. World-class product certification using erlang. *SIGPLAN Not.*, 37(12):25–34, 2002.

A Constraint Programming Approach to Bioinformatics Structural Problems

Pedro Barahona and Ludwig Krippahl

Dep. de Informática, Universidade Nova de Lisboa, 2825 Monte de Caparica, Portugal
ludi@di.fct.unl.pt, pb@di.fct.unl.pt

Abstract. In this paper we show how Constraint Programming (CP) techniques have been used to handle bioinformatics structural problems, namely in protein structure prediction and protein interaction (docking). Solving these problems requires innovative modelling of the problem variables and constraints, and the application of advanced CP features to handle the problems efficiently, namely the exploitation of global constraints and local search, in addition to more standard binary constraint propagation. Both applications, respectively PSICO (Processing Structural Information with Constraint programming and Optimisation), and BiGGER (Bimolecular complex Generation with Global Evaluation and Ranking) have been incorporated in a platform, Chemera, that aims at supporting (and has effectively supported, namely in protein docking), biochemists in their research.

1 Introduction

Bioinformatics is an increasingly important discipline where computer science methods are used to study biological entities and systems. This is especially important as a wealth of biological data have been gathered in recent years, in many cases freely accessible over the Web. By taking advantage of this availability, computational models may suggest what are the most promising outcomes, possibly decreasing the number (and cost) of experiments that are required to study certain biological properties.

Many interesting problems, requiring significant computational resources do arise in Bioinformatics. For example, sequencing problems are common, where one aims at reconstruct some large polymer (e.g. protein, DNA or RNA molecules) from a sequence of partially overlapping fragments of the polymer obtained in some experimental setting.

Other problems are related to the behaviour of biochemical systems, in particular metabolic pathways, that study the interaction of molecules along the time. Interesting pathways usually regard the processing of some biochemical molecules (for example, the citric acid cycle, glycolisis and other chemical reactions that are responsible for the metabolism of a cell), and are eventually related to gene expression, i.e. when genes become active and produce the corresponding enzymes and other proteins.

Finally, structural problems, such as the determination of the three-dimensional structure of proteins and other molecules, are also very important. Such determination is of particular interest in bioinformatics since in addition to other electro-chemical

M. Hanus (Ed.): PADL 2007, LNCS 4354, pp. 33–49, 2007.

properties (e.g. hidrophobicity, hidrophily, polarity) a key factor that determines whether two proteins interact is that proteins have shapes that allow them to spatially fit in the contact surface areas (active regions) .

This wide variety of problems demand for several distinct computational techniques, ranging from data mining and machine learning to explore similarities between the problem under study and problems already solved (e.g. homology studies), or a variety of simulation techniques to study, with some adequate level of abstraction, the dynamic behaviour of biochemical reaction networks [1]. Among these techniques, we have been applying, with considerable success, constraint programming to structural problems, namely the determination of protein structure and the study of protein interaction ("docking").

Constraint Programming is usually applied to constraint satisfaction problems (CSPs) by providing a declarative and efficient way of modelling such problems, through the specification not only of a set of variables and respective domains (often finite), but also the constraints that restrict the values that the variables can take (some variants to classical CSPs also include the addition of an optimisation function, or a partial satisfaction of the constraints). Non trivial problems are NP-complete or harder, and so a significant amount of search is required to solve instances of even of moderate size.

Several techniques are exploited in constraint programming to make search more efficient. In addition to the inevitable use of heuristics, search is interleaved with some kind of "reasoning", in that whenever a choice is performed, the consequences of such choice are analysed to make the subsequent search more informed and effective.

Some problems (typically large optimisation problems) are adequately addressed with local search techniques, where search is driven by the optimisation of some objective function (even for constraint satisfaction problems where that function may simply be a measure of the constraints violation, that is to be minimised). In this case, reasoning is largely related with the study of the neighbourhoods of current hypotheses, to allow better heuristics in the search for the optima of the objective (e.g. COMET[2]).

In complete methods, relying on backtrack search, reasoning is rather performed through various types of "constraint propagation". Such propagation, aims at decreasing the number of possible values for the variables not yet assigned specific values, and hence decrease the search space. Some basic techniques exist to deal with binary constraints. In particular, maintaining arc-consistency (usually with an AC-3 type algorithm [3]) enforces that values in a variable that share a constraint with another variable have support in the values of the latter variable, otherwise they can be discarded.

Moreover, constraint programming languages are also quite flexible, in that they allow a declarative specification of even quite complex constraints, in contrast with other declarative approaches to constraint solving (e.g. SAT or integer programming) where all constraints have to be converted into a rigid and expressively poor language (e.g. clauses and linear constraints). Constraint programming languages allow an easy combination of primitive constraints, into more complex ones, or even the specification of primitive global constraints, for which specific and efficient propagation methods exist that are seamlessly integrated into the general constraint propagation mechanisms [4]. The classical example is the global constraint all_different, that constrains a set of k variables to take distinct values and for which some graph-based algorithms propagate more efficiently than would the set with $k(k-1)/2$ difference constraints over all pairs of variables [5].

Despite the expressive power of constraint programming languages and systems, and the efficient search techniques provided, there is a non-negligible amount of ingenuity that is required to obtain the most adequate models to the problem in hand. This is particularly so in non-conventional problems, which might be usefully addressed by constraint programming only if an appropriate model is adopted, and if adequate and advanced constraint programming techniques are applied in the solving process.

In this paper we address the way in which, in our tool, CHEMERA (available in the Web [6]) two structural bioinformatics problems are modelled and solved by constraint programming techniques. Their models adopted unconventional domains, and their solving does apply some main features of CP, namely constraint propagation, improved propagation by means of global constraints and some complementarity between complete backtrack search methods and incomplete local search methods.

Section 2 introduces the main features of PSICO, the component that addresses the problem of structure determination of proteins, taking into account Nuclear Magnetic Resonance (NMR) induced constraints. Section 3 reports on BiGGER, and its use of constraint programming techniques to handle protein interaction, often referred to as protein docking. Section 4 discusses a number of ideas aimed at improving the current algorithms, specially for the problem of structure determination. The paper ends with a section on concluding remarks.

2 PSICO: Modelling Protein Structure

Constraint Programming has been used in protein structure prediction in two distinct approaches. In the first, the problem is addressed *ab initio*: all that is known is the primary structure of a protein (i.e. the sequence of its amino acid residues). In this case, the models assume that these residues are placed in a three dimensional lattice (e.g. cubic or more complex face-centred cubic lattices, as in [7]) and a solution should minimize some energy function. In practise, such function takes into account either the hydrophobic (H) or the hydrophilic, also known as polar (P), nature of the amino acids, and aims at maximizing the number of H-H contacts in the centre of the protein. Alternative models allow more sophisticated energy functions to minimise, and take into account secondary structures (alpha helices or beta-sheets) that might be known, or at least suspected from homology studies [8].

Although this H-P model is quite interesting from a computational viewpoint, it leads to significantly distorted solutions, since the dihedral angles that are possible (e.g. 90° in cubic lattices) are not those that are chemically admissible. Moreover, these models do not take into account the availability of biochemical data that should be used not only to test, but also to drive the search for a solution, in the spirit of constraint programming.

Hence, we adopted an alternative model for structure prediction that takes into account as much information as possible, including available experimental data. There are several sources of information that can help model the structure of a protein. First of all, the amino acid sequences of the protein chains determines most chemical bonds, restricting inter atomic distances in many atom pairs, angles formed by atom triplets, of even larger groups of atoms that are effectively rigidly bound together by the chemical bonds. NMR data provides distance constraints by showing that two atoms must be close enough for the Nuclear Overhauser Effect to be felt, limits the angles of rotation around some chemical bonds, or can even suggest limits for relative special orientations of groups of atoms with Residual Dipolar Coupling data. Furthermore, homology with known structures or modelling secondary structure can provide detailed information of the structure of parts of the protein being modelled.

We can divide this information into three types of constraints: distance constraints between two atoms, group constraints that fix the relative positions of a group of atoms in a rigid configuration, and torsion angle constraints that restrict the relative orientation of two groups joined together by a chemical bond.

The constraint programming approach that we adopt for protein structure determination is composed of two phases: firstly it adopts a backtrack search where enumeration of variables is interleaved with constraint propagation until an approximate solution is found. Secondly, this structure is improved by means of a local search optimisation.

2.1 Variable Domains and Propagation of Distance Constraints

The chemical information that is known from the protein sequence provides bond length and bond angle constraints. Bond length constraints are also distance constraints, and the bond angles can be modelled by sets of distance constraints. In fact, the structure and flexibility of an amino acid can be modelled by a conjunction of pair wise distance constraints between all the atoms. To model this information we consider two types of constraints: In constraints (eq. 1) and Out constraints (eq. 2).

$$\textit{In } \text{constraint} \quad \max(|x_1 - x_2|, |y_1 - y_2|, |z_1 - z_2|) \leq k \tag{1}$$

$$\textit{Out } \text{constraint} \quad |x_1 - x_2| \geq \alpha k \lor |y_1 - y_2| \geq \alpha k \lor |z_1 - z_2| \geq \alpha k \quad \alpha = \frac{1}{\sqrt{3}} \tag{2}$$

These two constraint types are used to model all the chemical structural information, whether it is known beforehand or from the NMR spectroscopy experiments. Notice that rather then considering Euclidean distances and spherical regions, we use an approximation that considers cuboid regions which are much easier to propagate, as discussed below.

The variables we wish to determine are the positions of the geometric centres of the atoms, that is, the (x, y, z) coordinates in a single variable with a three dimensional domain, and this domain is represented as a set of cuboid regions. One cuboid defines the Good region, which is the volume that contains the possible positions for the atom. A set of non-overlapping cuboids contained in the Good region defines the NoGoods region, which contains the positions from which the atom must be excluded (see Figure 1).

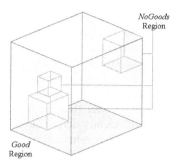

Fig. 1. The domain for the position of an atom is composed of two regions. The *Good* region is a cuboid that defines the positions for the atom that comply with the set of *In* constraints. The *NoGoods* region is a set of non-overlapping cuboids that define the volumes within the *Good* region from which the atom is excluded by the *Out* constraints.

We distinguished between the two types of distance constraints (In and Out) because of the way in which they are propagated (see Figure 2).

- The **In** *constraints* are propagated by simple intersection. The Good region of atom A will be the intersection of the current Good region of A with the neighbourhood of the Good region of atom B, defined as the Good region of B augmented by the distance value of the In constraint between A and B. The intersection of two cuboid blocks is very simple to calculate, requiring only Max and Min operations on the extremity coordinates, so propagation of In constraints is very efficient.

- For an **Out** *constraint* the propagation involves adding the exclusion region defined by the constraint to the NoGoods region of the affected atom. The most complex operation in this process is insuring that the NoGoods region consists of non-overlapping cuboids. This reduces propagation efficiency, but simplifies the task of determining the cases of failure when the NoGoods region becomes identical to the Good region.

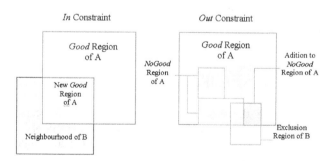

Fig. 2. This figure shows the propagation of both types of constraints. For *In* constraint propagation, the domain of atom A is reduced by intersecting the *Good* region of A with the neighbourhood of B. For *Out* constraint propagation a *NoGood* cuboid region is added, by intersecting the *Good* region of A with the exclusion region of B.

Arc-consistency is guaranteed by propagating the constraints on each atom that suffered a domain restriction until no domain changes. After complete propagation, one atom is selected for enumeration, and the propagation step is repeated.

Enumeration interleaves the arc-consistency enforcement following a first fail approach on a round robin system. First, the atom with the smallest domain that was not selected in the current enumeration round is selected for enumeration. Exception is made if the coordinate domain is smaller than 2.0Å for all three coordinates, in which case the atom is considered sufficiently determined and no domain reduction is necessary. The domain of this atom is then split into two similarly sized domains by 'cutting' across the longest coordinate axis (x, y or z) of the domain. The domain of the atom will be one of these two 'halves'.

Enumeration heuristics now come into play. One simple heuristic that was shown to be successful [9,10] was to choose for the new domain the half cuboid that is less occupied by the domains of all other atoms, but additional considerations such as the chemical nature of the amino acid or the prediction of local structures can play a role at this stage to inform the choice of which regions of the domain to eliminate.

Since the domain for the enumerated atom is reduced, constraints are then propagated (as discussed above), and then another atom is selected for enumeration (the atom with the smallest domain not selected yet). This process of selection and domain reduction is repeated until all atoms were selected once, after which a new round of enumeration starts. In case of failure it is possible to backtrack and try different domain reductions, but backtracking is limited both for practical reasons and because it is often the case that the set of constraints is inconsistent due to experimental noise, and in these cases the user needs some structure, even if only partially correct, to help correct the inconsistencies by reassigning the constraints.

2.2   Propagation of Global Rigid Group Constraints

The last section outlined the basic framework for PSICO: the domain representations, arc-consistency interleaved with a round-robin enumeration, and limited backtracking. The propagation of rigid group constraints extends this framework to include the information on the configuration of groups of atoms. These can be prosthetic groups, secondary structures like alpha-helices, or more complex domains obtained by homology modelling, for which we can know the relative positions of all atoms but which fits within the structure of the protein in an unknown position and orientation.

Since rigid groups include many atoms that may only move together, reasoning globally with all these atoms, i.e. maintaining generalised arc-consistency, achieves better propagation than simply considering, one at a time, distance constraints between all the pairs of the atoms in the group (simple arc-consistency). This improvement is typical of reasoning with global constraints in constraint programming settings, and close to all-different reasoning [5], although with different domains. This section briefly outlines how generalised arc consistency is achieved with global rigid-group constraints.

Given a fixed orientation, it is trivial to reduce the domains of the atoms in a rigid group. This requires simply that we determine the limits for the translations of the group that do not place any atom outside its domain. Denoting by w_c one of the coordinates of the centre of the group (x, y or z), by w_j the same coordinate for atom j, and by w_{max} and w_{min} the upper and lower limits, respectively, for that coordinate of a domain (of atom j or of the centre c), such limits are related by the following equations (note that the absolute values of w_c and w_j are irrelevant; only the coordinate difference w_c-w_j is important, and is independent of translation) :

$$w_{max\,c} = Min_{j=1}^{n}(w_{max\,j} + (w_c - w_j)) \qquad (3a)$$

$$w_{min\,c} = Max_{j=1}^{n}(w_{min\,j} + (w_c - w_j)) \qquad (3b)$$

Equations 3 assume a fixed orientation of the group, but we cannot make that assumption, since the group is free to rotate. Without loss of generality, we shall consider the case of the limits in the x and y coordinates as a function of a rotation around the z axis, centred on the centre point of the group.

To determine the limits for the placement of the group as a function of the rotation around one axis, considering the rotation around the other axes fixed, we need but intersect the contributions of all atoms to these limits (see details in [11]).

Now we need to extend this to rotations around all three axes. Dividing the rotations into finite intervals, each orientation corresponds to an interval of angles, instead of just a single angle, and each coordinate to an interval of values. This way each rotation can be divided into a manageable number of orientations. Nevertheless, whereas rotating coordinates around an angular value gives a single values for the coordinates, rotating around an interval of angles results in intervals of coordinates. However, as long as certain conditions are met (more specifically, that the intervals for the angles partition the rotation with a step size that is a sub-multiple of 90°) then the intervals of the corresponding coordinates are trivial to calculate (more details in [11]).

2.3 More on Global Constraints – Propagation of Torsion Angle Constraints

In some cases, it is possible for a molecule to change configuration by groups of atoms rotating around a chemical bond. It is this process that allows proteins to fold into their shapes, and the angle of such a rotation is called the torsion angle. Some experimental techniques may provide constraints on torsion angles, and this is useful information when modelling a protein structure.

The propagation of these constraints is an extension to the rigid group constraint propagation discussed in the previous section. We can consider that two rigid groups connected by a bond allowing rotation is a single rigid group if the torsion angle is fixed. If the torsion angle is an interval, we can account for the relative coordinates of all atoms in the two groups by using the corresponding intervals, in a way similar to that discussed in the previous section.

This procedure allows us to extend the rigid group constraint propagation to any number of rigid groups connected by torsion angles. There is a trade off between total group size and number of torsion angles to use, and the right trade off is also a function of the constraints on the torsion angles and the size of the atom domains at the time of propagation, so currently we are researching the best ways to optimise torsion angle constraint propagation taking into account all these factors.

2.4 Optimisation

Once enumeration terminates, each atom has a small cuboid domain, and a more exact position of the atom is obtained through an optimisation procedure, due to two main reasons. Firstly, enforcing smaller cuboids often leads to an exponential number of backtracks, unless a good heuristics is used. Secondly, if the geometric centre of the cuboids is considered the value for the atoms, then the resulting molecular structure does not respect the distance and angle values for the chemical bonds.

To address these problems, the Constraint Propagation method described so far, is complemented with a local search component that implements a simple torsion angle optimisation algorithm. Modelling the protein as a tree of rigid atom groups connected by rotatable bonds insures that the fine scale structure of the molecule is respected.

The minimisation proceeds in two steps. In the first step the torsion angle values for the torsion angle model are adjusted to minimize the distance between the atomic positions in the structure provided by the CP stage and the respective positions in the torsion angle model. This fits the torsion angle model to the CP solution, thus providing a chemically sound structure close to respecting the distance constraints (details can be found in [12]).

3 BiGGER: The Docking Algorithm

Another structural bioinformatics application where we have successfully applied constraint programming techniques is protein interaction (docking). A common trend is to model interactions using only knowledge derived from the structure and physicochemical properties of the proteins involved. Some algorithms have been developed [13, 14, 15] or adapted [16] to use data on the interaction mechanisms, but this approach is still the exception rather than the norm. BiGGER is one of these exceptions, as it has been developed from inception to help the researcher bring into the modelling process as much data as available, and Constraint Programming techniques have much improved the efficiency and expressiveness of earlier versions [17].

Again, not only simple propagation of constraints is obtained by maintaining arc-consistency, but also generalised arc consistency is achieved to deal with a special global constraint that can be used to enforce specific activity regions in the docking proteins.

At the core of our protein docking algorithm is the representation of the protein shapes and the measure of surface contact. The former is a straightforward representation using a regular cubic lattice of cells, similar to that commonly used in the Fast Fourier Transform (FFT) methods derived from [18]. In BiGGER the cells do not correspond to numerical values, but each cell can be either an empty cell, a surface cell, or a core cell. The surface cells define the surface of the structure, and the overlap of surface cells measures the surface of contact. Figure 3 illustrates these concepts, showing on the first two panels a cutaway diagram of the grid representing a protein structure, and on the third panel a cutaway diagram of two grids in contact, showing the contact region corresponding to a set of overlapping surface cells.

This representation has several advantages over the FFT approach, requiring about a thousand times less memory (approximately 15Mb in BiGGER vs. 8Gb for FFT in large proteins) and being up to ten times faster than FFT [17]. BiGGER also models side-chain flexibility implicitly by adjusting the core grid representation [13] and allows for hard or soft docking simulations depending on the nature of the interaction to model. Furthermore, this representation and the search algorithm can take advantage of information about the interaction to simultaneously improve the results and speed up the calculations.

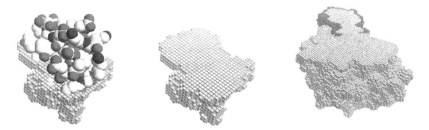

Fig. 3. The image on the left shows a protein structure overlaid on a cutaway of the respective grid, with spheres representing the atoms of the protein. The centre figure shows only the grid generated for this protein, cut to show the surface in light blue and the core region in grey. The rightmost image shows two grids (red and blue) in contact.

3.1 Restricting the Search to Surface Overlapping Regions

A significant proportion of all possible configurations for the two grids results in no surface overlap. Much can be gained by restricting the search to those configurations where surface cells of one grid overlap surface cells of the other. This is achieved by encoding the grids in a convenient way: instead of individual cells, grids are composed of lists of intervals specifying the segments of similar cells along the X coordinate. These lists are arranged in a two-dimensional array on the Y-Z plane.

This encoding not only reduces the memory requirements for storing the grids, but also leads naturally to searching along the X axis by comparing segments instead of by running through all the possible displacements along this coordinate. Given two surface segments, one from each structure and aligned in the same Y and Z coordinates, we can calculate the displacements where overlap will occur simply from the X coordinates of the extremities of the segments.

Representing by variable X, with domain Dx, the displacement of one structure relative to the other along the X direction, this approach of comparing segments efficiently enforces the constraint requiring surface overlaps, by reducing the domain of this variable to only those values where the constraint is verified. To begin with, each such variable is initialised to include all translations that may result in contacts by a bounds consistency check: if MaxA/MaxB and MinA/MinB are the maximum/minimum coordinate values along the X axis for the surface grid cells of the two structures, the domain of X is initialised to the interval [MinA-MaxB , MaxB-MinA]. This approach can be generalized for the translational search in the other 2 directions Y and Z.

3.2 Eliminating Regions of Core Overlap

Another important constraint in this problem is that core regions of the grids cannot overlap, for that indicates the structures are occupying the same space instead of being in contact. By identifying the configurations where such overlaps occur, it is possible to eliminate from consideration those surface segments on each structure that cannot overlap surface segments on the other structure without violating the core overlap constraint. Some surface segments can thus be discarded from each search along the X axis. Figure 4 illustrates this procedure.

One structure, labelled A, is shown in the centre of the image. The other structure, labelled B, will be moved along the horizontal direction to scan all possible configurations but, from the overlap of core segments, a set of positions along the horizontal direction can be eliminated. Structure B is shown in position 1 to the right of A and in position 39 to the left of A. Clearly, in this case, B cannot occupy some positions in the centre.

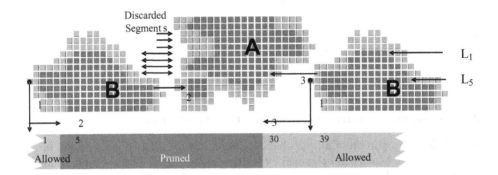

Fig. 4. Grid B is translated along the horizontal direction relative to grid A. The vertical arrows marked 1 indicate the position of B on the lower horizontal bar, which shows the allowed and forbidden values for the position of B. The arrows marked 2 and 3 show the allowed displacement of B. The group of horizontal arrows indicates segments to be discarded.

In particular, the domain of variable X, representing the displacement of one structure relative to the other along the X direction, can be pruned from the values 5 to 30. This is a contiguous interval in this example, but the domain of X can be an arbitrary set of intervals in the general case. This domain reduction due to the core overlap constraint propagates to the surface overlap, since some surface segments of A and B will not overlap in valid configurations. Some of these are shown in Figure 2 by the group of arrows to the left of structure A (Discarded Segments). For the last double arrow, for example, the surface cells of structures A and B would only overlap for X=7, a value pruned from the domain of X. In contrast, in the line below such overlap occurs for X = 3, a value kept in the domain. Thus the core overlap constraint allows us to reduce the number of surface segments to consider when counting surface overlaps.

The BiGGER algorithm imposes bounds consistency on these sets of core grids segments, which requires $O(k^2)$ operations, where k is the number of intervals defined by the core grid segments for each line and for each structure. This reduces the possible translation values, Dx, and affects the generation of the surface segments lists to take into account Dx, including only those segments that could overlap given this domain (again, by imposing bounds consistency on the intervals). Finally, the overlap of surface cells is determined for each allowed translation value in Dx. This requires testing the bounds of the matching surface segments in a way similar to imposing bounds consistency, which is of $O(k^2)$ for each line, and then counting the contacts along X, which is of $O(N)$.

The algorithm performs $O(N^2)$ steps by looping through the Dz and Dy, and in each of these steps it loops through the Z,Y plane twice to find the matching core and surface segments and compare the segment bounds. So each step in the z, y loop is $O(N^2k^2)$, where k is the number of segments per line. Except for fractal structures, k is a small constant. For convex shapes, for example, k is always two or less, and even for complex shapes like proteins k is seldom larger than two. Thus the time complexity of the search algorithm when imposing bounds constraints on the overlap of surface and core grid cells is $O(N^4)$, very close to the $O(N^3Log(N))$ of the FFT method. Furthermore, the comparisons done in the BiGGER algorithm are much faster and this constant factor makes BiGGER more efficient for values of N up to several hundred [17]. Finally, the space complexity of BiGGER is $O(N^2)$, significantly better and with a lower constant factor than the FFT space complexity of $O(N^3)$.

3.3 Restricting the Lower Bounds on Surface Contact

Branch and Bound is a common technique that Constraint Programming often uses in optimisation problems, to restrict the domains of the variables to where it is still possible to obtain a better value for the function to optimise. In this case, we wish to optimise the overlap of surface cells, and restrict the search to those regions where this overlap can be higher than that of the lowest ranking model to be kept.

This constraint is applied to the Z and Y coordinate search loops, by counting the total surface cells for each grid as a function of the Z coordinate (that is, the sum over each X, Y plane) and as a function of each Y, Z pair (that is, the sum of each line in the X axis). The determination of the Z translation domain considers the list of total surface cells for each X,Y plane along the Z axis. For each Z translation value these two lists will align in a different way, as the one structure is displaced in the Z direction relative to the other. The minimum of each pair of aligned values gives the maximum possible surface overlap for that X,Y plane at this Z translation, and the sum of these minima gives the maximum possible surface overlap for this Z translation. Since there are $O(N)$ possible Z translations to test and, for each, $O(N)$ values to compare and add, this step requires $O(N^2)$ operations.

The same applies to restricting the Y translation domain, but taking into account the current value of variable Z. This is also an $O(N^2)$ operation identical to the pruning of the Z domain, but must be repeated for each value of the z translation variable, adding a total time complexity of $O(N^3)$ to the algorithm. Since the BiGGER algorithm has a time complexity of $O(N^4)$, these operations do not result in a significant efficiency loss.

By setting a minimum value for the surface contact count, or by setting a fixed number of best models to retain, this constraint allows the algorithm to prune the search space so as to consider only regions where it is possible to find matches good enough to include in the set of models to retain. In general, this pruning results in a modest efficiency gain of up to 30% in medium-sized grids, but with decreasing returns as higher grid sizes lead to thinner surface regions and shift the balance between the total surface counts and the size of the grid [17]. However, this can benefit some applications like soft docking [13], where the surface and core grids are manipulated to model flexibility in the structures to dock, or if the minimum acceptable surface contact is high.

3.4 Constraining the Search Space to Active Regions

In some cases there is information about distances between points in the structures, information that can be used to restrict the search region. If this information is a conjunction of distance limits, then it is trivial to restrict the search to the volumes allowed by all the distances. However, real applications may be more complex.

For modelling protein interactions, it is often the case that one can obtain data on important residues or atoms from such techniques as site directed mutagenesis or NMR titrations, or even from theoretical considerations, but it is rare to be absolutely certain of these data. The most common situation is to have a set of likely distance constraints of which not all necessarily hold. Typically, we would like to impose a constraint of the form:

At least K atoms of set A must be within R of at least one atom of set B   (4)

where set A is on one protein and set B on the other, and R a distance value. This constraint results in combinatorial problem with a large number of disjunctions, since the distances need only hold for at least one of any combination of K elements of A.

Since the real-space (geometrical) search of BiGGER can be seen as three nested cycles spanning the Z, Y, and X coordinates, from the outer to the inner cycle, we can decompose the enforcement of constraint (4) by projecting it in each of the three directions:

At least K atoms of set A must be within R_ω of at least one atom of set B   (5)

where R_ω replaces the Euclidean distance R and represents the modulus of coordinate differences on one axis Z, Y or X. R_ω has the same value of R; the different notation is to remind us that this is not a Euclidean distance value, but its projection on one coordinate axis. This makes the constraint slightly less stringent, by considering the distance to be a cube of side 2R instead of a sphere of diameter 2R, but this can be easily corrected by testing each candidate configuration to see if it also respects Euclidean distance.

The propagation algorithm is the same for each axis and consists of two steps. The first step is to determine the neighbourhood of radius R of atoms in group B, projected on the coordinate axis being considered. The next step is to generate a list of segments representing the displacements for which at least K atoms of group A are inside the segments defining the neighbourhood R of the atoms in group B.

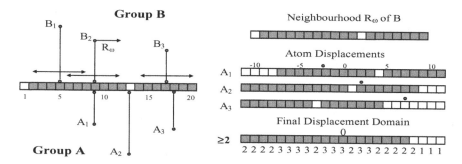

Fig. 5. Generating the displacement domain in one dimension. The left panel shows the generation of the neighbourhood of radius R of group B. The panel on the right shows the allowed displacements for each atom, and the final displacement domain for a K value of 2.

The calculation of the neighbourhood of B in some coordinate (either X, Y or Z) is illustrated in Figure 5. The positions of atoms B1, B2 and B3 in this coordinate are respectively 5, 9 and 17. Their neighbourhoods within a distance 3 are (2;8), (6;12) and (14;20). Merging the two first intervals, the neighbourhood 3 of the atom set B is thus (2;12) and (14;20).

To calculate the displacement values that place an atom of group A inside the neighbourhood of group B we only have to shift the segments defining the neighbourhood of B by the coordinate value of the atom. For example, atom A1, with coordinate 9, lies inside the neighbourhood 3 of B if its displacement lies in the range (-7;3) or (5;11). Similarly, atoms A2 and A3, with coordinate values 13 and 18, respectively may be displaced by (-11;-1) or (1;7) and (-16;-6) or (-4;2).

Once we have the displacement segments for all atoms, we must generate the segments describing the region at least K atoms are in the neighbourhood of B, which is a simple counting procedure (hence, constraint (5) need not be limited to specifying a lower bound for the distances to respect. The value of K can also be an upper bound, or a specific value, or even any number of values). In this case, there are at least two atoms of set A within neighbourhood 3 of atom set B if the displacement lies in ranges (-11;3) and (5;7). In ranges (-7;-6) and (-4;-1) all 3 A atoms are in the neighbourhood 3 of B.

The propagation of constraints of type (5) thus restrict the translation domains that are used in the translation search (see last section). The time complexity of enforcing constraint (2) in one axis is O(a+b+N), where a is the number of atoms in group A and b the number of atoms in group B, and N is the grid size. Since this must be done for the translation dimensions the overall complexity contribution is $O(N^3)$, which does not change the $O(N^4)$ complexity of the geometric search algorithm, and pruning the search space speeds up the search considerably [17].

4   Results and Further Work

Previous results show that BiGGER can be a powerful modelling tool when used in this manner, even when the experimental data are only applied after the search stage to score the models produced [13, 14, 19, 20, 21, 22, 23, 24, 25].

As to PSICO, it still is under development, namely to integrate the propagation of global constraints in the general algorithm. Initial tests performed with PSICO with real data (the Desulforedoxin dimer, with 520 atoms and about 8000 constraints where over 800 are provided from NMR data and the rest from amino acid knowledge) shown acceptable results achieved in 10 minutes, 1 minute for the CP phase, and 9 minutes for various runs of the optimisation phase to produce 15 distinct solutions.

This is significantly faster than the reference system currently used in this area (DYANA [26]) that uses a simulated approach to the problem and took 10 hours to solve the problem. Nevertheless, the accuracy achieved with DYANA is significantly better, achieving RMSD distances of about 1 Å, between the predicted and the actual structures, compared with 2.3 Å, achieved by PSICO. Although significant, this error does not prevent PSICO to assist biochemists in the interpretation of NMR. In fact, in earlier phases, distances are not assigned to the correct atom pairs, and so a fast, if only approximate, interpretation is quite useful to alert biochemists that some of the distance constraints should be revised.

Although the integration of global rigid body constraints has not been done yet, we expect that PSICO should improve considerably with such integration. Preliminary results have shown that the propagation of alpha-helices with 20 atoms or over (i.e. with 5 residues or more) typically decreases the union of the domains of the atoms by a factor of 10, with no sensible increase in run time [11]. However, run times depend significantly on the size of the rigid bodies that are considered and the actual propagation policy, i.e. the interplay between propagation of fast binary constraints, and heavier global constraints. The tuning of this propagation will be possible with Casper, a constraint propagation system that we started developing recently and that will be tested soon with PSICO problems [27].

Of course, the choice of the rigid bodies to consider is also a key factor for the integration of rigid body constraints. Currently, secondary structures such as alpha-helices and beta-sheets can be predicted quite accurately by homology reasoning, taking into account the vast amount of proteins whose structure is already known, and maintained in the PDB data bank, publicly accessible via the Web. In fact, this is a study we are currently undertaking in the Rewerse European Network of Excellence, that aims at developing Semantic Web tools and apply them to Bioinformatics, among other domains [28].

Regardless of the rigid body global constraints, PSICO should perform better if better enumeration heuristics, namely value choice heuristics were used. The heuristics that is still used, choose the half domain less occupied by the domains of all other atoms, does not take into consideration any biochemical properties of the amino acids. If these are taken into consideration, an initial data mining study was performed at amino acid level to predict whether the amino acids are buried in the protein complex or at its surface, with a success rate of around 80% [29]. This is quite close to another study we have performed that indicates a sensible decrease in the overall RMSD error of different proteins if this rate of success was achieved (but at an atom level). For example, before the optimisation phase, we achieved RMSDs below 4Å if the rate of success in the heuristics is 80%, rather than around 7Å when choices are correct only 50% of the time [30]. As with global constraints, more data mining and homology studies should be performed in the PDB data to improve the quality of the heuristics being used.

Finally, no heuristic is perfect, and a pure backtrack search will very likely be insufficient, given the size of the problems. A possible trade-off between completeness of search and efficiency is the use of limited discrepancy search, where regions of the search space are visited only if they do not involve overriding the heuristic choice more than a limited amount of times (the discrepancy level accepted [31]). Nevertheless this discrepancy search might have to be complemented with some form of local search in the first choices, which are critical for the performing of backtrack search, and which are very badly informed in the early stages of the search, where the likely positions of the atoms are still very much undefined. This is also a feature of the Casper system that is planned for the near future.

5 Conclusions

Constraint Programming is a computational paradigm quite adequate to address combinatorial problems given, on the one hand, its declarative nature that allows problems to be easily modelled and adapted and, on the other hand, the efficiency of the underlying constraint solvers. Of course, many problems are adequately addressed with Constraint Programming only if adequate models are used, which might require some degree of ingenuity from the users.

In this paper we have shown that structural bioinformatics problems can be handled quite successfully with a constraint programming approach, making it possible to incorporate many sources of information, including experimental data (e.g. NMR data) which very likely will be necessary to handle the difficult problems arising in this domain.

Although in the heart of the algorithms being used, constraint programming is likely to be complemented with other advanced techniques, namely data mining on various databanks, increasingly available in the Web, for the development of complete practical applications. This has been shown in the applications described in this paper, for which we expect to obtain soon better results with the integration of such complementary techniques.

Acknowledgements. We thank Nuno Palma and José Moura for their role in the development of BiGGER and Chemera. Developments of Chemera are currently being funded by the European Commission and by the Swiss Federal Office for Education and Science within the 6th Framework Program project REWERSE number 506779 (cf. http://rewerse.net).

References

1. N. Chabrier and F. Fages. The biochemical abstract machine BIOCHAM. In C. Christophe, H.P. Lenhof, and M. F. Sagot, editors, Proceedings of the European Conference on Computational Biology, ECCB'03, pages 597-599, Paris, France. System available at http://contraintes.inria.fr/BIOCHAM, September 2003.
2. Laurent Michel, Pascal Van Hentenryck: Parallel Local Search in Comet, CP'2005 (Procs.), Peter van Beek (Ed.), Lecture Notes in Computer Science, vol. 3709, Springer, pp. 430-444, October, 2005.

3. A.K. Mackworth and E.C. Freuder, The complexity of some polynomial network consistency algorithms for constraint satisfaction problems, Artificial Intelligence, 25(1):65–73, 1985,

4. N. Beldiceanu, Global Constraint Catalog, http://www.emn.fr/x-info/sdemasse/gccat/.

5. J.-C. Régin, A Filtering Algorithm for Constraints of Difference in CSPs, Proceedings of AAAI-94, pp.362-367, 1994.

6. http://www.cqfb.fct.unl.pt/bioin/chemera/.

7. Backhofen R. , Will S. A Constraint-Based Approach to Fast and Exact Structure Prediction in Three-Dimensional Protein Models, Constraints, Vol.11, N. 1, Springer, January 2006

8. Dovier A., Burato M. and Fogolari F., Using Secondary Structure Information for Protein Folding in CLP(FD), In Procs. Workshop on Functional and Constraint Logic Programming, ENTCS, Vol 76, 2002

9. Krippahl, L., Barahona, P., PSICO: Solving Protein Structures with Constraint Programming and Optimisation, Constraints 2002, 7, 317-331

10. Krippahl, L., Barahona, P., Applying Constraint Programming to Protein Structure Determination, Principles and Practice of Constraint Programming, Springer, 1999 289-302

11. Krippahl L. and Barahona P., Propagating N-Ary Rigid-Body Constraints, Principles and Practice of Constraint Programming, CP'2003 (Procs.), Francesca Rossi (Ed.), Lecture Notes in Computer Science, vol. 2833, Springer, pp. 452-465, October, 2003.

12. Krippahl L, Barahona P. PSICO: Solving Protein Structures with Constraint Programming and Optimisation, Constraints 2002, 7, 317-331

13. Palma PN, Krippahl L, Wampler JE, Moura, JJG. 2000. BiGGER: A new (soft) docking algorithm for predicting protein interactions. Proteins: Structure, Function, and Genetics 39:372-84.

14. Krippahl L, Moura JJ, Palma PN. 2003. Modeling protein complexes with BiGGER. Proteins: Structure, Function, and Genetics. V. 52(1):19-23.

15. Dominguez C, Boelens R, Bonvin AM. HADDOCK: a protein-protein docking approach based on biochemical or biophysical information. J Am Chem Soc. 2003 Feb 19;125(7):1731-7.

16. Moont G., Gabb H.A., Sternberg M. J. E., Use of Pair Potentials Across Protein Interfaces in Screening Predicted Docked Complexes Proteins: Structure, Function, and Genetics, V35-3, 364-373, 1999

17. Krippahl L. and Barahona P., Applying Constraint Programming to Rigid Body Protein Docking, Principles and Practice of Constraint Programming, CP'2005 (Procs.), Peter van Beek (Ed.), Lecture Notes in Computer Science, vol. 3709, Springer, pp. 373-387, October, 2005.

18. Katchalski-Katzir E, Shariv I, Eisenstein M, Friesem AA, Aflalo C, Vakser IA. 1992 Molecular surface recognition: determination of geometric fit between proteins and their ligands by correlation techniques. Proc Natl Acad Sci U S A. 1992 Mar 15;89(6):2195-9.

19. Pettigrew GW, Goodhew CF, Cooper A, Nutley M, Jumel K, Harding SE. 2003, The electron transfer complexes of cytochrome c peroxidase from Paracoccus denitrificans. Biochemistry. 2003 Feb 25;42(7):2046-55.

20. Pettigrew GW, Prazeres S, Costa C, Palma N, Krippahl L, Moura I, Moura JJ. 1999. The structure of an electron transfer complex containing a cytochrome c and a peroxidase. J Biol Chem. 1999 Apr 16;274(16):11383-9.

21. Pettigrew GW, Pauleta SR, Goodhew CF, Cooper A, Nutley M, Jumel K, Harding SE, Costa C, Krippahl L, Moura I, Moura J. 2003. Electron Transfer Complexes of Cytochrome c Peroxidase from Paracoccus denitrificans Containing More than One Cytochrome. Biochemistry 2003, 42, 11968-81

22. Morelli X, Dolla A., Czjzek M, Palma PN, Blasco, F, Krippahl L, Moura JJ, Guerlesquin F. 2000. Heteronuclear NMR and soft docking: an experimental approach for a structural model of the cytochrome c553-ferredoxin complex. Biochemistry 39:2530-2537.

23. Morelli X, Palma PN, Guerlesquin F, Rigby AC. 2001. A novel approach for assessing macromolecular complexes combining soft-docking calculations with NMR data. Protein Sci. 10:2131-2137.

24. Palma PN, Lagoutte B, Krippahl L, Moura JJ, Guerlesquin F. Synechocystis ferredoxin / ferredoxin - NADP(+)-reductase/NADP+ complex: Structural model obtained by NMR-restrained docking. (2005) FEBS Lett. 2005 Aug 29;579(21):4585-90.

25. Impagliazzo A, Krippahl L and Ubbink M. Pseudoazurin : Nitrite Reductase Interactions (2005) ChemBioChem 6, 1648-1653

26. Güntert, P., Mumenthaler, C. & Wüthrich, K. (1997). Torsion angle dynamics for NMR structure calculation with the new program DYANA. J. Mol. Biol. 273, 283-298.

27. M. Correia, P. Barahona and F. Azevedo, CaSPER: A Programming Environment for Development and Integration of Constraint Solvers, in Proceedings of the First International Workshop on Constraint Programming Beyond Finite Integer Domains (BeyondFD'05), Azevedo et al. (Editors), pages 59-73, 2005.

28. Krippahl, L. Integrating Web Resources to Model Protein Structure and Function. RW-SISS-'2006 (Procs.), Pedro Barahona (Ed.), Lecture Notes in Computer Science, vol. 4126, Springer, pp. 184-196, September 2006.

29. J.C. Almeida Santos, Mining Protein Structure Data, M.Sc. Thesis, New University of Lisbon, 2006

30. Correia M. and Barahona P., Machine Learned Heuristics to Improve Constraint Satisfaction, 17th Brazilian Symposium on Artificial Intelligence, SBIA'04 (Procs.), Ana.L.C. Balzan and Sofiane Labidi (eds.), LNCS, vol. 3171, Springer, pp.103-113, Maranhão, Brazil, 2004

31. W. Harvey and M. Ginsberg, Limited Discrepancy search, in Proceedings of IJCAI, International Joint Conference on Artificial Intelligence, C. Mellish (ed.), Montreal, 1995.

Rewriting Haskell Strings

Duncan Coutts[1], Don Stewart[2], and Roman Leshchinskiy[2]

[1] Programming Tools Group
Oxford University Computing Laboratory
[2] Computer Science & Engineering
University of New South Wales
duncan.coutts@comlab.ox.ac.uk, {dons,rl}@cse.unsw.edu.au

Abstract. The Haskell *String* type is notoriously inefficient. We introduce a new data type, *ByteString*, based on lazy lists of byte arrays, combining the speed benefits of strict arrays with lazy evaluation. Equational transformations based on term rewriting are used to deforest intermediate ByteStrings automatically. We describe novel fusion combinators with improved expressiveness and performance over previous functional array fusion strategies. A library for ByteStrings is implemented, providing a purely functional interface, which approaches the speed of low-level mutable arrays in C.

Keywords: Program fusion, Deforestation, Functional programming.

1 Introduction

Haskell can be beautiful. Here we have a small Haskell program to compute the hash of the alphabetic characters in a file:

$$return \cdot foldl'\ hash\ 5381 \cdot map\ toLower \cdot filter\ isAlpha\ =\ll\ readFile\ f$$
$$\textbf{where}\ hash\ h\ c\ =\ h * 33\ +\ ord\ c$$

and an equivalent naive C implementation:

```
int c;
long h = 5381;
FILE *fp = fopen(f, "r");
while ((c = fgetc(fp)) != EOF)
  if (isalpha(c))
      h = h * 33 + tolower(c);
fclose(fp);
return h;
```

Although elegant, the naive Haskell program is many times slower than the naive C version! Sadly it is all too common an experience that idiomatic Haskell programs dealing with strings and I/O can have poor performance.

With some care, it is possible to produce a reasonable Haskell implementation a few times slower than the C version, but at the expense of simplicity and elegance. This is unsatisfying, as the benefits of higher abstraction are abandoned.

M. Hanus (Ed.): PADL 2007, LNCS 4354, pp. 50–64, 2007.

Ideally, we would have our cake and eat it too. That is, we would like to program in a high-level declarative style and also produce fast code that is competitive with C:

import *Data.ByteString.Lazy.Char8* **as** *B*
return · *B.foldl' hash* 5381 · *B.map toLower* · *B.filter isAlpha* =≪ *B.readFile f*
  where *hash h c* = *h* ∗ 33 + *ord c*

By replacing the string type with our *ByteString* representation, Haskell is able to approach the speed of C, while still retaining the elegance of the idiomatic implementation. With *stream fusion* enabled, it actually beats the original C program (Figure 1). Only by sacrificing clarity and explicitly manipulating mutable blocks is the C program able to outperform Haskell.

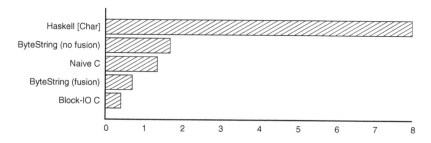

Fig. 1. Relative running times (seconds)

The main contribution of this paper is to introduce a new system for fusion, based on *streams*, offering greater expressiveness and generality than has been possible with previous work on functional array fusion [3,4]. Secondly, we describe a full scale, successful implementation of stream fusion for byte arrays, providing a fast *ByteString* type for Haskell. The implementation utilises existential types [10], the Haskell foreign function interface [2] and compiler rewrite rules [11], while presenting the user with a familiar, purely functional interface. The fusion techniques presented are not restricted to arrays or to Haskell, and should be generally applicable to sequence-like data structures, including lists.

The use of fusible array combinators dramatically improves both the time and space performance of I/O and string-based Haskell programs. Indeed, we are finally able to realise the performance promise of declarative programming in Haskell. The ByteString library is shipped with the latest Haskell implementations. The performance results therefore have practical impact, as the library is already used in performance-critical applications [1].

The remainder of the paper is organised as follows: in Section 2 we describe briefly the *ByteString* data types, both strict and lazy versions. Section 3 gives an overview of related fusion systems before presenting fusion based on streams and its application to *ByteStrings*. Section 4 explains the concrete implementation of the *ByteString* types. Section 5 presents benchmarks and finally in Section 6 we suggest further work before concluding.

2   Representing Strings

When the designers of Haskell chose a representation for strings they chose simplicity and elegance over performance:

> **type** *String* = [*Char*]

The representation is certainly convenient. A wide range of polymorphic list functions are available, and the recursive structure of the list type makes it easy to write inductively defined functions. The use of a concrete, rather than abstract, data type, allows for a very expressive programming style using pattern matching.

The representation is also undeniably inefficient; for both processing and input/output. A linked list of boxed characters gives poor data density and often poor locality of reference. With the heap representation used by the Glasgow Haskell Compiler (GHC) [14] on a 32 bit machine the [*Char*] type uses 12 bytes per character[1]. This means only 5 characters fit into a 64 byte cache line.

The obvious solution to the performance problems is to use arrays of unboxed bytes. The first step is to implement an abstract type, *ByteString*, internally represented by unboxed byte arrays, along with a suite of operations over this type similar to those available for the standard *String* type. Full details of the representation are deferred to Section 4.1.

The lazy [*Char*] representation means that it is not necessary to keep the whole string resident in memory if it can be generated and consumed incrementally. Haskell supports this programming style by providing "lazy I/O": functions that transparently interleave processing of data with I/O, enabling programs to run in constant space.

A *ByteString* representation based on unboxed byte arrays, however, forces the entire string to be resident at all times – lazy I/O is impossible. When working with files larger than available memory, a strict *ByteString* representation can be simply unusable. Forcing users to explicitly manage data in blocks, as C programmers typically must do, would be a great shame in a language built on lazy evaluation. The solution to restore laziness is to define a lazy list structure containing strict elements:

> **import qualified** *Data.ByteString* **as** *Strict*
> **newtype** *ByteString* = *LBS* [*Strict.ByteString*]

This representation provides the best of both worlds, enabling both the performance benefits of strict *ByteStrings* and lazy processing of streams. The representation is described in more detail in Section 4.2.

3   Fusion

The program presented in the introduction is essentially a pipeline of simple computations. This is a typical example of high-level Haskell code: the ability to

---

[1] *Char* boxes are preallocated by GHC as an optimisation, reducing the space from 20 to 12 bytes per character.

formulate complex algorithms as compositions of primitive combinators is one of the main strengths of the functional paradigm. However, extensive optimisation is required to compile programs written in this style to efficient code. In particular, a naive implementation would create a large number of intermediate data structures, resulting in suboptimal performance with respect to both space and time.

Eliminating intermediate results is particularly important in array-based programs. Consider, for instance, the computation *sum (enumFromTo 0 n)*. With lists, Haskell's non-strictness ensures that *enumFromTo* produces one element at a time which is then immediately consumed by *sum*. Thus, although an intermediate list is created the computation can still run in constant space. In the case of arrays, however, the entire intermediate array must be allocated and filled before *sum* can be applied to it. In addition to requiring $\mathcal{O}(n)$ space, this evaluation strategy is also ill-suited to modern hardware, especially with respect to cache behaviour.

If we want to generate efficient code for such computations we have to ensure that the intermediate data structure is eliminated automatically. In the context of inductive data structures, in particular lists, this problem is known as *deforestation* [15] and has been studied extensively [9]. Array fusion, on the other hand, has received comparatively little attention. In the following, we discuss a number of approaches to fusion for both arrays and lists, before describing the system used in the *ByteString* library.

3.1   Fusion Strategies

The Glasgow Haskell Compiler makes implementing fusion particularly easy due to its support for programmer-defined rewrite rules [11] which are applied by the compiler during optimisation. This allows us to specify custom equational transformations as part of the library without changing the compiler, in a manner similar to the list fusion system currently used by GHC. This flexibility has let us experiment with a number of fusion systems in the *ByteString* library. We review the most important ones below.

foldr/build. The most popular approach to list deforestation, and indeed the one used by GHC, is *foldr/build* fusion [7,6,5,8,13]. It requires basic list operations to be written in terms of two combinators:

$$foldr :: (a \rightarrow b \rightarrow b) \rightarrow b \rightarrow [a] \rightarrow b$$
$$build :: (\forall b. (a \rightarrow b \rightarrow b) \rightarrow b \rightarrow b) \rightarrow [a]$$

Here, *foldr* is the list catamorphism, and *build* is an abstract list constructor. The fusion rule:

⟨**foldr/build fusion**⟩ ∀ *g k z* . *foldr k z (build g)* ↦ *g k z*

eliminates intermediate lists by passing the elements constructed by *g* directly to the consumer *k*. Though only a limited range of functions are fusible, this system works well and, despite initial appearances, is even applicable to non-inductive sequences such as arrays [7]. However *array* fusion based on *foldr/build* is currently not efficient enough to be practical. Fused array code requires a particular form of higher-order function that cannot be compiled to efficient code by current versions of GHC. For the same reason, GHC cannot produce efficient code for a fused *foldl* under this approach, greatly limiting the application of *foldr/build* to arrays, where many key functions make use of *foldl* traversals (for example, *sum*).

destroy/unfoldr. Just as with *foldr/build* fusion, *destroy/unfoldr* fusion [12] defines two combinators, one for production and one for consumption:

$$destroy :: (\forall b. (b \rightarrow Maybe\ (a, b)) \rightarrow b \rightarrow c) \rightarrow [a] \rightarrow c$$
$$unfoldr :: (b \rightarrow Maybe\ (a, b)) \rightarrow b \rightarrow [a]$$

The production of lists is captured by the list anamorphism *unfoldr*. It produces a list from the seed b and a stepper function which, given the current seed, either generates the next element and the new seed, or returns *Nothing* ending the list. List consumption is encapsulated by *destroy*. As before, intermediate lists are eliminated by a fusion rule which ensures that produced elements are immediately passed on to the consumer:

⟨**destroy/unfoldr fusion**⟩ $\forall\ g\ f\ e$. $destroy\ g\ (unfoldr\ f\ e) \longmapsto g\ f\ e$

A major advantage of *destroy/unfoldr* is its support for *foldl* and *zip*-like algorithms, which cannot be implemented easily in the *foldr/build* framework.

One aspect that feels somewhat suboptimal is that defining functions that both produce and consume lists (such as *map*) is not totally straightforward and the full fusion transformation for them requires many steps, including an additional *destroy/destroy* rule.

Functional Array Fusion. Chakravarty and Keller [3,4] introduce a fusion system designed specifically for array code. It is based on a single combinator which captures left-to-right array traversals:

$$loop :: (s \rightarrow a \rightarrow (s, Maybe\ a)) \rightarrow s \rightarrow Array\ a \rightarrow (Array\ a,\ s)$$

The semantics of a traversal is given by a stepper function which, given a state and an array element, produces a new state and, optionally, a new element. The main fusion rule combines adjacent loops by suitably composing the stepper functions:

⟨**loop/loop fusion**⟩ $\forall\ f\ g\ s\ t$.
$loop\ f\ s \cdot fst\ \cdot loop\ g\ t \longmapsto loop\ (fuse\ f\ g)\ (s, t)$

While this system has been shown to work well for standard array algorithms such as *map*, *filter* and *scan*, it does not readily support more complex computations, in particular those which process arrays from right to left or consume multiple arrays. In particular, zips can only be fused in this framework if the array type is polymorphic in the type of the elements which *ByteString* is not. Furthermore, array transformers that produce more elements than they consume cannot be implemented at all; this rules out a fusible *concatMap*.

3.2 Stream Fusion

Of the three fusion systems, our contribution is most closely related to the *destroy/unfoldr* system and indeed inherits many of its benefits.

Both *foldr/build* and *destroy/unfoldr* reflect the inductive structure of lists, effectively requiring fusible algorithms to process elements from head to tail. An array fusion framework, however, should support other access patterns if we are to effectively make use of $\mathcal{O}(1)$ array indexing. Thus, we would like to decouple the order in which array elements are read or written from the computation performed for each element. In general, we are interested in a range of single-pass algorithms which access each element exactly once. Such algorithms can be split into three phases:

– read the array producing a stream of elements,
– process the elements transforming the stream, and
– write the resulting stream into a new array.

With such a separation, access patterns can be fully captured by the read and write phases, without affecting the processing phase. Furthermore, in a pipeline composed of such computations, adjacent write/read phases can be eliminated provided they access elements in the same order.

Obviously, a crucial question is how streams of elements are represented. Since they will always be used sequentially, lists seem to be an obvious choice. However, this would leave us with the problem of eliminating intermediate lists in addition to fusing the write/read phases. We can do better than that by encapsulating a list anamorphism:

```
data Step s  = Done
          | Yield Word8 s
          | Skip s
data Stream = ∃s. Stream (s → Step s) s Int
```

Here, a *Stream* is defined by an existentially wrapped seed and a stepper function which, in each step, can indicate one of three possible results: no more elements will be produced (*Done*); a new element is produced together with a new seed (*Yield*); or a new seed is returned without producing an element (*Skip*). The last alternative, while not strictly necessary, leads to more efficient code. Streams also store a hint on the number of elements. This helps to reduce the number of costly array reallocations in the write phase. For the *ByteString* library we restrict ourselves to streams of *Word8*. The above definition, however, can be easily made polymorphic in the type of elements. For efficiency reasons, we make extensive use of strictness annotations, omitted here for clarity.

We can now easily convert an array to a stream by reading the elements from left to right (we defer the discussion of other access patterns to Section 3.6):

```
readUp   :: ByteString → Stream
readUp s = Stream next 0 n
   where
      n              = length s
      next i | i < n    = Yield (index s i) (i + 1)
             | otherwise = Done
```

The implementation of $writeUp :: Stream \rightarrow ByteString$, which constructs an array from a stream, is omitted for space reasons but is equally straightforward.

Crucially, converting a stream to an array and then back is just the identity operation on streams. Hence, the two conversions can be eliminated, avoiding the creation of the intermediate array. This insight is captured by the following rewrite rule, which is central to our fusion framework:

⟨**readUp/writeUp fusion**⟩ $readUp \cdot writeUp \;\mapsto\; id$

3.3   Stream Transformers

The reading and writing phases of array algorithms are captured by $readUp$ and $writeUp$, respectively, but how do we implement the processing phase? In general, an array transformer of type $ByteString \rightarrow ByteString$ will have the form $writeUp \cdot h \cdot readUp$ where h is a stream transformer of type $Stream \rightarrow Stream$. For instance, we can implement map as follows:

$$map :: (Word8 \rightarrow Word8) \rightarrow ByteString \rightarrow ByteString$$
$$map\, f \;=\; writeUp \cdot mapS\, f \cdot readUp$$

The actual computation is performed by $mapS$, which applies f to each element of a stream:

$$mapS :: (Word8 \rightarrow Word8) \rightarrow Stream \rightarrow Stream$$
$$mapS\, f\, (Stream\ next\ s\ n) \;=\; Stream\ next'\ s\ n$$
$\quad$**where**
$\qquad next'\ s =$ **case** $next\ s$ **of**
$\qquad\qquad Done \quad\;\; \rightarrow\ Done$
$\qquad\qquad Yield\ x\ s' \rightarrow\ Yield\ (f\ x)\ s'$
$\qquad\qquad Skip\ s' \quad\;\rightarrow\ Skip\ s'$

With these definitions we can already fuse simple map pipelines:

$\quad map\, f \cdot map\, g$
$= writeUp \cdot mapS\, f \cdot readUp \cdot$ $\qquad$ {inline map ×2}
$\quad\; writeUp \cdot mapS\, g \cdot readUp$
$= writeUp \cdot mapS\, f \cdot mapS\, g \cdot readUp$ $\quad${$readUp/writeUp$ fusion}

Here, eliminating the $readUp \cdot writeUp$ has brought the two stream transformers together. One might expect that a separate rewrite rule is required for the two applications of $mapS$ to be fused, however, as the definition of $mapS$ is non-recursive, the standard optimisations performed by GHC are sufficient[2].

Indeed, it is precisely the desire to avoid recursion in stream transformers which has led us to allow stepper functions to return a new seed without producing a new element. Consider the following definition of $filter$:

$$filter :: (Word8 \rightarrow Bool) \rightarrow ByteString \rightarrow ByteString$$
$$filter\, p \;=\; writeUp \cdot filterS\, p \cdot readUp$$

and the corresponding stream transformer:

---

[2] This is quite similar to $destroy/unfoldr$ fusion where the compiler is expected to automatically eliminate temporary $Maybe$ values.

```
filterS :: (Word8 → Bool) → Stream → Stream
filterS p (Stream next s n) = Stream next' s n
    where
      next' s = case next s of
          Done                           → Done
          Yield x s' | p x               → Yield x s'
                     | otherwise → Skip s'
          Skip s'                        → Skip s'
```

Note how *next'* yields *Skip s'* for each deleted element. The alternative — recursively skipping to the next element satisfying the predicate — would prevent pipelines involving *filter* from being optimised satisfactorily.

3.4 Folding

Pure consumers, such as folds, are similarly easy to implement in the stream fusion framework. These algorithms only have a reading and a processing phase, so, for instance, *foldl'* is implemented as:

```
foldl' :: (a → Word8 → a) → a → ByteString → a
foldl' f z = foldlS' f z · readUp
```

where *foldlS'* folds a stream from left to right:

```
foldlS' :: (a → Word8 → a) → a → Stream → a
foldlS' f z (Stream next s n) = loop z s
    where
      loop z s = case next s of
          Done    → z
          Yield x s' → loop (f z x) s'
          Skip s'    → loop z s'
```

Some fold-like algorithms can produce a result without necessarily traversing the entire array. A prime example is *find* which searches for the first element satisfying a given predicate. We would like such computations to terminate as soon as possible while still being fusible. With *foldr/build* fusion this can only be done by employing laziness while with streams (and *destroy/unfoldr*) it can be done directly and efficiently. As before, we split the algorithm into two phases:

```
find  :: (Word8 → Bool) → ByteString → Maybe Word8
find p = findS p · readUp
```

In contrast to the algorithms presented so far, *findS* does not consume the entire stream. Instead, it returns as soon as it encounters an element which satisfies the predicate:

```
findS :: (Word8 → Bool) → Stream → Maybe Word8
findS p (Stream next s n) = loop s
    where
      loop s = case next s of
          Done                           → Nothing
          Yield x s' | p x               → Just x
                     | otherwise → loop s'
          Skip s'                        → loop s'
```

3.5   Fusing Pipelines

We are now in the position to demonstrate how the program presented in Section 1 is transformed by GHC using our fusion framework. For simplicity, let us just consider the inner pipeline, omitting I/O-related functions:

$$
\begin{aligned}
& foldl'\ f\ z \ \cdot\ map\ g \ \cdot\ filter\ h \\
={}& foldlS'\ f\ z \ \cdot\ readUp \ \cdot\ writeUp \ \cdot\ mapS\ g && \{\text{inline } foldl',\ map \\
& \qquad\qquad \cdot\ readUp \ \cdot\ writeUp \ \cdot\ filterS\ h \ \cdot\ readUp && \text{and } filter\} \\
={}& foldlS'\ f\ z \ \cdot\ mapS\ g \ \cdot\ filterS\ h \ \cdot\ readUp && \{readUp/writeUp \text{ fusion}\}
\end{aligned}
$$

Note how the original code, which used three loops and two intermediate arrays, has been *automatically* transformed into a single array traversal. Moreover, GHC is able to further optimise the code by inlining and combining the stream transformers and, thus, eliminating intermediate *Step* values. Overall, stream fusion improves the performance of this example by a factor of around 2.4.

3.6   Down Loops

Unlike lists, arrays provide $\mathcal{O}(1)$ indexing, making left-to-right and right-to-left traversals equally efficient. Several important functions, most prominently *foldr* and its strict version *foldr'*, are best implemented as down loops. Fortunately, we can easily extend our framework with functions for reading and writing arrays from right to left:

$$
\begin{aligned}
readDn &:: ByteString \to Stream \\
writeDn &:: Stream \to ByteString
\end{aligned}
$$

Adding a fusion rule for these is straightforward:

$$\langle \mathbf{readDn/writeDn\ fusion} \rangle \quad readDn \cdot writeDn \ \mapsto\ id$$

We are thus able to fuse both up and down loops equally well.

3.7   Bidirectional Loops

Combinations of up and down loops are more problematic. It is clear that it is not generally possible to directly combine up *and* down traversals into a single traversal. However, there are several important special case functions for which it would be valid to do so. Consider:

$$
\begin{aligned}
& foldr'\ f\ z \ \cdot\ map\ g \\
={}& foldrS'\ f\ z \ \cdot\ readDn \ \cdot\ writeUp \ \cdot\ mapS\ g \ \cdot\ readUp && \{\text{inline } foldr' \text{ and } map\}
\end{aligned}
$$

and we can fuse no further. However, *map* is able to generate the same result traversing either up or down, so a valid optimisation would be instead to *map* the stream in reverse, enabling fusion:

$$
\begin{aligned}
& foldrS'\ f\ z \ \cdot\ readDn \ \cdot\ writeDn \ \cdot\ mapS\ g \ \cdot\ readDn \\
={}& foldrS'\ f\ z \ \cdot\ mapS\ g \ \cdot\ readDn && \{readDn/writeDn \text{ fusion}\}
\end{aligned}
$$

We need a way to specially tag functions whose semantics allow them to be safely applied to either up or down streams. There is a difficulty though, as any change in stream direction, to fuse one *readDn/writeUp* pair, will require flipping other *readUp*s into *readDn*s. To deal with this we define wrappers over functions categorised by their direction and result type. We define:

$$producerDn \quad :: Stream \rightarrow ByteString$$
$$consumerDn \quad :: (Stream \rightarrow a) \rightarrow (ByteString \rightarrow a)$$
$$transformerDn \quad :: (Stream \rightarrow Stream) \rightarrow (ByteString \rightarrow ByteString)$$

$$producerDn \; f \quad = writeDn \; f$$
$$consumerDn \; f \quad = f \cdot readDn$$
$$transformerDn \; f = writeDn \cdot f \cdot readDn$$

and matching *Up* versions. From these definitions, and the existing *read/write* fusion rules, we can derive:

⟨**consumerDn/producerDn fusion**⟩ ∀ *f g* .
   consumerDn f (*producerDn g*) ↦ *f g*

⟨**consumerDn/transformerDn fusion**⟩ ∀ *f g* .
   consumerDn f · *transformerDn g* ↦ *consumerDn* (*f* · *g*)

⟨**transformerDn/producerDn fusion**⟩ ∀ *f g* .
   transformerDn f (*producerDn g*) ↦ *producerDn* (*f g*)

⟨**transformerDn/transformerDn fusion**⟩ ∀ *f g* .
   transformerDn f · *transformerDn g* ↦ *transformerDn* (*f* · *g*)

The rules for up loops follow the same pattern. We can now tag our traversal-independent functions as *bidirectional*, with special loop primitives:

$$producerBi \quad :: Stream \rightarrow ByteString$$
$$consumerBi \quad :: (Stream \rightarrow a) \rightarrow (ByteString \rightarrow a)$$
$$transformerBi :: (Stream \rightarrow Stream) \rightarrow (ByteString \rightarrow ByteString)$$

Their implementation are that of the *Up* or *Down* versions; here we will use the *Up* definition. Their use however must satisfy these side conditions:

$$\forall f . producerBi \; f \quad = reverse \cdot producerBi \; f$$
$$\forall f . consumerBi \; f \quad = consumerBi \; f \cdot reverse$$
$$\forall f . transformerBi \; f = reverse \cdot transformerBi \; f \cdot reverse$$

Traversals that do satisfy these conditions include:

$$replicate \; x \; n = producerBi \quad (replicateS \; x \; n)$$
$$sum \quad = consumerBi \quad (foldlS' \; (+) \; 0)$$
$$map \; f \quad = transformerBi \; (mapS \; f)$$

Using the side conditions we can derive the fusion rules for bidirectional loops. For the derivations we will make use of a *reverse* lemma: that *readUp* · *reverse* = *readDn* and *readDn* · *reverse* = *readUp*. There are many derived fusion rules; as an example, to fuse a *foldr'* with *map* we would have:

$$consumerDn \; f \; \cdot \; transformerBi \; g$$
$$= consumerDn \; f \; \cdot \; reverse \; \cdot$$
$$\qquad transformerBi \; g \cdot reverse \qquad \{\text{bidirection side condition}\}$$
$$= f \; \cdot \; readDn \; \cdot \; reverse \; \cdot \qquad \{\text{definition of } consumerDn \text{ and}$$
$$\qquad writeUp \; \cdot \; g \; \cdot \; readUp \; \cdot \; reverse \qquad \text{definition of } transformerBi\}$$

$$
\begin{array}{ll}
= f \cdot readUp \cdot writeUp \cdot g \cdot readDn & \{reverse \text{ lemma} \times 2\} \\
= f \cdot g \cdot readDn & \{Up/Up \text{ fusion}\} \\
= consumerDn\ (f \cdot g) & \{\text{definition of } consumerDn\}
\end{array}
$$

giving us the rule:

⟨consumerDn/transformerBi fusion⟩ $\forall\ f\ g$.

　　$consumerDn\ f \cdot transformerBi\ g\ \mapsto\ consumerDn\ (f \cdot g)$

and allowing us to fuse our example:

$$
\begin{array}{ll}
foldr'\ f\ z\ \cdot\ map\ g & \\
= consumerDn\ (foldrS'\ f\ z) \cdot transformerBi\ (mapS\ g) & \{\text{inline } foldr' \text{ and } map\ \} \\
= consumerDn\ (foldrS'\ f\ z\ \cdot\ mapS\ g) & \{\text{fusion}\}
\end{array}
$$

Being able to fuse bidirectional functions, such as *map*, *filter* and *length*, with such simplicity, is a great advantage: there is no penalty for using either up or down loops. The programmer can switch between *foldl'* and *foldr'* as their program requires. In contrast, *foldr*/*build*, and other fusion systems designed for inductive structures, have much greater difficulty with direction changes.

4   Implementation

4.1   ByteString

We implement a complete list-like interface to the *ByteString* type. To support an inductive view of strings we need a representation that supports *head* and *tail* efficiently. The simplest representation would be to use an array of unboxed bytes. However, such a structure cannot directly support *head* or *tail* without copying. The addition of offset and length fields is required. A zero-copy substring can then be constructed by simply modifying the length and offset fields.

For pragmatic reasons, instead of using Haskell's native unboxed arrays, we use a *ForeignPtr* to a contiguous block of bytes. The advantage is that this allows memory for the string to be allocated either on the Haskell GC-managed heap, or outside of Haskell (with a finaliser function to control deallocation). We can thus share *ByteStrings* with libraries written in foreign languages, such as C, without copying. For example, it is possible to memory-map a file directly to a *ByteString*, and to attach a finaliser to unmap the file when the garbage collector determines it is no longer in use. The concrete representation of *ByteStrings* is thus merely the pointer, offset and length:

data *ByteString* = *BS* !(*ForeignPtr Word8*) !*Int* !*Int*

GHC is able to optimise this representation by unboxing the *ForeignPtr* and the two integers into the *ByteString* constructor. There is therefore only a single indirection to access the string data.

4.2   Lazy ByteString

Lazy *ByteStrings* are represented as a list of strict *ByteString* chunks. There is some redundancy in this representation as zero-sized chunks might appear in the list, yet have no semantic value. To avoid this redundancy, empty list elements are disallowed, simplifying the logic required to manipulate lazy *ByteStrings*.

Profiling was used to find an optimal chunk size: too small, and performance approaches that of a *[Char]* structure, too large (larger than the L2 cache) and performance also falls away. In practice, a chunk size that allows the working set to fit comfortably in the L2 cache has been found to be best.

There are some additional advantages to the chunked representation: some operations requiring copying in the strict *ByteString* case only need manipulation of the spine of the lazy *ByteString* structure. For example, *append* runs in $\mathcal{O}(n/c)$ time (for chunk size c), versus $\mathcal{O}(n)$ for the strict version, with similar results for *concat*, *cons* and *snoc*. For these gains, we willingly pay a small overhead: the extra indirection from the list spine and the extra cases to consider when processing the more-complex representation.

5 Results

Comparing Haskell Lists and ByteStrings. Figure 2 compares standard *[Char]* library functions to their equivalent lazy *ByteString* implementations, applied to a 5M input string. Care is taken to explicitly force the evaluation of lazy lists, ensuring the cost of their construction is measured. As expected the lazy *ByteString* type is dramatically faster than *[Char]*. Memory usage of the fused *ByteString* is also *95% less* than that of the *[Char]* version.

Comparative Fusion Strategies. In order to quantify the effect of stream fusion, we implemented the complete functional array fusion described by Chakravarty and Keller [3,4]. The original formulation, based on the *loop* combinator, only fuses functions that make "up" traversals of arrays. We extended this system to also support fusion of down and bidirectional array traversals. In Figure 3 we compare the running time of a range of fusible strict *ByteStrings* expressions, implemented either via streams or *loop*. Each column represents a fusible expression, and we test all array traversal combinations. Results are averaged over 10 runs, with the cache dirtied between runs. The stream-based implementation of *ByteStrings* runs *on average 41% faster* than the *loop*-based implementation, and *up to 88% faster* in the best case. We believe this is because the *loop* system needs more glue code to construct the fused versions. It appears that this glue code cannot always be fully eliminated and this may also interfere with additional optimisations.

Effect of Fusion. Figure 4 measures the effect fusion has on strict *ByteStrings*, by measuring running time with and without the stream fusion rule enabled. When stream fusion occurs it greatly improves the running time of array code. Over the micro benchmark suite the average speed increase due to fusion is 74%, and 89% in the best case. The memory usage decreases by around 85% when fusion is enabled, due to the deforestation of intermediate arrays.

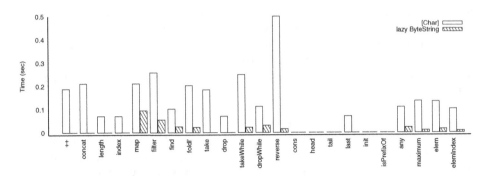

Fig. 2. [*Char*] and lazy *ByteString* : running time

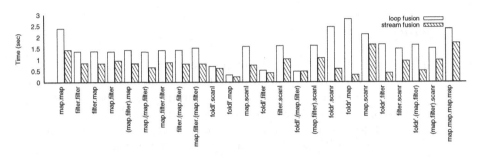

Fig. 3. Fusion strategies: loop versus stream fusion

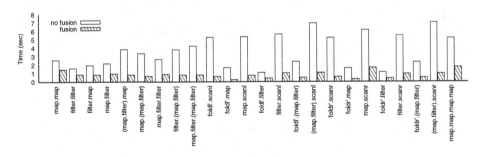

Fig. 4. Effect of fusion: streams with and without fusion

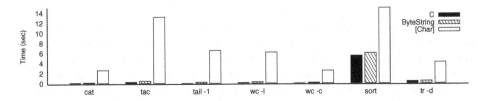

Fig. 5. Comparative results for C, ByteString and [Char] Unix tools

Comparing with C. Performance was measured against a range of standard Unix tools implemented in C in Figure 5. We measure both *ByteString* and *[Char]* implementations (one line Haskell programs) against their C equivalent. Although the C programs use a wide variety of optimisations (such as *seek*), the *ByteString* implementations are certainly competitive.

6   Further Work

More remains to be done, and this work has highlighted some promising directions for improving the performance of various aspects of Haskell.

Haskell lists. Adapting the polymorphic Haskell [a] type to use stream fusion, as a potential solution to the limitations of *foldr/build* fusion, seems a fruitful area to pursue.

Code generation. The object code GHC produces from stream combinators is fast enough that several low level issues become significant. For example, improving GHC's ability to arrange code blocks to make best use of the branch-prediction behaviour of modern CPUs is one area we wish to investigate.

Multiple traversals. A range of common functions traverse two or more streams simultaneously: for example, *append* or *zip*. Developing efficient stream fusion techniques for such functions is ongoing work.

7   Conclusion

By exploiting equational transformations via rewrite rules, it is possible to automatically fuse a wide range of array-based functions. This work goes beyond previous functional array fusion techniques by enabling fusion of bidirectional traversals and short-circuiting loops. Stream fusion is not limited to a single concrete type, but provides a general fusion mechanism for arbitrary data types expressible as streams. To demonstrate the application of stream fusion we have implemented a high-performance string processing library for Haskell, providing C-like speed, yet retaining idiomatic Haskell brevity and clarity. The source code for the *ByteString* library, all examples and a list of applications are available online [1].

Acknowledgements. We are indebted to Simon Peyton Jones for clarifying and extending GHC's rewrite rules and optimiser, which has been important to the success of this work, and to Simon Marlow for help with the GHC storage manager and *ForeignPtr* optimisations. The design of the stream fusion combinators benefited from discussions with Janis Voigtländer. We thank the anonymous referees for their helpful comments. We are also grateful to Manuel Chakravarty, Bertram Felgenhauer, Spencer Janssen, Neil Mitchell, Andres Löh, Elizabeth Baldwin, Suzie Allen and Audrey Tang for feedback on drafts.

References

1. The website accompanying this paper. http://www.cse.unsw.edu.au/~dons/papers/CSL06.html.
2. M. M. T. Chakravarty et al. *The Haskell 98 Foreign Function Interface 1.0: An Addendum to the Haskell 98 Report*, 2004. http://www.cse.unsw.edu.au/~chak/haskell/ffi/.
3. M. M. T. Chakravarty and G. Keller. Functional array fusion. In X. Leroy, editor, *Proceedings of the Sixth ACM SIGPLAN International Conference on Functional Programming*, pages 205–216. ACM Press, 2001.
4. M. M. T. Chakravarty and G. Keller. An approach to fast arrays in Haskell. In J. Jeuring and S. P. Jones, editors, *Lecture Notes for The Summer School and Workshop on Advanced Functional Programming 2002*, pages 27–58. Springer-Verlag, 2003. LNCS 2638.
5. O. Chitil. Typer inference builds a short cut to deforestation. In *ICFP '99: Proceedings of the fourth ACM SIGPLAN international conference on Functional programming*, pages 249–260, New York, NY, USA, 1999. ACM Press.
6. A. Gill. *Cheap Deforestation for Non-strict Functional Languages*. PhD thesis, University of Glasgow, January 1996.
7. A. Gill, J. Launchbury, and S. Peyton Jones. A short cut to deforestation. In *Conference on Functional Programming Languages and Computer Architecture*, pages 223–232, June 1993.
8. P. Johann. Short cut fusion: Proved and improved. In *SAIG 2001: Proceedings of the Second International Workshop on Semantics, Applications, and Implementation of Program Generation*, pages 47–71, London, UK, 2001. Springer-Verlag.
9. E. Meijer, M. Fokkinga, and R. Paterson. Functional programming with bananas, lenses, envelopes and barbed wire. In J. Hughes, editor, *Proceedings 5th ACM Conf. on Functional Programming Languages and Computer Architecture, FPCA'91, Cambridge, MA, USA, 26–30 Aug 1991*, volume 523, pages 124–144. Springer-Verlag, Berlin, 1991.
10. N. Perry. *The Implementation of Practical Functional Programming Languages*. PhD thesis, Imperial College, 1991.
11. S. Peyton Jones, A. Tolmach, and T. Hoare. Playing by the rules: rewriting as a practical optimisation technique in GHC. In R. Hinze, editor, *2001 Haskell Workshop*. ACM SIGPLAN, September 2001.
12. J. Svenningsson. Shortcut fusion for accumulating parameters & zip-like functions. In *ICFP '02: Proceedings of the seventh ACM SIGPLAN international conference on Functional programming*, pages 124–132, New York, NY, USA, 2002. ACM Press.
13. A. Takano and E. Meijer. Shortcut deforestation in calculational form. In *Conf. Record 7th ACM SIGPLAN/SIGARCH Int. Conf. on Functional Programming Languages and Computer Architecture, FPCA'95*, pages 306–313. ACM Press, New York, 1995.
14. The GHC Team. The Glasgow Haskell Compiler (GHC). http://haskell.org/ghc, 2006.
15. P. Wadler. Deforestation: transforming programs to eliminate trees. *Theoretical Computer Science, (Special issue of selected papers from 2nd European Symposium on Programming)*, 73(2):231–248, 1990.

Instantly Turning a Naive Exhaustive Search into Three Efficient Searches with Pruning

Takeshi Morimoto, Yasunao Takano, and Hideya Iwasaki

The University of Electro-Communications
1-5-1 Chofugaoka, Chofu, Tokyo, Japan
{morimoto,yasunao}@ipl.cs.uec.ac.jp, iwasaki@cs.uec.ac.jp

Abstract. A technique is described that enables purely functional programmers to write efficient search programs in the same form as simple and naive but exhaustive search programs. It performs pruning while retaining a simple program form by exploiting a lazy data structure, an *improving sequence*, which is a monotonical sequence of approximation values that approach the final value. If some approximation value in an improving sequence has sufficient information to yield the result of some part of the program, the computations that produce the values remaining after the approximation can be pruned. On the basis of an exhaustive search program, which can be regarded as the specification of a problem, three important search algorithms, namely best-first, depth-first branch-and-bound, and iterative-deepening, can be obtained by using suitable functions defined on improving sequences. Two specific examples, the eight puzzle problem and the knapsack problem in Haskell, demonstrate that the technique is practical.

Keywords: intermediate results, purely functional data structures, improving sequences, lazy evaluation.

1 Introduction

We have developed a technique that enables purely functional programmers to write efficient search programs in the same form as simple and naive but exhaustive search programs.

It preserves the clarity of the program form by exploiting a lazy data structure, an *improving sequence* [9], which is a monotonical sequence of approximation values that are gradually improved on the basis of some ordering relation so that they approach the final value. If some approximation value within the improving sequence has sufficient information to yield the result of some part of the program, the computations that produce the values remaining after the approximation value can be pruned. By using improving sequences together with suitable functions defined on the sequences, we can rewrite naive and exhaustive search programs, which can be regarded as the problem specification, into efficient search programs.

M. Hanus (Ed.): PADL 2007, LNCS 4354, pp. 65–79, 2007.

We define functions on improving sequences to implement three important search algorithms [13]: best-first [7], depth-first branch-and-bound [11], and iterative-deepening [10].

The organization of this paper is as follows. In Section 2, we begin by reviewing the definition and usage of improving sequences in Haskell [1]. We then show, in Section 3, the typical form for an exhaustive search program and apply improving sequences to the program while maintaining its simple form. In the following three sections, we define functions that enable a simple improving sequence-based program to implement the three search algorithms. In Section 7, we modularize the functions into higher-order functions, and in Section 8 we present specific examples, namely the eight puzzle problem and the knapsack problem. Finally, we discuss related work in Section 9, and conclude with a brief summary in Section 10.

The Haskell source code described in this paper is available via the web at `http://ipl.cs.uec.ac.jp/%7Emorimoto/is/bf-dfbb-id/`.

2   Improving Sequences

Improving sequences [9] enable exhaustive programs to be rewritten into more efficient ones with pruning without spoiling the simple forms that are easily understood. An improving sequence is a lazy monotonical sequence of approximation values that are gradually improved on the basis of some ordering relation so that they approach the final value. When sufficient information is provided by an approximation value, reading the next approximation value in a demand-driven manner enables unnecessary computations in the improving sequence to be eliminated.

2.1   Definition in Haskell

Each element of an improving sequence is a lazy data structure consisting of an approximation value, its remaining computations, and some ordering binary relation that is totally defined. Each remaining computation is also an improving sequence. An improving sequence is constructed in such a way that two adjacent values in the sequence have a binary relation. We can thus use an approximation value together with the binary relation to judge the necessity of the remaining computations.

In Haskell, an improving sequence is defined as a particular data type:

```
data Ord a => IS a = a :? IS a | E deriving Eq
```

Expression `x :? xs` denotes an improving sequence consisting of approximation value `x` and its remaining computations, `xs`. Operator `<` of the `Ord` type class is used as the ordering binary relation. Hence, the type of approximation values must be an instance of `Ord`. An improving sequence may be finite or infinite. If a sequence is finite, data constructor `E` denotes the termination of the sequence; it indicates that the current value cannot be further improved. For instance, 0 :? 1 :? 2 :? 3 :? E denotes an improving sequence whose values are gradually improved from initial value 0 to final value 3 based on relation < defined on Int.

The above definition of improving sequences resembles that of lazy lists. However, we introduce the new type IS instead of using lists for clarity of exposition.

2.2 Use of Improving Sequences

We illustrate the definition of functions that use improving sequences and the use of improving sequences to eliminate unnecessary computations by considering function length, which returns the length of a given list.

```
length :: [a] -> Int -> Int
length []     n = n
length (x:xs) n = length xs (n+1)
```

The second argument of length is an accumulative parameter that holds the number of elements in the list investigated so far; its initial value is 0. Assume that we want to determine the value of 1 < length [1..100] 0. Since operator < is strict in both operands, length [1..100] 0 is evaluated until 100. It is compared with 1, and True is returned as the final answer.

$$
\begin{aligned}
 & \quad 1 < \text{length } [1..100] \; 0 \\
\Rightarrow & \quad 1 < \text{length } [2..100] \; 1 \\
\Rightarrow & \quad 1 < \text{length } [3..100] \; 2 \\
 & \quad \vdots \\
\Rightarrow & \quad 1 < 100 \\
\Rightarrow & \quad \text{True}
\end{aligned}
$$

However, because length [1..100] 0 is called in the context of the comparison to 1, the final answer could be determined to be True at the point of the second recursive call, length [3..100] 2, in which the second argument guarantees that the length is at least 2. Thus, the remaining recursive calls are not needed.

We can prune such unnecessary computations by using improving sequences. First, we rewrite the definition of length so that it returns not an integer but an improving sequence of integers. The definition of a function that returns an improving sequence can be obtained by adding expressions that denote the termination and an approximation during the computation. Function length terminates its computation and returns value n when the given list is empty. Otherwise, it is certain that the length is at least n, so length constructs a structure whose approximation value is n and whose remaining computation is length xs (n+1). Therefore, the new definition of length can be obtained by adding :? E in the former case and adding n :? to denote the approximation in the latter case.

```
length :: [a] -> Int -> IS Int
length []     n = n :? E
length (x:xs) n = n :? length xs (n+1)
```

For example, `length [9,4] 0` returns `0 :? 1 :? 2 :? E`. As shown above, a function that returns an improving sequence retains the same form as that of its simple and naive original definition.

The following comparison operator is used instead of `<` to prune unnecessary computations.

```
(.<) :: Ord a => a -> IS a -> Bool
n .< E         = False
n .< (x :? xs) = if n < x then True else n .< xs
```

Operator `.<` judges whether the first argument (an ordinary value) is less than the final value of the second argument (an improving sequence). The second clause of the above definition refers to intermediate result `x` of the second argument. Pruning using this operator is achieved when `.<` judges that `n` is less than `x`; `True` is immediately returned without investigating the sequence any further. As a result, we can prune the computation that calculates `length [4..100] 3` as follows.

```
      1 .< (length [1..100] 0)
  ⇒   1 .< (0 :? length [2..100] 1)
  ⇒   1 .< (1 :? length [3..100] 2)
  ⇒   1 .< (2 :? length [4..100] 3)
  ⇒   True
```

Thus, improving sequences enable us to attain both program efficiency and clarity.

The functions on improving sequences used in this paper are defined as follows.

```
approx   :: Ord a => IS a ->    a
finalize :: Ord a => IS a -> IS a

approx   (x :? xs) = x
finalize (x :? E)  = x :? E
finalize (x :? xs) = finalize xs
```

Function `approx` returns the approximation value of a given sequence, and function `finalize` returns a sequence whose first value is the final value of a given sequence.

2.3   Converting Ordering Relation

Values in an improving sequence of type `IS a` are improved on the basis of `<` defined on type `a`, which is an instance of `Ord`. How do we make an improving sequence whose values are improved based on another ordering relation, e.g. `>`, other than `<`? The answer is to define a new type and appropriately define ordering relation `<`.

```
newtype Gt a = Gt a deriving Eq
instance Ord a => Ord (Gt a) where
    (Gt x) < (Gt y)  = y < x
```

The values of an improving sequence on `Gt a` are inversely improved on binary relation `>` on type a. For instance, `Gt 2 :? Gt 1 :? Gt 0 :? E` is a sequence that decreases on `Gt Int`. By using operator `>?`

```
(>?) :: Ord a => a -> IS (Gt a) -> IS (Gt a)
x >? xs = Gt x :? xs
```

we can write this sequence as `2 >? 1 >? 0 >? E`, which is more readable.

Type `Gt a` replaces binary relation `<` of an improving sequence with `>` on type a. Similarly, types `LtE a` and `GtE a` are defined to describe improving sequences based on relations `<=` and `>=` on type a, respectively.

```
(LtE x) < (LtE y)  =  x < y || x .== y
(GtE x) < (GtE y)  =  y < x || y .== x
```

Operator `.==` judges the equality of its operands using operator `<` on type class `Ord`.

```
(.==) :: Ord a => a -> a -> Bool
x .== y  =  (x < y) == (y < x)
```

For instance, both `Gt 1 .== Gt 1` and `LtE 1 .== LtE 1` return `True`. Operators that construct an improving sequence on `LtE` and `GtE` are defined as `<=?` and `>=?`, respectively. For consistency with operators `>?`, `<=?`, and `<=?` introduced here, we use `<?` as an alias of `:?`, except for the pattern part of the function definitions.[1]

```
(<?) :: Ord a => a -> IS a -> IS a
(<?) = (:?)
```

Because the binary relation of an improving sequence on type a depends only on a, functions and operators defined on improving sequences can be used on any kind of sequence. It may seem somewhat unusual that the sense of `<` is reversed by `Gt a`. However, by the introduction of `Gt a`, tedious definitions of similar comparison operators like `.>` are not needed. For example, operator `.<` in the previous section can be reused to compare an improving sequence based on `>` with some value.

3   Search Problem

The search problem is to find the least cost to a goal state reachable from a given initial state. Generally speaking, the search space for states grows exponentially, so the choice of search algorithm is critical for search programming. As mentioned in Introduction, there are three important search algorithms [13]: best-first, depth-first branch-and-bound, and iterative-deepening. We implemented functions for them by using improving sequences.

---

[1] It would be better if we could define `<?` as a data constructor of `IS a`. However, it is impossible to do so because Haskell requires that the name of a data constructor begins with `:`.

An exhaustive search uses a naive algorithm that searches the entire state-space, so its program is terribly inefficient. However, it is simple enough to regard as a specification for solving the problem.

The typical form of an exhaustive search program is

```
search :: s -> c
search state
  | isGoal state = cost state
  | otherwise    =
    minimum [search s | s <- children state, legal s]
```

where `isGoal state` judges whether `state` is a goal state, `cost state` returns the actual cost of `state`, `children state` returns a list of the next states of `state`, and `legal state` judges whether `state` is legal.

Using this definition, we can write an improving sequence-based program as follows.

```
search :: Ord c => s -> IS c
search state
  | isGoal state = cost state <? E
  | otherwise    = eval state <?
    minimum' [search s | s <- children state, legal s]
```

The additional expressions are `<? E` for the termination and `eval state <?` to indicate the approximation value at the current stage of computation, where `eval state` returns a lower bound (evaluated value) of the cost of `state`. Function `minimum' :: [IS c] -> IS c` is used instead of `minimum :: [c] -> c` because this `search` returns an improving sequence. The need for the remaining computations can be judged using the approximation value, `eval state`. Therefore by defining a suitable `minimum'`, we can obtain efficient programs for the three search algorithms. The next three sections describe the three algorithms.

4   Best-First Search

A best-first search (BFS) is a generic algorithm that expands the most promising choice by using some evaluation function. Different evaluation functions lead to different versions of the best-first search. For example, if the evaluation function returns a depth from the initial state, the best-first search becomes a breadth-first search. If the function returns the cost of the path from the initial state to the current state, the search becomes a Dijkstra's single-source shortest-path search [3]. If the function returns the sum of the cost from the initial state and the estimated cost of the path from the current state to the goal, the search becomes A* search [5].

To obtain a BFS program based on the exhaustive search program described in the previous section, we simply use function `minimumB` instead of `minimum'`.

```
searchB,  search :: Ord c => s -> IS c
searchB = search
search state
  | isGoal state = cost state <? E
  | otherwise    = eval state <?
    minimumB [search s | s <- children state, legal s]
```

In this program, `eval` is the evaluation function for the BFS.

Function `minimumB` is defined in terms of function `minB` with two arguments, similar to Burton's *minimum* function [2].

```
minimumB :: Ord a => [IS a]          -> IS a
minB     :: Ord a =>  IS a -> IS a -> IS a

minimumB = foldl1 minB
minB E ys = E
minB xs E = E
minB xxs@(x :? xs) yys@(y :? ys)
  | x == y     = x <? minB  xs  ys
  | x <  y     = x <? minB  xs yys
  | otherwise = y <? minB xxs  ys
```

Essentially, `minB` merges two improving sequences in the order of binary relation `<`, but, when one of the sequences terminates, the rest of the other sequence is discarded. Therefore this means that all computations in the discarded sequence are eliminated. Function `minimumB` implements a BFS because it first chooses the minimum cost (approximation value) among the improving sequences given in a list and prunes those sequences whose cost is greater than the minimum cost. For example, consider the following example.

```
      minB (2 <? E) (1 <? minB (3 <? xs) (4 <? ys))
  ⇒  1 <? minB (2 <? E) (minB (3 <? xs) (4 <? ys))
  ⇒  1 <? minB (2 <? E) (3 <? minB  xs  (4 <? ys))
  ⇒  1 <? 2 <? minB  E  (3 <? minB  xs  (4 <? ys))
  ⇒  1 <? 2 <? E
```

The computation whose approximation value is 1 is evaluated first, because it is the most promising candidate. Next, the computation whose approximation value is 2 is evaluated. Then, because the minimum cost is determined to be 2, computations whose approximation value is 3, which is greater than the minimum cost, are eliminated.

For improving sequences of `Gt a`, `minimumB` returns an improving sequence that approaches the minimum value of `Gt a`, which is the maximum of `a`. Hence, the following aliases are useful for readability when using improving sequences of `Gt a` or `GtE a`.

```
maximumB = minimumB
```

5   Depth-First Branch-and-Bound Search

A depth-first branch-and-bound (DFBB) search starts with an upper bound on the minimum cost and then searches the entire state-space in a depth-first manner. Whenever a new goal whose cost is lower than the best one found so far is found, the upper bound is updated with the cost of this new goal. Any state whose cost equals or exceeds the current bound is eliminated.

To create a DFBB search program, we add upper bound u as an argument to search and use minimumD u for minimum'. Function minimumD u searches in a depth-first manner and prunes using upper bound u. This search starts with an initial upper bound, uinit.

```
searchD :: Ord c => s          -> IS c
search  :: Ord c => s -> IS c -> IS c

searchD state = search state (uinit <? E)
search  state u
  | isGoal state = cost state <? E
  | otherwise    = eval state <?
    minimumD u [search s | s <- children state, legal s]
```

Note that search state returns a function that takes argument u and returns an improving sequence.

Function minimumD searches each child in a depth-first manner as long as the cost of a state is lower than the current upper bound. Whenever a better new goal is found, the upper bound is updated. Let dfbb u f be a function that searches child f in a depth-first manner under upper bound u. We define minimumD as follows.

```
minimumD :: Ord a => IS a -> [IS a -> IS a] -> IS a
dfbb     :: Ord a => IS a -> (IS a -> IS a) -> IS a

minimumD = foldl dfbb
dfbb u f = finalize (minB u (f u))
```

To understand the behavior of minimumD, consider the case in which the second argument of minimumD is a list of two elements, [f,g].

```
minimumD u [f,g] = dfbb (dfbb u f) g
```

First, minimumD searches first child f under bound u; it then searches the second child g using the search result for the first child as a new bound. Function dfbb gives a bound to a child and then searches the child. Function minB u, defined in the previous section, prunes a child state whose cost equals or exceeds upper bound u; finalize implements depth-first behavior.

As shown above, we can construct a DFBB search program by simply adding argument u to search, applying minimumD, and setting an initial value for u.

6   Iterative-Deepening Search

An iterative-deepening (ID) search repeats a series of depth-first searches while updating the cost threshold used for pruning. In each iteration, a branch of the search tree is pruned if the cost of the path from the root to the branch exceeds the cost threshold for that iteration. The initial threshold is the cost of the initial state, and the threshold for each succeeding iteration is the minimum cost that is greater than the previous threshold. The algorithm terminates when a goal whose cost does not exceed the current threshold is found. Since no state whose cost is less than the cost threshold exists, the threshold used in each iteration is a lower bound of the actual cost. Therefore, the first goal chosen for expansion has the least cost. Special cases of an ID search include a depth-first iterative-deepening (DFID) search whose `eval` returns a depth from the initial state and an iterative-deepening-A* (IDA*) search whose `eval` is the same as A*'s.

We construct an ID search program by adding threshold t as an argument to function `search` and using function `minimumI t` for `minimum'` to search in a depth-first manner until the cost of some state exceeds t. Function `search` is repeated by function `iter`, which iterates a search, deepening the threshold until the goal is reached.

```
searchI :: Ord c => s       -> IS c
search  :: Ord c => s -> c -> IS c

searchI = iter . search
search state t
  | isGoal state = cost state <? E
  | otherwise    = eval state <?
    minimumI t [search s | s <- children state, legal s]
```

Function `minimumI` searches each given child in a depth-first manner until the cost of a state exceeds the threshold for the current iteration. In a search for some child, if a goal whose cost is not greater than the threshold is found, the goal is returned and searches for remaining children are pruned. Otherwise, the minimum value among the costs of children is selected as the new threshold for the next iteration.

Let `dfs` be a function that searches each child and `mn` be a function that chooses a minimum result among the children. Function `minimumI` is defined as

```
minimumI :: Ord a => a -> [a -> IS a] -> IS a
minimumI t = foldl1 (mn t) . map (dfs t)
```

Function `dfs t` gives threshold t to a child and searches the child until its value exceeds t or it finds a goal.

```
dfs  :: Ord a => a -> (a -> IS a) -> IS a
dfs' :: Ord a => a ->       IS a  -> IS a
```

```
dfs  t f              = dfs' t (f t)
dfs' t s@(x :? xs) = if (x < t || x .== t) && xs /= E
                      then dfs' t xs else s
```

Function `mn t` first searches the first child. If a goal whose cost equals `t` is found, it is returned. Otherwise, `mn t` searches the second child and returns a better result.

```
mn :: Ord a => a -> IS a -> IS a -> IS a
mn t xs ys = if x .== t || x < y || x .== y
             then xs else ys
             where x = approx xs
                   y = approx ys
```

Function `iter` repeats the search with an initial threshold. Since the argument of `iter` is function `f`, which takes a threshold and searches from an initial state, the approximation of the initial state, `approx (f undefined)`, is given as the initial threshold, where `undefined` denotes ⊥. Although `undefined` is used, it causes no problem because, in the evaluation of the approximation, `undefined` is never needed. If a goal is found at some iteration step, the search terminates; otherwise, it re-searches with a new threshold.

```
iter  :: Ord a => (a -> IS a)        -> IS a
iter' :: Ord a => (a -> IS a) -> a -> IS a

iter f   = iter' f (approx (f undefined))
iter' f t = let x :? xs = dfs t f in
                x <? if xs == E then E else iter' f x
```

As shown above, we can construct an ID search program by simply adding argument `t` to `search` and using `minimumI` and `iter`.

7 Modularization Using a Higher-Order Function

For clarity and modularity, it might be useful to describe the three search programs in terms of a common higher-order function.

In the exhaustive search program described in Section 3, we parameterize `minimum'` and recursively call `search`.

```
search rec min state
  | isGoal state = cost state <? E
  | otherwise    = eval state <?
    min [rec s | s <- children state, legal s]
```

Programs for BF, DFBB, and ID searches can be defined in terms of higher-order function `search` as follows.

```
toBF srch = srchB
  where srchB = srch srchB minimumB

toDFBB srch uinit = \state -> srchD state uinit
  where srchD s u = srch srchD (minimumD u) s

toID srch = iter . srchI
  where srchI s t = srch srchI (minimumI t) s

searchB = toBF    search
searchD = toDFBB search uinit
searchI = toID    search
```

Note that we define a different higher-order function, namely toBF, toDFBB, and toID, for the BF, DFBB, and ID searches. By defining an appropriate exhaustive search function whose minimum function and recursively-called function are parameterized and then giving the function to toBF, toDFBB, and toID, we can easily obtain functions for the three algorithms.

8 Examples

8.1 Eight Puzzle Problem

The eight puzzle problem is a classic search problem. It involves eight square tiles numbered from 1 to 8 that are placed on a 3×3 board, leaving one position blank. The task is to reposition the tiles from a given initial configuration by sliding them one at a time until reaching the goal configuration in Fig. 1.

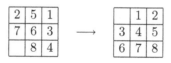

Fig. 1. Initial and goal configurations of eight puzzle problem

We describe programs that search for a path along which the tiles are slid that minimizes the number of moves, i.e., the cost. The result is a pair consisting of the cost and the path. Ordering the pairs by cost is done using the CostPath type.

```
newtype CostPath c p = CP (c,p) deriving Eq
cost (CP (c,p)) = c
instance (Ord c,Eq p) => Ord (CostPath c p) where
    x < y  =  cost x < cost y
```

We describe an exhaustive search program without improving sequences.

```
pz (CP (cost,path), conf)
  | isGoal conf = CP (cost,path)
  | otherwise   =
      minimum [pz (CP (cost+1, mv:path), cf) |
                     (mv,cf) <- children conf]
```

Variables `path` and `cost` are a path and its cost, respectively, from an initial configuration to the current configuration `conf`. If `conf` is the goal, function `pz` returns `CP (cost,path)` and terminates the computation. Otherwise, because `conf` is not the goal, `pz` searches the next configurations of `conf` and chooses the minimum cost from the results. Function `isGoal` judges whether a given configuration is the goal, function `children` returns a list of pairs of move `mv` and configuration `cf`, each of which is obtained by a single sliding of a tile from the current configuration.

We rewrite the exhaustive program into an improving sequence-based one. Since different paths may have the same cost, we use improving sequences based on relation `<=`. Similar to the case of `search` in Section 3, expressions that denote the termination and approximation of the current computation are added to the definition of the exhaustive program. In the computation of the approximation, we use Manhattan distance md, which is the distance between two points measured along axes:

$$md\ (x_1, y_1)\ (x_2, y_2) = |x_1 - x_2| + |y_1 - y_2| . \tag{1}$$

For each tile, the Manhattan distance between the current position and the goal is the minimum cost of reaching the goal. Thus, the sum of the Manhattan distances for all tiles from the current configuration to the goal, namely `md conf`, can be regarded as a lower bound on cost.

```
pz rec min (CP (cost,path), conf)
  | isGoal conf = CP (cost,path) <=? E
  | otherwise   = CP (cost + md conf, path) <=?
      min [rec (CP (cost+1, mv:path), cf) |
              (mv,cf) <- children conf]
```

The programs for the three algorithms are obtained by giving `pz` to `toBF`, `toDFBB`, and `toID` with an appropriate initial upper bound, `uinit`.

```
pzB = toBF   pz
pzD = toDFBB pz uinit
pzI = toID   pz
```

8.2   Knapsack Problem

The knapsack problem is, given a certain capacity knapsack and items of various values and sizes, to find the most valuable set of items that fit in the knapsack. The number of items of each type is unbounded. For simplicity, we assume that the types of items are sorted in descending order of per-size value.

An exhaustive search program without improving sequences is defined as

```
ks (sum,cap,[]) = sum
ks (sum,cap,items@((val,size):rest))
   | cap <  0 = 0
   | cap == 0 = sum
   | cap >  0 = maximum [ks (sum+val, cap-size, items),
                         ks (sum,     cap,      rest )]
```

Variable sum is the accumulative value of the items packed so far, variable cap is the remaining capacity, and variable items is a list of the items. Each item consists of a pair of its value (val) and its size (size). If the list of items is empty, ks returns sum. Otherwise, cap < 0 checks for an illegal situation, and cap == 0 checks the room for packing. The ks (sum+val,cap-size,items) corresponds to the case where the first item (val,size) is packed, and ks (sum,cap,rest) corresponds to the case where the first type of item is not longer packed.

In this problem, we want to maximize the total value of the items in the knapsack, so improving sequences based on >= are used. A program using improving sequences is

```
ks rec max (sum,cap,[]) = sum >=? E
ks rec max (sum,cap,items@((val,size):rest))
   | cap <  0 = 0    >=? E
   | cap == 0 = sum >=? E
   | cap >  0 = sum+(val/size)*cap >=?
                    max [rec (sum+val, cap-size, items),
                         rec (sum,     cap,      rest )]
```

The approximation is an ideal total value, the value that would be attained if the remaining capacity was completely filled with the most valuable items. Since items is sorted in descending order of per-size value, the ideal total value is the product of the (val/size) ratio of the headmost item of items multiplied by the remaining capacity.

The programs for the three algorithms are constructed by simply giving ks as arguments of toBF, toDFBB, and toID with an appropriate initial lower bound linit.

```
ksB = toBF   ks
ksD = toDFBB ks linit
ksI = toID   ks
```

9   Discussion and Related Work

We used a naive exhaustive search program that produces the entire state-space (search space) as lazy data structures with improving sequences. In this case, the exhaustive search program specifies the problem. To implement pruning, it is necessary to restrict the state-space to be searched; improving sequences coupled with lazy evaluation are the keys to accomplishing this. An important feature of improving sequences is the raising of intermediate results generated during the computation into first-class objects. This enables us to refer to the intermediate results, determine the need for the remaining computations on the basis of the intermediate results, and control the computation process. Since each minimum function (`minimumB`, `minimumD`, and `minimumI`) for improving sequences demands only parts of the state-space and uses intermediate results in its own way, we can implement different search algorithms while retaining the clarity of an exhaustive search program.

Similar to our approach, Hughes and Swierstra [8] implemented parser combinators for ambiguous grammars. They defined a data structure and a function, which correspond to `IS a` and `minB`, respectively, and represented a parse process in a breadth-first manner by incorporating the depth into the data structure. In contrast, we implemented *three* search algorithms in terms of the *general* data structure, improving sequences.

Erwig proposed type class `SearchProblem` [4] to support functional search programming. In his approach, users write a program in such a way that it satisfies the specification of type class `SearchProblem`. Our approach for the description of search programs is different; it does not impose any definition form for search. As long as the user defines an exhaustive search function in terms of improving sequences with parameterizations of minimum and recursively-called functions, the user can obtain efficient search programs by giving an exhaustive search function to `toBF`, `toDFBB`, and `toID`.

Van Hentenryck and Michel [12] separated a search algorithm from a state-space in a nondeterministic object-oriented language COMET. They defined class `SearchController` to abstract search algorithms and used an instance of `Search Controller` for each algorithm. The objective of their research is similar to ours, but the approaches are different; they developed the new language and implemented the pruning using continuations, which are first-class objects in COMET, while we defined the new data type `IS` in an existing functional language Haskell.

10   Conclusion

We have presented purely functional implementations of three important search algorithms, best-first, depth-first branch-and-bound (DFBB), and iterative-deepening (ID), that enable us to write efficient search programs with pruning in the same form as a simple and naive but exhaustive search program. We use improving sequences that contain intermediate results of computations to judge the need for the remaining computations. In addition, we defined higher-order functions that parameterize the minimum (or maximum) function and obtain three kinds of efficient search programs, while retaining the clarity of an exhaustive search program, by giving suitable minimum functions defined on improving sequences as actual parameters. Our implementations are more comprehensive than a previous implementation of only the best-first search algorithm [2] because DFBB and ID search programs can be constructed in the same fashion as a best-first search program. We are going to apply our technique using improving sequences to other interesting search problems like limited discrepancy search [6].

Acknowledgments. We would like to thank the anonymous referees for their helpful comments.

References

1. Bird, R.: *Introduction to Functional Programming using Haskell.* Prentice Hall (1998)
2. Burton, F.W.: Encapsulating Non-determinacy in an Abstract Data Type with Determinate Semantics. *Journal of Functional Programming* (1991) 1(1):3-20
3. Dijkstra, E.W.: A Note on Two Problems in Connexion with Graphs. *Numerische Mathematik* (1959) 1:269-271
4. Erwig, M.: Escape from Zurg: An Exercise in Logic Programming. *Journal of Functional Programming* (2004) 14(3):253-261
5. Hart, R.E., Nilsson, N.J., Raphael, B.: A Formal Basis for the Heuristic Determination of Minimum Cost Paths. *IEEE Transactions on Systems Science and Cybernetics* (1968) 4(2):100-107
6. Harvey, W.D., Ginsberg, M.L.: Limited Discrepancy Search. *Proc. International Joint Conference on Artificial Intelligence (IJCAI'95)* (1995) 607-613
7. Horowitz, E., Sahni, S.: *Fundamentals of Computer Algorithms.* Computer Science Press (1978)
8. Hughes, R.J.M., Swierstra, S.D.: Polish Parsers, Step by Step. In *Proc. International Conference on Functional Programming (ICFP'03)* (2003) 239-248
9. Iwasaki, H.: Pruning Unnecessary Computations using Improving Sequences. In *Proc. Asian Workshop on Programming Languages and Systems (APLAS'02)* (2002) 46-57
10. Korf, R.E.: Depth-First Iterative Deepening: An Optimal Admissible Tree Search. *Artificial Intelligence* (1985) 27:97-109
11. Lawler, E.L., Woods, D.: Branch-and-Bound Methods: A Survey. *Operations Research 14* (1966) 4:699-719
12. Van Hentenryck, P., Michel, L.: Non-deterministic Control for Hybrid Search. In *Proc. International Conference on Integration of AI and OR Techniques in Constraint Programming for Combinatorial Optimization Problems (CP-AI-OR'05)* (2005) 380-395
13. Vempaty, N.R., Kumar, V., Korf, R.E.: Depth-First vs Best-First Search. In *Proc. National Conference on Artificial Intelligence (AAAI'91)* (1991) 434-440

Algebraic Knowledge Discovery Using Haskell

Jens Fisseler[1], Gabriele Kern-Isberner[2], Christoph Beierle[1],
Andreas Koch[1], and Christian Müller[1]

[1] Department of Computer Science, University of Hagen, 58084 Hagen, Germany
Tel.: (+49) 2331 987-4294; Fax: (+49) 2331 987-4288
{jens.fisseler,christoph.beierle}@fernuni-hagen.de
[2] Department of Computer Science, University of Dortmund, 44227 Dortmund,
Germany
Tel.: (+49) 231 755-2779; Fax: (+49) 231 755-2405
gabriele.kern-isberner@cs.uni-dortmund.de

Abstract. While declarative programming languages are often considered to be applicable to "toy problems" only, we present an example of a real-world programming task realized with a functional programming language. CONDORCKD is a novel algebraic knowledge discovery algorithm completely implemented in Haskell. We give an overview of CONDORCKD and describe our experiences gained during its development, including the implementation of a graphical user interface and a novel approach to compute the cycles of an undirected graph.

1 Introduction

Knowledge discovery and data mining algorithms put high demands on their implementation languages when it comes to speed and the ability to handle huge amounts of data. Because of this, mainly imperative languages like C++ or Java have been used for implementing data mining software [15]. To the best of our knowledge, there are very few examples of data mining algorithms implemented in functional languages ([3] describes one such example), although logical languages like Prolog are very popular in the subarea of *Inductive Logic Programming* [12].

In [6, 7], a novel approach to knowledge discovery employing algebraic methods is presented. When evaluating several programming languages for implementing this approach, we were looking for a language which would make it easy to transfer the mathematical, high-level specification of the algorithm into program code, and that would allow us to quickly implement a working prototype which we could further refine easily. As functional programming languages have a reputation for higher productivity than their imperative counterparts, we evaluated several functional languages and finally chose Haskell, for several reasons. Its clean syntax seemed well suited to express our mathematical specification, it offered a comprehensive standard library and good development tool support. We also hoped to turn our prototype into a usable product, without having to recode the algorithm in another language because of severe performance penalties.

M. Hanus (Ed.): PADL 2007, LNCS 4354, pp. 80–93, 2007.

In Section 2, we give a short overview of our algebraic knowledge discovery algorithm, before further elaborating on our choice of Haskell in Section 3. As an important part of our implementation, a novel algorithm for enumerating the cycles of an undirected graph is discussed in Section 4. Our general experiences in using Haskell for implementing quite a demanding algorithm are stated in Section 5, and Section 6 contains some concluding remarks and points out future work.

2   Knowledge Discovery by Reversing Inductive Knowledge Representation

In a very general sense, the aim of knowledge discovery is to reveal *structures of knowledge* which can be seen as *structural relationships*, being represented by rules, often also called conditionals in this paper. There are two key ideas underlying the approach we used for our implementation: First, knowledge discovery is understood as a process which is inverse to inductive knowledge representation. So the relevance of discovered information is judged with respect to the chosen induction method. Second, the link between structural and numerical knowledge is established by an algebraic theory of conditionals, which makes it possible to consider complex interactions between rules [6]. By applying this theory, we develop an algorithm that computes sets of probabilistic rules from distributions. The inductive representation method used here is based on maximizing entropy, an information theoretical principle (*ME-principle* [13]), so that the discovered rules can be considered as being most informative in a strict, formal sense. This approach is described in detail in [7]; we will give a brief overview in this section, also presenting a small running example that will help illustrating both the method and the implementation.

Example 1. Suppose in our universe are *animals* (A), *fish* (F), *aquatic beings* (Q), *objects with gills* (G) and *objects with scales* (S). The following table may reflect our observations:

object	freq.	prob.	object	freq.	prob.
$afqgs$	59	0.5463	$a\overline{f}qgs$	11	0.1019
$afqg\overline{s}$	21	0.1944	$a\overline{f}qg\overline{s}$	9	0.0833
$afq\overline{g}s$	6	0.0556	$a\overline{f}q\overline{g}\,\overline{s}$	2	0.0185

We are interested in any relationship between these objects, e.g., to what extent can we expect an animal that is an aquatic being with gills to be a fish? This relationship is expressed by the *conditional* $(f|aqg)$, which is read as "f, under the condition a and q and g". If P is the probability distribution given by the table above and $x \in [0, 1]$ is a probability value, P satisfies the *probabilistic conditional* $(f|aqg)[x]$, written as $P \models (f|aqg)[x]$ iff for the conditional probability, it holds that $P(f|aqg) = x$. In our example, it is easily calculated that $P \models (f|aqg)[0.8]$.

Our method is a *bottom-up approach*, starting with conditionals with long premises, and shortening these premises to make the conditionals most expressive but without losing information, in accordance with the information inherent to the data. It is able to make use of structural information obtained from the data due to its algebraic foundations for probabilistic conditionals, which represent conditionals by group generators and take kernels of group homomorphisms as structural invariants of probability distributions (for further details, cf. [6, 1]). An overview of the algorithm in pseudocode (using lists for set representations) is given in Figure 1 and its data flow is illustrated in Figure 2; both will be explained in a bit more detail in the following. The algorithm has been implemented as a component of the CONDOR system (for an overview, cf. [2])

Algorithm CKD
(Conditional Knowledge Discovery)

Input :   A frequency/probability distribution
Output :   A set of probabilistic conditionals

$calculateRules :: Dist \rightarrow [Rule]$
$calculateRules\ dist$
$\quad = solveAllEqs\ dist\ (equations\ dist)$
$\quad\quad (pruneBasicRules\ dist\ (allBasicRules\ dist))$

$solveAllEqs :: Dist \rightarrow [Equation] \rightarrow [Rule] \rightarrow [Rule]$
$solveAllEqs\ \_\ []\ rules = rules$
$solveAllEqs\ dist\ eqs\ rules$
$\quad = \textbf{case}\ (solveAnyEq\ dist\ eqs\ rules)\ \textbf{of}$
$\quad\quad\quad Just\ (newEqs,\ newRules) \rightarrow solveAllEqs\ dist\ newEqs\ newRules$
$\quad\quad\quad Nothing \rightarrow rules$

$equations :: Dist \rightarrow [Equation]$
$equations\ dist = map\ (cycleToEquation\ dist)\ (findEvenCycles\ dist)$

Fig. 1. High-level description of our CKD algorithm [7]. Note that the definitions of some functions have been left out for clarity of presentation.

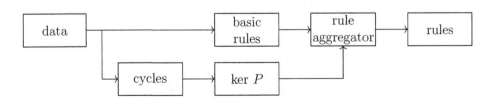

Fig. 2. Dataflow of the CONDORCKD algorithm

The frequency distributions calculated from data are mostly sparse, full of zeros, with only scattered clusters of non-zero probabilities. In our approach, these zero values are treated as non-knowledge without structure. They play a prominent role in setting up a set $\mathcal{S}_0$ of *basic rules* of manageable size in the beginning. In order to represent missing information in a most concise way, *null-conjunctions* (i.e. conjunctions of literals, with frequency 0) are calculated from the *basic tree of conjunctions* the leaves of which either correspond to actually occurring data, or to feature combinations not having been recorded at all. Aggregating the latter ones yields a set NC of most concise conjunctions of probability 0.

Next, the numerical relationships in P have to be explored to set up the so-called kernel of P, $ker\ P$. We only use conjunctions with non-zero probabilities for this purpose. It turns out that any such relationship corresponds to a simple cycle of even length (i.e. involving an even number of vertices) in an associated graph. Therefore, the search for numerical relationships holding in P amounts to searching for such cycles in a graph. Finally, as the last step of the initialization, the kernel of a structure homomorphism, $ker\ g$, has to be computed from $ker\ P$ with respect to the set $\mathcal{S}_0$ of conditionals. In this way, algebraic representations of numerical probabilistic information are obtained, which are encoded as equations holding in groups associated with the respective set of conditionals. Solving these equations successively yields modifications both on the groups and on the appertaining conditionals.

So, in the main loop of the algorithm CKD, the sets $\mathcal{K}$ of group elements and $\mathcal{S}$ of conditionals are subject to change. In the beginning, $\mathcal{K} = ker\ g$ and $\mathcal{S} = \mathcal{S}_0$; in the end, $\mathcal{S}$ will contain the discovered conditional relationships. Note that no probabilities are used in this main loop – only structural information (derived from numerical information) is processed. It is only afterwards, that the probabilities of the conditionals in the final set $\mathcal{S}$ are computed from P, and the probabilistic conditionals are returned.

Example 2. We continue Example 1. First, the set NC of *null-conjunctions* has to be calculated from the data; here, we find $NC = \{\overline{a}, \overline{q}, \overline{f}\,\overline{g}\}$ – no object matching any one of these partial descriptions occurs in the data base. These null-conjunctions are crucial to set up a starting set $\mathcal{S}_0 = \mathcal{B}$ of basic rules of feasible size:

$$\mathcal{B} = \{\phi_{f,1} = (f|aqgs) \quad \phi_{g,1} = (g|afqs) \quad \phi_{s,1} = (s|afqg) \quad \phi_{a,1} = (a|\top)$$
$$\phi_{f,2} = (f|aqg\overline{s}) \quad \phi_{g,2} = (g|afq\overline{s}) \quad \phi_{s,2} = (s|afq\overline{g})$$
$$\phi_{f,3} = (f|\overline{g}) \quad\quad \phi_{g,3} = (g|\overline{f}) \quad\quad \phi_{s,3} = (s|a\overline{f}qg) \quad \phi_{q,1} = (q|\top)\}$$

The next step is to analyze numerical relationships in P. In this example, we find two numerical relationships that hold with near equality:

$$P(a\overline{f}qgs) \approx P(a\overline{f}qg\overline{s}) \quad \text{and} \quad P(\frac{afqgs}{afqg\overline{s}}) \approx P(\frac{afq\overline{g}s}{afq\overline{g}\,\overline{s}})$$

These relationships are translated into algebraic group equations and help modifying the set of rules. For instance, $\phi_{f,1}$ and $\phi_{f,2}$ are joined to yield $(f|aqg)$, and

$\phi_{s,3}$ is eliminated. As a final output, the CKD algorithm returns the following set of conditionals:

Conclusion	Premise	Prob.
A=YES		1.0
F=YES	G={NO}	1.0
F=YES	A={YES}, Q={YES}, G={YES}	0.8
Q=YES		1.0
G=YES	F={NO}	1.0
G=YES	A={YES}, F={YES}, Q={YES}	0.91
S=YES	A={YES}, F={YES}, Q={YES}	0.74

This result can be interpreted as follows: All objects in our universe are aquatic animals which are fish or have gills (corresponding to the four rules with probability 1.0). Aquatic animals with gills are mostly fish (with a probability of 0.8), aquatic fish usually have gills (with a probability of 0.91) and scales (with a probability of 0.74).

Note that our system actually has generated the LATEX-code for the table given above as output. The only modification necessary was to adapt the table width to the column width.

3   Using Haskell for Data Mining

When beginning with the implementation of the CONDORCKD algorithm, we had to choose a suitable programming language. As we had an abstract, high-level description of the algorithms and their corresponding data structures, we were looking for a programming language that would make it easy to transfer these algorithms from their mathematical description to an executable form. We also wanted to be able to quickly implement a prototype so to review the results of the algorithms and further refine them. In order to do this, it should be possible for people with less a background in programming to look at the code and get a rough idea of what it would do. This led us to favor functional programming languages over imperative ones.

As indicated in Section 2, the description of the CONDORCKD algorithm was given in pseudocode with a strong mathematical flavor. This was very convenient during the implementation, as the specification was already decomposed into many intertwined functions and utilized set-based syntax for describing collections of data with certain properties and constraints. These mathematical concepts were easily and rapidly coded in Haskell, whereas Haskell's concise syntax allowed us to stay very close to the original specification.

Figure 3 very briefly illustrates the CONDOR system that is completely implemented in Haskell. It takes data in the form of CSV or ARFF files (these are widely used formats for exchanging tabular data used in data mining systems,

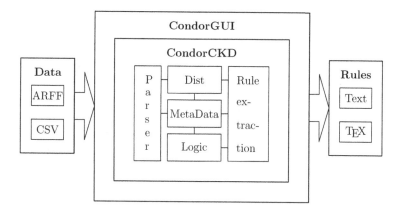

Fig. 3. Overview of the CONDOR system

see e.g. [15]) as input. The parser of the CONDORCKD component reads these input files and makes the data available to functions generating the internal representations of probability distributions, including meta data about the involved variables. Using a logic representation component, probabilistic rules are extracted from the probability distribution and are presented both in a simple text format (ready for further processing) as well as in a polished LATEX version. The complete user interaction is supported by a graphical user interface which is also completely implemented in Haskell.

4 Enumerating all Cycles of an Undirected Graph – A Functional Programming Challenge

As described in Section 2, one of the most important parts of the CONDORCKD algorithm is the computation of the simple cycles of the neighbor-graph. These depict numerical relationships in the input data, which are used for aggregating the basic rules.

4.1 Cycles in an Undirected Graph

For an undirected graph $G = (V, E)$ with edges $E \subseteq \{\{u, v\} \mid u, v \in V, u \neq v\}$, a *simple cycle* (of length k) is a sequence $\langle v_0, v_1, \ldots, v_k, v_0 \rangle$ of pairwise distinct vertices $v_i \in V$. We are interested in computing *all* simple cycles with even length up to a certain maximum length $k_{\max} \in \{2, 4, 6, \ldots\}$. This cycle length restriction is necessary, as the number of simple cycles can be exponential in the number of vertices.

There are several approaches to compute the simple cycles of an undirected graph [11], of which the *vector space* approach and *search-based algorithms* are the most important ones.

Every spanning tree T of an undirected graph partitions the graph edges into two disjoint sets, the tree edges and *back edges*, which close a cyclic path in T.

Every back edge $e \in E \setminus T$ induces one so-called *fundamental cycle* when added to T. All cycles (and edge-disjoint unions of cycles) of an undirected graph can be expressed as a combination of such fundamental cycles, thus forming a vector space over the finite field $GF(2)$, with the vector addition corresponding to the symmetric difference on the edge sets of subgraphs, cf. [11]. A fundamental cycle set $\{S_1, S_2, \ldots, S_{|E|-|V|+1}\}$ corresponding to a spanning tree T is a basis of this vector space. Whereas in principle one could enumerate every possible combination of fundamental cycles, only a small fraction of these are cycles, the rest being edge-disjoint unions of cycles. Although several vector space algorithms have been developed [11], very little has been done regarding pruning these unnecessary computations, let alone incorporating cycle length restrictions.

Search-based algorithms use a modified depth-first search with backtracking, during which edges are appended to a path until a cycle is found. Careful pruning of the search space is necessary to ensure that every cycle is generated exactly once and that little unnecessary work is done. To this end, most algorithms impose a certain ordering on the graph vertices and initiate a search only in certain vertices, see [11].

4.2   A Combined Approach

Although search-based algorithms are the fastest known algorithms for enumerating all cycles, even their running times on several of our problems were prohibitively large. But combining search-based and vector-space algorithms allowed for some further reduction of the search-space.

The key to our new algorithm is the fact that every fundamental cycle has one special edge that is not a member of any other fundamental cycle – the back edge closing a path in the corresponding spanning tree, thus yielding this fundamental cycle. Assume a fixed ordering of the elements of a given fundamental cycle set $\{S_1, S_2, \ldots, S_{|E|-|V|+1}\}$. Recall that every cycle c can be written as a combination of several fundamental cycles $S_{i_1}, S_{i_2}, \ldots, S_{i_n}$, w.l.o.g. $i_1 < i_2 < \cdots < i_n$. At least one edge must have been removed from every S_i, otherwise one or more of the S_i would be part of c as a whole, which means c would be a disjoint union of cycles. Thus, in order to compute all cycles containing the back edge of S_i, $1 \leq i \leq |E| - |V| + 1$, we can restrict the graph to be searched to the subgraph induced by $S_1 \cup \cdots \cup S_i$. This restriction of the search to an induced subgraph is what speeds up our algorithm.

Our cycle enumeration algorithm can be described by three steps:

1. Compute a set of fundamental cycles $\{S_1, S_2, \ldots, S_{|E|-|V|+1}\}$.
2. For every S_i, compute a subgraph G_i. G_i is the union of a subset of the fundamental cycles $S_1, \ldots, S_i$, and is defined by the cycles of the equivalence class of S_i with respect to the transitive closure of the relation $R_\cap^i$,

$$R_\cap^i := \{(S_r, S_t) \mid S_r, S_t \in \{S_1, \ldots, S_i\} \wedge S_r \cap S_t \neq \emptyset\}.$$

3. Conduct a search-based cycle enumeration in each of these subgraphs G_i, starting at one of the vertices incident to the back edge of S_i.

We have compared the running time[1] of our algorithm (column "FCs + DFS") and that of a standard search-based algorithm (DFS) on three different graphs, and the preliminary results are encouraging (see Figure 4).

Graph	Max. cycle length	#Cycles	FCs + DFS	DFS
A	10	2827	0:00:01	0:00:02
	12	16699	0:00:05	0:00:13
	14	119734	0:00:45	0:08:13
	16	890204	0:05:48	7:23:54
B	10	2929	0:00:04	0:00:06
	12	23021	0:00:42	0:01:28
	14	222459	0:09:11	0:42:09
C	6	2927	0:00:10	0:01:26
	8	18695	0:00:36	0:02:13
	10	268097	0:13:51	0:30:27

Fig. 4. Runtime comparison

Although there are several approaches to functional graph algorithms described in the literature (cf. [4]), they all need to support the marking of already processed parts of the graph, either by threading a state parameter through the function calls, or by hiding the state inside an appropriate graph ADT. As our novel cycle enumeration algorithm is still part of our research, we have opted for an initial implementation using an explicit state parameter. Despite leading to a computational overhead, this allowed us to easily "glue" the functions for the subgraph generation and the search-based cycle enumeration together, without having to deal with the additional complexity of a state monad. Having obtained encouraging results with our current version, we are currently reimplementing it using the stated-monad based approach described in [8], in order to compare both variants with respect to memory consumption and runtime behaviour.

5   Lessons Learned

After introducing the CONDORCKD algorithm and pointing out some important parts of our implementation, we now want to give an overview of our general experience in using a functional programming language for implementing a knowledge discovery algorithm. One thing to note is that some of the programmers involved in the implementation of the CONDOR system only had very little previous experience with Haskell, consisting mostly of an introductory university course in functional programming.

---

[1] Using GHC 6.4.1 with optimization turned on and code generation via C. The executables were running on an AMD Athlon64-3200+ in 32bit-mode with 1GB RAM, using Linux.

5.1   Clean and Concise Syntax

As stated in Section 3, Haskell's concise syntax allowed us to stay close to the original specification, thereby making a quick implementation of a prototype possible, which could be refined afterwards. The often mentioned brevity of functional programs applies to CONDORCKD, too. Our functions generally consist of only a few lines, few have more than a dozen.

In our experience, the brevity results from our extensive use of higher-order functions (like *map*, *filter* and *fold*) in combination with Haskell's automatic memory management. Thus our experiences correspond the well-known observation that the (functional) programmer generally does not have to deal with traversal of data structures or memory management, but can focus on the data manipulation itself.

5.2   Strong Typing

Haskell's type system is often emphasized as one of the language's most important features in helping the user writing correct programs, and we can only support this claim. When writing a new module function, we have made a habit of writing its type signature first, then implementing its body. This way, the compiler or interpreter would complain about type mismatches, which easily occur when writing new functions not used by or not using other module functions. Writing a type signature was hence an additional tool in forcing all CONDOR programmers to think about the function once again instead of quickly hacking it down.

It could be argued that other languages like C++ or Java also feature an expressive type system, but Haskell's type system offers additional benefits. Whereas a C++ or Java compiler will only issue a warning or an error when the arguments given to a function or its return value don't match its declaration, a Haskell compiler can infer the type of a function based on its arguments. By comparing this type to the type signature of the function, it is often quite easy to find the bug resulting in the type mismatch.

Algebraic data types are another important part of Haskell's type system we heavily relied upon when developing CONDORCKD. In conjunction with *pattern matching*, algebraic types allow the processing of data based on its structural properties. Because pattern matching is the only way to extract data from algebraic types, incomplete patterns will cause the compiler to issue a warning, thus forcing the programmer to rethink the boundary conditions of his data types. Whereas in the beginning, those programmers in our team with only little previous experience with Haskell complained about too many warnings, in the end they appreciated these Haskell features.

5.3   A Comprehensive Standard Library

In addition to powerful language features, the number of available libraries is also an important factor with respect to programmer productivity.

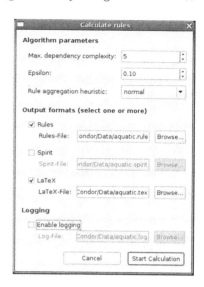

Fig. 5. The graphical user interface

We extensively used the *Haskell Hierarchical Libraries* while implementing the CONDORCKD algorithm, especially the collection types *Map* and *Set*. They allow for similar processing as lists, as they also offer the probably most often used (list) manipulation functions *map*, *filter* and *fold*. This made it easy to change functions processing lists to utilize a more adequate collection type, which we did at various places during our system development.

Other libraries that were important during the development of CONDORCKD are PARSEC [10], used for reading data from files and parsing user input, and the GUI-libraries wxHaskell and gtk2hs.

5.4 Implementing a Graphical User Interface

From the start, CONDORCKD has been developed with the end user in mind, whom we wanted to offer a comfortable user interface to make working with CONDORCKD as convenient as possible. To this end, we have developed a graphical user interface, initially using the wxHaskell library [9]. Though we were satisfied at first, because wxHaskell allowed us to develop a single GUI for different platforms, after a while slightly varying behaviour of certain GUI elements surfaced, which we could not track down to either wxHaskell, wxWidgets or some platform-specific library. As the development of wxHaskell seemed to have come to a halt, we decided to reimplement our GUI, using the gtk2hs[2] library. This library is under active development, and is also supported on Linux and Windows, our two main development platforms.

Two screenshots of the dialog windows can be seen in Figure 5. The screenshot on the left shows the main window, from which the user can initiate actions like

---

[2] http://www.haskell.org/gtk2hs/

loading a probability distribution from a file, or computing probabilistic rules from the current distribution. After loading a probability distribution, the main window also gives information about the variables pertaining to the current distribution, and also enables the user to query the (conditional) probability of certain logical expressions. The screenshot on the right-hand side of Figure 5 shows the dialog window for calculating rules from the current distribution. The user can adjust various parameters of the CKD-algorithm and can choose certain output formats for the rules.

Our experiences show that gtk2hs provides all the functionality needed to realize the GUI of the CONDOR system. Although the current GUI was developed with Linux, it worked out-of-the-box when run on Windows, without the need for a single platform-adjustment. This is a big plus, but as GTK+ is a toolkit originally developed for Unix-like systems, some parts of it may alienate Windows users. Haskell would clearly benefit from a platform-independant GUI library, like wxHaskell was intended to be.

5.5   A Suitable Development Environment

We used two Haskell implementations during the development of CONDORCKD. Initial development was done with Hugs[3], because its interactive interpreter made the incremental development very convenient. But as the project's code size grew and the algorithms needed to be tested on real-world data, better run-time performance was required and we switched to GHC[4], which has an interactive environment, too, but also the ability to generate executables.

Debugging was mainly done by interactive testing of functions and excessive printing of intermediate data whenever possible, which we consider unwise in retrospect. We are planning to use Hood [5] for debugging during further development of CONDORCKD.

Profilers proved to be another invaluable development tool for us, enabling the exact location of performance bottlenecks, even more so with lazy evaluation [14]. Fortunately, GHC includes support for space and time profiling, and this helped increasing our algorithms' performance on several occasions, although *how* to improve performance was not always obvious, see Section 5.6.

5.6   Dealing with Laziness and Excessive Memory Consumption

When we had a prototypical implementation of CONDORCKD at hand and started testing it on real-world data sets, Haskell's lazy evaluation caused some performance problems by delaying many computations. Although lazy evaluation can be a clear benefit, as it allows for quite elegant solutions, and also CONDOR-CKD relies on lazy evaluation in the implementation of several functions, it is quite a hindrance for high-performance code.

---

[3] http://www.haskell.org/hugs/
[4] http://www.haskell.org/ghc/

Lazy evaluation makes reasoning about run-time performance and memory consumption much more difficult than eager evaluation, because the evaluation order of expressions is not easily assessed for all but the most simple programs, and sometimes a lot of unevaluated expressions fill up the heap. Thus we have made heavy use of GHC's profiling capabilities in improving the run-time behaviour and memory consumption of CONDORCKD, although finding the right places for inserting "*seq*" and "*$!*", two functions used for improving the strictness of other functions, was not always obvious. It often was a trial-and-error process, and included the inspection of the core code generated by GHC in order to assess the strictness of certain functions. If Haskell is to be used for real-world projects, it clearly needs better ways for improving the strictness of functions, because using "*seq*" and "*$!*" is cumbersome and makes the resulting code much more difficult to read, loosing some of the conciseness emphasized in Section 5.1. Hopefully this will be remedied with the introduction of the so-called *bang patterns*[5] proposed for the upcoming Haskell' standard. These would offer additional syntax which enables the programmer to provide function parameters with a strictness annotation, thus making the implementation of strict functions much easier.

Memory consumption was further reduced by using appropriate data types. For example, CONDORCKD uses a lot of small objects for representing *conjunctions* – simple logical formulas representing the premises of rules. Initially, these conjunctions where implemented using nested lists of *Int*s, causing every list element to occupy three words of memory. As the flexibility offered by lists was not really needed for representing conjunctions, we replaced them by unboxed arrays of *Int*s, leading to some serious reduction in memory requirements, and also better run-time performance. Another way of reducing the memory needs was using strictness flags ("!") to enforce the evaluation of the arguments of data constructors to remove some laziness. In combination with the "UNPACK" pragma, this also improved the run-time performance of CONDORCKD.

6   Conclusions and Further Work

We have introduced our implementation of CONDORCKD, a novel algorithm for knowledge discovery based on the principle of maximum entropy. We used Haskell for its implementation, where our choice was based on our expectation to be able to quickly implement the algorithm based on its abstract, high-level description. Haskell has lived up to our expectations, as a prototype was implemented quite rapidly, though optimizing its run-time behaviour and memory consumption was a lengthier – and sometimes problematic – process. Nonetheless, the resulting code displays the brevity ascribed to functional programs, as the whole *documented* codebase involves little more than 9000 lines of code, including a GUI. An implementation written in C++ or Java can be expected to be several times larger, and despite being optimized, the Haskell code still closely resembles its abstract description, a definite advantage over imperative languages.

---

[5] http://hackage.haskell.org/trac/haskell-prime/ticket/76

Currently, we are planning to further refine and enhance our algorithm and its implementation. This includes work to further reduce the memory consumption, but also trying to utilize external data storage, because when analyzing large and complex data sets, the intermediate data structures computed by our algorithm, especially the cycles (see Section 4), will definitely be too large to fit into even todays computer's main memory.

Acknowledgements. We'd like to thank the anonymous reviewers for their helpful comments. The research reported here was partly supported by the DFG – Deutsche Forschungsgemeinschaft (grant BE 1700/5-3).

References

[1] C. Beierle and G. Kern-Isberner. An alternative view of knowledge discovery. In *Proceedings of the 36th Annual Hawaii International Conference on System Sciences, HICSS-36*, page 68.1. IEEE Computer Society, 2003.

[2] C. Beierle and G. Kern-Isberner. Modelling conditional knowledge discovery and belief revision by abstract state machines. In E. Boerger, A. Gargantini, and E. Riccobene, editors, *Abstract State Machines 2003 – Advances in Theory and Applications, Proceedings 10th International Workshop, ASM2003*, pages 186–203. Springer, LNCS 2589, 2003.

[3] A. Clare and R. D. King. Data mining the yeast genome in a lazy functional language. In V. Dahl and P. Wadler, editors, *Practical Aspects of Declarative Languages, 5th International Symposium, PADL 2003, Proceedings*, volume 2562 of *Lecture Notes in Computer Science*, pages 19–26. Springer, 2003.

[4] M. Erwig. Inductive graphs and functional graph algorithms. *Journal of Functional Programming*, 11(5):467–492, 2001.

[5] A. Gill. Debugging haskell by observing intermediate data structures. *Electronic Notes in Theoretical Computer Science*, 41(1), 2000.

[6] G. Kern-Isberner. Solving the inverse representation problem. In *Proceedings 14th European Conference on Artificial Intelligence, ECAI'2000*, pages 581–585, Berlin, 2000. IOS Press.

[7] G. Kern-Isberner and J. Fisseler. Knowledge discovery by reversing inductive knowledge representation. In *Proceedings of the Ninth International Conference on the Principles of Knowledge Representation and Reasoning, KR-2004*, pages 34–44. AAAI Press, 2004.

[8] D. J. King and J. Launchbury. Structuring depth-first search algorithms in Haskell. In *Proceedings of the 22nd ACM SIGPLAN-SIGACT Symposium on Principles of Programming Languages (POPL'95)*, pages 344–354. ACM Press, 1995.

[9] D. Leijen. wxHaskell – a portable and concise GUI library for Haskell. In *ACM SIGPLAN Haskell Workshop (HW'04)*. ACM Press, 2004.

[10] D. Leijen and E. Meijer. Parsec: Direct style monadic parser combinators for the real world. Technical Report UU-CS-2001-27, Department of Computer Science, Universiteit Utrecht, 2001.

[11] P. Mateti and N. Deo. On algorithms for enumerating all circuits of a graph. *SIAM Journal on Computing*, 5(1):90–99, 1976.

[12] S. Muggleton and L. De Raedt. Inductive logic programming: Theory and methods. *Journal of Logic Programming*, 19/20:629–679, 1994.

[13] J.B. Paris. *The uncertain reasoner's companion – A mathematical perspective.* Cambridge University Press, 1994.

[14] C. Runciman and D. Wakeling. Heap profiling of lazy functional programs. *Journal of Functional Programming*, 3(2):217–245, 1993.

[15] I. H. Witten and E. Frank. *Data Mining: Practical Machine Learning Tools and Techniques.* Morgan Kaufmann, 2005.

Applications, Implementation and Performance Evaluation of Bit Stream Programming in Erlang

Per Gustafsson[1] and Konstantinos Sagonas[2]

[1] Uppsala University and Ericsson AB, Sweden
[2] National Technical University of Athens, Greece

Abstract. Writing code that manipulates bit streams is a painful and error-prone programming task, often performed via bit twiddling techniques such as explicit bit shifts and bit masks in programmer-allocated buffers. Still, this kind of programming is necessary in many application areas ranging from decoding streaming media files to implementing network protocols. In this paper we employ high-level constructs from declarative programming, such as pattern matching at the bit level and bit stream comprehensions, and show how a variety of bit stream programming applications can be written in a succinct, less error-prone, and totally memory-safe manner. We also describe how these constructs can be implemented efficiently. The resulting performance is superior to that of other (purely) functional languages and competitive to that of low-level languages such as C.

1 Introduction

Binary data is everywhere. Many applications such as processing network data, encoding and decoding streaming media files, file compression and decompression, cryptography etc. need to process such data. Consequently, programmers often find themselves wanting to write programs that manipulate bit streams. In imperative languages such as C, processing of bit streams typically happens using so called *bit twiddling* techniques that involve combinations of shifts, bitwise operators and explicit masks on programmer-allocated buffers. In general, bit twiddling obfuscates the intention of the programmer, is often error-prone, and leads to code that is unnecessarily verbose, hard to read and modify. Furthermore, bit twiddling code tends to lose the connection with the specification of the data format which is to be processed.

Declarative languages can in principle avoid these shortcomings since they allow for high-level manipulation of data. Unfortunately, the ability to do so comes with a catch. For example, the pattern matching facilities offered by most functional languages are tightly coupled to constructor-based datatypes. As a result, programmers who want to manipulate bit streams have to choose between the lesser of the following two evils: either pay a significant cost in time and space and convert binary data to a symbolic representation, or resort to an imperative style of programming using bit twiddling techniques on byte arrays. In typical applications which require bit stream manipulation, performance considerations are paramount. As a result, in most practical uses, the imperative style of programming wins although there is no fundamental reason for declarative languages to lack constructs for efficient bit stream manipulation.

M. Hanus (Ed.): PADL 2007, LNCS 4354, pp. 94–108, 2007.

Since 2001, the functional language Erlang comes with a *byte-oriented* datatype (called *binary*) and with constructs to do pattern matching on a binary [13]. We have been heavily involved in this work and implemented a scheme for native code compilation of binaries and designed efficient algorithms for constructing deterministic pattern matching automata for byte-based binaries [7]. In last year's Erlang workshop we put forward a proposal [6] for lifting the restriction that Erlang binaries are sequences of bytes rather than bits and described the semantics of bit-level pattern matching on a bit-level binary (called *bit stream*). We have subsequently realized this proposal and describe its applications and implementation in this paper.

More specifically, the contributions of this paper are as follows:

- We explain how declarative programming constructs such as pattern matching and comprehensions brought down to the bit level can simplify bit stream programming (Sect. 2) and show how these constructs allow us to obtain compact and elegant solutions to important real-world applications (Sect. 3).
- We describe how these bit-level constructs can be implemented efficiently (Sect. 4).
- Finally, we compare the efficiency and ease of programming of using this approach to writing bit stream applications, with that of using other languages, both functional and imperative (Sect. 5).

2   Bit Stream Programming in Erlang

We show the features and expressive power of bit stream manipulation in Erlang through a series of examples. A more detailed and formal treatment can be found in [6].

2.1   Constructing and Matching a Bit Stream

This first example is very simple. It shows how to construct a bit stream and how such a stream can be deconstructed using bit-level pattern matching.

```
case <<8:4, 63:6>> of
    <<A:7, B/bitstr>> -> {A,B}
end
```

The expression <<8:4, 63:6>> evaluates to a ten-bit bit stream were its first four bits are the four low bits of the integer 8 and its last six bits are the six low bits of the integer 63. This creates the bit stream <<1000111111>>. For succinctness, we will denote such a bit stream as <<143:8, 3:2>>, which means that the first eight bits of the bit stream represented as an unsigned integer is 143 and the last two bits are the integer 3.

The case statement binds the variable A[1] to an integer constructed from the first seven bits in the bit stream, namely 39 (1000111). Because of the explicit type specifier bitstr rather than integer which is the default, B gets bound to the remaining bit stream <<7:3>>. As a result, the case expression evaluates to {39,<<7:3>>}.

Another useful feature of bit streams is the ability to have arithmetic expressions as sizes of bit stream segments. This is shown in the next example.

---

[1] All variables in Erlang start with a capital letter.

```
 0                   1                   2                   3
 0 1 2 3 4 5 6 7 8 9 0 1 2 3 4 5 6 7 8 9 0 1 2 3 4 5 6 7 8 9 0 1
+-+-+-+-+-+-+-+-+-+-+-+-+-+-+-+-+-+-+-+-+-+-+-+-+-+-+-+-+-+-+-+-+
|Version|  IHL  |Type of Service|          Total Length         |
+-+-+-+-+-+-+-+-+-+-+-+-+-+-+-+-+-+-+-+-+-+-+-+-+-+-+-+-+-+-+-+-+
|         Identification        |Flags|      Fragment Offset    |
+-+-+-+-+-+-+-+-+-+-+-+-+-+-+-+-+-+-+-+-+-+-+-+-+-+-+-+-+-+-+-+-+
|  Time to Live |    Protocol   |         Header Checksum        |
+-+-+-+-+-+-+-+-+-+-+-+-+-+-+-+-+-+-+-+-+-+-+-+-+-+-+-+-+-+-+-+-+
|                       Source Address                          |
+-+-+-+-+-+-+-+-+-+-+-+-+-+-+-+-+-+-+-+-+-+-+-+-+-+-+-+-+-+-+-+-+
|                    Destination Address                        |
+-+-+-+-+-+-+-+-+-+-+-+-+-+-+-+-+-+-+-+-+-+-+-+-+-+-+-+-+-+-+-+-+
|                    Options                    |    Padding     |
+-+-+-+-+-+-+-+-+-+-+-+-+-+-+-+-+-+-+-+-+-+-+-+-+-+-+-+-+-+-+-+-+
```

```
parse_IP_packet(
    <<Version:4, IHL:4, ToS:8, TotalLength:16,
      Identification:16, Flags:3, FragOffset:13
    TimeToLive:8, Protocol:8, Checksum:16
    SourceAddress:32,
    DestinationAddress:32,
    OptionsAndPadding:((IHL-5)*32)/bitstr,
    Data/bitstr>>) when Version =:= 4 ->
    ...
```

Fig. 1. Internet Protocol datagram header (from RFC 791) and parsing of an IPv4 packet in Erlang

2.2 Parsing IP Packets

In RFC 791 [14] the IP header is exemplified with the diagram shown in the left part of Figure 1. Note the close resemblance between this representation and the bit stream pattern shown in the right part of the figure which parses an IPv4 packet header.

For the most part, this is similar to the previous example except that this pattern is used in a function head rather than a `case` statement. Note also that the pattern expresses the meaning of the `IHL` field, which contains the IP header length in 32-bit words. Since the non-optional part of the IP header consists of five 32-bit words, the options and padding will take up `(IHL-5)*32` bits. This is expressed by using an arithmetic expression as the size of a segment. Because this arithmetic expression can refer to variables bound earlier in the binary pattern, as in this example, the matching has to respect the corresponding left-to-right ordering constraints between segments.[2]

2.3 Iterating and Filtering a Bit Stream

Consider a variation of the `drop_third` program introduced in [17] that requires inspecting bits besides counting them. The task is to drop from a bit stream of size exactly divisible by three all 3-bit chunks that begin with a zero. Using pattern matching on bit streams this task can be performed with the program in Figure 2. The solution is both natural and straightforward. The first clause describes what should happen if the first bit in a 3-bit chunk is one: we keep that chunk and add it to the resulting stream. The second clause handles the case where the first bit is a zero: we discard that 3-bit chunk. Finally the last clause handles the

```
drop_0XX(<<1:1, X:2, Rest/bitstr>>) ->
    <<1:1, X:2, drop_0XX(Rest)>>;
drop_0XX(<<0:1, _:2, Rest/bitstr>>) ->
    drop_0XX(Rest);
drop_0XX(<<>>) ->
    <<>>.
```

Fig. 2. `drop_0XX` using bit stream pattern matching

case where there are no more chunks: we return the empty bit stream.

Contrast this with a program written in a language that does not support manipulation of bit streams at the bit level very well such as C or Java. The programmer would have to

---

[2] Arithmetic expressions as sizes of segments are not allowed in Erlang/OTP R11B-1 (or prior). Instead, size expressions can only be variables or constants.

keep track of which bits to extract from the current byte of the incoming bit stream, use bit masks and shifts to extract each triple, and calculate how much padding is needed in the output stream. Being able to express pattern matching at the bit level, Erlang programmers are allowed to write declarative specifications of their intentions without having to worry about low-level details such as padding.

2.4 Inverting a Bit Stream Using a Comprehension

Another way to write code which iterates over a bit stream is to use a bit stream comprehension [6]. This is a construct analogous to a list comprehension [18], which in turn is an expression that is syntactic sugar for the combination of map, filter and concat on lists. For a simple example use of a bit stream comprehension consider the task of inverting all bits in a bit stream. The bsnot function below performs this task.

```
bsnot(BitStr) ->
    << bnot(X):1 || <<X:1>> <= BitStr >>.
```

The meaning of this comprehension is: iterate through each bit in the bit stream, invert it using the built-in bnot operator, and put it into the resulting bit stream.

2.5 Iterating and Filtering a Bit Stream Using Comprehensions

For a slightly more involved example consider the drop_0XX function of Section 2.3. Using bit stream comprehensions, drop_0XX would be written more succinctly as:

```
drop_0XX(BitStr) ->
    << <<1:1,X:2>> || <<1:1,X:2>> <= BitStr >>.
```

This comprehension works as follows. If the first three bits of the bit stream match the pattern <<1:1,X:2>> then place those bits in the resulting stream; otherwise drop these bits. Repeat until no bits remain in the bit stream. That is the pattern works as both a filter and a generator. To make this more explicit we can write a drop_0XX function which is equivalent with the previous one using an explicit filter in the following manner:[3]

```
drop_0XX(BitStr) ->
    << X:3 || <<X:3>> <= BitStr, 2#100 =< X >>.
```

In bit stream comprehensions, sometimes more complicated, perhaps user-defined, filtering is needed. In the following example, we are given a string represented as a bit stream and want to extract all non-digit characters from this string and store each of the digits in four bits:[4]

```
compact_digits(String) ->
    << (X-$0):4 || <<X:8>> <= String, is_digit(X) >>.

is_digit(X) when $0 =< X, X =< $9 -> true;
is_digit(_) -> false.
```

---

[3] In Erlang, 2#100 represents the number four in base two.

[4] In Erlang, '$' is an operator which given a character returns the ASCII value of that character.

3 Applications

3.1 UU-Encoding

UU-encoding is an old binary-to-text encoding scheme where groups of three binary bytes are encoded in four characters. This is done by dividing the three binary bytes into four groups of six bits. Then 32 is added to each six bit group which turns them into characters. The cores of these encoding and decoding scheme essentially become one-liners using Erlang's bit stream programming facilities.

```
uuencode(BitStr) ->
   << (X+32):8 || <<X:6>> <= BitStr >>.

uudecode(Text) ->
   << (X-32):6 || <<X:8>> <= Text >>.
```

3.2 yEnc

The yEnc format is a newer encoding of binary files than UU-encoding where bytes which cannot be safely transmitted in text mode are escaped. Each byte in the original stream is encoded by adding 42 to it using 8-bit arithmetic. If the result is a critical character (i.e., NULL, TAB [ASCII 9], LF [ASCII 10], CR [ASCII 13] which are hard to transmit over some networks or '=' [ASCII 61] which is used as an escape character), the character is encoded using two bytes: the first byte is '=' [ASCII 61] and the second byte is the critical value plus 64. To encode a binary file in the yEnc format [8], we can use the bit stream comprehension in the following program:

```
yenc(Bin) ->
   << yenc_byte(Byte) || <<Byte:8>> <= Bin >>.

yenc_byte(Byte) ->
   Enc = (Byte+42 rem 256),
   case is_critical(Enc) of
     true  -> <<61:8, (Enc+64):8>>;
     false -> <<Enc:8>>
   end.
```

3.3 μ-Law

Audio files are nowadays transmitted over the network using a variety of formats. One such format, designed to be space efficient, is μ-law compressed files [10]. Such files are compressed to half the size of the original audio as each 16-bit sample is translated into an 8-bit representation.

μ-law encoding. The encoding method is non-trivial but still quite simple. First the Sound sample is transformed from 2's complement form to a Biased sign magnitude form where the magnitude is an integer in the range [132..32767]. This can be done easily with the bit stream comprehension:

```
   << to_sign_magn(Sample) || <<Sample:16/integer-signed>> <= Sound >>
```

which simply takes each 16-bit sample in 2's complement form. This is achieved by using the `signed` specifier in the pattern. The `to_sign_magn` function is then applied to this value. This function is defined as follows:

```
to_sign_magn(Sample) ->
  <<sign(Sample):1, (min(abs(Sample), 32635)+132):15>>.
```

i.e., it transforms the sample from 2's complement form into sign magnitude form and increases the magnitude with 132.

In the next step, this representation is translated to an 8-bit representation where the first bit represents the sign, the next three bits represent the position of the first 1 in the magnitude, and the last four bits represent the values of the four bits following the leading 1. This can also be done with a comprehension of the form:

```
<< to_byte(S,M) || <<S:1,M:15/bitstr>> <= Biased >>
```

In this case, S contains the sign bit and M is a bit stream consisting of 15 bits representing the magnitude of the sample. These are used as arguments to the `to_byte` function which is defined as follows:

```
to_byte(Sign, Magn) -> to_byte(Sign, Magn, 7).

to_byte(Sign, <<1:1, Mantissa:4, _/bitstr>>, N) ->
  <<Sign:1, N:3, Mantissa:4>>;
to_byte(Sign, <<0:1, Rest/bitstr>>, N) ->
  to_byte(Sign, Rest, N-1).
```

This function searches for the position of the first 1 in the `Magn` bit stream. Since the range of the magnitude is 132–32676 there will be at least one 1 in the first 8 bits and recursion will stop. The position of the first 1 is therefore coded in the following way:

```
7 6 5 4 3 2 1 0
```

Thus, if the third bit contains the first 1, its position is 5. The following four bits are called the mantissa. In the byte created by the `to_byte` function the first bit contains the sign, the following three bits contain the position, and the last four bits contain the mantissa.

Finally, we take the 1's complement of this value using the `bsnot` operator of Section 2.4. The complete code for μ-law encoding is shown in the appendix.

μ-law decoding. To decode these values we start by taking their 1's complement. We then translate the bytes to sign magnitude form again with this comprehension:

```
Biased = << to_short(Sign, Exp, Mantissa) ||
              <<Sign:1,Exp:3,Mantissa:4>> <= Encoded >>
```

where the `to_short` function is defined in the following way:

```
to_short(Sign, Exp, Mantissa) ->
  <<Sign:1, 1:(8-Exp), Mantissa:4, 1:1, 0:(2+Exp)>>.
```

That is, put the `Sign` bit first, then put the leading one in the correct place followed by the mantissa and an additional 1 and fill the remaining bits with zeroes.

Finally, we must translate the sign magnitude representation into 2's complement representation and remove the bias. This is done with the comprehension:

```
<< unbias(Sign,Magn) || <<Sign:1,Magn:15>> <= Biased >>
```

where the function `unbias` is defined as follows:

```
unbias(0, Magn) -> <<(Magn - 132):16>>;
unbias(1, Magn) -> <<(132 - Magn):16>>.
```

3.4 PNG

The Portable Network Graphics (PNG) file format [16,11] is a rather recent format for picture files intended to replace the widely-used but patent-based GIF format. The structure of the PNG format is quite simple. It consists of an initial signature and then a series of chunks. Each of the chunks consists of a length field, a type field, the chunk data, and a checksum. A certain type of chunk contains the raw compressed data whereas the rest of the chunks contains meta data. Assuming that the PNG variable is bound to a bit stream where we have removed the signature from the original file, we can recreate the raw data in order to decompress it using the following bit stream comprehension.

```
<< RawData || <<Length:32, 73:8,68:8,65:8,84:8,
                RawData:(Length*8)/bitstr, _Crc:32>> <= PNG >>
```

The sequence of numbers $73,68,65,84$ is the content of the type field for the chunk containing raw data. This means that only the chunks that contain raw data match the generator pattern and only the data from those chunks makes up the resulting bit stream. We can then decompress this data and use the uncompressed data and the chunks containing meta data to generate the picture.

3.5 Huffman

Huffman encoding is a variable length encoding of characters. The mapping between the variable length codes and the static codes is described by a *Huffman tree*. This tree is a binary tree where the leaves are static codes. The mapping from the dynamic length codes to the static codes is encoded in the path from the root to a leaf. For example, if a leaf contains the static code 32 and is reached from the root by taking the left branch, then the right branch and finally the left branch, this means that 010 maps to 32.

To decode a Huffman encoded bit stream we can use Program 1. The main decoding function has four clauses. The first is taken if we have reached a leaf in the Huffman tree. If this is the case we add the value in that leaf to the output and recurse. The second clause is taken if we are at a branch and the value of the next bit is zero. In that case we take the left branch. The third clause is taken if the next bit was one and in that case we choose the right branch. The fourth and final clause is taken when there are no more bits left to decode which means that we are done.

Program 1. Function for decoding a Huffman encoded bit stream

```
huffman_decode(BitStr, Tree) ->
  huffman_decode(BitStr, Tree, Tree).

huffman_decode(Rest, Char, Tree) when is_char(Char) ->
  [Char | huffman_decode(Rest, Tree, Tree)];
huffman_decode(<<0:1,Rest/bitstr>>, {Left,_}, Tree) ->
  huffman_decode(Rest, Left, Tree);
huffman_decode(<<1:1,Rest/bitstr>>, {_,Right}, Tree) ->
  huffman_decode(Rest, Right, Tree);
huffman_decode(<<>>, _, _) ->
  [].
```

4   Implementation

Having seen constructs and typical applications of bit stream manipulation, let us now see how we efficiently implement these constructs.

4.1   Internal Representation of Bit Streams

We have chosen an internal representation of bit streams which has the property that the space overhead of storing each stream is constant, independent of the size of the stream. The representation uses two different structures: a *base stream* and a *sub-stream*. The base stream contains a header, a size field expressing the size of the bit stream in bits, and an array of data which contains the actual bit sequence. For a bit stream with bit size n, the bit sequence starts with the first bit in the data array and ends at the n-th bit in the array. The sub-stream structure contains a header field, a size field, an offset field, and a pointer to a base stream. Let us denote the content of the size field by n, the content of the offset field by o and the base stream that the sub-stream is pointing to by BS. Then the bit sequence that the sub-stream represents starts with o-th bit of the data array of the base stream BS and ends with the (o+n-1)-th bit of the data array of BS.

Figure 3 shows the representation of a base stream and two sub-streams. In our implementation, the header, size and offset fields are all word-sized even though they look smaller in the figure. The header field stores the size in words of the structure and a runtime tag which identifies the object as a base stream (or sub-stream). In the figure, A, B, and C are all variables bound to binaries. A is bound to the base stream <<47:8,47:8,101:8,1:7>>, B is bound to the sub-stream <<25:5>> marked with a black border in the figure and C is bound to the sub-stream <<47:8,101:8>> which is marked with a grey background in the figure.

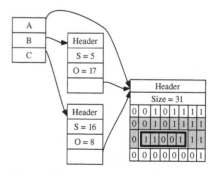

Fig. 3. Internal representation of bit streams

4.2   Implementation of Bit Stream Construction

Bit stream construction is aided by two low-level auxiliary functions:

put_integer() which given a pointer, an offset in bits, a size in bits, and an integer (a
   fixnum or a bignum) and writes size bits of the integer starting at offset bits from
   the pointer, and
put_bitstr() which given a pointer, an offset in bits, a size in bits, and a bit stream
   writes the first size bits of the bit stream starting at offset bits from the pointer.

A bit stream construction expression of the form $<\!\!<\!\texttt{ve}_1\!:\!\texttt{se}_1/\texttt{t}_1,\ldots,\texttt{ve}_n\!:\!\texttt{se}_n/\texttt{t}_n\!\!>\!\!>$
is translated using these functions as follows. We start by evaluating all the value and
size expressions and end up with an expression of the form $<\!\!<\!\texttt{v}_1\!:\!\texttt{s}_1/\texttt{t}_1,\ldots,\texttt{v}_n\!:\!\texttt{s}_n/\texttt{t}_n\!\!>\!\!>$
where all the $\texttt{v}_i$:s are values and all the $\texttt{s}_i$:s are non-negative integers. If any $\texttt{s}_i$ is a neg-
ative value, a run-time exception is raised.

   Then, we perform the following operations:

1. Calculate the resulting size of the bit stream as $\sum_{i=1}^{n} s_i$.
2. Allocate a base stream with a large enough data array to hold all the bits of the bit
   stream, initialize data_ptr to a pointer to the beginning of the data array and set
   offset to 0.
3. For each segment, do the following:
   (a) If $\texttt{t}_i$ is integer we call put_integer(data_ptr, offset, $\texttt{s}_i$, $\texttt{v}_i$)
   (b) If $\texttt{t}_i$ is bitstr we call put_bitstr(data_ptr, offset, $\texttt{s}_i$, $\texttt{v}_i$)
   (c) Set offset to offset+$\texttt{s}_i$
4. After all segments are processed, return the base stream.

4.3   Implementation of Bit Stream Pattern Matching

We only describe the case of matching a bit stream against a single binary pattern. For
a thorough treatment of how to efficiently match a (byte-aligned) binary against many
patterns simultaneously refer to our prior work [7] which describes effective algorithms
for constructing deterministic binary pattern matching automata.

   The matching is aided by two low-level auxiliary functions:

get_integer() which returns an integer given a pointer to some data, an offset in bits
   into that data, and the number of bits that should be used to create the integer, and
get_bitstr() which creates a sub-stream from an offset, a size and a pointer to a base-
   binary.

   To match $<\!\!<\!\texttt{X}_1\!:\!\texttt{e}_1/\texttt{t}_1,\ldots,\texttt{X}_n\!:\!\texttt{e}_n/\texttt{t}_n\!\!>\!\!>$ against a bit stream BitStr we perform
the matching in the manner described below.

1. Create a matching state from BitStr. The state contains the following information:
   data_ptr a pointer to the data
   offset the present offset into the data
   end the offset of the last bit in the stream
   orig_ptr a pointer to the base stream which contains the data
2. For each segment, perform the following tasks:
   (a) Evaluate $\texttt{e}_i$, the size expression of the first segment to the integer $\texttt{s}_i$.
   (b) Check whether offset+$\texttt{s}_i \leq$ end, or else the matching fails.

(c) If t_i is `integer` then X_i = get_integer(data_ptr, offset, s_i)
(d) If t_i is `bitstr` then X_i = get_bitstr(offset, s_i, orig_ptr)
(e) Set offset to offset+s_i
3. Check whether offset == end. If so, the matching succeeds, otherwise it fails.

A tail segment (i.e., a last segment of the form X_n/`bitstr`) is handled specially: we bind X_n to get_bitstr(offset, end, orig_ptr) and set the value of offset to end.

Also, note that we described the case where all segments are of the form $X_i : e_i / t_i$ where X_i is a variable. If some X_i is not a variable but has a value v_i we simply add an equality test that checks that v_i is equal to the value returned from either get_integer or get_bitstr. If not equal, the matching fails. Otherwise the matching continues with the next segment.

4.4 Efficient Abstractions and Alternatives

With the contiguous internal representation of Sect. 4.1 bit stream pattern matching is fast but building bit streams piece by piece is expensive. Still, on top of our representation we can build two efficient abstractions, *segmented bit streams* and *buffers*.

Segmented bit streams. A segmented bit stream consists of a list of (possibly segmented) streams and represents the stream that is formed if the streams in the list are concatenated. Thus, a segmented bit stream is a (deep) list of bit streams. This abstraction makes it easy and cheap to concatenate a new bit stream to an existing segmented bit stream: all we need to do is to put it first in the list. Then, to efficiently turn a segmented bit stream into a regular contiguous bit stream we introduce a built-in called list_to_bitstr which simply transforms a (deep) list of bit streams into a single, contiguous one. This way, constructing a bit stream of size n piecemeal from some other streams can be done in $O(n)$ as opposed to $O(n^2)$ if segmented bit streams are not used. However, note that in the worst case (when each element in the list is a one-bit stream), the segmented bit streams abstraction has a significant space overhead.

Buffers. The idea of the buffer abstraction is taken from the Lua programming language [9]. A buffer is basically a list of bit streams with the following invariant: each bit stream in the list is strictly smaller than the next bit stream in the list. Note that, since the representation is a list of bit streams, the list_to_bitstr built-in can then be used to turn a buffer into a contiguous bit stream. However, since we need to maintain the invariant that bit streams in the list are increasing in size, sometimes we need to concatenate bit streams directly when adding streams to the buffer. This makes construction of a buffer more expensive than constructing a segmented bit stream, but the invariant keeps the space overhead lower for a buffer than for a segmented bit stream, since the maximal length of the list is $O(\sqrt{n})$ if the total number of bits is n.

Currently, neither *buffers* nor *segmented bit streams* have any support on the language level. This means that e.g. to use bit stream pattern matching on a buffer, the buffer must first be explicitly converted to a contiguous representation using list_to_bitstr.

4.5 Implementation of Bit Stream Comprehensions

The implementation of bit stream comprehensions requires considering the implications of the chosen underlying representation. If we choose to implement bit stream comprehension naïvely, constructing a new bit stream in each iteration the cost of the comprehension would be quadratic in the number of iterations.

Naturally we can do better than this. One possible choice is to use segmented bit streams, i.e. build a list of bit streams and then use the list_to_bitstr built-in to convert the list into a bit stream. Another possibility is to collect all of the bit streams in a list accumulator and at the same time calculate the sum of the sizes of the streams in the list. In this way we find out the size of the resulting bit streams and create a list whose elements are the streams in reverse order. We can then allocate a large enough base stream and copy the bit streams in the list into the data array of that base stream.

Though both these solutions have linear complexity, we can decrease the constant factors significantly whenever it is possible to compute an upper bound on the size of the resulting bit stream. In these cases we allocate a base stream in advance and write the results to the base stream as the bit stream comprehension is evaluated.

When is it possible to compute an upper bound on the resulting bit stream? Let us consider the case when we only have one generator, which is by far the most common situation. In such a case, the bit stream comprehension looks as follows:

$$\texttt{<<}\ e\texttt{:}se\texttt{/}t\ \texttt{||}\ \texttt{<<}e_1\texttt{:}se_1\texttt{/}t_1\texttt{,}\ldots\texttt{,}e_n\texttt{:}se_n\texttt{/}t_n\texttt{>>}\ \texttt{<=}\ \texttt{BitStr},e_f\ \texttt{>>}$$

If all of the size expressions ($se, se_1, \ldots, se_n$) can be evaluated before the bit stream comprehension starts being evaluated, then we can calculate how many bits of the input bit stream are consumed in each iteration ($\sum_{i=1}^{n} se_i$) and how many bits might be produced in each iteration (se). That is, if $\texttt{BitStr}$ has size m the maximal number of bits in the resulting binary is: $(m \times se)/\sum_{i=1}^{n} se_i$.

On the other hand, in some cases it is impossible to calculate a tight upper bound on the size of the resulting binary. One example is this comprehension:

$$\texttt{<<}\ \texttt{42:N}\ \texttt{||}\ \texttt{<<S:8,N:(S*S)>>}\ \texttt{<=}\ \texttt{BitStr}\ \texttt{>>}$$

Luckily, such comprehensions are rather rare in practice. Thus, in our implementation we chose to stick to a simple implementation of bit stream comprehensions, namely that which uses segmented binaries flattened by a call to list_to_bitstr for such uncommon cases. For cases when a tight upper bound can be calculated we use the method which preallocates a base stream of suitable size.

5   Performance

From Section 3 it should be clear that bit-level binaries and comprehensions allow for flexible manipulation of bit streams. Still, these constructs are to be used in applications where speed of processing is a prime consideration. Thus, it is imperative that the performance of the underlying implementation is competitive with both imperative languages using bit shifts and bit masks on byte arrays and with other high-performance functional languages using bit or byte arrays for representing bit streams.

Notice however that bit streams in Erlang are immutable data structures. The language provides no support for destructive updates. Also, notice that memory management for bit streams is automatic and a responsibility of the underlying runtime system, not of the programmer. Thus comparing the performance of functional vs. imperative

drop_0XX This is the program from Section 2.3. It takes a bit stream and removes all 3-bit chunks that start with a 0. In the benchmark, the size of the input stream is about 28.5 million bits; the size of the resulting bit stream is about 8 million bits. We perform 10 iterations.

five11 Implements the IS-683 PRL protocol. Reads a file whose first 16 bits represent an integer that describes how many PRL packets the file contains. Each packet starts with a 5-bit integer describing how many channels the packet contains and is followed by that number of 11-bit channel descriptors. The output is a list of channel descriptors for each packet. The input data consists of 496 different packets (16 of each possible size) and is decoded 10,000 times.

huffman The input is a file containing the huffman tree and a message encoded using this tree. The benchmark recreates the original message. The size of the encoded file is 747,647 bytes and the decoded file consists of 3,568,560 bytes. The file is decoded 10 times.

uudecode This benchmark decodes a file that has been uuencoded. The size of the encoded input file is 747,647 bytes and the size of the decoded output file is 542,623 bytes. The file is decoded 100 times.

uuencode This benchmark uuencodes a file. The input file consists of 542,623 bytes and the encoded output consist of 747,647 bytes. The file is encoded 100 times.

Fig. 4. Description of the benchmarks

languages in applications which manipulate bit streams has a bit of an "apples and oranges" flavor, especially since different styles of programming are often employed.

Still, this performance comparison is interesting. We will base it on the programs described in Figure 4 which spend the bulk of their work in bit stream manipulation.

We have implemented these benchmarks in three different functional languages, namely Erlang with all the extensions described in this paper, Haskell and O'Caml. In addition, we wrote C and Java versions of the first three benchmarks and found publicly available **uudecode** and **uuencode** C programs on the net which we converted to appropriate benchmarks and translated to Java. Our intention was to eliminate any traces of possible favoritism for some language and any inefficiencies due to our programming skills. So, we requested the help of Haskell and O'Caml experts to perform any efficiency improvements they saw fit, provided that the programs remain functional: i.e., use no mutation in the part of the program for which measurements are taken. On the other hand, the imperative languages are free to—and indeed do—use destructive assignments on all benchmarks.

The compilers that we used are the Glasgow Haskell Compiler version 6.4.1, the O'Caml 3.09.1 native code compiler, and GCC 3.4.2 for C and Java (gcj). For Erlang we used the HiPE native code compiler in the pre-release of Erlang/OTP R11B-2. The machine we used is a 2.4 GHz Pentium 4 with 1 GB of memory running Fedora Core 3.

5.1   Runtime Performance

Figure 5 shows performance results. We can see that Erlang enhanced with the constructs described in this paper is competitive in speed with other state-of-the-art functional languages in programs that manipulate bit streams. This is not due to Erlang's overall performance compared with Haskell and O'Caml. Instead, it is due to having these constructs in the language and having the compiler generate reasonably efficient

	Runtimes (in secs)					Lines of code				
	Functional			Imperative		Functional			Imperative	
Benchmark	Erlang	Haskell	O'Caml	C	Java	Erlang	Haskell	O'Caml	C	Java
drop_0XX	2.09	5.85	2.25	0.96	1.99	2	47	45	26	47
five11	4.97	8.65	7.69	9.79	18.41	9	38	23	64	78
huffman	2.29	7.38	10.81	0.97	1.75	14	30	54	67	81
uudecode	3.21	6.04	2.65	0.86	0.97	20	91	65	43	57
uuencode	2.85	7.77	2.82	1.04	0.98	25	70	70	54	64

Fig. 5. Time performance and succinctness of programming in different languages

code for them. Also, at least for these programs, the performance of the functional way of manipulating low-level representations is not so far away from that obtained using C with destructive assignment and programmer-controlled memory management.

Some runtime numbers stick out and require explanation. The bad performance of O'Caml on **huffman** is due to extensive garbage collection; the program spends more than half of its time doing GC. Also, the bad performance of imperative languages on **five11** is partly due to the nature of the task, which is not tailored to accessing bits in a multiple-of-eight fashion, and partly due to calling individual `malloc`:s and `free`:s (in C) for each channel description rather than allocating a big memory area once and partitioning it to each channel using programmer-controlled pointer bumping.

5.2   Succinctness and Ease of Programming

Performance is only part of the story. Ease of programming is equally important. It is very difficult to quantify this dimension, but the lines of code required to perform these tasks in different languages provide some rough estimate. As seen in Figure 5, the Erlang solutions are 2–20 times more compact than solutions in other functional languages. Once again, this is not due to the functional core part of Erlang; it is due to the ability to manipulate bit streams declaratively.

We have used the following rules when counting line numbers:

– We only counted lines directly involved in performing the tasks required by the benchmarks, not lines needed for I/O or for measuring execution times.
– We did not count blank lines, comments, type specifications of functions, strictness annotations, or lines containing only one keyword.
– No line was allowed to be wider than 80 characters.

We have made all these benchmark programs publicly available and annotated their source code with line numbers to see exactly which lines we count in the different benchmarks. Their annotated source code is at http://user.it.uu.se/~pergu/bitbench. Input data for running these programs, further information, as well as a pre-release of the Erlang/OTP system we have used are also accessible from the same site.

6 Related Work

Currently, very few general purpose languages provide constructs for direct manipulation of binary data down at the bit level, let alone efficient ones. Bit streams are typically represented as character arrays and their bit-level manipulation is performed by the programmer using explicit bit shifts and bit masks. Doing so is both exacting and error-prone. But since this kind of programming is commonplace in domains such as cryptography, data communication and multimedia programming, a plethora of domain-specific languages targeting these areas come with some ability to manipulate bit streams.

Cryptol [12] and SLED [15] are domain specific languages in the field of cryptology and machine language manipulation, respectively. They both allow bit-level pattern matching, but the size of the fields in the patterns are fixed at compile time.

Solar-Lezama et al. have proposed BitStream, a language for manipulating binaries in the coding and cryptography area [17]. The dataflow programming model used in BitStream is radically different from ours, as is the methodology to achieve both correct and efficient programs which requires the programmer to first write a simple reference implementation and then sketch a more efficient implementation which is rejected by the compiler if it is not equivalent to the reference implementation. For some applications, BitStream achieves good performance, on par with hand-optimized C programs.

In the area of data communication Chandra and McCann [2] have proposed a type system which can be used to describe how network packets are structured at the bit level. Back has proposed the DataScript [1] language which is both a constraint-based specification language for specifying binary data formats and a scripting language for manipulating such formats. DataScript is based on Java and does not support pattern matching. The PADS [4] language, proposed by Fisher and Gruber, allows description of any ad hoc data format and comes with the ability to automatically generate tools that manipulate such formats. In the context of the PADS project, Fisher, Walker, and Mandelbaum have recently developed a calculus of dependent types [5] which is suitable to use as a semantic foundation for the whole family of data description languages.

The previous examples of related work are all in one way or another domain-specific. Diatchki, Jones and Leslie [3], proposed a language extension for general purpose languages that allows pattern matching on fixed-width bit data types. Their proposal would make it easier to use a high-level functional language similar to Haskell to perform low-level tasks like writing device drivers or implementing operating systems. What distinguishes their work from ours is that 1) they only consider bit data whose representation fits in the registers of a machine while we do not have any such constraint, and 2) that their implementation comes in the form of an interpreter rather than being fully integrated in a general purpose programming language.

7 Concluding Remarks

The treatment of bit-level data is a neglected area in general-purpose programming languages and most declarative languages are no exceptions. This is unfortunate since there are many applications out there craving for language constructs which remove the need for tedious and error-prone bit-twiddling, while still achieving decent performance.

Armed with bit stream comprehensions and the ability to perform pattern matching at the bit level without being hampered by artificial restrictions (e.g., always having to create bit streams whose length is a multiple of eight) we have shown how a variety of important "real-world" bit stream applications can be programmed both succinctly and efficiently. We see very little reason for bit streams not to co-exist with other complex terms such as lists or tuples, or for Erlang to be an exception in providing such support. Perhaps this paper paves the way in this direction.

References

1. G. Back. Datascript — a specification and scripting language for binary data. In *Generative Programming and Component Engineering*, pages 66–77. Springer, Sept. 2002.
2. S. Chandra and P. J. McCann. Packet types. In *Proceedings of the Second ACM SIGPLAN Workshop on Compiler Support for System Software*. ACM Press, May 1999.
3. I. S. Diatchki, M. P. Jones, and R. Leslie. High-level views on low-level representations. In *Proceedings of the Tenth ACM SIGPLAN International Conference on Functional Programming*, pages 168–179. ACM Press, Sept. 2005.
4. K. Fisher and R. Gruber. PADS: A domain-specific language for processing ad hoc data. In *Proceedings of the ACM SIGPLAN Conference on Programming Language Design and mplementation*, pages 295–304. ACM Press, June 2005.
5. K. Fisher, Y. Mandelbaum, and D. Walker. The next 700 data description languages. In *Conference Record of the 33rd ACM SIGPLAN-SIGACT Symposium on Principles of Programming Languages*, pages 2–15. ACM Press, Jan. 2006.
6. P. Gustafsson and K. Sagonas. Bit-level binaries and generalized comprehensions in Erlang. In *Proceedings of the Fourth ACM SIGPLAN Erlang Workshop*, pages 1–8. Sept. 2005.
7. P. Gustafsson and K. Sagonas. Efficient manipulation of binary data using pattern matching. *Journal of Functional Programming*, 16(1):35–74, Jan. 2006.
8. J. Helbing. yEnc: Efficient encoding for Usenet and eMail, June 2002. See also www.yenc.org.
9. R. Ierusalimschy. *Programming in Lua*. Lua.org, second edition, Mar. 2006.
10. International Telecommunication Union. *G.711: Pulse code modulation (PCM) of voice frequencies*. Series G: Transmission Sytems and Media, Digital Systems and Networks. Standardization Sector of ITU, Geneva, Switzerland, Nov. 1998.
11. Joint ISO/IEC International Standard and W3C Recommendation. Portable network graphics (PNG) specification, W3C/ISO/IEC version, Nov. 2003.
12. J. R. Lewis and B. Martin. Cryptol: high assurance, retargetable crypto development and validation. In *MILCOM 2003 2003 IEEE Military Communications Conference*, volume 2, pages 820– 825. IEEE, Oct. 2003.
13. P. Nyblom. The bit syntax - the released version. In *Proceedings of the Sixth International Erlang/OTP User Conference*, Oct. 2000. Available at http://www.erlang.se/euc/00/.
14. J. Postel. RFC 791: Internet Protocol, Sept. 1981. Obsoletes RFC0760. Status: STANDARD.
15. N. Ramsey and M. F. Fernandez. Specifying representations of machine instructions. *ACM Trans. Prog. Lang. Syst.*, 19(3):492–524, 1997.
16. G. Roelofs. *PNG: The Definite Guide*. O'Reilly and Associates, June 1999. See also www.libpng.org/pub/png/.
17. A. Solar-Lezama, R. Rabbah, R. Bodík, and K. Ebcioğlu. Programming by sketching for bit-streaming programs. In *Proceedings of the ACM SIGPLAN Conference on Programming Language Design and Implementation*, pages 281–294. ACM Press, June 2005.
18. P. Wadler. List comprehensions. In S. L. Peyton Jones, editor, *The Implementation of Functional Programming Languages*, chapter 7, pages 127–138. Prentice-Hall, 1987.

Automatic Incrementalization of Prolog Based Static Analyses

Michael Eichberg, Matthias Kahl, Diptikalyan Saha[1], Mira Mezini, and Klaus Ostermann

Software Technology Group, Darmstadt University of Technology
[1]Computer Science Department, Stony Brook University
{eichberg,kahl,mezini,ostermann}@st.informatik.tu-darmstadt.de,
[1]dsaha@cs.sunysb.edu

Abstract. Modern development environments integrate various static analyses into the build process. Analyses that analyze the whole project whenever the project changes are impractical in this context. We present an approach to *automatic incrementalization* of analyses that are specified as tabled logic programs and evaluated using *incremental tabled evaluation*, a technique for efficiently updating memo tables in response to changes in facts and rules. The approach has been implemented and integrated into the Eclipse IDE. Our measurements show that this technique is effective for automatically incrementalizing a broad range of static analyses.

1 Introduction

Static analysis is becoming increasingly important for software developers [2]. For example, many APIs and frameworks define restrictions that cannot be expressed by function or method signatures alone. If such restrictions are not statically checked, subtle bugs can arise at runtime.[1] Enforcement of style or design guidelines, detection of bug patterns and security holes are other example areas of applying static analyses [1,15,19].

In this context, static analyses are most effective when they are integrated into the build process of integrated development environments (IDEs). This allows analyses to run "behind the scenes", ensuring continuous quality inspection during project development and providing the developer with immediate feedback.

However, such an integration also puts constraints on the time and space complexity of static analyses to be integrated; long build times that slow down the code-save-build cycle are unacceptable. To this end, it is desirable to compute the result of static analyses in an incremental way, whenever possible.

One option is to design an incremental version of each single static analysis. While this may be acceptable for standard analyses, it would be very inconvenient for analyses that are specific to a particular domain, framework, or company; in the latter case, it should be easy to extend the set of applicable analyses with little effort. The obligation to design an incremental version of each individual new analysis would be a major burden.

---

[1] For examples cf. Enterprise JavaBeans 3.0 Specification – Core Contracts and Requirements.

M. Hanus (Ed.): PADL 2007, LNCS 4354, pp. 109–123, 2007.

The work presented in this paper proposes *automatic incrementalization of static analyses* as a key technique for extensible static analysis platforms that are integrated into the incremental build process offered by modern IDEs.

We consider an analysis to be *incremental* if the following holds: Let R be the current result of the analysis. Then, in response to the next changes made to the code, the analysis only reprocesses those parts of the code that are necessary to compute the new result from R. Determining the set of software elements to reanalyze in an incremental step is not trivial: A single change might require reanalyzing multiple classes. Yet, typically this reanalyzed set represents only a small fraction of the whole project.

In our proposal, analyses are specified as Prolog programs that operate on a logic database containing a representation of the source code. New analyses can be defined declaratively, which is important for our goal of an extensible set of analyses. Specifically, we use *tabled logic programs* [5,9,31] which employ memoization to cache and reuse intermediate results. Tabling removes some of the shortcomings of Prolog's evaluation strategy, especially its susceptibility to infinite looping. For example, termination is guaranteed for Datalog programs (an important subset of Prolog); as such, it is suitable for a variety of static analyses.

Our basis of automatic incrementalization of static analysis is *incremental tabled evaluation* [26,27,28,29,30] which efficiently updates the memoized information in response to the changes in the underlying data. We use the incremental algorithm for *general logic programs* presented in [29] that is implemented on top of the tabled Prolog system XSB (ver. 2.7.1)[2]. The advantage of basing the specification and evaluation of static analyses on incremental tabled evaluation is that analyses become incremental for free, by simply declaring them as tabled. Hence, results produced by previous evaluations of analyses are automatically kept up-to-date and invalidated when needed. Incremental tabled evaluation has been tested for a few exemplary analyses (e.g. pointer analysis, push-down model checking) for C programs in [27,28]. The work presented here generalizes and extends these preliminary results.

The contributions of this paper are as follows: FIRST, this is the first proposal to use automatic incrementalization for analyses (of Java code) that are integrated into the incremental build process of modern IDEs. To facilitate data-flow dependent analyses, a 3-address based representation in static single assignment form is used as the foundation. SECOND, we extended the capabilities of the incremental tabled evaluation algorithm. Specifically, we incorporated functionality to abolish incrementally maintained tables when they are no longer needed. THIRD, we prove the effectiveness of automatic incrementalization for a broad range of static analyses and for large changes.

The remainder of this paper is organized as follows. In Section 2, we discuss the implementation of analyses in Prolog as well as their automatic incrementalization. The section ends with an overview how the analyses are embedded into the incremental build process of Eclipse. Section 3 evaluates the proposed approach. The paper ends with the discussion of related work followed by a short summary and outlook to future work.

---

[2] http://xsb.sourceforge.net

```
1  package bat;
2      public class Node{  void accept(Visitor visitor){visitor.visit(this);} }
3      public class SubNode extends Node{ /* empty */ }
4
5      @Visitor(Node.class)
6      public class StructureVisitor{  public void visit(Node node){...} }
```

Listing 1.1. Sample source code

```
1  % class(PackageName,ClassName,AccessSpecifier,IsAbstract,IsFinal,SuperClass)
2  % classAnn(Class,Annotation)
3  % method(Id,DeclaringClassName,Name,AccessSpecifier,...,ReturnType,
          ListofParam,ListofAnnotations)
4
5  class('bat',ref('bat.Node'),public,false,false,ref('java.lang.Object')).
6  method(4,ref('bat.Node'),'accept',default,...,void,[parameter(ref('bat.Visitor'),[])],[]).
7
8  class('bat',ref('bat.StructureVisitor'),public,false,false,ref('java.lang.Object')).
9  classAnn(ref('bat.StructureVisitor'),annotation(type('Visitor'),value(ref('bat.Node')))).
10 method(2,ref('bat.StructureVisitor'),'visit',public,...,void,[parameter(ref('bat.Node'),[])
       ],[]).
11
12 class('bat',ref('bat.SubNode'),public,false,false,ref('bat.Node')).
```

Listing 1.2. Encoding of sample source code as Prolog database

2   Analyses in Tabled Prolog Integrated into an IDE

2.1   Data Model and Prolog Based Analyses

We use two example analyses to illustrate our approach to specifying static analyses as tabled Prolog queries.

The first analysis detects violations of a best practice in applying the Visitor pattern [17]. The best practice states that a visitor is expected to implement a special visit method for each type in the hierarchy it visits. The second analysis detects methods which return the self reference `this`. Such data-flow analyses are often required when implementing advanced type systems, such as, Confined Types [32].

For illustration of the analysis which detects violations of the Visitor pattern, consider the Java code in Listing 1.1. The classes `Node` (Line 2) and `StructureVisitor` (Line 6) are defined together at some point in time. Later on, the class `SubNode` (Line 3) is added to the code base. This violates the best practice, since `StructureVisitor` does not implement a `visit` method for `SubNode`. Nevertheless, the compiler will not generate any warning. A Prolog-based static analysis for detecting such a violation is shown in the following.

Listing 1.2 shows a Prolog encoding of the source code. A class fact (Line 5, 8, or 12) consists of the package name, the fully-qualified class name, the visibility, boolean

```
1  % the subtype relation is computed by invInherits and transInvInherits
2  invInherits(SuperClass,Class):- class(_,Class,_,_,_,SuperClass).
3  % transitive reflexive hull of invInherits
4  :- table transInvInherits/2.
5  transInvInherits(X,Y) :- invInherits(X,Y).
6  transInvInherits(X,X).
7  transInvInherits(X,Y) :- invInherits(X,Z), transInvInherits(Z,Y).
8
9  :- table visitor/1.
10 visitor(Class):- classAnn(Visitor,annotation(type('Visitor'),value(Node))),
11                      transInvInherits(Node,Class),
12                      not(method(_,Visitor,'visit',_,_,_,_,_,_,_,[parameter(
                          Class,_)],_)).
```

Listing 1.3. Visitor Query

values denoting whether the class is final or abstract, and the name of the superclass. The first value in `method` facts (e.g. 4 in Line 6) is a generated unique identifier for a method; after that, the declaring class is specified, followed by the method's name, its visibility (`default`), an encoding of the method's modifiers using boolean values (omitted for brevity), the return type, the parameter types along with parameter annotations and the list of declared exceptions.[3]

The analysis is specified as the `visitor(Class)` query in Listing 1.3 Line 10. The query identifies visitor classes that do *not* implement a visit method for every subtype of the annotation parameter, but which are marked with the `@Visitor(Type)` annotation. For doing so, the query first selects classes with the `@Visitor` annotation to get the root of the visited hierarchy: `Node` in our example. Next, it applies the rule `transInvInherits/2` to find all classes which extend `Node`; for any such class, the query verifies that the `Visitor` has a corresponding visit method and if not the class is bound to the variable `Class`.

For each answer to the query, i.e., each binding of the variable `Class`, a warning message is generated indicating that the class violates the best practice.

The second example analysis, which checks that a method does not return the self reference (`this`), illustrates writing analyses using the 3-address based code representation in static single assignment form. A violation is shown in Line 4 on the left hand side of the following listing: `this` is assigned to the variable `o` which may be returned later on.

```
1  public Object violate(){
2      Object o;
3      if (...)
4          o = this;
5      else
6          o = null;
7      return o;
8  }
```

```
1  method(4,ref('C'),'violate',public,...).
2      if(4,2,4,...,operator,...,1).
3      label(4,3,4).
4      goto(4,4,4,2).
5      label(4,5,1).
6      label(4,7,2).
7      phi(4,8,8,p7,[phiElem(this,4),phiElem(null,1)
           ]).
8      return(4,9,8,p7).
```

---

[3] All facts are properly indexed (not shown in the listing) for efficient query response.

The Prolog encoding of the method is shown on the right hand side. In general, the first value of each fact (Lines 2–8) is the id of the method and the second one is the number of the instruction. The third value is the line number of the corresponding source code — except for `labels` (Lines 3,5,6) where the third value is a method-wide unique id. The last values of `if` and `goto` statements (Lines 2,4) are the id's of labels which are the jump targets. Labels are also defined for each basic block of the control flow graph. The `phi` statement is a result of the transformation into static single assignment form and states that the value of the variable p7 (Line 7) is control flow dependent: If the id of the basic block of the last executed instruction is 4 the value of p7 will be `this`. If the basic block's id is 1 the value will be `null`.

The query to detect the violation is shown in the Listing below. The helper predicate `initializedWithThis/2` (Lines 1,2) binds its second argument to a variable directly initialized with `this` or `this` itself. The analysis is defined in Lines 4 – 6. Line 5 binds `RetVal` to variables that are directly or indirectly initialized with `this`. Line 6 succeeds for those methods that return such a value.

```
1 | initializedWithThis(MethodID, Variable) :-
2 |     phi(_,_,_,Variable,Phis), member(phiElem(this,_),Phis).
3 |
4 | returnsThis(MethodID) :-
5 |     initializedWithThis(MethodID, Val), propagate(Val, RetVal),
6 |     return(MethodID,_,_,RetVal).
```

The tabled predicate `propagate/2` (Line 2,3) is the reflexive and transitive closure of all initializations of a variable; `dpropagate/2` (Line 1) implements the initialization relation.

```
1 | dpropagate(V1, V2) :- phi(_,_,_,V2,Phis), member(phiElem(V1,_), Phis).
2 | propagate(V,V).
3 | propagate(V1,V2) :- dpropagate(V1,V3), propagate(V3,V2).
```

As shown by the `propagate/2` predicate, analyzing the data-flow is simplified as each variable is initialized exactly once and the data-flow is explicitly encoded in the phi facts.

2.2 Tabled Evaluation

Tabled logic programs declare certain predicates as tabled. Recursive predicates (for ensuring termination) and predicates that are reused multiple times are good candidates to be declared as tabled. Tabled resolution systems evaluate programs by memoizing subgoals of tabled predicates (referred to as *calls*) and their provable instances (referred to as *answers*) in a set of tables.

Calls are stored in a call table and all answers corresponding to a call are stored in a corresponding answer table. During resolution, if a subgoal is present in the call table, then it is resolved against the answers recorded in the corresponding answer table (*answer clause resolution*); otherwise, the subgoal is entered in the call table, its answers are computed by resolving the subgoal against program clauses (*program clause resolution*), and are entered in the answer table.

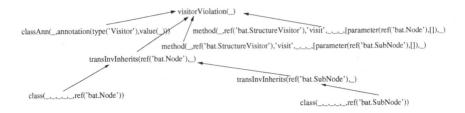

Fig. 1. Called-by Graph for Visitor Example

We exemplify the principles of tabling with the visitor example. As shown in Listing 1.3 Line 4, the recursive predicate `transInvInherits/2` is declared as tabled. Also the top level predicate `visitor/1` is declared as tabled (Line 9); a query `visitor(Class)` can be resolved by looking up the `visitor(Class)`'s answer table if the latter is non-empty. When `visitor(Class)` is executed for the first time, tabling creates an entry `visitor(Class)` in the call table and uses the rule for the `visitor` predicate to find results.

Resolving the first subgoal of the `visitor` predicate binds the variables `Node` and `Visitor` to `ref('bat.Node')` and `ref('bat.StructureVisitor')` respectively. The `transInvInherits/2` predicate is evaluated with the call `transInvInherits(ref('bat.Node'),Class)`, which is stored in the call table. The answers `Class=ref('bat.Node')` and `Class=ref('bat.Subnode')` of this call are obtained by resolution of the second clause of `transInvInherits/2`, and by resolution of the first clause of `transInvInherits/2` and `invInherits/2`, respectively. These answers are stored in the answer table of the `transInvInherits(ref('bat.Node'),Class)` call. The resolution of the last subgoal in the body of the `visitor` predicate generates only the answer `Class=ref('bat.Subnode')` for the call `visitor(Class)`, as the last subgoal fails for the substitution `Class=ref('bat.Node')`. Since `visitor/1` is tabled, any subsequent `visitor(X)` call will be resolved from its answer table.

2.3   Incremental Evaluation

Any change to a Java program causes the addition and deletion of facts to the Prolog fact base. Changes in the fact base can, in turn, render already evaluated tables stale: They may not have all the answers or the answers in the tables may be incorrect. The *non-incremental* approach to this problem is to abolish all the call and answer tables, and reissue the query. This is often wasteful, especially when the effect of the changes to the fact base is small. On the contrary, the incremental evaluation algorithm, that we use, tries to identify the calls that are *changed* and reissues only these calls. The algorithm is presented in [29] and is shortly described in the following.

A call is deemed changed iff the set of answers corresponding to the call before the change differs from that after the change. However, it is not possible to identify the set of changed calls before reevaluating any calls. Thus the incremental algorithm in [29] *over-approximates* the set of changed calls by the set of *affected calls*, which are calls that can be potentially changed.

To determine the set of affected calls, the incremental algorithm maintains a data structure which keeps the dependency between calls and facts that can be changed (known as *volatile* facts). The data structure, known as *called-by graph*, is central to the incremental algorithm and is described below using our visitor example.

The called-by graph is a directed graph whose nodes consist of calls and subgoals that unify with the volatile predicates. A path from a node c_1 to node c_2 indicates that c_1 is a tabled subgoal (or a call to a volatile predicate) that was called while resolving the tabled subgoal c_2. Each edge describes the immediate dependency between calls. The graph captures the dependencies between tabled calls and calls to volatile predicates. It is first generated in the initial (non-incremental) run, and maintained over subsequent incremental runs.

The called-by graph for `visitor(Class)` is given in Figure 1. The edges from nodes `classAnn(_,annotation(type('Visitor'),value(_)))`, `transInvInherits(ref('bat.Node'),_)`, and two `method` nodes to node `visitor(_)` correspond to the first, second and two calls to the third subgoal in the body of clause `visitor(Class)`, respectively.

The incremental algorithm works in two phases: an *invalidation* phase and a *reevaluation* phase. The invalidation phase finds affected calls by bottom-up traversal of the called-by graph starting from the vertices that unify with added or deleted facts. Edges in the called-by graph are directed from callee to caller which enables us to compute the affected calls by traversing the called-by graph. For an illustration, consider the addition of a `StructureVisitor.visit(bat.SubNode)` method. This adds a fact similar to the one in Line 10 of Listing 1.2, which instead of `bat.Node` refers to `bat.SubNode`. The invalidation phase determines the `visitor(_)` call as affected, because the added fact unifies with the `method` node of the called-by graph that has `ref('bat.SubNode')` as a parameter, which, in turn, has a path to node `visitor(_)`.

If an added/deleted fact does not unify with any leaf of the called-by graph, none of the calls are affected, i.e., the change has no effect to the present set of calls and answers. For example, if we add a class `bat.Foo` that does not affect the class hierarchy of `bat.Node`, none of the existing leaves will unify with the added class fact for `bat.Foo`. Hence, none of the existing calls are affected and reevaluated. Nonetheless, a non-incremental evaluation will reevaluate all existing calls.

The specific actions taken in the invalidation phase, e.g., whether the affected calls are deleted or not, depend on the strategy of the reevaluation phase of the algorithm. However, for brevity we only describe the implemented reevaluation strategy in the following.

The algorithm approximates the changed set, called the *recomputed* set which represents the smallest set of calls that need to be reevaluated. The intuition behind the recomputed set is based on the following observations:

– Every changed call needs to be reevaluated.
– Every call that immediately depends on a changed call needs to be reevaluated (even if it itself is not changed). Note that the called-by graph contains no

qualitative information on *how* the change of a call affects another. Only the program has this information embedded in it and, hence, the only way to determine whether or not such a call changes, is to reevaluate it.

– If a reevaluated call is in a strongly connected component (SCC), then all calls in that SCC need to be reevaluated.

The algorithm reevaluates only the calls in the recomputed set. Two basic mechanisms are used to accomplish this:

1. Determine whether a reevaluated call is changed by comparing its answer table before and after update.
2. Evaluate the calls "bottom-up" through the called-by graph: Trigger reevaluations at higher levels only if the lower-level calls have changed.

For illustration, consider the change of the visibility modifier of `bat.SubNode`. It causes the call `transInvInherits(ref('bat.SubNode'),Class)` to be reevaluated but without any changes. Hence, the calls to `transInvInherits( ref('bat.Node'),Class)` and `visitor(Class)` are not recomputed. Thus, among the three affected tabled calls the algorithm recomputes only one call.

2.4   Deletion of Incrementally Maintained Tables

The algorithm presented in [29] incrementally maintains tables in response to changes to volatile predicates. The data structures and tables are maintained as long as the session is running. However, in our case a user can always select or deselect analyses and in case that an analysis is deselected, the maintenance of the tables that are used solely by the deselected analysis is no longer necessary. Deletion of such tables is important to reclaim unused resources and to avoid the unnecessary maintenance during incremental builds. In this paper, we therefore extend the functionality of incremental tabled evaluation to enable reclamation of incremental tables.

We provide a builtin `abolish_call(C)` which takes as the argument an incremental call C which is intended to be abolished and tries to abolish C and all calls that are directly or indirectly called by C. For example, when the visitor analysis is deselected, `abolish_call(visitor(_))` is executed. Subsequently all table space of the calls identified by `abolish_call` is reclaimed.

Below we define the set of calls that are deleted when a particular incremental call is called for deletion.

Definition 1. *Given a called-by graph $G = (V, E)$, the set $not\_deleted(C)$ defines the set of calls that should not be deleted when $abolish\_call(C)$ is called. The set $not\_deleted(C)$ is the least set satisfying the relation below:*
$C' \in not\_deleted(C)$ if

– *C is not reachable (reflexive and transitive) from C' in called-by graph*
– *$\exists C'' \in not\_deleted(C)$ and $(C', C'') \in E$ (i.e C'' depends on C').*

The set of deleted calls (denoted by $deleted(C)$) due to abolishing incremental call C is the complement of the set $not\_deleted(C)$ over all incrementally maintained calls present in the called-by graph.

We developed a called-by graph based algorithm for determining the set $deleted(C)$. The algorithm is non-trivial because of cycles in called-by graphs. It has three phases: marking, checking assumption, and deletion. The marking phase overapproximates the calls that need to be deleted and subsequent phases prune the overapproximation. Due to limited space we do not provide the algorithm here, but it can be found in an accompanying technical report [16].

2.5 IDE Integration

We have integrated the XSB Prolog engine — extended with the algorithm for incremental tabled evaluation as described in the previous sections — with the Eclipse IDE using Magellan[4]. Magellan takes care of translating every source-file of a project into its corresponding Prolog encoding. More specifically, the BAT bytecode toolkit[5] is used to convert Java class files to a 3-address based representation in static single assignment form [12] and then to convert this data into its Prolog encoding.

A full build process runs as follows: FIRST, the Prolog database is cleared, the rules used by the selected analyses are added to the database, and the Prolog facts for all Java class files are generated and added to the database. SECOND, Magellan executes the Prolog-based analyses. Each Prolog query is wrapped into a small Java class, which is responsible for (a) calling the Prolog engine to execute the query, and (b) post-processing the results, e.g., by retrieving the source code locations and by adding the error messages to Eclipse's problem view.

An incremental build maintains the database rather than rebuilding it from scratch: FIRST, whenever a document is added, changed, or removed Magellan calls the maintenance analysis and passes on the information about the edited documents. Currently, the units of change are whole classes, i.e., even when a single class' comment is modified, the maintenance analysis retracts all facts related to that class from the database and adds the class again. SECOND, the maintenance analysis then adds/removes the facts corresponding to the edited classes to/from the database and calls `update` on the Prolog database to propagate the changes to the tables. THIRD, Magellan re-evaluates the queries by simply reading the values of the corresponding tables and updates dependent IDE views such as the problems view correspondingly.

3 Evaluation

In this section, we evaluate the performance of our approach. First, the set of analyses that are used for the evaluation is presented. After that we discuss the evaluation setup and the performance figures.

3.1 Used Analyses

The analyses used for the evaluation require different kinds of information about the code and are ordered w.r.t. the extent of the required information.

---

[4] http://www.st.informatik.tu-darmstadt.de/Magellan
[5] http://www.st.informatik.tu-darmstadt.de/BAT

The first analysis detects classes which violate the contract defined in java.lang. Object stating that subclasses should always implement the equals(...) and hashCode() methods pairwise. A violation of this contract in a class C can lead to subtle errors when instances of C are stored in, e.g., HashSets.

The second analysis detects covariant definitions of equals(Object). Such definitions are error prone, as methods with covariant parameter definitions do not override methods defined in superclasses.

The two analyses above require only information about method signatures. The third analysis is the previously discussed analysis that checks the implementation of the Visitor design pattern [17]; hence, it requires type hierarchy information.

Finally, we added a set of 17 analyses for controlling aliasing in object-oriented systems based on confined types [32]; the basic idea is to confine the creation of aliases to a certain protection domain, in this case, to a Java package. These analyses require information about the type hierarchy and the method implementations, e.g., to analyze that a confined type is not casted to an unconfined type. Four of these analyses also require (intra-procedural) data-flow information.

3.2   Evaluation Setup and Results

The evaluation was done on a P IV, 3 Ghz with 1024 MB RAM and Sun JDK 5.

The analyzed test project is the BAT bytecode toolkit (cf. Section 2.5). This project consists of 22 packages, 790 classes, 45 interfaces, 55068 methods and approx. 395.000 facts are required to represent the method implementations. BAT contains an interface called IStructureElement which is implemented by 252 non-abstract classes. The visitor attached with this interface contains 504 methods. Applied on this project, the visitor query (Listing 1.3) produced 2 warnings; further, one class was identified that violated the equals/hashCode contract, and three covariant definitions of equals were found.

The test set was supplemented by 17 classes from a second project spread over 3 packages which implement a small part of a public key infrastructure. Initially, confined types were used in two of the packages. When performing the changes described in Table 1, classes in the third package were also made confined. Initially, 17 different errors related to confined types were in the code.

In case of a full build, the time to create the Prolog facts takes 3300 msecs. This includes the transformation of the Java files into the 3-address representation and the creation of the Prolog facts; to add the generated facts to the database, XSB requires another 5200 msecs. Since all tables are initally empty, the first evaluation of the queries takes 328 msecs.

Changes shown in Table 1 were executed in the given order. The first eight changes affect core classes of the BAT project by modifying a comment, adding a field, adding a method, renaming a class file, or adding a new class. Changes 9 to 16 simulate the use of confined types in the project by marking classes as confined or unconfined.

To better assess the effect of a change, the number of affected classes is shown in the third column of Table 1; further, the number of methods defined by the classes and the total number of facts that were removed and added is given. In the fourth column, the results produced by the queries after performing the changes is given: The first is

Table 1. Change description and timing results

Run	Description of the Changes	removed / added Classes, Methods, Facts	Results	msecs. no incr. XSB	msecs. incr. XSB
1	inserted two empty lines into a class	1, 504, 2779 / 1, 504, 2779	1/3/2/17	673	390
2	deleted a small method and the implementation of another small method	1, 504, 2779 / 1, 503, 2771	1/3/3/17	627	390
3	created a new field along with the corresponding getter method; further a new empty method is created in a different class	2, 41, 430 / 2, 43, 447	1/3/3/17	468	156
4	ten fields and corresponding getters and setters are created	1, 9, 40 / 1, 29, 141	1/3/3/17	454	78
5	refactored the name of a class which has 6 children; hence 7 classes are affected	7, 112, 2690 / 7, 112, 2690	1/3/3/17	812	578
6	added a blank into the comment of a small class	1, 9, 41 / 1, 9, 41	1/3/3/17	437	78
7	deleted six small methods as a whole and also deleted the content of another six methods	1, 503, 2771 / 1, 497, 2723	1/3/9/17	669	390
8	added a new class which implements an interface	0, 0, 0 / 1, 3, 11	1/3/10/17	406	63
9	added a new method which leads to a violation of a widening constraint	1, 3, 15 / 1, 4, 19	1/3/10/18	389	48
10	added a new method	1, 3, 15 / 1, 4, 18	1/3/10/18	392	78
11	deleted the method which was added in the previous change	1, 4, 18 / 1, 3, 15	1/3/10/18	405	78
12	changed the superclass, modified a small method, added a new field and a another small method which violates a widening constraint	1, 3, 15 / 1, 4, 31	1/3/10/25	453	141
13	created a new interface which is implemented by two classes, deleted parts of a method	3, 9, 72 / 2, 9, 65	1/3/10/25	454	172
14	declared a class as confined	1, 5, 32 / 1, 5, 32	1/3/10/24	454	141
15	changed the implementation of a method	1, 4, 19 / 1, 4, 22	1/3/10/24	469	78
16	a new field is added to three different confined classes	3, 10, 69 / 3, 10, 73	1/3/10/27	500	187
in average				*ø503,8*	*ø190,4*

the number of violations of the `equals`/`hashCode` contract, the second is the number of covariant `equals` methods, the third is the number of violations related to the `Visitor` design pattern, and the fourth is the number of violations of confinement rules.

The last two columns of Table 1 compare the time required to update the database and to retrieve the new set of results using tabling without incremental evaluation of XSB and using tabling with incremental evaluation.

The numbers for incremental evaluation (last column in Table 1) result from summing the time for removing and adding facts with the time for incrementally maintaining the tables. All queries are evaluated in roughly 0 msecs independent of the code change that triggers the evaluation. This is because query results are tabled and the extraction of the answers from a table only depends on the number of identified errors. With non-incremental evaluation, the time to execute the queries also remains constant at roughly 300 msecs. The difference between this 300 msecs and the numbers in the corresponding column in Table 1 is spent to add/remove facts.

To summarize, we the draw following conclusions: FIRST, the approach is fast enough to execute a reasonable number of analyses along with the incremental build process for projects with at least 1000 classes; executing all discussed analyses simultaneously is feasible. Even in case of changes that affect large numbers of facts (Runs 1,2,5,7) the execution times are acceptable. SECOND, in comparison to non-incremental evaluation, our system is between 1.4 and 8 times faster. In case of non-incremental evaluation, the queries need to be reevaluated from scratch after every change; in particular it is necessary to explicitly delete all tables, as the tables are not maintained incrementally. THIRD, most of the time required by the incremental build goes to maintain the tables. This time is largely dependent on the number of facts that need to be removed and added. Hence, if the granularity of a change would be more fine-grained than an entire class, the overall time could be further improved.

4 Related Work

Writing analyses using a logic language, such as, Prolog is not new. Many classical program analysis problems can be readily encoded into deductive frameworks [13] and various practical implementations have been stemmed based on such encodings. E.g., Besson and Jensen [3] discuss the implementation of a class analysis using Datalog.

Various approaches use declarative query languages to implement static analyses [34,14,21]. For example, the Program Query Language (PQL) presented in [23] allows programmers to express queries in application specific context and allows them to specify actions along with the queries. PQL is then transformed into Datalog which is evaluated using the BDD based evaluation framework BDDBDDB. Soul [35] is a logic meta-language implemented in Smalltalk to express and extract structural relationships (Prolog like) in class-based object-oriented systems. ASTLOG [11] is also a Prolog like language to identify bug patterns primarily in C/C++ code. ASTLOG directly operates on top of the source syntactic structures to get a better performance when compared with using a Prolog database. Spine [4] is a typed first-order logic similar to Prolog for describing design patterns and their constraints. Given a Spine specification of a design pattern the Hedgehog proof system [4] is then used to reason about the implementation of design patterns in Java. However, none of the above techniques supports incrementalization, i.e., in case of small changes to the source code, all analyses have to be repeated for the whole program to get an up-to-date view.

CodeQuest [18] uses Datalog for querying code. Unlike the above approaches, it realizes the importance of incremental updates. CodeQuest incrementally maintains the database of facts. When notified by the Eclipse platform about a change to a compilation unit, CodeQuest removes from the database all facts that are directly or indirectly related to the compilation unit (determined using ad-hoc stored procedures); it then reparses the compilation unit and populates the database with the new facts. Compared to CodeQuest, our approach also employs incremental maintenance of query results.

The problem of incremental evaluation has been addressed in various fields of research, such as view maintenance in databases, model checking, program analysis, logic programming, functional programming, attribute grammar evaluation, and AI. In the focus of this discussion is only the problem of incremental evaluation in the area of program analysis. Most of the existing work addressing incremental evaluation in the latter area is catered toward particular kinds of static analyses, e.g., pointer analysis, data-flow analysis, MOD analysis, and verification of safety properties, and cannot be readily generalized to a wide range of analyses.

An incremental alias analysis is presented in [37] which is based on Landi-Ryders's flow- and context-sensitive alias analysis [20]. A variety of incremental algorithms have been developed for data flow analysis problems. Some of them use the elimination method [6,8,25]; others are based on restarting iterations [24], while both techniques are combined in [22]. A comparison of incremental iterative algorithms for data flow analysis can be found in [7]. The effectiveness of incremental analysis has been shown for MOD analysis of C programs [36]. Pollock and Soffa [24] presented a precise incremental iterative algorithm using change classification and reinitialization for bitvector problems. In [10], an algorithm is presented that incrementally analyzes the verification of safety properties of a program. In [33], an incremental algorithm is presented which analyzes part of the program assuming no previous analysis result. This algorithm monitors the analysis results incrementally in each phase to direct the analysis in those parts of the program which offer the highest expected optimized return. This work does not consider the problem of updating existing analysis results to reflect the effect of program changes.

The above approaches to incremental evaluation of static analysis are specific to the analysis considered and the used techniques are not easy to generalize for incremental evaluation of other static analyses. The first step toward developing techniques for automatic incrementalization of a broad range of analysis is the work by Saha and Ramakrishnan on incremental evaluation of tabled logic programs [26,28,30]. Tabled logic programs offer a declarative way of encoding a large variety of program analysis [13]. As discussed in this paper, incremental tabled evaluation offers a generic approach to incrementalizing static analysis.

5   Summary and Future Work

In this paper, we proposed to use incremental tabled Prolog for the automatic incrementalization of static analyses. This enables developers to write static analyses with the full-build case in mind. The analyses are automatically incrementalized by the Prolog engine, i.e., in case of changes to the fact-base only the necessary parts of the project are reanalyzed. The analyses are implemented on top of a 3-address based representation in SSA form. This representation proved to be well-suited for intra-procedural data-flow analyses and enables an efficient implementation of static analyses.

The automatic incrementalization frees the developer from the burden of developing incremental algorithms for each single analysis and, thus, facilitates the development of new domain and project specific static analyses. As shown in the evaluation section, the proposal significantly improves the performance of static analyses compared to their non-incremental versions and enables to tightly integrate them with the incremental build process of an IDE.

Further performance improvements will be in the focus of future work. One possibility to improve performance is by decreasing the change granularity, which is currently at the class level. By pushing the granularity down, e.g., to the level of instructions, further overall performance improvements are expected.

References

1. K. Ashcraft and D. Engler. Using programmer-written compiler extensions to catch security holes. In *Proceedings of the Symposium on Security and Privacy*. IEEE, 2002.
2. T. Ball, B. Cook, V. Levin, and S. K. Rajamani. Slam and static driver verifier: Technology transfer of formal methods inside Microsoft. In *Proceedings of IFM*. Springer, 2004.
3. F. Besson and T. P. Jensen. Modular class analysis with datalog. In *Proceedings of SAS*. Springer, 2003.
4. A. Blewitt, A. Bundy, and I. Stark. Automatic verification of java design patterns. In *Proceedings of ASE*. IEEE, 2001.
5. R. Bol and L. Degerstadt. Tabulated resolution for well-founded semantics. In *Proceedings of ILPS*. MIT Press, 1993.
6. M. Burke. An interval-based approach to exhaustive and incremental interprocedural data-flow analysis. *TOPLAS*, 12(3), 1990.
7. M. G. Burke and B. G. Ryder. A critical analysis of incremental iterative data flow analysis algorithms. *IEEE Transactions on Software Engineering*, 16(7), 1990.
8. M. D. Carroll and B. G. Ryder. Incremental data flow analysis via dominator and attribute update. In *Proceedings of POPL*. ACM, 1988.
9. W. Chen and D. S. Warren. Tabled evaluation with delaying for general logic programs. *Journal of the ACM*, 43(1), 1996.
10. C. L. Conway, K. S. Namjoshi, D. Dams, and S. A. Edwards. Incremental algorithms for inter-procedural analysis of safety properties. In *Proceedings of CAV*. Springer, 2005.
11. R. F. Crew. Astlog: A language for examining abstract syntax trees. In *Proceedings of DSL*. USENIX, 1997.
12. R. Cytron, J. Ferrante, B. K. Rosen, M. N. Wegman, and F. K. Zadeck. Efficiently computing static single assignment form and the control dependence graph. *ACM Transactions on Programming Languages and Systems*, 13(4), 1991.
13. S. Dawson, C. R. Ramakrishnan, and D. S. Warren. Practical program analysis using general purpose logic programming systems — a case study. In *Proceedings of PLDI*. ACM, 1996.
14. M. Eichberg, M. Mezini, K. Ostermann, and T. Schäfer. Xirc: A kernel for cross-artifact information engineering in software development environments. In *Proceedings of WCRE*. IEEE, 2004.
15. M. Eichberg, T. Schäfer, and M. Mezini. Using annotations to check structural properties of classes. In *Proceedings of FASE*. Springer, 2005.

16. Michael Eichberg, Matthias Kahl, Diptikalyan Saha, Mira Mezini, and Klaus Oster-
    mann.   Automatic incrementalization of static analyses.   Technical report, 2006.
    (http://www.st.informatik.tu-darmstadt.de/Magellan).
17. E. Gamma, R. Helm, R. Johnson, and J. Vlissides. *Design Patterns: Elements of Reusable
    Object-Oriented Software*. Addison Wesley, 1995.
18. Elnar Hajiyev, Mathieu Verbaere, and Oege de Moor.   Codequest: Scalable source code
    queries with datalog. In *Proceedings of ECOOP*. Springer, 2006.
19. D. Hovemeyer and W. Pugh. Finding bugs is easy. *SIGPLAN Not.*, 39(12), 2004.
20. W. Landi and B. G. Ryder. A safe approximate algorithm for interprocedural pointer aliasing.
    In *Proceedings of PLDI*. ACM, 1992.
21. Y. A. Liu, T. Rothamel, F. Yu, S. D. Stoller, and N. Hu. Parametric regular path queries. In
    Proceedings of PLDI. ACM, 2004.
22. T. J. Marlowe and B. G. Ryder.   An efficient hybrid algorithm for incremental data flow
    analysis. In *Proceedings of POPL*. ACM, 1990.
23. M. Martin, B. Livshits, and M. S. Lam. Finding application errors and security flaws using
    PQL: a program query language. In *Proceedings of OOPSLA*. ACM, 2005.
24. L. L. Pollock and M. L. Soffa. An incremental version of iterative data flow analysis. *IEEE
    Transactions on Software Engineering*, 15(12), 1989.
25. B. G. Ryder and M. C. Paull. Incremental data-flow analysis algorithms. *ACM Transactions
    on Programming Languages and Systems*, 10(1), 1988.
26. D. Saha and C. R. Ramakrishnan.   Incremental evaluation of tabled logic programs.   In
    Proceedings of ICLP. Springer, 2003.
27. D. Saha and C. R. Ramakrishnan. Incremental and demand-driven points-to analysis using
    logic programming. In *Proceedings of PPDP*. ACM, 2005.
28. D. Saha and C. R. Ramakrishnan. Symbolic support graph: A space-efficient data structure
    for incremental tabled evaluation. In *Proceedings of ICLP*. Springer, 2005.
29. D. Saha and C. R. Ramakrishnan. Incremental evaluation of tabled prolog: Beyond pure
    logic programs. In *Proceedings of PADL*. Springer, 2006.
30. D. Saha and C. R. Ramakrishnan.   A local algorithm for incremental evaluation of logic
    programs. In *Proceedings of ICLP*. Springer, 2006.
31. H. Tamaki and T. Sato. OLDT resolution with tabulation. In *Proceedings of ICLP*. Springer,
    1986.
32. J. Vitek and B. Bokowski. Confined types in java. *Software Practice and Experience*, 31(6),
    2001.
33. F. Vivien and M. C. Rinard. Incrementalized pointer and escape analysis. In *Proceedings of
    PLDI*. ACM, 2001.
34. J. Whaley and M. S. Lam. Cloning-based context-sensitive pointer alias analysis using binary
    decision diagrams. In *Proceedings of PLDI*. ACM, 2004.
35. R. Wuyts. Declarative reasoning about the structure of object-oriented systems. In *Proceed-
    ings of TOOLS-USA*. IEEE, 1998.
36. J. Yur, B. G. Ryder, W. Landi, and P. Stocks.   Incremental analysis of side effects for C
    software system. In *Proceedings of ICSE*. ACM, 1997.
37. J. Yur, B. G. Ryder, and W. A. Landi.   An incremental flow- and context-sensitive pointer
    aliasing analysis. In *Proceedings of ICSE*. IEEE, 1999.

Verification of Java Bytecode Using Analysis and Transformation of Logic Programs

E. Albert[1], M. Gómez-Zamalloa[1], L. Hubert[2], and G. Puebla[2]

[1] DSIC, Complutense University of Madrid, E-28040 Madrid, Spain
[2] CLIP, Technical University of Madrid, E-28660 Boadilla del Monte, Madrid, Spain
{elvira,mzamalloa,laurent,german}@clip.dia.fi.upm.es

Abstract. State of the art analyzers in the Logic Programming (LP) paradigm are nowadays mature and sophisticated. They allow inferring a wide variety of global properties including termination, bounds on resource consumption, etc. The aim of this work is to automatically transfer the power of such analysis tools for LP to the analysis and verification of Java bytecode (JVML). In order to achieve our goal, we rely on well-known techniques for meta-programming and program specialization. More precisely, we propose to partially evaluate a JVML interpreter implemented in LP together with (an LP representation of) a JVML program and then analyze the residual program. Interestingly, at least for the examples we have studied, our approach produces very simple LP representations of the original JVML programs. This can be seen as a decompilation from JVML to high-level LP source. By reasoning about such residual programs, we can automatically prove in the CiaoPP system some non-trivial properties of JVML programs such as termination, run-time error freeness and infer bounds on its resource consumption. We are not aware of any other system which is able to verify such advanced properties of Java bytecode.

1 Introduction

Verifying programs in the (Constraint) Logic Programming paradigm —(C)LP— offers a good number of advantages, an important one being the maturity and sophistication of the analysis tools available for it. The work presented in this paper is motivated by the existence of *abstract interpretation*-based analyzers [3] which infer information on programs by interpreting ("running") them using abstract values rather than concrete ones, thus, obtaining safe approximations of programs behavior. These analyzers are parametric w.r.t. the so-called abstract domain, which provides a finite representation of possibly infinite sets of values. Different domains capture different properties of the program with different levels of precision and at different computational costs. This includes error freeness, data structure shape (like pointer sharing), bounds on data structure sizes, and other operational variable instantiation properties, as well as procedure-level properties such as determinacy, termination, non-failure, and bounds on resource consumption (time or space cost), etc. CiaoPP [9] is the *abstract interpretation*-based preprocessor of the Ciao (C)LP system, where analysis results have been applied to perform high- and low-level optimizations and *program verification*.

M. Hanus (Ed.): PADL 2007, LNCS 4354, pp. 124–139, 2007.

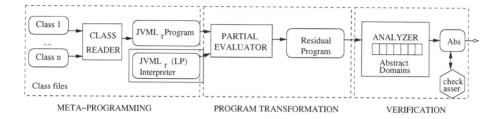

Fig. 1. Verification of Java Bytecode using Logic Programming Tools

A principal advantage of verifying programs on the (LP) *source* code level is that we can infer complex global properties (like the aforementioned ones) for them. However, in certain applications like within the context of mobile code, one may only have the *object* code available. In general, analysis tools for such low-level languages are unavoidably more complicated than for high-level languages because they have to cope with complicated and unstructured control flow. Furthermore, as the JVML (Java Virtual Machine Language, i.e., Java bytecode) is a stack-based language, stacks cells are used to store intermediate values, and therefore their type can change from one assignment to another, and they can also be used to store 32 bits of a 64 bit value, which make the inference of stack information much more difficult. Besides, it is a non trivial task to specify/infer global properties for the bytecode by using pre- and post-conditions (as it is usually done in existing tools for high-level languages).

The aim of this work is to provide a practical framework for the verification of JVML which exploits the expressiveness, automation and genericity of the advanced analysis tools for LP source. In order to achieve this goal, we will focus on the techniques of meta-programming, program specialization and static analysis that together support the use of LP tools to analyze JVML programs. Interpretative approaches which rely on CLP tools have been applied to analyze rather restricted versions of high-level imperative languages [13] and also assembly code for PIC [8], an 8-bit microprocessor. However, to the best of our knowledge, this is the first time the interpretative approach has been successfully applied to a general purpose, realistic, imperative programming language.

Overview. Fig. 1 presents a general overview of our approach. We depict an element within a straight box to denote its use as a program and a rounded box for data. The whole verification process is split in three main parts:

1. *Meta-programming.* We use LP as a language for representing and manipulating JVML programs. We have implemented an automatic translator, called CLASS_READER, which given a set of .class files {Class 1,..., Class n} returns P, an LP representation of them in JVML$_r$ (a representative subset of JVML presented in Sect. 2). Furthermore, we also describe in Sect. 3 an interpreter in LP, called JVML$_r$_INT, which captures the JVM semantics. The interpreter has been extended in order to compute *execution traces*, which will be very useful for reasoning about certain properties.

2. *Partial evaluation.* The development of partial evaluation techniques [10] has allowed the so-called "interpretative approach" to compilation which consists in specializing an interpreter w.r.t. a fixed object code. We have used an existing PARTIAL_EVALUATOR for LP in order to specialize the JVML$_r$_INT w.r.t. P. As a result, we obtain I_P, an LP residual program which can be seen as a decompiled and translated version of P into LP (see Sect. 4).

3. *Verification of Java bytecode.* The final goal is that the JVML program can be verified by analyzing the residual program I_P obtained in Step 2) above by using state-of-the-art ANALYZERs developed for LP, as we will see in Sect. 5.

The resulting scheme has been implemented and incorporated in the CiaoPP preprocessor. Our preliminary experiments show that it is possible to infer global properties of the computation of the residual LP programs. We believe our proposed approach is very promising in order to bring the analysis power of declarative languages to low-level, imperative code such as Java bytecode.

2   The Class Reader (JVML to JVML$_r$ in LP)

As notation, we use *Prog* to denote LP programs and *Class* to denote .class files (i.e., JVML classes). The input of our verification process is a set of .class files, denoted as $C_1 \ldots C_n \in Class$, as specified by the Java Virtual Machine Specification [12]. Then, the CLASS_READER takes $C_1 \ldots C_n$ and returns an LP file which contains all the information in $C_1 \ldots C_n$ represented in our JVML$_r$ language. JVML$_r$ is a representative subset of the JVML language which is able to handle: classes, interfaces, arrays, objects, constructors, exceptions, method call to class and instance methods, etc. For simplicity, some other features such as packages, concurrency and types as float, double, long and string are left out of the chosen subset. For conciseness, we use JVML$_r$-*Prog* to make it explicit that an LP program contains a JVML$_r$ representation. The differences between JVML and JVML$_r$ are essentially the following:

1. *Bytecode factorization.* Some instructions in JVML have a similar behavior and have been factorized in JVML$_r$ in order to have fewer instructions[1]. This makes the JVML$_r$ code easier to read (as well as the traces which will be discussed in Sect. 3) and the JVML$_r$_INT easier to program and maintain.

2. *References resolution.* The original JVML instructions contain indexes onto the *constant-pool* table [12], a structure present in the .class file which stores different kinds of data (constants, field and method names, descriptors, class names, etc.) and which is used in order to make bytecode programs as compact as possible. The CLASS_READER removes all references to the constant-pool table in the bytecode instructions by replacing them with the complete information to facilitate the task of the tools which need to handle the bytecode later.

---

[1] This allows covering over 200 instructions of JVML in 54 instructions in JVML$_r$.

```
1  class(
2    className(packageName(''),shortClassName('Rational')),final(false),public(true),
3    abstract(false),className(packageName('java/lang/'),shortClassName('Object')),[],
4    [field(
5      fieldSignature(
6        fieldName(
7          className(packageName(''),shortClassName('Rational')),shortFieldName(num)),
8          primitiveType(int)),
9        final(false),static(false),public,initialValue(undef)),
10     field(
11       fieldSignature(
12         fieldName(
13           className(packageName(''),shortClassName('Rational')),shortFieldName(den)),
14           primitiveType(int)),
15         final(false),static(false),public,initialValue(undef))],
16     [method(
17       methodSignature(
18         methodName(
19           className(packageName(''),shortClassName('Rational')),shortMethodName('<init>')),
20           [primitiveType(int),primitiveType(int)],none),
21         bytecodeMethod(3,2,0,methodId('Rational_class',1),[]),
22         final(false),static(false),public),
23     method(
24       methodSignature(
25         methodName(
26           className(packageName(''),shortClassName('Rational')),shortMethodName(exp)),
27           [primitiveType(int)],
28           refType(classType(className(packageName(''),shortClassName('Rational'))))),
29         bytecodeMethod(4,4,0,methodId('Rational_class',2),[]),
30         final(false),static(false),public),
31     method(
32       methodSignature(
33         methodName(
34           className(packageName(''),shortClassName('Rational')),shortMethodName(expMain)),
35           [primitiveType(int),primitiveType(int),primitiveType(int)],
36           refType(classType(className(packageName(''),shortClassName('Rational'))))),
37         bytecodeMethod(3,4,0,methodId('Rational_class',3),[]),
38         final(false),static(true),public)]).
```

Fig. 2. Extract of the Program Fact Describing the Rational Class of Running Example

The Ciao file generated by the CLASS_READER contains the bytecode instructions for all methods in $C_1 \ldots C_n$, represented as a set of facts; and also, a single fact obtained by putting together all the other information available in the .class files (class name, methods and fields signatures, etc.).

Example 1 (running example). Our running example considers a main Java class named **Rational** which represents rational numbers using two attributes: **num** and **den**. The class has a constructor, an instance method **exp** for computing the exponential of rational numbers w.r.t. a given exponent (the result is returned on a new rational object), and a static method **expMain** which given three integers, creates a new rational object using the first two ones as numerator and denominator, respectively, and invokes its **exp** method using the third argument as parameter. Finally, it returns the corresponding rational object. This example features arithmetic operations, object creation, field access, and invocation of both class and instance methods. It also shows that our approach is not restricted to intra-procedural analysis.

In Fig. 2, we show the extract of the program fact corresponding to class **Rational**. Line numbers are provided for convenience but they are not part of the

```
1  class(
2    className(packageName(''),shortClassName('Rational')),final(false),public(true),
3    abstract(false),className(packageName('java/lang/'),shortClassName('Object')),[],
4    [field(
5       fieldSignature(
6          fieldName(
7             className(packageName(''),shortClassName('Rational')),shortFieldName(num)),
8          primitiveType(int)),
9       final(false),static(false),public,initialValue(undef)),
10    field(
11       fieldSignature(
12          fieldName(
13             className(packageName(''),shortClassName('Rational')),shortFieldName(den)),
14          primitiveType(int)),
15       final(false),static(false),public,initialValue(undef))],
16    [method(
17       methodSignature(
18          methodName(
19             className(packageName(''),shortClassName('Rational')),shortMethodName('<init>')),
20          [primitiveType(int),primitiveType(int)],none),
21       bytecodeMethod(3,2,0,methodId('Rational_class',1),[]),
22       final(false),static(false),public),
23    method(
24       methodSignature(
25          methodName(
26             className(packageName(''),shortClassName('Rational')),shortMethodName(exp)),
27          [primitiveType(int)],
28          refType(classType(className(packageName(''),shortClassName('Rational'))))),
29       bytecodeMethod(4,4,0,methodId('Rational_class',2),[]),
30       final(false),static(false),public),
31    method(
32       methodSignature(
33          methodName(
34             className(packageName(''),shortClassName('Rational')),shortMethodName(expMain)),
35          [primitiveType(int),primitiveType(int),primitiveType(int)],
36          refType(classType(className(packageName(''),shortClassName('Rational'))))),
37       bytecodeMethod(3,4,0,methodId('Rational_class',3),[]),
38       final(false),static(true),public)]).
```

Fig. 3. Extract of the Bytecode facts of our Running Example

code. The description of the field num appears in Lines 4-9, den in L.10-15 and the methods in L.16-38. For conciseness, only methods actually used are shown. The first method (L.16-22) is a constructor that takes two integers (L.20) as arguments. The second method (L.23-30) is named exp (L.26), it is an instance method (cf. static(false) L.30)) and takes an integer (L.27) as a parameter and returns an instance of Rational (L.28). Finally, the last method (L.31-38), expMain, is a class method (cf. static(true) L.38), that takes as parameters three integers (L.35) and returns an instance of Rational (L.36).

Fig. 3 presents the bytecode facts corresponding to the methods exp and expMain. Each fact is of the form bytecode(PC,MethodID,Class,Inst,Size), where Class and MethodID, respectively, identify the class and the method to which the instruction Inst belongs. PC corresponds to the program counter and Size to the number of bytes of the instruction in order to be able to compute the next value of the program counter. The class method number 3 (i.e., expMain) creates first an instance of Rational (Instructions 0-6) and then invokes the instance method exp (I.9-10). The bytecode of the method number 2 (i.e., exp), can be divided in 3 parts. First, the initialization (I.0-3) of two local variables, say x_2 and x_3, to 1. Then, the loop body (I.4-25) first compares the exponent to 0 and, if it is less or equal to 0, exits the loop by jumping 23 bytes ahead (I.4-5). Then, the current value of x_2 (`iload`) and the denominator (`aload` and `getfield`) are retrieved (I.8-10), multiplied and stored in x_2 (I.13-14). The same is done for x_3 with the numerator in I.15-21. Finally, the value of the exponent is decreased by one (I.22) and PC is decreased by 21 (I.25) i.e., we jump back to the beginning of the loop. After the loop, the method creates an instance of `Rational`, stores the result (I.28-34), and returns this object (I.37).

3   Specification of the Dynamic Semantics

(C)LP programs have been used traditionally for expressing the semantics of both high- and low-level languages [13,17]. In our approach, we express the JVML semantics in `Ciao`. The formal JVML specification chosen for our work is Bicolano [14], which is written with the Coq Proof Assistant [1]. This allows checking that the specification is consistent and also proving properties on the behavior of some programs.

In the specification, a state is modeled by a 3-tuple[2] $\langle Heap, Frame, Stack\text{-}Frame \rangle$ which represents the machine's state where $Heap$ represents the contents of the heap, $Frame$ represents the execution state of the current $Method$ and, $StackFrame$ is a list of frames corresponding to the call stack. Each frame is of the form $\langle Method, PC, OperandStack, LocalVar \rangle$ and contains the stack of operands $OperandStack$ and the values of the local variables $LocalVar$ at the program point PC of the method $Method$. The definition of the dynamic semantics is based on the notion of $step$.

Definition 1 ($step \xrightarrow{L}_P$). *The dynamic semantics of each instruction is specified as a partial function $step : \text{JVML}_r\_Prog \times State_{JVM} \to State_{JVM} \times Step\_Name$ that, given a program $P \in \text{JVML}_r\_Prog$ and a state $S \in State_{JVM}$, computes the next state $S' \in State_{JVM}$ and returns the name of the step $L \in Step\_Name$. For convenience, we write $S \xrightarrow{L}_P S'$ to denote $step(P, S) = (S', L)$.*

In order to formally define our interpreter, we need to define the following function which iterates over the steps of the program until obtaining a final state.

Definition 2 ($\xrightarrow{T}{}^{*}_P$). *Let $\xrightarrow{T}{}^{*}_P$ be a relation on $State_{JVM}$ with $S \xrightarrow{T}{}^{*}_P S'$ iff:*

- *there exists a sequence of steps L_1 to L_n such that $S \xrightarrow{L_1}_P \ldots \xrightarrow{L_n}_P S'$,*
- *there is no state $S'' \in State_{JVM}$ such that $S' \xrightarrow{L}_P S''$, and*
- *$T \in Traces$ such that $T = [L_1, \ldots, L_n]$ is the list of the names of the steps.*

We can now define a general interpreter which takes as parameters a program and a *method invocation specification* (MIS in the following) that indicates: 1)

---

[2] Both in Bicolano and in our implementation there is another kind of state for exceptions, but we have omitted it from this formalization for the sake of simplicity.

the method the execution should start from, 2) the corresponding effective parameters of the method which will often contain logical variables or partially instantiated terms (and should be interpreted as the set of all their instances) and 3) an initial heap. The interpreter relies on an EXECUTE function that takes as parameters a program $P \in$ JVML$_r$_$Prog$ and a state $S \in State_{JVM}$ and returns (S', T) where $S \xrightarrow{T}{}^{*}_{P} S'$.

The following definition of JVML$_r$_INT computes, in addition to the return value of the method called, also the trace which captures the computation history. Traces represent the semantic steps used and therefore do not only represent instructions, as the context has also some importance. They allow us to distinguish, for example, for a same instruction, the step that throws an exception from the normal behavior. E.g., `invokevirtual_step_ok` and `invokevirtual_step_-NullPointerException` represent, respectively, a normal method call and a method call on a null reference that throws an exception.

Definition 3 (JVML$_r$_INT). *Let M be a* MIS *that contains a method signature, the parameters for the method and a heap, written as $M \in$ MIS. We define a general interpreter* JVML$_r$_INT$(P, M) = (R, T)$ *with*

- *$S = initialState(P, M)$, where function initialState builds, from the program P and the* MIS *M, a state $S \in State_{JVM}$,*
- EXECUTE$(P, S) = (S', T)$ *and*
- *$R = result\_of(S')$ is the result of the execution of the method specified by M (the value on top of the stack of the current frame of S').*

This definition of JVML$_r$_INT returns the trace and the result of the method but it is straightforward to modify the definitions of JVML$_r$_INT and EXECUTE to return less information or to add more. This gives more flexibility to our interpretative approach when compared to direct compilation: for example, if needed, we can return in an additional argument a list containing the information about each state which we would like to *observe* in order to prove properties which may require a deeper inspection of execution states.

4   Automatic Generation of Residual Programs

Partial evaluation (PE) [10] is a semantics-based program optimization technique which has been deeply investigated within different programming paradigms. The main purpose of PE is to specialize a given program w.r.t. the *static data*, i.e., the part of its input data which is known—hence it is also known as *program specialization*. The partially evaluated (or residual) program will be (hopefully) executed more efficiently since those computations that depend only on the static data are performed once and for all at PE time. We use the partial evaluator for LP programs of [15] which is part of `CiaoPP`. Here, we represent it as a function PARTIAL_EVALUATOR: $Prog \times Data \rightarrow Prog$ which, for a given program $P \in Prog$ and static data $S \in Data$, returns a residual program $P_S \in Prog$ which is a *specialization* [10] of P w.r.t. S.

The development of PE, program specialization and related techniques [6,10,7] has led to an alternative approach to compilation (known as the first Futamura projection) based on specializing an interpreter with respect to a fixed object program. The success of the application of the technique involves eliminating the overhead of parsing the program, fetching instructions, etc., and leading to a residual program whose operations mimic those of the object program. This can also be seen as a translation of the object program into another programming language, in our case Ciao. The *residual* program is ready now to be, for instance, efficiently executed in such language or, as in our case, accurately analyzed by tools for the language in which it has been translated. The application of this interpretative approach to compilation within our framework consists in partially evaluating the JVML$_r$_INT w.r.t. $P = $ CLASS_READER$(C_1, \ldots, C_n)$ and a MIS.

Definition 4 (LP residual program). *Let* JVML$_r$_INT $\in$ *Prog be a* JVML$_r$ *interpreter,* $M \in$ MIS *and* $C_1, \ldots, C_n \in$ *Class be a set of classes. The* LP *residual program,* I_P, *for* JVML$_r$_INT *w.r.t.* $C_1, \ldots, C_n$ *and* M *is defined as* $I_P =$ PARTIAL_EVALUATOR*(*JVML$_r$_INT, (CLASS_READER$(C_1, \ldots, C_n), M$))*.

Note that, instead of using the interpretative approach, we could have implemented a compiler from Java bytecode to LP. However, we believe that the interpretative approach has at least the following advantages: 1) more flexible, in the sense that it is easy to modify the interpreter in order to observe new properties of interest, see Sect. 3, 2) easier to trust, in the sense that it is rather difficult to prove (or trust) that the compiler preserves the program semantics and, it is also complicated to explicitly specify what the semantics used is, 3) easier to maintain, new changes in the JVM semantics can be easily reflected in the interpreter by modifying (or adding) a proper "step" definition, and 4) easier to implement, provided a powerful partial evaluator for LP is available.

Example 2 (residual programs). We now want to partially evaluate our implementation of the interpreter which does not output the trace (see Sect. 3) w.r.t. the bytecode method expMain in Ex. 1, an empty heap and three free variables as parameters. The size of the program to be partially evaluated (i.e., interpreter) is 86,326 bytes (2,240 lines) while the size of the data (i.e., bytecode representation) is 16,677 bytes (101 lines) of JVML$_r$. The partial evaluator has different options for tuning the level of specialization. For this example, we have used local and global control strategies based on *homeomorphic embedding* (see [11]).

We show in Fig. 4 the residual program resulting of such automatic PE. The parameters A, B and C of expMain/5 represent the numerator, denominator and exponent, respectively. The fourth and fifth parameters represent, respectively, the top of the stack and the heap where the method result (i.e., an object of type Rational in the bytecode) will be returned. In particular, the result corresponds to the second element, ref(loc(2)), in the heap. Note that this object is represented in our LP program as a list of two atoms, the first one corresponds to attribute num and the second one to den. The first two rules for expMain/5 are the base cases for exponents C = 0 and C = 1, respectively. The third rule, for C > 1, uses an auxiliary recursive predicate execute/6 which computes A^{C+1}

```
expMain(A,B,C,ref(loc(2)),heap([[num(int(A)),num(int(B))],
            [num(int(1)),num(int(1))]])) :- C=<0 .
expMain(A,B,C,ref(loc(2)),heap([[num(int(A)),num(int(B))],
            [num(int(A)),num(int(B))]])) :- C>0, F is C-1, F=<0 .
expMain(A,B,C,D,E) :- C>0, H is C-1, H>0, I is A*A,
            J is B*B, K is H-1, execute(A,B,K,I,J,E,D) .

execute(A,B,C,D,E,heap([[num(int(A)),num(int(B))],
            [num(int(D)),num(int(E))]]),ref(loc(2)))) :- C=<0 .
execute(A,B,C,D,E,G,L) :- C>0, N is D*A, O is E*B, P is C-1,
            execute(A,B,P,N,O,G,L) .
```

Fig. 4. Residual Exponential Program without Trace

and B^{C+1} and returns the result in the second element of the heap. It should be noted that our PE tool has done a very good job by transforming a rather large interpreter into a small residual program (where all the interpretation overhead has been removed). The most relevant point to notice about the residual program is that we have converted low level jumps into a recursive behavior and achieved a very satisfactory translation from the Java bytecode method expMain. Indeed, it is not very different from the Ciao version one could have written by hand, provided that we need to store the result in the fifth argument of predicate expMain/5 as an object in the heap, using the corresponding syntax.

While the above LP program can be of a lot of interest when reasoning about functional properties of the code, it is also of great importance to augment the interpreter with an additional argument which computes a trace (see Def. 3) in order to capture the computation history. The residual program which computes execution traces is expMain/4, which on success contains in the fourth argument the execution trace at the level of Java bytecode (rather than the top of the stack and the heap). Below, we show the recursive rule of predicate execute/8 whose last argument represents the trace (and corresponds to the second rule of execute/7 without trace in Fig. 4):

```
execute(B,C,D,E,F,G,I,[goto_step_ok,iload_step,if0_step_continue,
        iload_step,aload_step_ok,getfield_step_ok,ibinop_step_ok,
        istore_step_ok,iload_step,aload_step_ok,getfield_step_ok,
        ibinop_step_ok,istore_step_ok,iinc_step|H]) :-
    D>0, I is E*B, J is F*C, K is D-1, execute(B,C,K,I,J,G,I,H) .
```

As we will see in the next section, this trace will allow observing a good number of interesting properties about the program.

5 Verification of Java Bytecode Using LP Analysis Tools

Having obtained an LP representation of a Java bytecode program, the next task is to use existing analysis tools for LP in order to infer and verify properties about the original bytecode program. We now recall some basic notions on *abstract interpretation* [3]. *Abstract interpretation* provides a general formal framework for computing safe approximations of program behaviour. In this framework, programs are interpreted using *abstract values* instead of *concrete values*. An abstract value is a finite representation of a, possibly infinite, set of concrete values in the concrete domain D. The set of all possible abstract values constitutes the *abstract domain*, denoted D_α, which is usually a complete lattice or cpo which is ascending chain finite. Abstract values and sets of concrete values are related by an *abstraction* function $\alpha : 2^D \to D_\alpha$, and a *concretization* function $\gamma : D_\alpha \to 2^D$. The concrete and abstract domains must be related in such a way that the following condition holds [3]: $\forall x \in 2^D : \gamma(\alpha(x)) \supseteq x$ and $\forall y \in D_\alpha : \alpha(\gamma(y)) = y$. In general, the comparison in D_α, written $\sqsubseteq$, is induced by $\subseteq$ and α.

We rely on a generic analysis algorithm (in the style of [9]) defined as a function ANALYZER: $Prog \times AAtom \times ADom \to AApprox$ which takes a program $P \in Prog$, an abstract domain $D_\alpha \in ADom$ and a set of abstract atoms $S_\alpha \in AAtom$ which are descriptions of the entries (or calling modes) into the program and returns $Approx_\alpha \in AApprox$. Correctness of analysis ensures that $Approx_\alpha$ safely approximates the semantics of P. We denote that S_α and $Approx_\alpha$ are abstract semantic values in D_α by using the same subscript α.

In order to verify the program, the user has to provide the intended semantics $Assert_\alpha$ (or specification) as a semantic value in D_α in terms of *assertions* (these are linguistic constructions which allow expressing properties of programs) [16]. This intended semantics embodies the requirements as an expression of the user's expectations. The *verifier* has to compare the (actual) inferred semantics $Approx_\alpha$ w.r.t. $Assert_\alpha$. We use the *abstract interpretation*-based verifier integrated in CiaoPP. It is dealt here as a function AI_VERIFIER: $Prog \times AAtom \times ADom \times AAssert \to boolean$ which for a given program $P \in Prog$, a set of abstract atoms $S_\alpha \in AAtom$, an abstract domain $D_\alpha \in ADom$ and an intended semantics $Assert_\alpha$ in D_α succeeds if the approximation computed by ANALYZER$(P, S_\alpha, D_\alpha) = Approx_\alpha$ entails that P satisfies $Assert_\alpha$, i.e., $Approx_\alpha \sqsubseteq Assert_\alpha$.

Definition 5 (verified bytecode). *Let $I_P \in Prog$ be an LP residual program for JVML$_r$_INT w.r.t. $C_1, \ldots, C_n \in Class$ and $M \in$ MIS (see Def. 3). Let $D_\alpha \in ADom$ be an abstract domain, $S_\alpha \in AAtom$ be a set of abstract atoms and $Assert_\alpha \in D_\alpha$ be the abstract intended semantics of I_P. We say that $(C_1, \ldots, C_n, M)$ is verified w.r.t. $Assert_\alpha$ in $ADom$ if AI_VERIFIER$(I_P, S_\alpha, D_\alpha, Assert_\alpha)$ succeeds.*

In principle, any of the considerable number of abstract domains developed for *abstract interpretation* of logic programs can be applied to residual programs, as well as to any other program. In addition, arguably, analysis of logic programs is inherently simpler than that of Java bytecode since the bytecode programs decompiled into logic programs no longer contain an operand stack for arithmetic and execution flow is transformed from jumps (since loops in the Java program are compiled into conditional and unconditional jumps) into recursion.

5.1   Run-Time Error Freeness Analysis

The use of objects in Ex. 1 could in principle issue exceptions of type NullPointerException. Clearly, the execution of the expMain method will not produce any exception, as the unique object used is created within the method. However, the JVM is unaware of this and has to perform the corresponding run-time test. We illustrate that by using our approach we can statically verify that the previous code cannot issue such an exception (nor any other kind of run-time error).

First, we proceed to specify in Ciao the property "goodtrace" which encodes the fact that a bytecode program is run-time error free in the sense that its execution does not issue NullPointerException nor any other kind of run-time error (e.g., ArrayIndexOutOfBoundsException, etc). As this property is not predefined in Ciao, we declare it as a regular type using the regtype declarations in CiaoPP. Formally, we define this property as a *regular unary logic* program, see [5]. The following regular type goodtrace defines this notion of safety for our example (for conciseness, we omit the bytecode instructions which do not appear in our program):

```
:- regtype goodtrace/1.
goodtrace(T) :- list(T,goodstep).

:- regtype goodstep/1.
goodstep(iinc_step).          goodstep(aload_step_ok).          goodstep(invokevirtual_step_ok).
goodstep(iload_step).         goodstep(if0_step_jump).          goodstep(invokestatic_step_ok).
goodstep(normal_end).         goodstep(const_step_ok).          goodstep(if0_step_continue).
goodstep(new_step_ok).        goodstep(return_step_ok).         goodstep(if_icmp_step_jump).
goodstep(pop_step_ok).        goodstep(astore_step_ok).         goodstep(putfield_step_ok).
goodstep(dup_step_ok).        goodstep(istore_step_ok).         goodstep(getfield_step_ok).
goodstep(goto_step_ok).       goodstep(ibinop_step_ok).         goodstep(if_icmp_step_continue).
goodstep(areturn_step_ok).    goodstep(invokespecial_step_here_ok).
```

Next, the version with traces of the residual program in Fig. 4 is extended with the following assertions:

```
:- entry expMain(Num,Den,Exp,Trace):(num(Num),num(Den),num(Exp),var(Trace)).
:- check success expMain(Num,Den,Exp,Trace) => goodtrace(Trace).
```

The entry assertion describes the valid external queries to predicate expMain/4, where the first three parameters are of type num and the fourth one is a variable. We use the "success" assertion as a way to provide a partial specification of the program. It should be interpreted as: for all calls to expMain(Num,Den,Exp, Trace), if the call succeeds, then Trace must be a goodtrace.

Finally, we use CiaoPP to perform regular type analysis using the *eterms* domain [18]. This allows computing safe approximations of the success states of all predicates. After this, CiaoPP performs compile-time checking of the success assertion above, comparing it with the assertions inferred by the analysis, and produces as output the following assertion:

```
:- checked success expMain(Num,Den,Exp,Trace) => goodtrace(Trace).
```

Thus, the provided assertion has been *validated* (marked as checked).

5.2   Cost Analysis and Termination

As mentioned before, *abstract interpretation*-based program analysis techniques allow inferring very rich information including also resource-related issues. For example, CiaoPP can compute upper and lower bounds on the number of execution steps required by the computation [9,4]. Such bounds are expressed as functions on the sizes of the input arguments. Various metrics are used for the "size" of an input, such as list-length, term-size, term-depth, integer-value, etc. Types, modes, and size measures are first automatically inferred by the analyzers and then used in the size and cost analysis.

Let us illustrate the cost analysis in CiaoPP on our running example. We consider a slightly modified version of the residual program in Fig. 4 in which we have eliminated the accumulating parameter due to a current limitation of the cost analysis in CiaoPP. The cost analysis can then infer the following property of the recursive predicate execute/5 (and a similar one of expMain/4) using the same entry assertion as in Sect. 5.1:

```
:- true pred execute(A,B,C,D,E): (num(A),num(B),num(C),var(D),var(E))
       => ( num(A), num(B), num(C), num(D), num(E),
            size_ub(A,int(A)), size_ub(B,int(B)), size_ub(C,int(C)),
            size_ub(D,expMain(int(A),int(C)+1)+int(A)),
            size_ub(E,expMain(int(B),int(C)+1)+int(B)) )
     + steps_ub(int(C)+1).
```

which states that execute/5 is called in this program with the first three parameters being of type num (i.e., bound to numbers) and two variables. The part of the assertion after the => symbol indicates that on success of the predicate all five parameters are bound to numbers. This is used by the cost analysis in order to set the integer-value as size-metric for all five arguments. The first three arguments are input to the procedure and thus their size (value) is fixed. The last two arguments are output and their size (value) is a function on the value of (some of) the first three arguments. The upper bound computed by the analysis for D (i.e., the fourth argument) is $A^{C+1} + A$. Note that this is a correct upper bound, though the most accurate one is indeed A^{C+1}. A similar situation occurs with the upper bound for the fifth argument (E). Finally, the part of the assertion after the + symbol indicates that an upper bound on the number of execution steps is $C + 1$, which corresponds to a linear algorithmic complexity. This is indeed the most accurate upper bound possible, since predicate execute/5 is called $C + 1$ times until C becomes zero. Note that, in this case, we do not mean the number of JVM steps in Def. 1, but the number of computational steps.

CiaoPP's termination analysis relies on the cost analysis described in the previous section. In particular, it is able to prove termination of a program provided it obtains a non-infinite upper bound of its cost. Following the example of Sect. 5.2, CiaoPP is able to turn into checked status the following assertion (and the similar one for expMain/4): ":- check comp execute(A,B,C,D,E) + terminates". which ensures that the execution of the recursive predicate always terminates w.r.t. the previous entry.

6   Experiments and Discussion

We have implemented and performed a preliminary experimental evaluation of our framework within the CiaoPP preprocessor [9], where we have available a partial evaluator and a generic analysis engine with a good number of abstract domains, including the ones illustrated in the previous section. Our interpretative approach has required the implementation in Ciao of two new packages: the CLASS_READER (1141 lines of code) which parses the .class files into Ciao and the JVML$_r$_INT interpreter for the JVML$_r$ (3216 lines). These tools, together with a collection of examples, are available at: http://cliplab.org/Systems/jvm-by-pe.

Table 1 studies two crucial points for the practicality of our proposal: the size of the residual program and the relative efficiency of the full transformation+analysis process. As mentioned before, the algorithms are parametric w.r.t. the abstract domain. In our experiments we use *eterms*, an abstract domain based on regular types, that is very useful for reasoning about functional properties of the code, run-time errors, etc., which are crucial aspects for the safety of the Java bytecode. The system is implemented in Ciao 1.13 [2] with compilation to WAM bytecode. The experiments have been performed on an Intel P4 Xeon 2 GHz with 4 GB of RAM, running GNU Linux FC-2, 2.6.9.

The input "program" to be partially evaluated is the JVML$_r$_INT interpreter in all the examples. Then, the first group of columns **Bytecode** shows information about the input "data" to the partial evaluator, i.e., about the .class files. The columns **Class** and **Size** show the names of the classes used for the experiments and their sizes in bytes, respectively. The second column **Method** refers to the name of the method within each class which is going to form the MIS, i.e., to be the starting point for PE and context-sensitive program analysis. We use a set of classical algorithms as benchmarks. The first 9 methods belong to programs with iterations and static methods but without object-oriented features, where **mod**, **fact**, **gcd** and **lcm**, compute respectively the modulo, factorial, greatest-common-divisor and least-common-multiple (two versions); the **Combinatory** class has different methods for computing the number of selections of subsets given a set of elements for every ordering/repetition combination. The next two benchmarks, **LinearSearch** and **BinarySearch**, deal with arrays and correspond to the classic linear and binary search algorithms. Finally, the last four benchmarks correspond to programs which make extensive use of object-oriented features such as instance method invocation, field accessing and setting, object creation and initialization, etc.

The information about the "output" of the PE process appears in the second group of columns, **Residual**. The columns **Size** and **NUnfs** show the size in bytes of each residual program and the number of unfolding steps performed by the partial evaluator to generate it, respectively. We can observe that the partial evaluator has done a good job in all examples by transforming a rather large interpreter (86,326 bytes) in relatively small residual programs. The sizes range from 317 bytes for **m2** (99.4% reduction) to 4.911 for **Lcm2** (83.6 %). The number of required unfolding steps explains the high PE times, as we discuss

Table 1. Sizes of residual programs and transformation and analysis times

Class	Bytecode Size	Method	Residual Size	NUnfs	Trans	Times (ms) PE	Ana	Total
Mod	314	mod	956	1645	18	1244	59	1322
Fact	324	fact	1007	1537	19	1432	74	1525
Gcd	265	gcd	940	1273	18	1160	125	1303
Lcm	299	lcm	2260	4025	21	5832	817	6670
Lcm2	547	lcm2	4911	3724	26	3963	1185	5174
Combinatory	703	varNoRep	1314	1503	32	1837	87	1955
Combinatory	703	combNoRep	2177	2491	34	3676	150	3860
Combinatory	703	combRep	2151	3033	29	5331	950	6310
Combinatory	703	perm	1022	1256	29	1234	65	1328
LinearSearch	318	search	3114	8832	22	45228	296	45546
BinarySearch	412	search	3670	14117	23	72945	313	73282
Np	387	m2	317	527	20	502	12	534
ExpFact	890	main	2266	8353	35	23773	95	23903
Rational	559	expMain	3131	6613	31	13692	16	13739
Date	602	forward	11046	26982	36	80960	218	81213

below. A relevant point to note is that, for most programs, the size of the LP translation is larger than the original bytecode. This can be justified by the fact that the resulting program does not only represent the bytecode program but it also makes explicit some internal machinery of the JVM. This is the case, for instance, of the exception handling. As there are no Ciao exceptions in the residual program, the implicit exceptions in JVML have been made explicit in LP. Furthermore, the Java bytecode has been designed to be really compact, while the LP version has been designed to be easier to read by human beings and contains type information that must be inferred on the JVML. It should not be difficult to reduce the size of the residual bytecode if so required by, for example, simply using short identifiers.

The final part of the table provides the times for performing the transformations and the analysis process. Execution times are given in milliseconds and measure *runtime*. They are computed as the arithmetic mean of five runs. For each benchmark, **Trans**, **PE** and **Ana** are the times for executing the CLASS_READER, the partial evaluator and the analyzer, respectively. The column **Total** accumulates all the previous times. We can observe that most of the time is due to the partial evaluation phase (and this time is directly related to the number of unfolding steps performed). This is to be expected because the specialization of a large program (i.e., the interpreter) requires to perform many unfolding steps in all the examples (ranging from 14.117 steps for **search** in **BinarySearch** to 527 for **m2**), plus many additional generalization steps which are not shown in the table. The analysis time is then relatively low, as the residual programs to be analyzed are significantly smaller than the program to be partially evaluated.

As for future work, we plan to obtain accurate bounds on resource consumption by considering the traces that the residual program contains and the concrete cost of each bytecode instruction. Also, we are in the process of studying the scalability of our approach to the verification of larger Java bytecode programs. We also plan to exploit the advanced features of the partial evaluator which integrates abstract interpretation [15] in order to handle recursion.

Acknowledgments. This work was funded in part by the Information Society Technologies program of the European Commission, Future and Emerging Technologies under the IST-15905 *MOBIUS* project, by the Spanish Ministry (TIN-2005-09207 *MERIT*), and the Madrid Regional Government (S-0505/TIC/0407 *PROMESAS*). The authors would like to thank David Pichardie and Samir Genaim for useful discussions on the Bicolano JVM specification and on termination analysis, respectively.

References

1. B. Barras et al. The Coq proof assistant reference manual: Version 6.1. Technical Report RT-0203, 1997. citeseer.ist.psu.edu/barras97coq.html.
2. F. Bueno, D. Cabeza, M. Carro, M. Hermenegildo, P. López, and G. Puebla (Eds.). The Ciao System. (v1.13). At `http://clip.dia.fi.upm.es/Software/Ciao/`.
3. P. Cousot and R. Cousot. Abstract Interpretation: a Unified Lattice Model for Static Analysis of Programs by Construction or Approximation of Fixpoints. In *Proc. of POPL'77*, pages 238–252, 1977.
4. S. Debray, P. López, M. Hermenegildo, and N. Lin. Estimating the Computational Cost of Logic Programs. *Proc. of SAS'94*, LNCS 864, pp. 255–265. Springer.
5. T. Früwirth, E. Shapiro, M.Y. Vardi, and E. Yardeni. Logic programs as types for logic programs. In *Proc. LICS'91*, pages 300–309, 1991.
6. Yoshihiko Futamura. Partial evaluation of computation process - an approach to a compiler-compiler. *Systems, Computers, Controls*, 2(5):45–50, 1971.
7. J. Gallagher. Transforming logic programs by specializing interpreters. In *Proc. of the 7th. European Conference on Artificial Intelligence*, 1986.
8. Kim S. Henriksen and John P. Gallagher. Analysis and specialisation of a pic processor. In *SMC (2)*, pages 1131–1135. IEEE, 2004.
9. M. Hermenegildo, G. Puebla, F. Bueno, and P. López. Integrated Program Debugging, Verification, and Optimization Using Abstract Interpretation. *Science of Computer Programming*, 58(1–2):115–140, October 2005.
10. N.D. Jones, C.K. Gomard, and P. Sestoft. *Partial Evaluation and Automatic Program Generation*. Prentice Hall, New York, 1993.
11. M. Leuschel. On the power of homeomorphic embedding for online termination. *Proc. of SAS'98*, pages 230–245, 1998. Springer-Verlag.
12. T. Lindholm and F. Yellin. *The Java Virtual Machine Specification*. A-W, 1996.
13. J.C. Peralta, J. Gallagher, and H. Sağlam. Analysis of imperative programs through analysis of CLP. In *Proc. of SAS'98*, LNCS 1503, pp. 246–261, 1998.
14. D. Pichardie. Bicolano (Byte Code Language in cOq). http://www-sop.inria.fr/everest/personnel/David.Pichardie/bicolano/main.html.
15. G. Puebla, E. Albert, and M. Hermenegildo. Abstract Interpretation with Specialized Definitions. In *Proc. of SAS'06*, LNCS. Springer, 2006. To appear.

16. G. Puebla, F. Bueno, and M. Hermenegildo. An Assertion Language for CLP. In *Analysis and Visualization Tools for CP*, pages 23–61. Springer LNCS 1870, 2000.
17. Brian J. Ross. The partial evaluation of imperative programs using prolog. In *META*, pages 341–363, 1988.
18. C. Vaucheret and F. Bueno. More Precise yet Efficient Type Inference for Logic Programs. In *Proc. of SAS'02*, pages 102–116. Springer LNCS 2477, 2002.

Combining Static Analysis and Profiling for Estimating Execution Times

Edison Mera[1], Pedro López-García[1], Germán Puebla[1],
Manuel Carro[1], and Manuel V. Hermenegildo[1,2]

[1] Technical University of Madrid
edison@clip.dia.fi.upm.es, {pedro.lopez,german,mcarro,herme}@fi.upm.es
[2] University of New Mexico
herme@unm.edu

Abstract. Effective static analyses have been proposed which infer bounds on the number of resolutions. These have the advantage of being independent from the platform on which the programs are executed and have been shown to be useful in a number of applications, such as granularity control in parallel execution. On the other hand, in distributed computation scenarios where platforms with different capabilities come into play, it is necessary to express costs in metrics that include the characteristics of the platform. In particular, it is specially interesting to be able to infer upper and lower bounds on actual execution times. With this objective in mind, we propose an approach which combines compile-time analysis for cost bounds with a one-time profiling of a given platform in order to determine the values of certain parameters for that platform. These parameters calibrate a cost model which, from then on, is able to compute statically time bound functions for procedures and to predict with a significant degree of accuracy the execution times of such procedures in that concrete platform. The approach has been implemented and integrated in the `CiaoPP` system.

Keywords: Execution Time Estimation, Cost Analysis, Profiling, Resource Awareness, Cost Models, Mobile Computing.

1   Introduction

Predicting statically the running time of programs has many applications ranging from task scheduling in parallel execution to proving the ability of a program to meet strict time constraints in real-time systems. A starting point in order to attack this problem is to infer the computational complexity of such programs. This is one of the reasons why the development of static analysis techniques for inferring cost-related properties of programs has received considerable attention. However, in most cases such cost properties are expressed using platform-independent metrics. For example, [5,4] present a method for automatically inferring functions which capture an upper bound on the number of resolution steps or reductions that a procedure will execute as a function of the size of its input data. In [12,11] the method of [5,11] was fully automated in the context of a practical compiler and in [6,11] a similar approach was applied in order to also obtain lower bounds, which are specially relevant in parallel

M. Hanus (Ed.): PADL 2007, LNCS 4354, pp. 140–154, 2007.

execution. Such platform-independent cost information (bounds on number of reductions) has been shown to be quite useful in various applications. This includes, for example, scheduling parallel tasks [11,12,8]. In a typical scenario, these tasks will be executed in a single parallel machine, where all processors are typically identical. Therefore, the deduced number of reductions can actually be used as a relative measure in order to compare to a first degree of approximation the amount of work under the tasks.

However, in distributed execution and other mobile/pervasive computation scenarios, where different platforms come into play with each platform having different computing power, it becomes necessary to express costs in metrics that can be later instantiated to different architectures so that actual running time can be compared using the same units. This applies also to heterogeneous parallel computing platforms. With this objective in mind, we present a framework which combines cost analysis with profiling techniques in order to infer functions which yield bounds on platform-dependent *execution times* of procedures. Platform-independent cost functions are first inferred which are parametrized by certain constants. These constants aim at capturing the execution time of certain low-level operations on each platform. For each execution platform, the value of such constants is determined experimentally once and for all by running a set of synthetic benchmarks and measuring their running times with a profiling toolkit that we have also developed. Once these constants are determined, they are fed into the model with the objective of predicting with a certain accuracy execution times. We have studied a relatively large number of cost models, involving different sets of constants in order to explore experimentally which of the models produces the most precise results, i.e., which parameters model and predict best the actual execution times of procedures. In doing this we have taken into account the trade-off between simplicity of the cost models (which implies efficiency of the cost analysis and also simpler profiling) and the precision of their results. With this aim, we have started with a simple model and explored several possible refinements.

In addition to cost analysis, the implementation of profilers in declarative languages has also been considered by various authors, with the aim of helping to discover why a part of a program does not exhibit the expected performance. Debray [3] showed the basic considerations to have in mind when profiling Prolog programs: handling backtracking and failure. Ducassé [7] designed and implemented a trace analyzer for Prolog which can be applied to profiling. Sansom and Peyton Jones [14] focused on profiling of functional languages using a semantic approach and highlighted the difficulty in profiling such kind of languages. Jarvis and Morgan [13] showed how to profile lazy functional programs. Brassel et al. [1] solved part of the difficulty in profiling when considering special features in functional logic programs, like sharing, laziness and non-determinism. We will use also profiling but, since our aim is to *predict* performance, profiling will in our case be aimed at calibrating the values for some constants that appear in the cost functions, and which will be instrumental to forecast execution times for a given platform and cost model. Therefore we will not use profiling with just some fixed input arguments, but with a set of programs and input arguments which we hope will be representative enough to derive meaningful characteristics of an execution platform.

2 Static Platform-Dependent Cost Analysis

In this Section we present the compile-time cost bounds analysis component of our combined framework. This analysis has been implemented and integrated in CiaoPP [9] by extending previous implementations of reduction-counting cost analyses. The inferred (upper or lower) bounds on cost are expressed as functions on the sizes of the input arguments and use several platform-dependent parameters. Once these parameters are instantiated with values for a given platform, such functions yield bounds on the execution times required by the computation on such platform. The analyzer can use several metrics for computing the "size" of an input, such as list length, term size, term depth, integer value, etc. Types, modes, and size measures are first automatically inferred by other analyzers which are part of CiaoPP and then used in the size and cost analysis.

2.1 Platform-Independent Static Cost Analysis

As mentioned before, our static cost analysis approach is based on that developed in [5,4] (for estimation of upper bounds on resolution steps) and further extended in [6] (for lower bounds). In these approaches the time complexity of a clause can be bounded by the time complexity of head unification together with the time complexity of each of its body literals. For simplicity, the discussion that follows is focused on the estimation of upper bounds. We refer the reader to [6] for details on lower-bounds analysis. Consider a clause C defined as "$H : -L_1, ..., L_m$". Because of backtracking, the number of times a literal will be executed depends on the number of solutions that the literals preceding it can generate. Assume that $\overline{n}$ is a vector such that each element corresponds to the size of an input argument to clause C and that each $\overline{n}_i$, $i = 1 \ldots m$, is a vector such that each element corresponds to the size of an input argument to literal L_i, τ is the cost needed to resolve the head H of the clause with the literal being solved, and Sols_{L_j} is the number of solutions literal L_j can generate. Then, an upper bound on the cost of clause C (assuming all solutions are required), $\mathrm{Cost}_C(\overline{n})$, can be expressed as:

$$\mathrm{Cost}_C(\overline{n}) \leq \tau + \sum_{i=1}^{m} (\prod_{j \prec i} \mathrm{Sols}_{L_j}(\overline{n}_j)) \mathrm{Cost}_{L_i}(\overline{n}_i), \tag{1}$$

Here we use $j \prec i$ to denote that L_j precedes L_i in the literal dependency graph for the clause.

Our current implementation also considers the cost of term creation for the literals in the body of clauses, which can affect the cost expression significantly. To further simplify the discussion that follows, we restrict ourselves to the simple case where each literal is determinate, i.e., produces at most one solution. In this case, equation (1) simplifies to:

$$\mathrm{Cost}_C(\overline{n}) \leq \tau + \sum_{i=1}^{m} \mathrm{Cost}_{L_i}(\overline{n}_i). \tag{2}$$

However, it should be pointed out that our implementation is not limited to deterministic programs: our cost analysis system indeed handles non determinism, i.e., the presence of several solutions for a given call.

A difference equation is set up for each recursive clause, whose solution (using as boundary conditions the cost of non-recursive clauses) is a function that yields the cost of a clause. The cost of a predicate is then computed from the cost of its defining clauses. Since the number of solutions generated by a predicate that will be demanded is generally not known in advance, a conservative upper bound on the computational cost of a predicate can be obtained by assuming that all solutions are needed, and that all clauses are executed (thus the cost of the predicate is assumed to be the sum of the costs of its defining clauses). If we take mutual exclusion among clauses into account, we can obtain a more precise estimate of the cost of a predicate: the complexity for deterministic predicates can be approximated by the maximum of the costs of mutually exclusive groups of clauses.

The analysis in [5,4] was primarily aimed at estimating resolution steps. However, the basic metric is open and can be tailored to alternative scenarios: more sophisticated and accurate measures can be used in place of the initially proposed ones (by, e.g., decomposing arbitrary unifications into simpler steps). In the rest of this section we explore this open issue more deeply and study how the original cost analysis can be extended in order to infer cost functions using more refined (and parametric) cost models. These will in turn make it possible to generate expressions which capture execution time (or, typically, a bound thereof) more accurately.

2.2 Proposed Platform-Dependent Cost Analysis Models

Since the cost metric which we want to use in our approach is execution time, we take τ (in expression 2) to include the time needed to resolve a literal G against the corresponding clause head H, but also the cost associated with selecting alternatives, the cost coming from setting up the body literals for execution, allocating activation records, etc. In the following, we will still refer to τ as the *clause head cost function* (but understanding that it now includes all these costs), and we will consider different definitions for τ, each of them yielding a different cost model. These cost models make use of a vector of platform-dependent constants, together with a vector of platform-independent metrics, each one corresponding to a particular low-level operation related to program execution. Examples of such low-level operations considered by the cost models are unifications where one of the terms being unified is a variable and thus behave as an "assignment", or full unifications, i.e., when both terms being unified are not variables, and thus unification performs a "test" or produces new terms, etc. Thus, we generalize τ to be a function parametrized by the cost model so that:

$$\tau(\Omega) = time(\Omega) \tag{3}$$

$time(\Omega)$ returns the time associated to a resolution step, including the aforementioned additional overheads. The parameter $\Omega = (\omega_1, \ldots, \omega_v)$ is a vector denoting which characteristics we want to take into account: every ω_i looks at a different indicator of the execution time. The family of cost models we will study assumes that $time(\Omega)$ is defined as follows:

$$time(\Omega) = time(\omega_1) + \cdots + time(\omega_v), \; v > 0 \qquad (4)$$

where each $time(\omega_i)$ contributes with the part of the execution time which depends on the feature ω_i. We also assume that:

$$time(\omega_i) = K_{\omega_i} \times I(\omega_i) \qquad (5)$$

where K_{ω_i} is a platform-dependent constant and $I(\omega_i)$ is a platform-independent cost function. I.e., K_{ω_i} expresses the cost of each unit of $I(\omega_i)$ in terms of time. Equation (4) can be written in vector notation as

$$time(\Omega) = \overline{K}_\Omega \bullet \overline{I(\Omega)} \qquad (6)$$

where $\overline{K}_\Omega = (K_{\omega_1}, \ldots, K_{\omega_v})$ and $\overline{I(\Omega)} = (I(\omega_1), \ldots, I(\omega_v))$ are vectors of platform-dependent constants and of platform-independent cost functions, respectively. Accordingly, we generalize equation (2) by introducing the clause head cost function τ as a parameter:

$$\mathsf{Cost}_\mathsf{C}(\Omega, \overline{n}) \leq \tau(\Omega) + \sum_{i=1}^{m} \mathsf{Cost}_{\mathsf{L}_i}(\Omega, \overline{n}_i). \qquad (7)$$

A cost model, of which we have tested several, is given by a particular definition of the parameter Ω. Every cost model is defined by the program characteristics taken into account by it. While a large number of indicators can be used, we have identified some of them as specially interesting. We list them below, giving a mnemonic to every ω_i and explaining the meaning of each $I(\omega_i)$.

In what follows we will say that an argument of a literal is an *output argument* if the term being passed by the calling literal is known to be a variable at run-time, and an *input argument* if it is not a variable. Run-time arguments can be classified as either input or output using well-known techniques for mode analyses (in our case, those provided by CiaoPP).

$I(step) = 1$ Every successful *head traversal* has a constant weight in the execution. I.e., in equation (5), we have:

$$time(step) = K_{step}$$

$I(vounif) =$ *the number of variables in the clause head which correspond to "output" argument positions.* This describes a component of the execution time that is directly proportional to the number of cases where both a goal argument and the corresponding head argument are variables. This should boil down to assignment (maybe with trailing).

$$time(vounif) = K_{vounif} \times I(vounif)$$

$I(viunif) =$ *the number of variables in the clause head which correspond to "input" argument positions.* This component corresponds to the number of non-variable goal arguments which are unified with a variable in the head. The unification for such arguments is also similar to an assignment with a small, constant cost. We assume that the cost of creating the input argument is constant. Given these assumptions:

$$time(viunif) = K_{viunif} \times I(viunif)$$

$I(gounif) =$ *The number of function symbols and constants in the clause head which appear in output arguments.* We are capturing here the size of the terms that are created when a variable in a goal is unified with a non-variable in the clause head.

$$time(gounif) = K_{gounif} \times I(gounif)$$

$I(giunif) =$ *The number of function symbols and constants in the clause head which appear in input arguments.* We assume that there is a component of the execution time which depends on the number of arguments in which neither the goal nor the clause head arguments are variables. For each of these arguments, we take into account the number of symbols in the clause head.

$$time(giunif) = K_{giunif} \times I(giunif)$$

$I(nargs) = arity(H)$ we are assuming that there is a component of the execution time that depends on the number of arguments in the clause head:

$$time(nargs) = K_{nargs} \times I(nargs) \tag{8}$$

This component is obviously redundant with respect to the previous ones, but we have included it as a statistical control: the experiments should show (and do show) that it is irrelevant when the others are used.

Clearly, other components can be included (such as whether activation records are created or not) but our objective is to see how far we can go with the components outlined above.

We adopt the same approach as [4,6] for computing bounds on cost of predicates from the computed values for the cost of the clauses defining it. However, we introduce the cost model τ as a parameter of these cost functions.

Let $\text{Cost}_p(\Omega, \overline{n})$ be a function which gives the cost of the computation of a call to predicate p for an input of size $\overline{n}$ (recall that the cost units depend on the definition of Ω). Given a predicate p, and a clause head cost function $time(\Omega)$ as defined in equation (6), we have that:

$$\text{Cost}_p(\Omega, \overline{n}) = \overline{K}_\Omega \bullet \overline{\text{Cost}_p}(\Omega, \overline{n}) \tag{9}$$

where

$$\overline{\text{Cost}_p}(\Omega, \overline{n}) = (\text{Cost}_p(I(\omega_1), \overline{n}), \ldots, \text{Cost}_p(I(\omega_v), \overline{n}))$$

Equation (9) gives the basis for computing values for constants K_{ω_i} via profiling (as explained in Section 3). Also, it provides a way to obtain the cost of a procedure expressed in a platform-dependent cost metric from another cost expressed in a platform-independent cost metric.

2.3 Dealing with Builtins

In this section we present our approach to the cost analysis of programs which call builtins, or more generally, predicates whose code is not available to the analyzer (external predicates). We will refer to all of them as builtins for brevity. We assume that a cost function is available (expressed via **trust** assertions [9]) for each such predicate. This cost function can be a constant in simple cases but more generally it will be a function that depends on sizes of the (input) arguments of the predicate. As an example, the cost of arithmetic predicates (such as =:=/2, =\=/2, or >/2) is approximated by a function that depends on the size (and types) of the arithmetic expressions that will appear as arguments.

Note that this is a significant change with respect to the cost analysis proposed in [4] since one of the simplifying assumptions made in that analysis was to not count calls to certain builtin as resolution steps (which meant that they were simply ignored in the cost analysis). While such an assumption made sense for inferring *number of resolution steps*, the assumption is not realistic for estimating *execution times*, since the time involved in executing such builtins is not negligible in general and thus has to be taken into account.

We have modeled this by assuming that each builtin contributes with a new component of the cost model to the execution time as expressed in Equation (4). Then, a new $time(\omega_i)$ is added for each builtin predicate **b/n** as follows:

$$time(b/n) = K_{b/n} \times I(b/n)$$

We now consider in more detail the case of arithmetic operators and discuss several possibilities. For the sake of accuracy, every arithmetic operator can be dealt with separately: let $\odot/n$ be an arithmetic operator. As usual, the execution time due to the total number of times that this operator is evaluated is given by:

$$time(\odot/n) = K_{\odot/n} \times I(\odot/n)$$

where $K_{\odot/n}$ approximates the time taken by the evaluation of the arithmetic operator $\odot/n$. $I(\odot/n)$ could be the number of times that the arithmetic operator is evaluated. With these assumptions, equation (9) (in Section 2.2) also holds for programs that perform calls to builtin predicates, say, for example, a builtin b/n, by introducing b/n and $\odot/n$ as new cost components of Ω.

Alternatively, $I(\odot/n)$ can be a cost function defined as:

$$I(\odot/n) = \sum_{a \in S} \texttt{EvCost}(\odot/n, a)$$

where S is the set of arithmetic expressions appearing in the clause body which will be evaluated; and $\texttt{EvCost}(\odot/n, a)$ represents the cost corresponding to the operator $\odot/n$ in the evaluation of the arithmetic term a, i.e.:

$$\texttt{EvCost}(\odot/n, A) = \begin{cases} 0 & \text{if } \texttt{atomic}(A) \vee \texttt{var}(A) \\ 1 + \sum_{i=1}^{n} \texttt{EvCost}(\odot/n, A_i) & \text{if } A = \odot(A_1, ..., A_n) \\ \sum_{i=1}^{m} \texttt{EvCost}(\odot/n, A_i) & \text{if } A = \hat{\odot}(A_1, ..., A_m) \wedge \hat{\odot} \neq \odot \end{cases}$$

For simplicity we can make the assumption that the cost of evaluating the arithmetic term t to which a variable appearing in A will be bound at execution time is zero (i.e., to ignore the cost of evaluating t). This can be a good approximation if in most cases t is a number and thus no evaluation of a complex expression is needed for it. This is the case in our simple benchmarks and our experimental results show good time predictions for arithmetic builtin predicates using just the simple cost model. On the other hand, a more refined cost model which assumes that cost is a function on the size of t will be needed for programs which evaluate symbolic arithmetic expressions.

Note that the simple models that we have discussed ignore the possible optimizations that the compiler might perform. We can take into account those performed by source-to-source transformation by placing our analyses in the last stage of the front-end, but at some point the language the compiler works with would be different enough as to require different considerations in the cost model.

3   Calibrating Constants Via Profiling

In order to compute values for the platform-dependent constants which appear in the different cost models proposed in Section 2.2, our calibration schema takes advantage of the relationship between the platform-dependent and -independent cost metrics expressed in Equation (9). In this sense, the calibration of the constants appearing in $\overline{K}_\Omega$ is performed by solving systems of linear equations (in which such constants are treated as variables).

Based on this expression, the calibration procedure consists of:

1. Using a selected set of calibration programs which aim at isolating specific aspects that affect execution time in general cases. For these calibration programs it holds that $\text{Cost}_\text{p}(I(\omega_i), \overline{n})$ is known for all $1 \leq i \leq v$. This can be done by using any of the following methods:
   - The analyzers integrated in the CiaoPP system infer the exact cost function, i.e., both upper an lower bounds are the same: $\text{Cost}_\text{p}^l(I(\omega_i), \overline{n}) = \text{Cost}_\text{p}^u(I(\omega_i), \overline{n}) = \text{Cost}_\text{p}(I(\omega_i), \overline{n})$,
   - $\text{Cost}_\text{p}(I(\omega_i), \overline{n})$ is computed by a profiler tool, or
   - $\text{Cost}_\text{p}(I(\omega_i), \overline{n})$ is supplied by the user together with the code of program p (i.e., the cost function is not the result from any automatic analysis but rather p is well known and its cost function can be supplied in a trust assertion).
2. For each benchmark p in this set, automatically generating a significant amount m of input data for it. This can be achieved by associating with each calibration program a data generation rule.
3. For each generated input data d_j, computing a pair $(\overline{C}_{p_j}, T_{p_j})$, $1 \leq j \leq m$, where:
   - T_{p_j} is the j-th observed execution time of program p with this generated input data.
   - $\overline{C}_{p_j} = \overline{\text{Cost}_\text{p}}(\Omega, \overline{n_j})$, where $\overline{n_j}$ is the size of the j-th input data d_j.
4. Using the set of pairs $(\overline{C}_{p_j}, T_{p_j})$ to set up the equation:

$$\overline{C}_{p_j} \bullet \overline{K}_\Omega = T_{p_j} \tag{10}$$

where $\overline{K}_\Omega$ is considered a vector of variables.

5. Setting up the (overdetermined) system of equations resulting from putting together all the equations (10) corresponding to all the calibration programs.
6. Solving the above system of equations using the least squares method (see, e.g., [15]). A solution to this system gives values to the vector $\overline{K}_\Omega$ and hence, to the constants K_{ω_i} which are the elements composing it.
7. Calculating the constants for builtins and arithmetic operators by performing repeated tests in which only the builtin being tested is called, accumulating the time, and dividing the accumulated time by the number of times the repeated test has been performed.

4   Assessment of the Calibration of Constants

We have assessed both the constant calibration process and the prediction of execution times using the previously proposed cost models in two different platforms:

- "Intel" platform: Dell Optiplex, Pentium 4 (Hyper threading), 2GHz, 512MB RAM memory, Fedora Core 4 operating System with Kernel 2.6.
- "PPC" platform: Apple iMac, PowerPC G4 (1.1) 1.5GHz, 1GB RAM memory, with Mac OS X 10.4.5 Tiger.

Equation (10) is, in general, overdetermined, and we plan to find an approximation which is "best" in some sense, by using the least squares method. We used the Householder transformation [10], which decomposes the $m \times n$ matrix $C = \{\overline{C}_{p_j}\}$ into the product of two matrices Q and U such that $C = Q \bullet U$, where Q is an orthonormal matrix (i.e., $Q^T \bullet Q = I$, the $m \times m$ identity matrix) and U an upper triangular $m \times n$ matrix. Then, multiplying both sides of equation (10) by Q^T and simplifying we can get:

$$U \bullet K = Q^T \bullet T = B$$

where, for clarity, we denote $K = \overline{K}_\Omega$, $T = T_{p_j}$ and $Q^T \bullet T = B$. We can take advantage of the structure of U and define V as the first n rows of U, n being the number of columns of C and b the first n rows of B, then K can be estimated solving the following upper triangular system, where $\hat{K}$ stands for the estimate for K:

$$V \bullet \hat{K} = Q^T \bullet T = b$$

Since this method is being used to find an approximate solution, we define the residual of the system as the value $R = T - C\hat{K}$.

Let $RSS = R \bullet R$ be the residual square sum, and let $MRSS = \frac{RSS}{m-n}$ be the mean of residual square sum, where m and n are the number of rows and columns of the matrix C respectively, and finally let $S = \sqrt{MRSS}$ be the estimation of the standard error of the model, S. In order to evaluate experimentally which models generate the best approximation of the observed time, we have compared the values of $MRSS$ (or S) for several proposed models.

Table 1 shows the considered models. Table 2 shows the estimated values for the vector K using the calibration programs in Table 3, as well as the standard

Table 1. List of cost models being applied

No.	Model
1	step nargs giunif gounif viunif vounif
2	step giunif gounif viunif vounif
3	step giunif gounif vounif
4	step

Table 2. Values (in nanoseconds) for vector constants in several cost models, sorted by standard error

Plat.	Model	S (μs)	$\overline{K}_\Omega$
Intel	1	6.2475	(21.27, 9.96, 10.30, 8.23, 6.46, 5.69)
	2	9.3715	(26.56, 10.81, 8.60, 6.17, 6.39)
	3	13.7277	(27.95, 11.09, 8.77, 7.40)
	4	68.3088	108.90
PPC	1	4.7167	(41.06, 5.21, 16.85, 15.14, 9.58, 9.92)
	2	5.9676	(43.83, 17.12, 15.33, 9.43, 10.29)
	3	16.4511	(45.95, 17.55, 15.59, 11.82)
	4	116.0289	183.83

error of the model, sorted from the best to the worst model. Note that the estimation of K only needs to be done once per platform. This took 15.62 seconds for the Intel platform and 17.84 seconds for the PPC, repeating the experiment 250 times for each calibration program. Our approach has been tested on the programs used in the calibration process itself for the considered models. Table 3 shows the error incurred in when an observed value is compared against an estimated value using the models in Table 1. It can be observed that the simpler models incur in significant errors while the more complex ones are more accurate

Table 3. Calibration programs used to estimate the constants and the estimation error

Program	Error (%)			
Model	1	2	3	4
Environment creation	20	16	12	73
Predicates with no arguments	10	6	2	85
Traverse a list without last call optimization	20	20	11	80
Traverse a list with last call optimization	53	50	32	88
Program (unifying deep terms) for which $I(giunif)$ is known	16	18	18	474
Program (unifying deep terms) for which $I(gounif)$ is known	0	4	2	409
Program (unifying flat terms) for which $I(giunif)$ is known	16	18	18	472
Program (unifying flat terms) for which $I(gounif)$ is known	5	10	8	386
Program for which $I(viunif)$ is known	9	11	36	735
Program for which $I(vounif)$ is known	1	2	11	227
Unify two list element by element	34	29	20	26
Predicate with many arguments	17	16	9	159

(understandable since these calibrators exercise just particular implementation aspects and are thus expected to deviate from any "normal" behaviour).

5   Assessment of the Prediction of Execution Times

We have tested the proposed cost models in a set programs not used in the calibration process in order to assess how well their execution time is predicted, without performing any runtime profiling on them. We have performed experiments with the 63 possible cost models resulting from selecting one or more of the components described in Section 2.2. For space reasons we only show the three most accurate cost models (according to a global accuracy comparison that will be presented later) plus the step model (number 4), which, despite its simplicity, has a special interest, as we will also see later. Experimental results are shown in Table 4, where the analyzers integrated in the CiaoPP system infer the exact platform-independent cost function for all the programs in that table, which means that the upper and lower bound are the same, i.e., $\text{Cost}_p^l(I(\omega_i), \overline{n}) = \text{Cost}_p^u(I(\omega_i), \overline{n}) = \text{Cost}_p(I(\omega_i), \overline{n})$. The first three rows for each test program show the three more accurate predictions along with the model used. The fourth row shows the prediction obtained by the cost model *step*, which assumes that the execution time is directly proportional to the number of resolution steps performed. Note that $\text{Cost}_C(I(step), \overline{n})$ gives the number of resolution steps performed by clause C. The row tagged as **Observed** corresponds to the actual measured timings, and the last row details the analysis time (roughly the same in all benchmarks, and which includes mode, type, and cost analysis).

The first column is the program name, the second is the cost model Ω (= vector of characteristics taken into account) and the third and fourth are the timing estimations corresponding to the "Intel" and "PPC" platforms. These are computed by using the average value of the constant $\overline{K}_\Omega$ as estimated in Table 2 with the formula:

$$\textbf{Estimate}_P = \overline{K}_\Omega \bullet \overline{\text{Cost}_p}(\Omega, \overline{n})$$

Deviations respect to the measured values are also shown between parenthesis in the column **Estimate$_P$**.

The observed execution times have been measured by running the programs with input data of a fixed size. We generated randomly 10 input data sets of fixed size, and for each data set we run 5 times every program. The observed execution time for the (fixed) input size was computed as the average of all runs.

Table 5 compares the overall accuracy of the four cost models already shown in Table 4, for the two considered platforms. The last column shows the global error and it is an indicator of the amount of deviation of the execution times estimated by each cost model with respect to the observed values. As global error we take the square mean of the errors in each example being considered in Table 4. By considering both platforms in combination we can conclude that the more accurate cost model is $\Omega = (steps, giunif, gounif, viunif, vounif)$. This cost model has an overall error of 14.66 % in the PPC platform and 31.06 % in

Table 4. Evaluation of execution time predictions

Program	Model	Estimate$_P$ Intel (μs)	(%)	PPC (μs)	(%)
evpol	1 step nargs giunif gounif viunif vounif	89.72	(44)	77.4	(23)
	2 step giunif gounif viunif vounif	85.06	(38)	74.96	(26)
	3 step giunif gounif vounif	82	(35)	70.28	(33)
	4 step	90.12	(45)	85.07	(13)
	Observed	58.43		97.08	
	Analysis time T_{ca} (s)	2.002		4.461	
hanoi	1 step nargs giunif gounif viunif vounif	319	(31)	398.5	(4)
	2 step giunif gounif viunif vounif	243.3	(3)	358.8	(7)
	3 step giunif gounif vounif	205.6	(14)	301.3	(25)
	4 step	340.7	(38)	538.6	(34)
	Observed	235.3		384.2	
	Analysis time T_{ca} (s)	2.145		4.903	
nrev	1 step nargs giunif gounif viunif vounif	131.3	(68)	179.4	(26)
	2 step giunif gounif viunif vounif	101.1	(39)	163.6	(16)
	3 step giunif gounif vounif	82.51	(18)	135.2	(3)
	4 step	144.4	(80)	243.8	(59)
	Observed	69.25		139.2	
	Analysis time T_{ca} (s)	2.022		4.691	
palind	1 step nargs giunif gounif viunif vounif	131.8	(18)	179.8	(5)
	2 step giunif gounif viunif vounif	101	(9)	163.7	(5)
	3 step giunif gounif vounif	86.91	(24)	142.1	(19)
	4 step	167.2	(43)	282.2	(52)
	Observed	110		171.6	
	Analysis time T_{ca} (s)	2		4.7	
powset	1 step nargs giunif gounif viunif vounif	537.5	(59)	727.9	(17)
	2 step giunif gounif viunif vounif	404.5	(28)	658.3	(7)
	3 step giunif gounif vounif	323.8	(5)	534.9	(14)
	4 step	448.7	(38)	757.4	(21)
	Observed	308.2		615	
	Analysis time T_{ca} (s)	2.07		4.636	
append	1 step nargs giunif gounif viunif vounif	50.29	(75)	68.72	(24)
	2 step giunif gounif viunif vounif	38.69	(44)	62.65	(15)
	3 step giunif gounif vounif	31.36	(22)	51.45	(5)
	4 step	54.56	(85)	92.1	(56)
	Observed	25.16		53.92	
	Analysis time T_{ca} (s)	1.932		4.441	

Table 5. Global comparison of the accuracy of cost models

Platform	Intel				PPC			
Model	1	2	3	4	1	2	3	4
Error (%)	53.17	31.06	21.48	58.45	18.72	14.66	19.44	43.04

the Intel platform. In the latter (obviously more challenging) architecture the model $\Omega = (steps, giunif, gounif, vounif)$ appears to be the best.

This is in line with the intuition that taking into account a comparatively large number of lower-level operations should improve accuracy. However, such components should contribute significantly to the model in order to avoid noise introduction. It is also interesting to see that including $nargs$ in the cost model does not further improve accuracy, as expected, since nargs is not independent from the four components giunif, gounif, viunif, vounif. In fact, including this component results in a less precise model in both platforms, due to the noise introduced in the model. Also, the cost model step deserves special mention, since it is the simplest one and, at least for the given examples, the error is smaller than we expected and better than more complex cost models not shown in the tables.

The disparity in the accuracy for both platforms can be attributed to a number of reasons, among them the difference in the internal architectures (number of registers, orthogonality in their usage, etc.), which make predicting execution characteristics in Intel processors harder. The weight of some constants can also differ from the calibration programs to the benchmarks due to, e.g., the state of the internal processor pipelines and state of registers. In our experience, the PPC architecture offers a more homogeneous behavior performance-wise.

Overall we believe that the results are encouraging in the sense that our combined framework predicts with an acceptable degree of accuracy the execution times of programs and paves the way for even more accurate analyses by including additional parameters.

6   Applications

The experimental results presented in Section 5 show that the proposed framework can be relevant in practice for estimating platform dependent cost metrics such as execution time. We believe that execution time estimates can be very useful in several contexts. As already mentioned, in certain mobile/pervasive computation scenarios different platforms come into play, with each platform having different capabilities. More concretely, the execution time estimates could be useful for performing resource/granularity control in parallel/distributed computing. This belief is based on previous experimental results, where it appeared from the sensitivity of the results observed in such experiments, that while it is not essential to be absolutely precise in inferring the best time estimates for a query, the number of reductions by itself was too rough a measure and the current time estimation approach could presumably improve on previous results.

One of the good features of our approach is that we can translate platform-independent cost functions (which are the result of the analyzer) into platform-dependent cost functions (using the relationship in expression (9)). A possible application for taking advantage of this feature is mobile code safety and in particular Proof-Carrying Code (PCC), a general approach in which the code supplier augments the program with a certificate (or proof). Consider a scenario where the producer sends a certificate with a platform-independent cost function (i.e., where the cost is expressed in a platform-independent metric) together with a calibration program. The calibration program includes a fixed set of calibration benchmarks. Then, the consumer runs (only once) the calibration program and computes the values for the constants appearing in the cost functions. Using these constants, the consumer can obtain platform-dependent cost functions [8].

Another application of the proposed approach is resource-oriented specialization. The proposed cost models, which include low-level factors for CLP programs, are more refined cost models than previously proposed ones and thus can be used to better guide the specialization process. The inferred cost functions can be used to develop automatic program transformation techniques which take into account the size of the resulting program, its run time and memory usage, and other low-level implementation factors. In particular, they can be used for performing self-tuning specialization in order to compare different specialized version according to their costs [2].

The use of a source-level characterization of the execution profile, which undoubtedly carries some lack of accuracy with it, can be applied not only to different architectures, but also to different compilation / execution schemes. By identifying a rich enough cost model, and using the calibration programs under a given execution model (and architecture), predictions about this execution model / architecture can be made. The advantage lies in that instrumenting the low-level representation used by the execution algorithm (e.g., WAM code & emulator, C code / assembler, or interpreters or virtual machines for other bytecode representations) is not needed: $\overline{K}_\Omega$ should get instantiated to the cost (or an approximation thereof) of every identified *basic* feature in the execution model under study.

7   Conclusions

We have developed a framework which allows estimating execution times of procedures of a program in a given execution platform. The method proposed combines compile-time (static) cost analysis with a one-time profiling of the platform in order to determine the values of certain constants. These constants calibrate a cost model from which time cost functions for a given platform can be computed statically. The approach has been implemented and integrated in the CiaoPP system. To the best of our knowledge, this is the first combined framework for estimating statically and accurately execution time bounds based on static automatic inference of upper and lower bound complexity functions plus experimental adjustment of constants. We have performed an experimental assessment of this implementation for a wide range of different candidate cost models and two execution platforms. The results achieved show that the combined framework predicts the execution times of programs with a reasonable degree of accuracy. We believe this is an encouraging result, since using a one-time profiling for estimating execution times of other, unrelated programs is clearly a challenging goal.

Also, we argue that the work presented in this paper presents an interesting trade-off between accuracy and simplicity of the approach. At the same time, there is clearly room for improving precision by using more refined cost models which take into account additional (lower level) factors. Of course, these models would also be more difficult to handle since on one hand they would require computing more constants and on the other hand they may require taking into account factors which are not observable at source level. This is in any case the subject of possibly interesting future work.

Acknowledgments. This work was funded in part by the IST program of the EU, Future and Emerging Technologies under the IST-15905 *MOBIUS* project, by the Spanish Ministry of Education under the TIN-2005-09207 *MERIT* project, and the Madrid Regional Government under the *PROMESAS* program. Manuel Hermenegildo is also supported by the Prince of Asturias Chair in Information Science and Technology at UNM.

References

1. B. Brassel, M. Hanus, F. Huch, J. Silva, and G. Vidal. Run-time profiling of functional logic programs. In *Proceedings of the International Symposium on Logic-based Program Synthesis and Transformation (LOPSTR'04)*, pages 182–197. Springer LNCS 3573, 2005.
2. S.J. Craig and M. Leuschel. Self-tuning resource aware specialisation for Prolog. In *Proc. of PPDP'05*, pages 23–34. ACM Press, 2005.
3. S. K. Debray. Profiling prolog programs. *Software Practice and Experience*, 18(9):821–839, 1983.
4. S. K. Debray and N. W. Lin. Cost analysis of logic programs. *ACM Transactions on Programming Languages and Systems*, 15(5):826–875, November 1993.
5. S. K. Debray, N.-W. Lin, and M. Hermenegildo. Task Granularity Analysis in Logic Programs. In *Proc. of the 1990 ACM Conf. on Programming Language Design and Implementation*, pages 174–188. ACM Press, June 1990.
6. S. K. Debray, P. López-García, M. Hermenegildo, and N.-W. Lin. Lower Bound Cost Estimation for Logic Programs. In *1997 International Logic Programming Symposium*, pages 291–305. MIT Press, Cambridge, MA, October 1997.
7. Mireille Ducassé. Opium: An extendable trace analyzer for prolog. *J. Log. Program.*, 39(1-3):177–223, 1999.
8. M. Hermenegildo, E. Albert, P. López-García, and G. Puebla. Abstraction Carrying Code and Resource-Awareness. In *Proc. of PPDP'05*. ACM Press, July 2005.
9. M. Hermenegildo, G. Puebla, F. Bueno, and P. López-García. Integrated Program Debugging, Verification, and Optimization Using Abstract Interpretation (and The Ciao System Preprocessor). *Science of Computer Programming*, 58(1–2):115–140, October 2005.
10. Alston S. Householder. Unitary Triangularization of a Nonsymmetric Matrix. *Journal ACM*, 5(4):339–342, October 1958. DOI:10.1145/320941.320947.
11. P. López-García. *Non-failure Analysis and Granularity Control in Parallel Execution of Logic Programs*. PhD thesis, Universidad Politécnica de Madrid (UPM), Facultad Informatica UPM, 28660-Boadilla del Monte, Madrid-Spain, June 2000.
12. P. López-García, M. Hermenegildo, and S. K. Debray. A Methodology for Granularity Based Control of Parallelism in Logic Programs. *J. of Symbolic Computation, Special Issue on Parallel Symbolic Computation*, 22:715–734, 1996.
13. S. A. Jarvis R. G. Morgan. Profiling large-scale lazy functional programs. *Journal of Functional Programing*, 8(3):201–237, May 1998.
14. Patrick M. Sansom and Simon L. Peyton Jones. Formally based profiling for higher-order functional languages. *ACM Transactions on Programming Languages and Systems*, 19(2):334–385, March 1997.
15. D. Wackerly, W. Mendenhall, and R. Scheaffer. *Mathematical Statistics With Applications 5th Edition*. P W S Publishers, 1995.

On Improving the Efficiency and Robustness of Table Storage Mechanisms for Tabled Evaluation

Ricardo Rocha

DCC-FC & LIACC
University of Porto, Portugal
`ricroc@ncc.up.pt`

Abstract. Most of the recent proposals in tabling technology were designed as a means to improve some practical deficiencies of current tabling execution models that reduce their applicability in particular applications. The discussion we address in this paper was also motivated by practical deficiencies we encountered, in particular, on the table storage mechanisms used for tabling support. To improve such mechanisms, we propose two new implementation techniques that make tabling models more efficient when dealing with incomplete tables and more robust when recovering memory from the table space. To validate our proposals, we have implemented them in the YapTab tabling system as an elegant extension of the original design.

1 Introduction

Tabling [1,2] is a technique of resolution that overcomes some limitations of traditional Prolog models in dealing with recursion and redundant sub-computations. As a result, in the past years several alternative tabling models have been proposed [3,4,5,6,7,8] and implemented in systems like XSB, Yap, B-Prolog, ALS-Prolog and Mercury.

More recently, the increasing interest in tabling technology led to further developments and proposals that improve some practical deficiencies of current tabling execution models. In [9], Sagonas and Stuckey proposed a mechanism, named *just enough tabling*, that offers the capability to arbitrarily suspend and resume a tabled evaluation without requiring full re-computation. In [10], Saha and Ramakrishnan proposed an incremental evaluation algorithm for maintaining the freshness of tables that avoids recomputing the full set of answers when the program changes upon addition or deletion of facts/rules. In [11], Rocha *et al.* proposed the ability to support dynamic mixed-strategy evaluation of the two most successful tabling scheduling strategies, batched and local scheduling.

All these recent proposals were designed as a means to improve the performance of particular applications in key aspects of tabled evaluation like recomputation and scheduling. The discussion we address in this work was also motivated by our recent attempt of applying tabling to Inductive Logic Programming (ILP) [12]. ILP applications are very interesting for tabling because they have huge search spaces and do a lot of re-computation. In [13] we showed

M. Hanus (Ed.): PADL 2007, LNCS 4354, pp. 155–169, 2007.

that tabling is indeed a promising approach to minimize re-computation in ILP systems and that one can have impressive gains through tabling. However, we found that current tabling execution models suffer from significant limitations that reduce their applicability in many ILP applications. Analysis showed two major issues with the table storage mechanisms used for tabling support.

A first problem is *incomplete tabling*. Tabling is about storing answers for subgoals so that they can be reused when a repeated call appears. On the other hand, most ILP algorithms are interested in example satisfiability, not in the answers: query evaluation stops as soon as an answer is found. This is usually implemented by *pruning* at the Prolog level. Unfortunately, pruning over tabled computations results in *incomplete tables*: we may have found several answers but not the complete set. Thus, usually, when a repeated call appears we cannot simply trust the answers from an incomplete table because we may lose part of the computation. The simplest approach, and the one that has been implemented in most tabling systems, is to throw away incomplete tables, and restart the evaluation from scratch. In this work, we propose a more aggressive approach where, by default, we keep incomplete tables around. Whenever a call for an incomplete table appears, we first consume the answers from the table. If the table is exhausted, then we will restart the evaluation from the beginning. The main goal of this proposal is to avoid re-computation when the already stored answers are enough to evaluate a repeated call.

A second problem is *memory recovery*. When we use tabling for applications that build very many queries or that store a huge number of answers, we can build arbitrarily many or very large tables, quickly running out of memory space. In general, we will have no choice but to throw away some of the tables (ideally, the least likely to be used next). Tabling systems have not really addressed this problem. At most, they have a set of tabling primitives that the programmer can use to dynamically abolish some of the tables. However, this can be hard to use and very difficult to decide what are the potentially useless tables that should be deleted. In this work, we propose a more suitable approach for large dynamic searches, a memory management strategy based on a *least recently used* algorithm, that dynamically recovers space from the least recently used tables when the system runs out of memory.

Both proposals have been implemented in the YapTab tabling system [14] with minor changes to the original design. Preliminaries results using the April ILP system [15] showed very substantial performance gains and a substantial increase of the size of the problems that can be solved by combining ILP with tabling. Despite the fact that we used ILP as the motivation for this work, our proposals are not restricted to ILP applications and can be generalised and applied to most other applications.

The remainder of the paper is organized as follows. First, we briefly introduce some background concepts and discuss the motivation for our work. Next, we present our proposals and describe the issues involved in providing engine support for integrating them in the YapTab tabling system. We then present some experimental results and outline some conclusions.

2   Background and Motivation

To discuss the motivation for our work, we start by introducing some basic concepts about tabling and ILP and then we address the practical deficiencies encountered when combining them.

2.1   Basic Tabling Definitions

The basic idea behind tabling is straightforward: programs are evaluated by storing answers for current subgoals in a proper data space, called the *table space*. Whenever a repeated call is found, the subgoal's answers are recalled from the table instead of being re-evaluated against the program clauses. The nodes in a tabled evaluation are classified as either: *generator nodes*, corresponding to first calls to tabled subgoals; *consumer nodes*, corresponding to repeated calls to tabled subgoals; or *interior nodes*, corresponding to non-tabled subgoals. Tabling based models have four main types of operations for definite programs:

1. The *tabled subgoal call* operation is a call to a tabled subgoal. It checks if the subgoal is in the table. If so, it allocates a consumer node and starts consuming the available answers. If not, it adds a new entry to the table, and allocates a new generator node.
2. The *new answer* operation checks whether a newly found answer is already in the table, and if not, inserts the answer. Otherwise, the operation fails.
3. The *answer resolution* operation checks whether extra answers are available for a particular consumer node and, if so, consumes the next one. If no unconsumed answers are available, it *suspends* the current computation and schedules a backtracking node to continue the execution.
4. The *completion* operation determines whether a tabled subgoal is *completely evaluated*. A table is said to be *complete* when its set of stored answers represent all the conclusions that can be inferred from the set of facts and rules in the program for the subgoal call associated with the table. Otherwise, it is said to be *incomplete*. A table for a tabled subgoal is thus marked as complete when, during evaluation, it is determined that all possible resolutions have been made and, therefore, no more answers can be found.

We could delay completion until the very end of the execution. Unfortunately, doing so would also mean that we could only recover space for consumers (suspended subgoals) at the very end of the execution. Instead we shall try to achieve *incremental completion* [16] to detect whether a generator node has been fully exploited and, if so, to recover space for all its consumers. Moreover, if we call a repeated subgoal that is already completed, then we can avoid consumer node allocation and perform instead what is called a *completed table optimization* [17]. This optimization allocates a node, similar to an interior node, that will consume the set of found answers executing compiled code directly from the table data structures associated with the completed subgoal.

2.2   Inductive Logic Programming

The fundamental goal of an ILP system is to find a consistent and complete theory (logic program), from a set of examples and prior knowledge, the *background knowledge*, that explains all given positive examples, while being consistent with the given negative examples. Since it is not usually obvious which set of hypotheses should be picked as the theory, an ILP system must traverse the *hypotheses space* searching for a set of hypotheses (clauses) with the desired properties.

Computing the coverage of a hypothesis requires, in general, running positive and negative examples against the clause. For instance, to evaluate if the hypothesis 'theory(X):- a1(X),a2(X,Y).' covers the example theory(p1), the system executes the goal once(a1(p1),a2(p1,Y)). The once/1 predicate is a primitive that prunes over the search space preventing the unnecessary search for further answers. It is defined in Prolog as 'once(Goal):- call(Goal),!.'. Note that the ILP system is only interested in evaluating the coverage of the hypothesis, and not in finding answers for the goal.

Now assume that the previous hypothesis obtains a *good coverage*, that is, the number of positive examples covered by it is high and the number of negative examples is low. Then, it is quite possible that the system will use it to generate more specific hypotheses such as 'theory(X):- a1(X),a2(X,Y),a3(Y).'. If the same example, theory(p1), is then evaluated against this new hypothesis, goal once(a1(p1),a2(p1,Y),a3(Y)), part of the computation will be repeated. For data-sets with a large number of examples, we can do an arbitrarily large amount of re-computation.

2.3   Tabling and Inductive Logic Programming

In previous work, we have already proposed two approaches of using tabling to minimize re-computation in ILP systems [13]. The first approach is simply to table subgoals. This approach requires minimal changes to the ILP system and comes for free if using a Prolog engine with tabling support. A second approach is to table prefixes, that is, replace the conjunction of subgoals in the hypotheses with proper tabled predicates inferred during execution. If we are able to table these conjunction of subgoals, we only need to compute them once. This strategy can be recursively applied as the system generates more specific hypotheses. This idea is similar to the *query packs* technique proposed by Blockeel *et al.* [18].

However, we have found two major problems with the table storage mechanisms currently used for tabling support that reduce their applicability in many ILP applications. One of these problems is memory recovery. To recursively table conjunction of subgoals, we need to store a large number of tables, and thus, we may increase the table memory usage arbitrarily and quickly run out of memory [13]. Therefore, at some point, we need to compromise efficiency and throw away some of the tables in order to recover space. A first approach is to let the programmer dynamically control the deletion of the tables. However, this puts the burden on the ILP designer, and in the worst case may result in removing useful tables. In order to allow useful deletion without compromising efficiency, we propose in this work a more robust approach, a memory management strategy based on a *least recently used* replacement algorithm that dynamically recovers space from the tables when the system runs out of memory.

The other problem is incomplete tabling. Consider again the evaluation of once(a1(p1),a2(p1,Y),a3(Y)) but now with a2/2 declared as tabled. Coverage computation with tabled evaluation works fine when examples are not covered by hypotheses. In such cases, all tabled subgoals in a clause are completed. For instance, when evaluating the goal once(a1(p1),a2(p1,Y),a3(Y)), if the subgoal a3(Y) never succeeds then, by backtracking, a2(p1,Y) will be completely evaluated. On the other hand, tabled evaluation can be a problem when examples are successfully covered by hypotheses. For example, if once(a1(p1),a2(p1,Y),a3(Y)) eventually succeeds, then the once/1 primitive will reclaim space by pruning the goal at hand. However, as a2(p1,Y) may still succeed with other answers for Y, its table entry cannot be marked as complete. Thus, when a repeated call to a2(p1,Y) appears, we cannot simply load answers from its incomplete table, because we may lose part of the computation. A question then arises: how can we make tabling worthwhile in an environment that potentially generates so many incomplete tables?

We first tackled this problem by taking advantage of YapTab's functionality that allows to combine different *scheduling strategies* within the same tabled evaluation [11]. Our results showed that best performance can be achieved when we evaluate some subgoals using *batched scheduling* and others using *local scheduling*. Batched scheduling is the default strategy, it schedules the program clauses in a depth-first manner as does the WAM. This strategy favors forward execution, when a new answer is found the evaluation automatically propagates the answer to solve the goal at hand. Local scheduling is an alternative strategy that tries to *force* completion before returning answers. The key idea is that whenever new answers are found, they are added to the table space, as usual, but execution fails. Answers are only returned when all program clauses for the subgoal at hand were resolved.

At first, local scheduling seems more attractive because it avoids incomplete tabling. When the once/1 primitive prunes the search space, the tables are already completed. On the other hand, if the cost of fully generating the complete set of answers is very expensive, then the ILP system may not always benefit from it. It can happen that, after completing a subgoal, the subgoal always succeeds just by using the initial answers, making it useless to compute beforehand the full set of answers. We believe that it is very difficult to define the best strategy to evaluate each subgoal. The approach we propose in this work can be seen as a compromise between the efficiency of batched scheduling and the effectiveness of local scheduling. We want to favor forward execution in order to quickly succeed with the coverage evaluation of the hypotheses, but we also want to be able to reuse the answers already found in order to avoid re-computation.

We next describe how we extended the YapTab tabling system to be more efficient when dealing with incomplete tables and more robust when recovering memory from the table space.

3   Incomplete Tabling

This section describes how we extended YapTab to support incomplete tabling. The main goal of our proposal is to avoid re-computation when the answers in an incomplete table are enough to evaluate a repeated call. To support that, we thus keep incomplete tables for pruned subgoals. Then, when a repeated call to a pruned subgoal appears, we start by consuming the available answers from its incomplete table, and only if we exhaust all such answers, we restart the evaluation from the beginning. Later, if the subgoal is pruned again, then the same process is repeated until eventually the subgoal is completely evaluated.

3.1   Implementation Details

In YapTab, tables are implemented using *tries* as proposed in [17]. An important data structure in the table space is the *subgoal frame*. For each different tabled subgoal call, a different subgoal frame is used to store information about the subgoal. In particular, part of that information includes a pointer to where answers are stored, the SgFr_answers field, and a flag indicating the state of the subgoal, the SgFr_state field (see Fig. 1 for details).

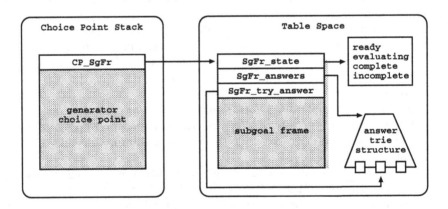

Fig. 1. Generator choice points and subgoal frames in YapTab

During evaluation, a subgoal frame can be in one of the following states: *ready*, i.e., without a corresponding generator in the choice point stack; *evaluating*, i.e., with a generator being evaluated; or *complete*, i.e., with the generator no longer present but with the subgoal fully evaluated. At the engine level, generator nodes are implemented as WAM choice points extended with two extra fields [11]. One of these fields, the CP_SgFr field, points to the associated subgoal frame in the table space.

To support incomplete tabling, we have introduced two minor changes to the subgoal frame data structure. First, a new *incomplete* state, marks the subgoals whose corresponding generators were pruned from the execution stacks. Second, when we are consuming answers from an incomplete table as a result of a repeated call to a previously pruned subgoal, a new SgFr_try_answer field marks the currently loaded answer (similarly to what consumer nodes have).

Handling incomplete tables also required minor changes to the tabled subgoal call operation. Figure 2 shows how we extended the tabled_subgoal_call() instruction to deal with incomplete tables.

```
tabled_subgoal_call(subgoal SG) {
  sg_fr = search_table_space(SG)      // sg_fr is the subgoal frame for SG
  if (SgFr_state(sg_fr) == ready) {
    gen_cp = store_generator_node(sg_fr)
    SgFr_state(sg_fr) = evaluating
    CP_AP(gen_cp) = failure_continuation_instruction()    // second clause
    goto next_instruction()
  } else if (SgFr_state(sg_fr) == evaluating) {
    cons_cp = store_consumer_node(sg_fr)
    goto answer_resolution(cons_cp)              // start consuming answers
  } else if (SgFr_state(sg_fr) == complete) {
    goto SgFr_answers(sg_fr)         // execute compiled code from the trie
  } else if (SgFr_state(sg_fr) == incomplete) {      // new block of code
    gen_cp = store_generator_node(sg_fr)
    SgFr_state(sg_fr) = evaluating
    first = get_first_answer(sg_fr)
    load_answer_from_trie(first)
    SgFr_try_answer(sg_fr) = first      // mark the current loaded answer
    CP_AP(gen_cp) = table_try_answer           // new instruction
    goto continuation_instruction()
  }
}
```

Fig. 2. Pseudo-code for tabled_subgoal_call()

The new block of code that deals with incomplete tables is similar to the block of code that deals with first calls to tabled subgoals (ready state flag). It also stores a generator node, but instead of using the program clauses to evaluate the subgoal call, as usual, it starts by loading the first available answer from the incomplete table. The subgoal's SgFr_try_answer field is made to point to this first answer. A second difference is that the failure continuation pointer of the generator choice point, the CP_AP field, is now updated to a special table_try_answer instruction.

When backtracking occurs, the table_try_answer instruction implements a variant of the answer resolution operation (see section 2.1). Figure 3 shows the pseudo-code for it. Initially, the table_try_answer instruction checks if there are more answers to be consumed, and if so, it loads the next one and updates the SgFr_try_answer field. When this is not the case, all available answers have been already consumed. Thus, we need to restart the computation from the beginning. The program counter is made to point to the first clause corresponding to the subgoal call at hand and the failure continuation pointer of the generator is updated to the second clause. At this point, the evaluation is in the same

```
table_try_answer(generator GEN) {
  sg_fr = CP_SgFr(GEN)
  last = SgFr_try_answer(sg_fr)              // get the last loaded answer
  next = get_next_answer(last)
  if (next) {                                // answers still available
    load_answer_from_trie(next)
    SgFr_try_answer(sg_fr) = next        // update the current loaded answer
    goto continuation_instruction()
  } else {                       // restart the evaluation from the first clause
    load_compiled_code(sg_fr)                    // adjust the program counter
    CP_AP(GEN) = failure_continuation_instruction()        // second clause
    goto next_instruction()
  }
}
```

Fig. 3. Pseudo-code for `table_try_answer()`

computational state as if we had executed a first call to the tabled subgoal call operation. The difference is that the table space for our subgoal already stores some answers.

We should remark that the use of generator nodes to implement the calls to incomplete tables is strictly necessary to keep unchanged all the remaining data structures and algorithms of the tabling engine. Note that, at the engine level, these calls are again the first representation of the subgoal in the execution stacks because the previous representation has been pruned.

3.2   Discussion

Let us consider again the previous ILP example and the evaluation of the goal `once(a1(p1),a2(p1,Y),a3(Y))` with predicate a2/2 declared as tabled. Consider also that, after a long computation for a2(p1,Y), we have found three answers: Y=y1, Y=y2, and Y=y3, and that a3(Y) only succeeds for Y=y3. Primitive `once/1` then prunes the goal at hand and a2(p1,Y) is marked as incomplete. Now assume that, later, the ILP system calls again a2(p1,Y) when evaluating a different goal, for example, `once(a2(p1,Y),a4(Y))`. If a4(Y) succeeds with one of the previously found answers, then no evaluation will be required for subgoal a2(p1,Y). This is the typical case where we can profit from having incomplete tables. The gain in the execution time is proportional to the cost of evaluating the subgoal from the beginning until generating the proper answer.

On the other hand, if a4(Y) does not succeed with any of the previously found answers, then a2(p1,Y) will be reevaluated as a first call. This means that the answers Y=y1, Y=y2 and Y=y3 will be generated again. However, as these answers are repeated, the evaluation will fail and a4(Y) will not be called again for them. The evaluation will fail until a non-repeated answer is eventually found. Thus, the computation time required to evaluate `once(a2(p1,Y),a4(Y))`, either with or without the incomplete table, is then equivalent. Therefore, we may not benefit from having maintained the incomplete table, but we do not pay any cost either.

Our proposal is close to the spirit of the *just enough tabling (JET)* proposal of Sagonas and Stuckey [9]. In a nutshell, the JET proposal offers the capability to arbitrarily suspend and resume a tabled evaluation without requiring any re-computation. The basic idea is that JET copies the execution stacks corresponding to pruned subgoals to an auxiliary area in order to be able to resume them later when a repeated call appears. The authors argue that the cost of JET is linear in the number of choice points which are pruned. However, to the best of our knowledge, no practical implementation of JET was yet been done.

Compared to JET, our approach does not require an auxiliary data space, does not require any complex dependencies to maintain information about pruned subgoals, and does not introduce any overhead in the pruning process. We thus believe that the simplicity of our approach can produce comparable results to JET when applied to real applications like ILP applications.

4   Memory Recovery

This section describes our proposal to handle tables when the system runs out of memory. We propose a memory management strategy that automatically recovers space from the least recently used tables. Note that this proposal is completely orthogonal to the previous one, that is, we can support either or both simultaneously. In what follows, we will thus consider the case where YapTab also includes support for incomplete tabling as described in the previous section.

4.1   Implementation Details

In YapTab, each tabled subgoal call is represented by a different subgoal frame in the table space. Besides this representation, a subgoal can also be represented in the execution stacks. First calls to tabled subgoals or calls to previously pruned subgoals are represented by generator nodes; repeated calls to tabled subgoals are represented by consumer nodes; and calls to completed subgoals are represented by interior nodes that execute compiled code directly from the answer trie structure associated with the completed subgoal. A subgoal is said to be *active* if it is represented in the execution stacks. Otherwise, it is said to be *inactive*. Inactive subgoals are thus only represented in the table space.

A subgoal can also be in one of the following states: ready, evaluating, complete or incomplete. The ready and incomplete states correspond to situations where the subgoal is inactive, while the evaluating state corresponds to a situation where the subgoal is active. The complete state is a special case because it can correspond to both active and inactive situations. In order to be able to distinguish these two situations, we introduced a new state named *complete-active*. We use the complete-active state to mark the completed subgoals that are also active in the execution stacks, while the previous complete state is used to mark the completed subgoals that are only represented in the table space. With this simple extension, we can now use the `SgFr_state` field of the subgoal frames to decide if a subgoal is currently active or inactive.

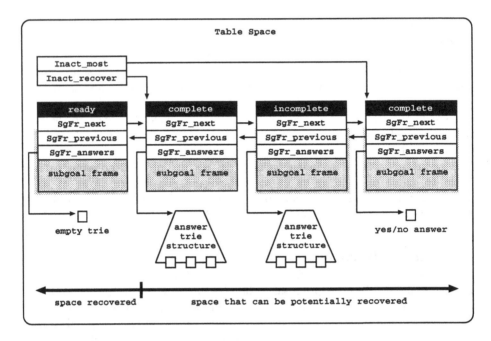

Fig. 4. Inactive subgoals in YapTab

Knowing what subgoals are active or inactive is important when the system runs out of memory. Obviously, active subgoals cannot be removed from the table space because otherwise we may lose part of the computation or produce errors. Therefore, when the system runs out of memory, we should try to recover space from the inactive subgoals. Figure 4 shows how we handle inactive subgoals in YapTab.

Subgoal frames corresponding to inactive subgoals are kept in a double linked list that is accessible by two new global registers. The Inact_most register points to the most recently inactive subgoal frame and the Inact_recover register

```
recover_space(structure data type STR_TYPE) {
  // STR_TYPE is the data type that we failed to allocate space for
  sg_fr = Inact_recover
  do {
    if (sg_fr == NULL)                        // end of list
      return
    if (get_first_answer(sg_fr)) {            // subgoal frame with answers
      free_answer_trie_structure(sg_fr)              // recover space
      SgFr_state(sg_fr) = ready              // reset the frame state
    }
    sg_fr = SgFr_next(sg_fr)
  } while (no_space_available_for(STR_TYPE))
  Inact_recover = sg_fr                       // update recover field
}
```

Fig. 5. Pseudo-code for recover_space()

points to the least recently inactive subgoal frame from where space can be potentially recovered. Two subgoal frame fields, SgFr_next and SgFr_previous, link the list. Space from inactive subgoals is recovered as presented next in Fig. 5.

The recover_space() procedure is called when the system fails to allocate memory space for a specific data type, the STR_TYPE argument. It starts from the subgoal frame pointed by the Inact_recover register and then uses the SgFr_next field to navigate in the list of inactive subgoals until at least a page of memory is recovered. YapTab uses a page-based memory allocation scheme where each page only stores data structures of the same type, and thus, to start using a memory page to allocate a different data structure, we first need to completely deallocate all the previous data structures from the page.

When recovering space, we only consider the subgoals that store at least one answer (completed subgoals with a yes/no answer are kept unchanged) and for these we only recover space from their answer trie structures. Through experimentation we found that, for a large number of applications, the space required by all the other table data structures is insignificant when compared with the space required by the answer trie structures (usually more than 99% of the total table space). Therefore, only sporadically, we are able to recover space from the non-answer related data structures. We thus argue that the potential benefit of recovering space from these structures does not compensate its cost.

During evaluation, an inactive subgoal can be made active again. This occurs when we execute a repeated call to an inactive subgoal. For such cases, we thus need to remove the corresponding subgoal frame from the list. On the other hand, when a subgoal turns inactive, its subgoal frame is inserted in the list as the most recently inactive frame. A subgoal turns inactive when it executes completion, it is pruned or it fails from an interior node that was executing compiled code from the answer trie structure.

```
tabled_subgoal_call(subgoal SG) {
    sg_fr = search_table_space(SG)      // sg_fr is the subgoal frame for SG
    if (SgFr_state(sg_fr) == ready) {
        remove_from_inactive_list(sg_fr)                            // new
        ...
    } else if (SgFr_state(sg_fr) == evaluating) {
        ...
    } else if (SgFr_state(sg_fr) == complete) {
        remove_from_inactive_list(sg_fr)                            // new
        SgFr_state(sg_fr) = complete-active                         // new
        trail(sg_fr)                                               // new
        goto SgFr_answers(sg_fr)      // execute compiled code from the trie
    } else if (SgFr_state(sg_fr) == complete-active) {      // new state
        goto SgFr_answers(sg_fr)      // execute compiled code from the trie
    } else if (SgFr_state(sg_fr) == incomplete) {
        remove_from_inactive_list(sg_fr)                            // new
        ...
    }
}
```

Fig. 6. Extended pseudo-code for tabled_subgoal_call()

This latter case can be complicated because we can have several interior nodes executing compiled code from the same answer trie. Only when the computation fails from the last (oldest) interior node should the corresponding subgoal be made inactive. To correctly implement that we use the trail stack. The call that first executes code for a completed subgoal changes the subgoal's state to complete-active and stores in the trail stack the reference to the subgoal frame. Further calls to the same subgoal (cases where the subgoal's state is now complete-active) are handled as before. Figure 6 shows how we extended the `tabled_subgoal_call()` instruction to support this.

When later backtracking occurs, we use the reference in the trail stack to correctly insert the subgoal in the list of inactive subgoals. This use of the trail stack does not introduce any overhead because the YapTab engine already uses the trail to store information beyond the normal variable trailing (to control dynamic predicates, multi-assignment variables and frozen segments).

4.2 Discussion

With this dynamic recovery mechanism, the programmer can now rely on the effectiveness of the memory management algorithm to completely avoid the problem of deciding what potentially useless tables should be deleted. Note, however, that we can still increase the table memory space arbitrarily. This can happen if the space required by the set of active subgoals exceeds the available memory space and we are not able to recover any space from the set of inactive subgoals. A possible solution for this problem is to store data externally using, for example, a database management system. We are already studying how this can be done, that is, how we can partially move tables to database storage and efficiently load them back to the tabling engine. This idea can also be applied to inactive subgoals and, in particular, we can eventually use our memory management algorithm, not to decide what tables to delete but, to decide what tables to move to the database.

5 Experimental Results

To evaluate the impact of our proposals, we ran the April ILP system [15] with YapTab. The environment for our experiments was a Pentium M 1600MHz processor with 1 GByte of main memory and running the Linux kernel 2.6.11.

We first experimented our support to incomplete tabling and, for that, we used a well-known ILP data-set, the *Mutagenesis* data-set, with two different configurations that we named *Mutagen1* and *Mutagen2*. The main difference between the configurations is that the hypotheses space is searched differently. Table 1 shows the running times, in seconds, for *Mutagen1* and *Mutagen2* using four different approaches to evaluate the predicates in the background knowledge: (i) without tabling; (ii) using local scheduling; (iii) using batched scheduling; and (iv) using batched scheduling with support for incomplete tabling. The running times include the time to run the whole ILP system. During evaluation,

Table 1. Running times, in seconds, with and without support for incomplete tabling

Tabling Mode	*Mutagen1*	*Mutagen2*
Without tabling	> 1 day	> 1 day
Local scheduling	153.9	143.3
Batched scheduling	278.2	137.9
Batched scheduling with incomplete tabling	122.9	117.6

Mutagen1 and *Mutagen2* call respectively 1479 and 1461 different tabled subgoals and, for batched scheduling, both end with 76 incomplete tables.

Our results show that, by combining batched scheduling with incomplete tabling, we can further speed up the execution for these kind of problems. Batched scheduling allows us to favor forward execution and incomplete tabling allows us to avoid re-computation. However, for some subgoals, local scheduling can be better than batched scheduling with incomplete tabling. We can benefit from local scheduling when the cost of fully generating the complete set of answers is less than the cost of evaluating the subgoal several times as a result of several pruning operations. Better results are thus still possible if we use YapTab's flexibility that allows to intermix batched with local scheduling within the same evaluation. However, from the programmer point of view, it is very difficult to define the subgoals to table using one or another strategy. We thus argue that our combination of batched scheduling with incomplete tabling is an excellent (and perhaps the best) compromise between simplicity and good performance.

We next show how we used another well-known ILP data-set, the *Carcinogenesis* data-set, to experiment with our second proposal. From our previous work on tabling conjunctions of subgoals, we selected one of the hypotheses that allocates more memory when computing its coverage against the set of examples in the *Carcinogenesis* data-set. That hypothesis is defined by a prefix that represents the conjunction of 5 tabled subgoals with a total of 20 arguments. Table 2 shows the running times in seconds (or *m.o.* for memory overflow) for computing its coverage with four different table limit sizes: 576, 384, 192 and 128 MBytes (the table limit size is defined statically when the system starts). In parentheses, it shows the number of executions of the `recover_space()` procedure.

Through experimentation, we found that this computation requires a total table space of 576 MBytes if not recovering any space, and a minimum of 160 MBytes if using our recovery mechanism (for Pentium-based architectures, YapTab allocates memory in segments of 32 MBytes). The results obtained with

Table 2. Running times, in seconds, with different table limit sizes

Tabling Mode	576MB	384MB	192MB	128MB
Local scheduling	15.2	15.9(95)	16.9(902)	*m.o.*(893)
Batched scheduling	11.4	12.6(62)	14.1(523)	*m.o.*(557)
Batched scheduling with incomplete tabling	11.1	12.3(91)	13.9(833)	*m.o.*(833)

this particular example show that batched scheduling with incomplete tabling is again the best approach. The results also suggest that our recovery mechanism is quite effective in performing its task (for a memory reduction of 66% in table space it introduces an average overhead between 10% and 20% in the execution time). The impact of our proposal in the execution time depends, in general, on the size of the table space and on the specificity of the application being evaluated, i.e., on the number of times it may call subgoals whose tables were previously deleted by the recovery procedure.

6   Conclusions

In this paper, we have discussed some practical deficiencies of current tabling systems when dealing with incomplete tabling and memory recovery. Incomplete tabling became a problem when, as a result of a pruning operation, the computational state of a tabled subgoal is removed from the execution stacks before being completed. On the other hand, memory recovery became a problem when we use tabling for applications that build very many queries or that store a huge number of answers, quickly running out of memory space.

To support incomplete tabling, we have proposed the ability to avoid re-computation by keeping incomplete tables for pruned subgoals. The typical case where we can profit from having incomplete tables is, thus, when the already stored answers are enough to evaluate repeated calls. When this is not the case, we cannot benefit from it but, on the other hand, we do not pay any cost either. To recover memory, we have proposed a memory management strategy that automatically recovers space from inactive tables when the system runs out of memory. Both proposals have been implemented in the YapTab tabling system with minor changes to the original design. To the best of our knowledge, YapTab is the first tabling system that implements support to incomplete tabling and memory recovery as discussed above. Preliminary results using the April ILP system showed very substantial performance gains and a substantial increase of the size of the problems that can be solved by combining ILP with tabling.

Acknowledgments

We are very thankful to Nuno Fonseca for his support with the April ILP System. This work has been partially supported by Myddas (POSC/EIA/59154/2004) and by funds granted to LIACC through the Programa de Financiamento Pluri-anual, Fundação para a Ciência e Tecnologia and Programa POSC.

References

1. Tamaki, H., Sato, T.: OLDT Resolution with Tabulation. In: International Conference on Logic Programming. Number 225 in LNCS, Springer-Verlag (1986) 84–98
2. Chen, W., Warren, D.S.: Tabled Evaluation with Delaying for General Logic Programs. Journal of the ACM **43** (1996) 20–74

3. Sagonas, K., Swift, T.: An Abstract Machine for Tabled Execution of Fixed-Order Stratified Logic Programs. ACM Transactions on Programming Languages and Systems **20** (1998) 586–634

4. Rocha, R., Silva, F., Santos Costa, V.: YapTab: A Tabling Engine Designed to Support Parallelism. In: Conference on Tabulation in Parsing and Deduction. (2000) 77–87

5. Demoen, B., Sagonas, K.: CHAT: The Copy-Hybrid Approach to Tabling. Future Generation Computer Systems **16** (2000) 809–830

6. Guo, H.F., Gupta, G.: A Simple Scheme for Implementing Tabled Logic Programming Systems Based on Dynamic Reordering of Alternatives. In: International Conference on Logic Programming. Number 2237 in LNCS, Springer-Verlag (2001) 181–196

7. Zhou, N.F., Shen, Y.D., Yuan, L.Y., You, J.H.: Implementation of a Linear Tabling Mechanism. Journal of Functional and Logic Programming **2001** (2001)

8. Somogyi, Z., Sagonas, K.: Tabling in Mercury: Design and Implementation. In: International Symposium on Practical Aspects of Declarative Languages. Number 3819 in LNCS, Springer-Verlag (2006) 150–167

9. Sagonas, K., Stuckey, P.: Just Enough Tabling. In: ACM SIGPLAN International Conference on Principles and Practice of Declarative Programming, ACM (2004) 78–89

10. Saha, D., Ramakrishnan, C.R.: Incremental Evaluation of Tabled Logic Programs. In: International Conference on Logic Programming. Number 3668 in LNCS, Springer-Verlag (2005) 235–249

11. Rocha, R., Silva, F., Santos Costa, V.: Dynamic Mixed-Strategy Evaluation of Tabled Logic Programs. In: International Conference on Logic Programming. Number 3668 in LNCS, Springer-Verlag (2005) 250–264

12. Muggleton, S.: Inductive Logic Programming. In: Conference on Algorithmic Learning Theory, Ohmsma (1990) 43–62

13. Rocha, R., Fonseca, N., Santos Costa, V.: On Applying Tabling to Inductive Logic Programming. In: European Conference on Machine Learning. Number 3720 in LNAI, Springer-Verlag (2005) 707–714

14. Rocha, R., Silva, F., Santos Costa, V.: On applying or-parallelism and tabling to logic programs. Journal of Theory and Practice of Logic Programming **5** (2005) 161–205

15. Fonseca, N.A., Silva, F., Camacho, R.: April - An Inductive Logic Programming System. In: European Conference on Logics in Artificial Intelligence. Number 4160 in LNAI, Springer-Verlag (2006) 481–484

16. Chen, W., Swift, T., Warren, D.S.: Efficient Top-Down Computation of Queries under the Well-Founded Semantics. Journal of Logic Programming **24** (1995) 161–199

17. Ramakrishnan, I.V., Rao, P., Sagonas, K., Swift, T., Warren, D.S.: Efficient Access Mechanisms for Tabled Logic Programs. Journal of Logic Programming **38** (1999) 31–54

18. Blockeel, H., Dehaspe, L., Demoen, B., Janssens, G., Ramon, J., Vandecasteele, H.: Improving the Efficiency of Inductive Logic Programming Through the Use of Query Packs. Journal of Artificial Intelligence Research **16** (2002) 135–166

Compiling Constraint Handling Rules for Efficient Tabled Evaluation*

Beata Sarna-Starosta[1] and C.R. Ramakrishnan[2]

[1] Dept. of Comp. Sci. & Engg., Michigan State University, East Lansing, MI 48824
bss@cse.msu.edu
[2] Dept. of Computer Science, University at Stony Brook, Stony Brook, NY 11794
cram@cs.sunysb.edu

Abstract. Tabled resolution, which alleviates some of Prolog's termination problems, makes it possible to create practical applications from high-level declarative specifications. Constraint Handling Rules (CHR) is an elegant framework for implementing constraint solvers from high-level specifications, and is available in many Prolog systems. However, applications combining the power of these two declarative paradigms have been impractical since traditional CHR implementations interact poorly with tabling. In this paper we present a new (set-based) semantics for CHR which enables efficient integration with tabling. The new semantics coincides with the traditional (multi-set-based) semantics for a large class of CHR programs. We describe CHRd, an implementation based on the new semantics. CHRd uses a distributed constraint store that can be directly represented in tables. Although motivated by tabling, CHRd works well also on non-tabled platforms. We present experimental results which show that, relative to traditional implementations, CHRd performs significantly better on tabled programs, and yet shows comparable results on non-tabled benchmarks.

1 Introduction

Constraint Logic Programming (CLP) is an elegant framework for encoding a wide variety of problems ranging from infinite-state system verification [7,6] to specification and analysis of security policies [3,15]. However, traditional CLP systems are unsuitable for directly evaluating these formulations since they use Prolog-style resolution strategy, and, consequently, inherit Prolog's weak termination (infinite looping) and efficiency (repeated subcomputations) problems. Tabled resolution [28,4] overcomes these problems by memoizing subgoals and computed answers during resolution, and reusing them. Prolog systems enhanced with tabling (e.g. XSB [19]) have supported the construction of efficient tools for program analysis and the verification of finite state systems [5,18] based on high-level logical specifications. Combining constraint processing with tabled resolution will enable evaluating complex applications, such as the analysis of infinite state systems, directly from high-level specifications.

Constraint Handling Rules (CHR) is a rule-based committed-choice language that is particularly well-suited for specifying constraint solvers at a high level [10]. CHR has been implemented in a variety of Prolog systems including SICStus [27], and hProlog [8]. The lack of tabled CLP systems was addressed by the recent port of hProlog's

---

* This research was supported in part by NSF grants CCR-0205376, CNS-0627447 and EIA-0000433, and ONR grant N00014-01-1-0744.

M. Hanus (Ed.): PADL 2007, LNCS 4354, pp. 170–184, 2007.

CHR to XSB [24] (called XSB-CHR in the remainder of this paper). However, as explained below, the data structures and algorithms used in traditional CHR systems are unsuitable for use with tabled resolution, leading to severe performance problems in XSB-CHR. This paper describes CHRd, an alternative implementation of CHR, that in addition to working with traditional Prolog systems, seamlessly integrates CHR with tabling. The efficiency of CHRd permits high-level implementations of applications combining constraint solving and tabling.

Background. Operationally, CHR programs can be viewed as rewriting rules. The constraint store is a multi-set of constraints, and the rules specify how the store should evolve. For instance, consider the CHR program for the partial order constraint:

Example 1
```
reflexivity  @ leq(X,X)                <=> true.
idempotence  @ leq(X,Y) \ leq(X,Y) <=> true.
antisymmetry @ leq(X,Y), leq(Y,X)  <=> X=Y.
transitivity @ leq(X,Y), leq(Y,Z)  ==> leq(X,Z).
```

Above, `reflexivity` and `antisymmetry` are *simplification* rules. The latter states that every pair of constraints in the store that match `leq(X,Y)` and `leq(Y,X)` should be *replaced* by the equality constraint `X=Y` (a built-in constraint solved by unifying X and Y). `transitivity` is a *propagation* rule. It states that for every pair of constraints that match the left hand side, the corresponding right hand side constraint should be *added* to the store. Since the constraint store is a multi-set, it may contain more than one instance of the same constraint. The *simpagation* rule `idempotence` (which combines simplification and propagation) ensures that the store is a set. It states that in the presence of one instance of `leq(X,Y)` (to the left of '\') another instance of `leq(X,Y)` should be replaced by `true` (i.e. removed from the store).

A rule becomes applicable when the store contains the constraints that match its left hand side. CHR evaluation proceeds by repeatedly selecting and firing an applicable rule (i.e. forward chaining) until no rule is applicable (i.e. a fixed point is reached).

Note that a propagation rule remains applicable even after it has been fired. Since the constraint store is a multi-set, re-firing a propagation rule will change the store, adding new copies of constraints. To avoid trivial nontermination due to firing the same propagation rule over and over again, the CHR operational semantics (and, subsequently, its implementations) maintain *propagation history*, a record of all instances of propagation rules that have been fired so far. A rule is applicable only if its instance is not in the propagation history.

Traditional CHR and Tabling. The idea of tabling is to record subgoals (calls) and their provable instances (answers) so that the results of a computation done in one context can be re-used in another. When tabling is integrated with constraint processing, we need to associate a constraint store with each call and answer to properly record the context of a computation. This leads to several efficiency problems. First, the CHR constraint store as well as its propagation history needs to be copied in and out of tables; traditional CHR representation of constraints (with their cyclic terms) are not well-suited for storage in tables. Second, as shown in [24], storing the propagation history imposes a heavy space burden, but not storing it leads to very high time overheads for re-propagating the constraints when they are retrieved from tables. Thus a port of a traditional CHR implementation to a tabled environment (represented by XSB-CHR) imposes significant performance penalties on tabled applications.

Our Solution. We combine CHR evaluation and tabling by taking a fundamentally different approach to CHR. We give CHR a set-based semantics that addresses the trivial nontermination problem *without the use of propagation history*. The new semantics is formulated so as to coincide with CHR's well-accepted semantics [9] for a large class of programs (see Section 3). In our implementation, called CHRd, we consider a syntactically restricted class called direct-indexed CHR, where all constraint terms in every rule head are connected by common variables. This class covers a large number of CHR-based constraint solvers. The restriction permits the constraint store to be represented in a distributed fashion, as a network of constraints on the individual variables (see Section 4). The distributed store and the absence of propagation history enables direct representation of constraint stores in tables, significantly reducing the time taken to switch between constraint stores in tabled evaluation. Our implementation has been integrated into XSB v3.0.1, and the latest version can be obtained from XSB's CVS repository at `http://xsb.sourceforge.net`.

CHRd enables us to efficiently evaluate applications that combine tabled evaluation and constraint processing, and to scale up to problem sizes of practical importance. A case in point is an application for the analysis of concurrent object-oriented systems based on a high-level formulation in terms of CHR rules and tabled logic programs [21]. The relatively good performance of CHRd is crucial to the success of this application. Moreover, CHRd itself is independent of tabling; its performance is comparable to that of existing CHR implementations on non-tabled platforms[1]. A detailed description of the experimental results appears in Section 5.

It should also be noted that *ground CHR*, a class that is of significant interest to the CHR community, is not direct-indexed. Nevertheless, ground CHR programs can be readily converted into programs that can be evaluated by CHRd (Section 4). Moreover, many of the recently developed CHR optimizations (e.g. selection of indexing structures) are valid for CHRd. We discuss the relationship between this paper and previous work on CHR and its implementations in Section 6.

2   Preliminaries

We use standard notions of variables, terms and substitutions [16]. We use t to refer to terms in general, c for *constraint* terms which have a constraint symbol as root, and b for built-in constraint terms which have a built-in constraint symbol as root. We use $vars(t)$ to refer to the set of variables in the term t. We write $\uplus$ to represent disjoint union, and $++$ to denote concatenation of ordered sequences. Sets and multi-sets are occasionally considered as sequences with non-deterministically chosen order of elements. Substitutions are denoted by θ, and a term t under θ is written as $t\theta$. We use upper-case letters such as G, S, etc. to denote collections (sets, multi-sets or sequences) and lower-case letters for elements of these collections.

CHR Syntax. A CHR program is a finite set of rules that specify how *user-defined* constraints are solved based on the host language's *built-in* constraints (e.g. Prolog predicates). CHR rules are of the form:

---

[1] The CHRd system for other platforms including hProlog and SWI-Prolog is available at `http://www.cse.msu.edu/~bss/chrd`.

$$label @ Head \left\{ \begin{matrix} \text{<=>} \\ \text{==>} \end{matrix} \right\} Guard \mid Body$$

Simpagation rules are the most general. They are of the form $H_1 \setminus H_2$ <=> $G \mid B$ where H_1 and H_2 are sequences of user-defined constraint terms (the *heads* of the rule), G (the *guard*) is a sequence of built-in constraints and B (the *body*) is a sequence of built-in and user-defined constraint terms. A rule specifies that when constraints in the store match H_1 and H_2 and the guard G holds, the constraints that match H_2 can be *replaced* by the corresponding constraints in B. The literal `true` represents an empty sequence of constraint terms. The guard part, $G \mid$, may be omitted when G is empty.

A simplification rule, which has the form H_2 <=> $G \mid B$ can be represented by a simpagation rule `true` $\setminus H_2$ <=> $G \mid B$. Similarly, a propagation rule, which has the form H_1 ==> $G \mid B$, can be represented by a simpagation rule $H_1 \setminus$ `true` <=> $G \mid B$.

CHR Semantics. CHR has a well-defined declarative as well as operational semantics [10,1]. The declarative interpretation of a CHR program P is given by the set of universally quantified formulas corresponding to the CHR rules, and an underlying consistent constraint theory CT. The constraint theory defines the meaning of host language constraints, the equality constraint '$=$', and the boolean atoms *true* and *false*.

The original operational semantics [1] is given in terms of a non-deterministic transition system. The evaluation of a program P is a path through the transition system. The transitions are made when a constraint is added from the goal to the store, or by firing any applicable program rule. The refined semantics ω_r [9] defines a more deterministic transition system, specifying, among others, the order in which rules are tried. Most CHR implementations are based on ω_r.

3   The Set-Based Operational Semantics

Our set-based operational semantics, called ω_{set}, is given in terms of a transition relation. The formulation of ω_{set} closely follows that of the refined operational semantics ω_r [9]. A state in the system is represented by a triple $\langle E, C_U, C_B \rangle_{\mathcal{V}, P}$ where E, called the *execution stack*, is an ordered sequence of constraint activation events; C_U, the user-defined constraint store, is a set of user-defined constraints, and C_B, the built-in constraint store, is a conjunction of built-in constraints; $\mathcal{V}$ is a sequence of variables; and P is the given CHR program. We omit either one or both of the subscripts $\mathcal{V}, P$ whenever clear from the context. In contrast, states in ω_r are quadruples $\langle E, C_U, C_B, \mathcal{T} \rangle_{\mathcal{V}, P}$ where $\mathcal{T}$ is the propagation history and C_U, the user-defined store, is a multi-set.

As in the refined operational semantics ω_r, different occurrences of constraint terms with the same symbol in the heads of rules are marked with an *occurrence* number corresponding to the order in which they appear in the CHR program (starting from 1). This numbering indicates the order in which the rules are tried, thus reducing non-determinism of program evaluation. Three kinds of activation events can appear in the execution stack:

- Inactive constraint: c is a user-defined or built-in constraint term;
- Active constraint: $c : j$ where c is a user-defined constraint term and j is a number, meaning that this term can match only with the j-th occurrence of the constraint symbol in the program; and

– Conditional activation: $(H_1 \backslash H_2), G \triangleright B$ where H_1 and H_2 are sets of user-defined constraint terms, G is a set of built-in constraint terms, and B is a sequence of user-defined and built-in constraint terms.

A CHR program is evaluated by forward chaining, and the evaluation stack is used to control this computation. The event at the top of the execution stack is the one *currently scheduled* for evaluation. The first two events above are also in ω_r; the conditional activation event is unique to ω_{set}[2]. An inactive constraint (the first event) corresponds to constraints that we have not yet begun processing; an active constraint corresponds to one that is being processed. The conditional activation event marks constraints that we will begin processing only when the conditions hold.

The initial state of the system is $\langle E, \emptyset, true \rangle_{V,P}$ where E is the sequence of constraints posed to the system, V is the set of variables in E, P is the CHR program. A successful terminating state of the system is of the form $\langle \top, C_U, C_B \rangle$, where $\top$ is an empty execution stack and $C_B \neq false$. A failed state is one where $C_B = false$. The *logical* reading of a state $\langle E, C_U, C_B \rangle_{V,P}$ is $\exists \bar{x}\ E \wedge C_U \wedge C_B$ where E and C_U denote conjunctions of their respective contents and $\bar{x}$ is the set of variables in the state that are not in V.

Note that a rule that was not applicable when a constraint was initially activated may become applicable when variables in that constraint are bound. We determine which constraints need to be reprocessed using the *wakeup* function defined below. We say that a built-in constraint b *affects* a user-defined constraint c in store C_U (denoted by $c \in affects(b, C_U)$) if the evaluation of b adds bindings to any variable in c. A variable x is *fixed* in the built-in store C_B (denoted by $x \in fixed(C_B)$) if there is only one value for x that makes C_B true. A constraint c in C_U is *fixed* in C_B (denoted by $c \in fixed(C_B, C_U)$) if $vars(c) \subseteq fixed(C_B)$. We need to reprocess the set of all constraints in C_U that are affected by b but are not fixed by C_B. Since these constraints have been activated before, we define the wakeup function to directly generate active constraints. Formally, $wakeup(b, C_U, C_B) = \{c{:}1\ |\ c \in affects(b, C_U) \wedge c \notin fixed(C_U, C_B)\}$.

3.1   Derivation Rules for ω_{set}

Derivations of ω_{set} are given by the relation $\mapsto_{set}$ which defines transitions of the form $\sigma_{src} \mapsto_{set} \sigma_{dst}$ according to the following rules. An example ω_{set} derivation for the leq program from Example 1 is shown in Fig. 1. We illustrate application of rules of $\mapsto_{set}$ with appropriate transitions in this derivation.

Activate: Let $\sigma_{src} = \langle [c|E], C_U, C_B \rangle$ and $c \notin C_U$. That is, c is an inactive user-defined constraint that is not already in the store. Then c is added to the CHR store and annotated to match its first occurrence in P. That is, $\sigma_{dst} = \langle [c{:}1|E], \{c\} \cup C_U, C_B \rangle$.

For example, the **Activate** transition in Fig. 1, lines (1–2), sets the currently scheduled constraint leq(A, B) to match the first occurrence of leq in the program, and adds it to the constraint store.

Default: If no other transition can be fired in a state $\sigma_{src} = \langle [c{:}j|E], C_U, C_B \rangle$, then the currently scheduled constraint $c{:}j$ is assigned the next occurrence number. That is, $\sigma_{dst} = \langle [c{:}j{+}1|E], C_U, C_B \rangle$.

---

[2] It should be noted that while formal definition of ω_r does not have conditional activation, most CHR *implementations* use this notion implicitly [12,22].

$$\langle [\texttt{leq}(A,B), \texttt{leq}(B,C), \texttt{leq}(A,C), \texttt{leq}(C,A)], \emptyset, true\rangle \tag{1}$$

$$\text{Activate} \mapsto_{set} \langle [\texttt{leq}(A,B):1, \texttt{leq}(B,C), \texttt{leq}(A,C), \texttt{leq}(C,A)], \{\texttt{leq}(A,B)\}, true\rangle \tag{2}$$

$$7*\text{Default} \mapsto_{set} \langle [\texttt{leq}(A,B):8, \texttt{leq}(B,C), \texttt{leq}(A,C), \texttt{leq}(C,A)], \{\texttt{leq}(A,B)\}, true\rangle \tag{3}$$

$$\text{Drop}^> \mapsto_{set} \langle [\texttt{leq}(B,C), \texttt{leq}(A,C), \texttt{leq}(C,A)], \{\texttt{leq}(A,B)\}, true\rangle \tag{4}$$

$$\begin{array}{c}\text{Activate}\\6*\text{Default}\end{array} \mapsto_{set} \langle [\texttt{leq}(B,C):7, \texttt{leq}(A,C), \texttt{leq}(C,A)], \{\texttt{leq}(A,B), \texttt{leq}(B,C)\}, true\rangle \tag{5}$$

$$\text{PropMatch} \mapsto_{set} \langle [(\texttt{leq}(A,B), \texttt{leq}(B,C)\backslash\emptyset), true \triangleright \texttt{leq}(A,C), \texttt{leq}(B,C):8,$$
$$\texttt{leq}(A,C), \texttt{leq}(C,A)], \{\texttt{leq}(A,B), \texttt{leq}(B,C)\}, true\rangle \tag{6}$$

$$\text{PropFire} \mapsto_{set} \langle [\texttt{leq}(A,C), \texttt{leq}(B,C):8, \texttt{leq}(A,C), \texttt{leq}(C,A)],$$
$$\{\texttt{leq}(A,B), \texttt{leq}(B,C)\}, true\rangle \tag{7}$$

$$\begin{array}{c}\text{Activate}\\7*\text{Default}\\\text{Drop}^>\end{array} \mapsto_{set} \langle [\texttt{leq}(B,C):8, \texttt{leq}(A,C), \texttt{leq}(C,A)],$$
$$\{\texttt{leq}(A,B), \texttt{leq}(B,C), \texttt{leq}(A,C)\}, true\rangle \tag{8}$$

$$\text{Drop}^> \mapsto_{set} \langle [\texttt{leq}(A,C), \texttt{leq}(C,A)], \{\texttt{leq}(A,B), \texttt{leq}(B,C), \texttt{leq}(A,C)\}, true\rangle \tag{9}$$

$$\text{Drop}^< \mapsto_{set} \langle [\texttt{leq}(C,A)], \{\texttt{leq}(A,B), \texttt{leq}(B,C), \texttt{leq}(A,C)\}, true\rangle \tag{10}$$

$$\begin{array}{c}\text{Activate}\\3*\text{Default}\end{array} \mapsto_{set} \langle [\texttt{leq}(C,A):4], \{\texttt{leq}(A,B), \texttt{leq}(B,C), \texttt{leq}(A,C)\}, true\rangle \tag{11}$$

$$\text{Simplify} \mapsto_{set} \langle [C = A], \{\texttt{leq}(A,B), \texttt{leq}(B,C)\}, true\rangle \tag{12}$$

$$\text{Solve} \mapsto_{set} \langle [\texttt{leq}(A,B):1, \texttt{leq}(B,C):1], \{\texttt{leq}(A,B), \texttt{leq}(B,C)\}, C = A\rangle \tag{13}$$

$$\begin{array}{c}3*\text{Default}\\\text{Simplify}\end{array} \mapsto_{set} \langle [C = B, \texttt{leq}(B,C):1], \{\texttt{leq}(A,B)\}, C = A\rangle \tag{14}$$

$$\text{Solve} \mapsto_{set} \langle [\texttt{leq}(A,B):1, \texttt{leq}(B,C):1], \{\texttt{leq}(A,B)\}, C = A \wedge C = B\rangle \tag{15}$$

$$\text{Simplify} \mapsto_{set} \langle [\texttt{leq}(B,C):1], \emptyset, C = A \wedge C = B\rangle \tag{16}$$

$$\begin{array}{c}7*\text{Default}\\\text{Drop}^>\end{array} \mapsto_{set} \langle [\,], \emptyset, C = A \wedge C = B\rangle \tag{17}$$

Fig. 1. Derivation for the `leq` program under ω_{set}

For example, each of the seven **Default** transitions in Fig. 1, lines (2–3), increments the occurrence index j of the currently scheduled constraint $\texttt{leq}(A,B):j$ until the occurrence number is 8. Since there are only seven occurrences of `leq` in the program, this enables the **Drop**$^>$ rule.

Drop$^>$: Let $\sigma_{src} = \langle [c:j|E], C_U, C_B\rangle$ where c does not have a j-th occurrence in P (i.e., all occurrences of c have been tried with the **Default** rule; see below). Then $c:j$ is popped from the execution stack. That is, $\sigma_{dst} = \langle E, C_U, C_B\rangle$.

For example, the **Drop$^>$** transition in Fig. 1, lines (3–4), pops $\texttt{leq}(A,B):8$ from the execution stack as there are only seven occurrences of `leq` in the program.

PropMatch: Let $\sigma_{src} = \langle [c:j|E], C_U, C_B\rangle$, the program P contain rule $R = c' : j, H_1'\backslash H_2' \mathrel{<=>} G \mid B$. Also let θ be a substitution s.t. $c'\theta = c$, $H_1'\theta$, $H_2'\theta$ and $\{c'\theta\}$ are all mutually disjoint subsets of C_U, and $CT \models C_B \to \exists \bar{x}(G\theta)$ where $\bar{x}$ are variables that occur in G but not in C_B. That is, there is a substitution under which the constraint store matches the heads of rule R and satisfies its guard. Then the currently scheduled constraint is assigned the next occurrence number. Moreover, *all* matching substitutions are computed iteratively, and the body constraints of R under these substitutions are pushed onto the stack. Note, however, that before a body constraint thus pushed on the stack is taken up for evaluation, some of the constraints used in the match may be removed from the store. Hence we create *conditional activations* for the body constraints. Formally, let $\{\theta_1, \dots, \theta_n\}$ be the set of all most general substitutions such that $c'\theta_i = c$, $H_1'\theta_i$, $H_2'\theta_i$ and $\{c'\theta_i\}$ are all mutually disjoint subsets of C_U, and $CT \models C_B \rightarrow \exists \bar{x}(G\theta_i)$. Let $\Gamma_i = (H_1'\theta_i \backslash H_2'\theta_i), G\theta_i \triangleright B\theta_i$. Then, $\sigma_{dst} = \langle [\Gamma_1, \ldots, \Gamma_n] \mathbin{+\!\!+} [c\!:\!j\!+\!1|E], C_U, C_B \rangle$.

For example, the **PropMatch** transition in Fig. 1, lines (5–6), matches the stored constraint $\texttt{leq(A,B)}$ and the currently scheduled constraint $\texttt{leq(B,C)}\!:\!7$ with the head of the $\texttt{transitivity}$ rule in the program. The occurrence index of the currently scheduled constraint is incremented by 1, and the corresponding body constraint $\texttt{leq(A,C)}$, annotated with the matched head constraints, is pushed onto the execution stack.

PropFire: Let $\sigma_{src} = \langle [(H_1 \backslash H_2), G \triangleright B|E], H_1 \uplus H_2 \uplus C_U, C_B \rangle$, such that $CT \models C_B \rightarrow \exists \bar{x}(G)$ where $\bar{x}$ are variables that occur in G but not in C_B. That is, a conditional activation event is on top of the stack such that the constraints in $H_1 \uplus H_2$ exist in the user-defined store, and the guard G is satisfied by the built-in store. Then the constraints in H_2 are removed from the user-defined store, and all constraints in B are pushed onto the evaluation stack. Formally, $\sigma_{dst} = \langle B \mathbin{+\!\!+} E, H_1 \uplus C_U, C_B \rangle$.

For example, the **PropFire** transition in Fig. 1, lines (6–7), verifies that the constraints $\texttt{leq(A,B)}$ and $\texttt{leq(B,C)}$, which matched the head of the $\texttt{transitivity}$ rule and caused pushing $\texttt{leq(A,C)}$ onto the execution stack, are present in the constraint store C_U, and schedules $\texttt{leq(A,C)}$ for evaluation.

PropDrop: Let $\sigma_{src} = \langle [(H_1 \backslash H_2), G \triangleright B|E], C_U, C_B \rangle$ such that either $(H_1 \uplus H_2) \not\subseteq C_U$ or $CT \not\models C_B \rightarrow \exists \bar{x}(G)$ where $\bar{x}$ are variables that occur in G but not in C_B. That is, a conditional activation event is on top of the stack, and its condition is not satisfied. Then the currently scheduled event is popped from the stack: $\sigma_{dst} = \langle E, C_U, C_B \rangle$.

Drop$^<$: Let $\sigma_{src} = \langle [c|E], C_U, C_B \rangle$ and $c \in C_U$. That is, c is an inactive constraint that is already in the store. Then c is popped from the execution stack: $\sigma_{dst} = \langle E, C_U, C_B \rangle$.

For example, the **Drop$^<$** transition in lines (9–10) of Fig. 1 pops $\texttt{leq(A,C)}$ from the execution stack since it is already in the constraint store.

Simplify: Let $\sigma_{src} = \langle [c\!:\!j|E], \{c\} \uplus H_1 \uplus H_2 \uplus C_U, C_B \rangle$ and the program P contain a matching rule R. I.e., $R = H_1'\backslash c' : j, H_2' <\!=\!> G \,|\, B$ and there is a substitution θ s.t. $H_1'\theta = H_1$, $H_2'\theta = H_2$, $c'\theta = c$, and $CT \models C_B \rightarrow \exists \bar{x}(G\theta)$ where $\bar{x}$ are variables that occur in G but not in C_B. Then $c\!:\!j$ is popped from the execution stack, all constraints matching H_2' are removed from the store, and R's body constraints under the substitution θ are pushed onto the stack. Formally, $\sigma_{dst} = \langle B\theta \mathbin{+\!\!+} E, H_1 \uplus C_U, C_B \rangle$

For example, the **Simplify** transition in Fig. 1 lines (11–12), matches the active constraint with $4th$ occurrence of $\texttt{leq}$ (i.e. the $\texttt{antisymmetry}$ rule), removes $\texttt{leq(A,C)}$, and adds the rule body $\texttt{C = A}$ to the stack.

Solve: Let $\sigma_{src} = \langle [b|E], C_U, C_B \rangle$ and b be a built-in constraint. Then b is added to the built-in store and all constraints affected by b but not fixed by C_B are pushed onto the execution stack. Formally, $\sigma_{dst} = \langle wakeup(b, C_U, C_B) \mathbin{+\!\!+} E, C_U, b \wedge C_B \rangle$.

For example, the **Solve** transition in Fig. 1, lines (14–15), processes the scheduled constraint $\texttt{C = B}$, by first adding $\texttt{C = B}$ to the built-in store. The affected constraint $\texttt{leq(A,B)}$ is re-activated, and made the new scheduled constraint.

The transitions **PropMatch**, **PropFire** and **PropDrop** directly correspond to the way constraint propagation is implemented. The universal search eliminates the problem of trivial nontermination due to repeated firing of a propagation rule for the same active constraint. Note that the propagation history used in ω_r serves to avoid the non-termination problem. In ω_{set}, **PropFire** performs actual propagation for the given matching to a propagation rule's head constraints, provided that matching conditions still hold. If the matching conditions do not hold, **PropDrop** prevents firing the rule's body constraints. The **Drop**$^<$transition ensures that the constraint store is a set, and the same constraint is not activated over and over again.

3.2 Properties of ω_{set}

It is easy to show that ω_{set} is sound with respect to CHR's declarative semantics:

Theorem 1 (Soundness). *Let P be a CHR program, CT be the consistent theory underlying the built-in constraints in P, G be a goal, $\langle G, \emptyset, true \rangle \mapsto^*_{set} \langle E, C_U, C_B \rangle$ be a derivation, and C be the logical reading of the final state. Then $P, CT \models C \leftrightarrow G$.*

This theorem is established by induction on the length of a derivation.

Relationship between ω_{set} and ω_r.   Since ω_{set} treats the constraint store as a set, programs for which ω_r places multiple occurrences of the same constraint in its store will have a different behavior under ω_{set} compared to ω_r. However, there are CHR programs for which the constraint store, even under ω_r, turns out to be a set. We call such programs set-CHR programs. Clearly, it is useful to compare the two semantics only for set-CHR programs.

In general, ω_{set} is not equivalent to ω_r. For instance, consider the evaluation of the CHR program in Fig. 2 in ω_{set} for the goal p(A, B). Starting from the empty constraint store, activation of p(A, B) will lead to store $\{p(A, B)\}$ (for brevity, we combine the user-defined and built-in stores in this example).

```
r1 @ p(X, Y) ==> q(X, Y).
r2 @ q(X, X) <=> X = a.
r3 @ q(X, Y) <=> X = Y.
```

Fig. 2. CHR program with different fixed points in ω_r and ω_{set}

Firing rule r1 takes us to $\{p(A, B), q(A, B)\}$. Note that the simplification rule r2 is not applicable in this store, but r3 is, leading to the store $\{p(A, B), A = B\}$. Since variables A and B have new bindings in the store, the constraint $p(A, B)$ will be woken up by the **Solve** transition. Rule r1 will be fired again, leading to the store $\{p(A, B), q(A, B), A = B\}$. Rule r2 is applicable in this store, yielding $\{p(a, a)\}$. The evaluation terminates after one more round of **Solve** and firing of r1 and r2.

The evaluation in ω_r leads to a different derivation. In ω_r, each constraint is given an identifier to distinguish between different occurrences of the same constraint in the multi-set store. Propagation history is maintained in terms of the identifiers of matching constraints. When the variables in a constraint get bound, the constraint's identifier is not changed. This means that if a propagation rule was fired once for a set of matching constraints, it will not be fired again even when the variables in its matching constraints are bound further. Thus evaluation of $p(A, B)$ in ω_r for the above example will proceed as in ω_{set} until we reach the store $\{p(A, B), A = B\}$. **Solve** will wake up $p(A, B)$, but rule r1 will not be applicable since it was fired before for the same constraint. Hence, ω_r terminates with the store $\{p(A, B), A = B\}$!

It appears that the state with which ω_r terminates is not a fixed point, and the propagation history makes ω_r terminate the fixed point computation early. For instance, the evaluation of $p(A, B)$ terminates with a store equivalent to $p(A, A)$. But evaluation of $p(A, A)$ will terminate with a different store: $p(a, a)$! In contrast, ω_{set}'s termination condition (presence of a constraint in the store) distinguishes between a constraint term under different substitutions, and hence does not abandon the fixed point computation early. In general, there are set-CHR programs and goals that terminate with ω_r but not with ω_{set} due to this difference in identifying fixed points.

Datalog-CHR is a class of CHR programs such that (i) there are no function symbols of arity ≥ 1, and (ii) every variable in a rule occurs on the rule's left hand side. For instance, the program in Fig. 2 is a Datalog-CHR program. For programs in this class, evaluation using ω_{set} will terminate whenever ω_r terminates.

4   Compiling CHR with Distributed Constraint Store

Direct-Indexed CHR. We now define a subclass of CHR programs for which we can use a simple and efficient constraint store representation. Note that in ω_{set} **Simplify** and **PropMatch** select a matching substitution in order to determine whether the rule is applicable for a given active constraint. This operation significantly affects the efficiency of a CHR implementation, and a considerable amount of work has gone into devising index structures to optimize it [13,23]. The matching procedure has two distinct parts: selecting from the store constraints that match the rule's head, and checking whether the guard is satisfiable under the matching substitution. The class of direct-indexed CHR programs, defined below, has a structure that simplifies the first part.

Each user-defined constraint in a direct-indexed program has a *mode* declaration that specifies the set of possible instances of the constraint that may appear in the store. Each argument of a constraint may have one of three modes: "v" if that argument remains free in any instance of the constraint in the store, "g" if that argument is a ground term all instances, and "?" if that argument is a variable or a constant in all instances[3].

Given a constraint term c, we use $avars(c)$ to denote the set of variables that appear at positions with mode "v". We assume that the mode declarations are consistent with the use of constraints in the rules and queries; and that all user-defined constraints have at least one position with mode "v".

The *matching graph* for a (multi-)set of constraints is a graph in which there is a vertex representing each constraint in the set, and there is an edge between every pair of constraints that share a "v"-moded variable. Formally,

Definition 1. *The matching graph of a set C of user-defined and built-in constraints is a labeled undirected graph $G = (V, E)$ where $V = C$, and E is the smallest set such that $\forall c_1, c_2 \in V, avars(c_1) \cap avars(c_2) \neq \emptyset \rightarrow (c_1, c_2, l) \in E$ where $l = avars(c_1) \cap avars(c_2)$.*

We can use the matching graph for a head of a CHR rule to drive the matching process. Given the vertex in the graph that matches the active constraint, we first can check whether its neighbors match any constraints in the store. Since a neighbor constraint shares unbound variables with the active constraint, we can index into the constraint store using this information, thereby speeding up matching. When the neighbors themselves are matched, we can traverse the graph further. Clearly, this process will not apply when there is a subset of head constraints that do not share variables with the remaining constraints in the head. The direct-indexed CHR is defined to disallow this condition. Formally:

---

[3] Similar declarations have been used in other CHR systems [23,13].

Definition 2. *A rule R in a CHR program is said to be direct-indexed if the matching graph for its head constraints is connected. A CHR program is direct-indexed if all its rules are direct-indexed. A CHR goal is direct-indexed if its matching graph is connected. A CHR derivation is direct-indexed if it evaluates a direct-indexed goal over a direct-indexed program.*

All valid CHRd derivations are direct-indexed. Many CHR specifications, e.g., `leq` from Example 1, are naturally direct-indexed, and all CHR specifications can be trivially translated to direct-indexed CHR programs. We describe the issues surrounding such a translation at the end of this section.

The Distributed Constraint Store Representation. Following other CHR implementations, we use attributed variables [11] to represent constraints. Attributed variables are associated with mutable data, and an user-defined unification handler is invoked whenever an attributed variable is unified. In our implementation, a variable's attribute represents the set of all the constraints the variable participates in, that is, the variable's local constraint store. The attribute is encapsulated in a *constraint attribute term (CAT)*. The CAT is different from a *suspension term*, which in other Prolog implementations of CHR represents a single stored constraint. The CAT of a variable is a vector whose size is determined at compile time based on the number and arity of the user-defined constraint symbols. For instance, if `a/2` and `b/1` are the only two user-defined constraint symbols, and `a(X,Y)` is the lone constraint in the store, then `X`'s CAT will be `v([attr(Y)],[],[])`, and `Y`'s CAT will be `v([],[attr(X)],[])`.

The constraint store is a collection of constraint variables and their CATs. It should be noted that, although each argument of a CAT is represented as a list, it is manipulated as though it is a set. When two constrained variables are unified, their CATs will be merged. Again, we treat the arguments of the CATs as sets and compute their pair-wise union. When a variable changes due to unification, all constraints in its CAT are considered to be in the *wakeup* set, and rules involving the constraints are re-fired.

The CHRd Compiler. Our compiler generates the code that faithfully implements the semantics ω_{set}, following the well-developed CHR-to-Prolog compilation schema [14]. In its current version, the compiler supports simple variants of the join-order, continuation, and late storage optimizations, standard in most of the traditional CHR systems.

Matching. CHRd's representation of the constraint store helps in quickly checking whether a matching constraint exists in the store. For instance, to select constraints of the form `a(U,Y)` for a particular variable `Y`, we need to simply inspect the *second* argument of `Y`'s CAT. This structure builds a single-level index on all arguments of a constraint. Although it is possible to build nested index structures within each argument of the CAT, this is not done in the current implementation of our system.

During an application of a propagation rule, first the **PropMatch** transition retrieves all constraints of a desired form (by accessing appropriate arguments in the CATs of the constrained variables) into a temporary data structure. After all matchings for therule's head have been collected, the **PropFire** transition evaluates each matching in turn against the corresponding substitution of the rule's guard and, when the guard is satisfied, fires the rule's body constraints under the same substitution.

```
gcd(0) <=> true.              :- mode gcd(v,g).
gcd(N) \ gcd(M) <=>           gcd(X,0) <=> true.
   N=<M | L is M-N, gcd(L).   gcd(X,N) \ gcd(X,M) <=>
                                 N=<M | L is M-N, gcd(X,L).
          (a)                              (b)
```

Fig. 3. (a) A ground CHR program; and (b) its translation into direct-indexed CHR

Evaluation of Ground CHR Programs. Consider the CHR program for evaluating the greatest common divisor of a set of integers given in Figure 3(a). When we pose two ground constraints, say gcd(12), and gcd(8), the program terminates with gcd(4) as the lone constraint in the store. The program is not direct-indexed since the matching graph for its second rule has two vertices and no edges (i.e. no shared variables).

Such programs can be trivially translated to direct-indexed CHR by adding an extra variable to each constraint. The direct-indexed CHR program equivalent to that in Figure 3(a) is given in Figure 3(b). The extra variable can be thought of as representing the constraint store itself. One salient point of the translation is that we now have a handle on a constraint store, and we can simultaneously create and manipulate multiple, possibly independent, stores. For instance, using the translated program, we can pose constraints gcd(A,12), gcd(A,9), and in the same computation pose gcd(B,45), gcd(B,30), and the two queries will be evaluated independently. Thus, we can consider the translated CHR program as operating over *local* constraint stores. The capacity for generating new constraint stores and manipulating them locally makes CHRd a good fit in a tabling system where each answer and call has an associated store.

5 Experimental Results

We now present the results of the experiments evaluating the performance of CHRd in tabled as well as non-tabled settings. All measurements were taken on a PC with 1.4 GHz Pentium-M processor and 512 MB RAM running Linux. The run time, given in milliseconds, is averaged over multiple tests. We have compared the performance of CHR and CHRd on XSB 3.0.1 (CHRd's native platform) and hProlog 2.4.35-32. We chose hProlog since it is the host for K.U.Leuven's CHR (KUL-CHR), currently the most representative of systems that efficiently implement Constraint Handling Rules.

Examples Using Tabled Evaluation. We evaluate the performance of CHRd for tabled programs using four examples: (1) truckload, a problem used in [24] to measure the performance of XSB-CHR;(2) buffer, the constraint-based verification of "in-order" message delivery property of a FIFO buffer; (3) dining_ph, deadlock analysis of a dining philosophers specification using synchronization contracts; and (4) fischer, a CHR-based implementation of reachability analysis for real-time systems.

Truckload is a variant of *knapsack*, the classical dynamic programming problem, for scheduling the delivery of packages using finite-capacity trucks to different destinations. Tabling ensures polynomial-time behavior. The base data for the problem, e.g. the attributes of packages were taken from [24].

Table 1. Run time (in ms.) for evaluation of tabled CHR programs

Benchmark	XSB-CHR	CHRd
truckload(300)	1870	243 (13%)
truckload(500)	2530	380 (15%)
fifo(240)	—	1580
fifo(320)	—	3730
dining_ph(6)	—	120
dining_ph(8)	—	980

The time taken to run truckload in XSB-CHR and CHRd for two truck capacities is given in Table 1. The percentage of time taken by CHRd w.r.t. XSB-CHR, given in parentheses, shows that CHRd is four times faster than XSB-CHR. The memory usage is similar on both systems.

The truckload problem is relatively small, and CHRd significantly outperformed XSB-CHR. The other tabled problems, taken from verification examples, are relatively large. As can be seen from the table, due to the more complex constraints and large number of table operations, XSB-CHR failed to work on these examples.

In [20] we presented a constraint-based algorithm for verifying a class of infinite-state systems called *data independent systems*. The rows labeled fifo(N) of Table 1 show the run time of a CHRd-based implementation of this algorithm for verifying the "in-order" message delivery property of an N-place FIFO buffer. The solver uses a reachability-based algorithm and hence needs tabling for termination. The original implementation for this problem (which used a meta-interpreter for constraint handling) is 2.5 times slower that the one based on CHRd.

Our deadlock detection framework [21] uses CHR to enforce correct synchronization of threads based on locally defined concurrency constraints, and reachability analysis to detect deadlocked states. Table 1 shows run time results for the evaluation of two configurations of N dining philosophers in which no deadlock was found.

Finally, we used CHRd to analyze *Fischer's protocol*, a mutual-exclusion protocol that is often used to benchmark real-time verification tools. We used CHR to specify a solver for the clock constraints. While CHRd was able to solve the verification problems for various instances of the protocol, XSB-CHR was unable to solve even a 2-process instance. However, the CHRd-based verifier is 2-5 times slower than a verifier that uses a hand-built (Prolog-based) clock constraint solver [17]. This example indicates that CHRd needs to be further optimized before it can compete with custom-built solvers for well-known constraint domains.

Non-tabled Examples. Table 2 compares CHRd running on XSB and hProlog, with each platform's original CHR system: XSB-CHR and KUL-CHR. The table shows the results for direct-indexed programs: cycle, a cycle of leq constraints on N variables; queens and zebra, two classical problems solved using finite-domain CHR; bool, N-digit binary addition; bool_chain, a cycle of "∧" constraints over N variables; alias, an encoding of Anderson's may-points-to analysis for C programs [2]; and ta, an evaluation of clock bounds on finite automata.

The table also shows results for ground CHR benchmarks: gcd described in Section 4; primes, a computation of prime numbers up to N; fib, a computation of first N Fibonacci numbers; and ram_simul, a simulator of a RAM machine. The ground CHR programs were evaluated directly by the native CHR systems on each platform. For CHRd, they were first translated as described in Section 4 and then ran.

Clearly, CHRd outperforms XSB-CHR for all tests. On hProlog, the performance of CHRd is close to, or better than, that of KUL-CHR for the direct-indexed programs. It should be noted that KUL-CHR is built to handle a more general class of CHR

Table 2. Runtime (in ms.) for evaluation of non-tabled CHR programs

	XSB		hProlog	
Benchmark	XSB-CHR	CHRd	KUL-CHR	CHRd
cycle(60)	11015	1500 (14%)	940	554 (59%)
queens(16)	9693	2520 (26%)	1250	820 (65%)
zebra(10)	45220	690 (2%)	1130	320 (28%)
bool(50000)	255810	1470 (1%)	770	1050 (136%)
bool_chain(400)	207420	16970 (8%)	680	610 (90%)
alias(m88ksim)	–	189	140	120 (86%)
alias(parser)	–	1134	3650	728 (20%)
ta(200)	5860	2090 (35%)	690	560 (75%)
gcd([3,10^6])	1010	945 (94%)	126	360 (300%)
primes(2000)	6871	2753 (40%)	500	1065 (213%)
fib(500)	3260	1250 (38%)	240	475 (198%)
ram_simul(40000)	–	2740	330	1170 (355%)

programs, and does not exploit the indexing available in direct-indexed programs. On the other hand, CHRd does not (currently) optimize the compilation based on the mode information, nor does it support the alternative index structures (e.g. hash tables) used in KUL-CHR. The significantly slower run times of our system for the ground benchmarks is due to the absence of such optimizations. We believe that adding these optimizations to CHRd will bring its performance closer to that of KUL-CHR.

6 Related Work and Discussion

Although the CHR framework was initially proposed for specifying constraint solvers, there is a growing body of work for using it as a full-fledged programming language. The semantics of the language and its implementation have evolved hand-in-hand. For instance, while the initial papers refer to the constraint store as a conjunction of constraints [10], the implementations represented the store using multi-set of terms. Subsequently, the formalization of its semantics in terms of multi-set rewriting have been widely accepted. The original operational semantics [10,1] has been refined [9] to reduce non-determinism and extend the class of programs amenable for evaluation. One of the stated motivations for the refined semantics was to bring the formalism closer to the popular implementations.

It was observed that the propagation history, a key structure of CHR semantics, contributed to significant performance issues when an existing CHR implementation was ported to a tabling environment [24]. When working with multi-set-based constraint store, it appears that propagation history is essential to provide a reasonable semantics. Our work can be viewed as an investigation into the effect of making the constraint store set-based. Note that bottom-up techniques for evaluating definite logic programs compute fixed points (minimal models) without maintaining something analogous to propagation history [16]. Our semantics ω_{set} extends this basic idea to work in the presence of simplification rules (i.e. non-monotonic changes to the store) and bindings on variables. As a result, we obtain a simpler semantics that is easier to implement in a tabled setting. We ensure that the new semantics is as close as possible to existing implementations by basing its formulation on refined semantics ω_r [9]. Although our semantics ω_{set} coincides with ω_r for a large class of constraint handlers written in CHR, the two semantics do not coincide in general. One problem of current interest is to identify the class of CHR programs for which the two semantics coincide.

Although traditional CHR implementations rely on central storage of constraints, direct indexing (storing constraints as variable attributes) has been recognized as more efficient. Therefore, many existing systems [14,23,13] store constraints both ways, using the central data structures only to access constraints when direct indexing is not available. Our work extends this approach by entirely eliminating central storage, and transforming programs that are not direct-indexed to simulate a store using another attributed variable. All CHR implementations we are aware of maintain a propagation history, which is eliminated in CHRd, thanks to its set-based semantics. Consequently, we have reduced the overheads of storing and manipulating constraint stores, leading to a scalable integration of CHR-based constraint solvers with tabled evaluation.

As mentioned before, CHR is being treated as a full-fledged programming language, and not just for writing constraint solvers. It has been shown that algorithms can be encoded in CHR and evaluated with no loss in their asymptotic-time complexity [25]. Recent works have addressed the space complexity of CHR programs [26]. In order to support the growing number of applications (most of them are ground CHR programs), a lot of effort has gone to optimizing central storage structures critical to performance of such programs. Works such as [13] propose analyses to determine the best index depending on the properties of the constraints specified in the program. Additionally, structures that guarantee efficient lookup (234-trees in [13] or hash tables in [23]) have replaced simple unordered lists that was used in early implementations [14]. In CHRd, the constraint set associated with each variable is defined as an unordered list, similar to that in [14]. Incorporating the results of indexing research will improve the CHRd implementation. Furthermore, for non-tabled programs, CHRd replaces the check on propagation history by a check on the constraint store. Our experience with CHRd indicates that constraint store checks can be done as efficiently as propagation history checks. There has also been analyses that determine whether propagation history can be eliminated [22]. Whether similar analyses can be used to eliminate explicit checks on the constraint store remains to be seen.

References

1. S. Abdennadher. Operational Semantics and Confluence of Constraint Propagation Rules. In *CP '97*, pages 252–266, 1997.
2. L. O. Anderson. *Program Analysis and Specialization for the C Programming Language*. PhD thesis, DIKU, Unversity of Copenhagen, 1994.
3. M. Y. Becker and P. Sewell. Cassandra: Flexible trust management, applied to electronic health records. In *IEEE Computer Security Foundations Workshop (CSFW)*, pages 139–154, 2004.
4. W. Chen and D. S. Warren. Tabled evaluation with delaying for general logic programs. *Journal of the ACM*, 43(1):20–74, 1996.
5. S. Dawson, C. R. Ramakrishnan, and D. S. Warren. Practical program analysis using general purpose logic programming systems — a case study. In *ACM PLDI*, 1996.

6. G. Delzanno and T. Bultan. Constraint-based verification of client-server protocols. In *CP*, pages 286–301, 2001.
7. G. Delzanno and A. Podelski. Model checking in CLP. In *TACAS*, pages 223–239, 1999.
8. B. Demoen. hProlog. `http://www.cs.kuleuven.ac.be/~bmd/hProlog/`.
9. G. J. Duck, P. J. Stuckey, M. J. G. de la Banda, and C. Holzbaur. The Refined Operational Semantics of Constraint Handling Rules. In *ICLP 2004*, pages 90–104, 2004.
10. T. Frühwirth. Theory and Practice of Constraint Handling Rules. *Journal of Logic Programming, Special Issue on Constraint Logic Programming*, 37(1-3):95–138, 1998.
11. C. Holzbaur. Metastructures versus Attributed Variables in the Context of Extensible Unification. In *PLILP '92*, pages 260–268, 1992.
12. C. Holzbaur, M. G. de la Banda, D. Jeffery, and P. J. Stuckey. Optimizing Compilation of Constraint Handling Rules. In *ICLP 2001*, volume 2237 of *Lecture Notes in Computer Science*, 2001.
13. C. Holzbaur, M. G. de la Banda, P. J. Stuckey, and G. J. Duck. Optimizing compilation of constraint handling rules in HAL. *Theory and Practice of Logic Programming*, 5(4-5, Special Issue on Constraint Handling Rules):503–531, 2005.
14. C. Holzbaur and T. W. Frühwirth. Compiling Constraint Handling Rules into Prolog with Attributed Variables. In *PPDP '99*, pages 117–133, 1999.
15. N. Li and J. C. Mitchell. Datalog with constraints: A foundation for trust management languages. In *PADL*, pages 58–73, 2003.
16. J. W. Lloyd. *Foundations of Logic Programming*. Springer, 1984.
17. G. Pemmasani, C. R. Ramakrishnan, and I. V. Ramakrishnan. Efficient model checking of real time systems using tabled logic programming and constraints. In *ICLP*, 2002.
18. C. R. Ramakrishnan, I. V. Ramakrishnan, S. A. Smolka, Y. Dong, X. Du, A. Roychoudhury, and V. N. Venkatakrishnan. XMC: A logic-programming-based verification toolset. In *CAV*, volume 1855 of *LNCS*, pages 576–580, 2000.
19. K. Sagonas, T. Swift, D. S. Warren, P. Rao, and J. Friere. The XSB logic programming system. `http://xsb.sourceforge.net`.
20. B. Sarna-Starosta and C. R. Ramakrishnan. Constraint-based model checking of data-independent systems. In *Intl. Conf. on Formal Engineering Methods (ICFEM)*, volume 2885 of *LNCS*, pages 579–598, 2003.
21. B. Sarna-Starosta, R. E. K. Stirewalt, and L. K. Dillon. A model-based design-for-verification approach to checking for deadlock in multi-threaded systems. In *18th International Conference on Software Engineering and Knowledge Engineering (SEKE)*, 2006.
22. T. Schrijvers. *Analyses, optimizations and extensions of Constraint Handling Rules*. PhD thesis, K.U.Leuven, 2005.
23. T. Schrijvers and B. Demoen. The K.U.Leuven CHR system: Implementation and application. In *First workshop on constraint handling rules: selected contributions*, pages 1–5, 2004. Published as technical report: Ulmer Informatik-Berichte Nr. 2004-01.
24. T. Schrijvers and D. S. Warren. Constraint handling rules and tabled execution. In *ICLP*, pages 120–136, 2004.
25. J. Sneyers, T. Schrijvers, and B. Demoen. The Computational Power and Complexity of Constraint Handling Rules. In *CHR 2005*, 2005.
26. J. Sneyers, T. Schrijvers, and B. Demoen. Memory reuse for CHR. In *ICLP 2006*, 2006.
27. Swedish Institute of Computer Science. SICStus Prolog System. `http://www.sics.se/isl/sicstuswww/site/index.html`.
28. H. Tamaki and T. Sato. OLDT resolution with tabulation. In *ICLP*, pages 84–98, 1986.

Prolog Performance on Larger Datasets

Vítor Santos Costa

COPPE/Sistemas, Universidade Federal do Rio de Janeiro, Brasil
vitor@cos.ufrj.br

Abstract. Declarative systems, such as logic programming, should be ideal to process large data sets efficiently. Unfortunately, the high-level nature of logic-based representations can cause inefficiencies, and may lead in some cases to unacceptable performance. We discuss how logic programming systems can accommodate large amounts of data in main memory. We use a number of real datasets to evaluate performance and discuss how a number of techniques can be used to improve memory scalability for such datasets.

1 Introduction

Computing systems are designed to process *data*. Technology has provided us with more and more sources of data, generating more and more data for analysis. The challenge is to be able to process such large amounts of data effectively. Declarative programming systems, such as logic programming, should be some of the most successful approaches toward such a goal, as they use a high-level representation of data (as a subset of First-Order Logic). This representation is widely understood and easy to reason on, and therefore to manipulate. Unfortunately, the high-level nature of logic-based representations can cause inefficiencies, leading to much worse performance than, say, data-base management systems.

Two approaches have been pursued to address this question. One is to use high-level programming as an interface to data-base technology [23,14]. Such an approach benefits from the extensive amount of work done in data-base management, but must address some difficulties. First, interfacing a data-base with a reasoning system is often expensive. Second, current data-base design is often tuned for specific types of queries. Tuning to different types of queries can be a difficult task. The limitations of these approaches suggest that one should also consider how to improve the design of logic programming systems so that they can cope with larger datasets. We discuss some of these challenges here.

Differently from data-bases, there is little motivation to implement logic programming systems that efficiently manage secondary storage. Thus, our interest is in how to accommodate large amounts of data in main memory. If, and only if, we can do so, the second consideration would be how to process such data effectively. To our knowledge most of the work so far has been on improving query execution. We believe this is because time scalability issues can arise even for smallish datasets. Fortunately, recent progress on techniques such

M. Hanus (Ed.): PADL 2007, LNCS 4354, pp. 185–199, 2007.

as tabling [9,27,33,16,26] or indexing [34,28] has shown that we can do useful work on larger datasets with Prolog, thus making space scalability an important consideration.

Space scalability issues reduce to how much data we can fit in main memory. We show that traditional WAM-based Prolog technology is not very effective towards this goal. Indeed, results on the YAP Prolog implementation demonstrate that incremental improvements can more than halve memory usage with relatively little effort. We further show that there is room for more aggressive improvements. This confirms our own experience in that Prolog systems can be used to effective process datasets with tens of millions of facts on standard 32-bit machines.

Our analysis is based on our experience with the YAP Prolog system. We compare YAP against other systems, mostly toward better understanding of what YAP does badly, and of how it can be improved. This work is therefore not intended as a comparison between Prolog systems, as several other parameters should be taken in consideration for a fair analysis. We do believe that our research will be of interest to logic programming implementers, and in general to the declarative programming community.

The paper is organised as follows. We briefly give an overview of the main players in Prolog implementation. Next, we discuss a number of datasets that we shall use as the basis for this work. We experiment these sets on a number of Prolog systems, and discuss some optimisations used to improve performance on the YAP system. Last, we discuss the results, and present some conclusions.

2   Prolog Data-Structures

Most Prolog systems use the Warren Abstract Machine (WAM) [32,1]. The WAM compiles a predicate to *indexing* code and as *clause* code. Often, each clause is compiled independently. The standard structure of the resulting code is shown in Figure 2. Indexing code is represented by the tall block to the left. Indexing code will always start by a switch on type instructions. Indexing code may also include a hash table that allows one to find all clauses matching the first argument. Last, it may have a sequence of choice-point manipulation instructions, linking every clause that matches the first argument. Usually, but not always, indexing code is stored as a single block. On the other hand, most WAM implementations compile clauses independently. Each clause always start with a choice-point manipulation instructions, followed by the actual clause code.

The actual structure of the clause code generated by a WAM compiler would be thus:

- A clause header, including a variety of information such as *flags* on clause status, the *procedure* we belong to, the *next* clause for this predicate, clause *size*, a *source* pointer. Dynamic clauses may have extra data such as timestamps [18].
- a *choice-point manipulation* instruction. Figure 2 shows how these instructions link the clause in a chain. Notice that this code is generated even if the code is always called deterministically.
- The actual clause-specific WAM code.

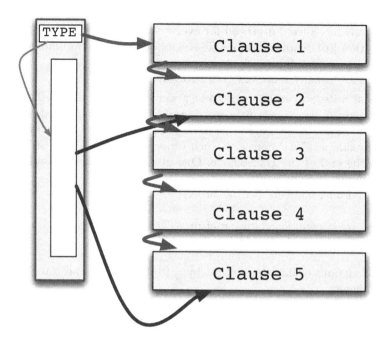

Fig. 1. Predicate Code

We will not describe WAM code here, but on average each symbol in the source code corresponds to a different clause. As an example, the clause-specific code for:

```
words_after_target_args(  pos(1),train,fold5,0).
```

would be:

```
get_structure    A1,pos/1
unify_integer    1
get_atom         A2,train
get_atom         A3,fold5
get_structure    A4,0
proceed
```

Notice that there is one instruction for token (excepting the separators, "," and brackets). We shall not discuss the WAM compilation process here. Instead, we focus on the building blocks we use for code: *instructions, atoms, integers,* and *floating-points.* In more details:

- An *instruction* is an *opcode* followed by a sequence of *operands*. WAM implementations may dispatch on the numeric opcode, or use a threaded emulator [5]. In the latter case, the opcode field would store a label. Operands would have at least 16 bits, and in some implementations such as YAP a word per operand [30]. Operands may also be *constants*, discussed next.

- A Prolog *atom* is usually represented as a pointer to a *symbol table*. This means one has a fixed overhead for every new atom. Afterwards, atom representation just requires a label. The symbol table may be implemented as a tree or as a hash table.
- Integers are usually represented in two ways:
  - *Small integers* can be made to fit a word (a word is usually label sized).
  - *Large integers* cannot fit a word, and thus need specialised processing. To our knowledge, processing of large integers differs across systems. As an example, YAP considers such objects as *blobs*, which are compiled at the end of the clause code. One alternative is to have all blobs for compiled code in a table.
- Floating-Point numbers can be processed in much the same way as large integers.
- Strings are a common data-structure. They can be processed as a list of numbers, or can have a specialised representation.

The actual amount of data-base spent by a Prolog system can thus be decomposed as follows:

$$(Clauses + Ind) + AtomTable + Extra + MM$$

Where *Extra* concerns extra data spent on predicate management and other data-base functionality, such as the Internal Data-Base, and MM corresponds to fields concerned with the Data-Base itself.

Our interest in this work are larger data-bases. Typically, such a data-base consists of a large number of very similar facts. We therefore expect *Extra* and MM to have little impact. Questions we try to address are: how to minimise *Clauses*? What is the relative value of *AtomTable*, and is it worth minimising? We will not discuss *Ind* much, as it depends hugely on the specific indexing algorithm.

3   Datasets

The motivation for this work is to support "large" datasets in Prolog. Our first step would be to agree on what does it mean for a Prolog dataset to be *large*? And, the second question would be: do such datasets exist?

As a starting point, we propose that a dataset is *large* if it includes over 1 MB of data (note that this is a Prolog point-of-view, such data sets would not be considered large in data-base technology). We consider eight such datasets in our experiments:

- *BC*: This dataset was developed at UW-Madison [10]. It contains data on 65000 thousand mammograms performed during three years at a Wisconsin hospital. The data follows the National Mammography Database (NMD) standard established by the American College of Radiology.

- *Cora*: The dataset was originally constructed by McCallum et al. [19]. We used the same version of the data as Kok and Domingos [17], but adapted to Prolog. Cora includes data on 1295 citations to 112 Computer Science papers.
- *EachMovie*: The EachMovie dataset was original developed at DECwrl labs [20]. It includes three tables. There is data on 1628 movies, including movie type, store-info, and a link to the IMDB data-base. There is data on 72000 people who voted on the movies. Input was voluntary, and may include age, gender and ZIP code. From ZIP code it is possible to estimate geographical location and to a good approximation average income. Last, there are 2.8 million votes. Votes can be organised by class and range from 0 to 5.
- *Gash:* The Gasch dataset consists of discretised gene expression data for DNA damage experiments on yeast from Gasch et al. [3,2]. The original continuous micro-array data was binarised by Ong [24].
- *IE:* This dataset was originally used by the Machine Learning System Gleaner [15] for the task of information extraction for a Protein Localization task [25].
- *Tea:* This dataset was is a Prolog representation of the Java SPEC benchmarks for program analysis [6].
- *Thrombin:* This dataset consists of structural information for a sequence of molecules that are associated with Thrombin, a coagulation protein that has many effects in the coagulation cascade. Each molecule may have a large number of different conformers. The dataset was used for the KDD cup 2001.
- *WNet:* this the Prolog version of the well-known of the lexical database for English WordNet [13].

These datasets reflect the author's personal experience, and are not meant to be a discussion of all larger Prolog applications. The BC, *Cora*, *EachMovie* applications were ported to Prolog by the author. Arguably, the datasets reflect a machine-learning bias, as all but *Tea* and *WNet* were developed for this style of tasks.

We used the Unix `sort` and `uniq` commands to remove duplicates, and the Unix command `grep` to remove comments. This introduced some syntax errors, we manually edited the resulting files to correct these bugs.

Table 1 shows dataset size. Application size ranges from 17MB and 366 thousand lines of code for `Thrombin` and 30MB and 260 thousand lines for `Cora` up to half almost half a of data GB and 8 million lines for `IE`. All datasets are structured, that is, data items use a single format throughout.

Datasets differ in a number of ways:

- *First Form:* Most datasets are in first normal form (only use constants), but not all of them. *IE* uses compound terms to represent example numbers. *Tea* has the richer structure: it uses compound-terms heavily to represent the Java code.
- *Predicates Distribution:* This property varies heavily across datasets. The two extremes are *BC* which includes over 50 predicates, all of the same

Table 1. Application

		Size in Lines	Size in MBytes
BC		2752	87
Cora		260	30
EachMovie		2857	70
Gasch		817	39
IE		7465	443
Tea		402	60
Thrombin		366	17
WNet		553	23

size, and *EachMovie* which includes 2 predicates, but where space is totally dominated by one of them (`vote`).

- *Constants:* Most datasets use *atoms* heavily. In some cases, such as *BC*, names correspond to labels: we thus have very few names that appear over and over again. In *IE* it is quite frequent to have atoms with long names, usually a concatenation of some properties.

  Small integers are used across all datasets. Floating-point numbers are used heavily in *Thrombin*, and to a lesser extent in *IE*. Strings are used in *Tea* to represent Java strings.

4   Prolog Performance

It is enlightening to just try to compile the datasets on different Prologs. We used in our experiments YAP-5.1.2, SWI Prolog 5.6.17, SICSTus Prolog 3.12.0, XSB 3.0.1 and ciao Prolog 1.10-p7. Note that our major goal in this experiment is to try to understand what different Prolog systems do well. We used stable versions of all systems except for YAP, development releases may have better performance. All experiments were performed on a 32-bit Linux machine, an AMD64 3.5+ running Ubuntu Linux x86 with kernel 2.6.15. The machine has 1GB of main memory.

We had difficulties in loading the datasets across the different Prolog systems. The major difference was in how the different Prologs scan strings. YAP and SWI would allow line breaks in strings, which is disallowed in other systems. Also, quotes are process differently across systems. The time in second to load the different datasets is shown in Table 2.

Surprisingly, only `YAP` and `SWI` could load all the datasets. We knew beforehand that YAP would be able to do so. `SWI` did well across the datasets. SICSTus had difficulties in two datasets: *IE* and *WNet*. In both cases the problem was a limitation on the maximum number of atoms the system can accommodate in its atom table. `XSB` had problems on the larger two datasets: loading *EachMovie* and *IE* eventually resulted in a segmentation violation. `ciao` inherits some of the difficulties with SICStus. It also would complain of memory allocation failure.

Table 2. Dataset Loading Time

‖	‖YAP	SWI	SICStus	XSB	ciao
BC	18.3	13.9	296	460	N/A
Cora	2.4	2.2	30	52	109
EachMovie	18.2	14.7	79	N/A	N/A
Gasch	5.9	5.1	101	201	N/A
IE	59.2	52.9	N/A	N/A	N/A
Tea	4.8	4.8	64.6	192	N/A
Thrombin	3.7	2.7	66.9	184	485
WNet	4.3	3.7	N/A	50	N/A

There is a huge difference in running-time between YAP and SWI on the other hand, and the other systems. The explanation is that most of the parsing and compilation code in YAP and SWI is written in C. This pays off well for large files. Note that SICStus, ciao and XSB generate compiled files which can load very quickly, so this problem would arise only once in the development process.

Table 3 shows database size in MB after loading each dataset. Note that there several important difference between YAP and the other systems. Usually, Prolog systems will generate the indexing code at the same time that they generate the clause code. YAP delays generating the indexing code until query execution. Also, YAP does not compile a choice-point manipulation instruction. These instructions will only be generated on demand. For both reasons, arguably numbers are biased to favour YAP.

Table 3. Application Size

‖	‖YAP	SWI	SICStus	XSB	ciao
BC	133	183	241	89	N/A
Cora	12	17	19	10.3	12.7
EachMovie	156	234	248	N/A	N/A
Gasch	45	60	64	39	N/A
IE	556	592	N/A	N/A	N/A
Tea	47	49	50	38	N/A
Thrombin	43	38	47	28	17.5
WNet	66	62	N/A	50	N/A

Usually, the systems tend to spend similar amounts of space. The exception is XSB, which tends to have better memory performance across the board. XSB does extremely well for *BC*. It also does very well for *Thrombin* and *Tea*. The results for ciao are also quite good. One reason is that YAP spends a single byte per WAM argument, whereas other systems spend a full word. YAP does quite well on *Cora*, and *EachMovie*, but does poorly on *Thrombin* and *WNet*.

4.1   Atom Space

The difficulties that SICStus and ciao had with *IE* and *WNet* suggest that the number of atoms and the size of the atom table, may also have a significant impact on system performance. To verify this, we instrumented YAP to report how many atoms were allocated, and how much space they occupied. The results on atom space are similar to the "string space" reported by XSB.

Table 4. Atom Space

‖	‖Number	Size in KBytes‖
‖BC	123	28‖
Cora	2444	111
EachMovie	6423	240
Gasch	6268	121
IE	391732	11777
Tea	164745	8479
Thrombin	12610	240
‖WNet	260775	12284‖

The results show that the text processing datasets, *IE*, *WNet*, and *Tea* have many more atoms than the others. *IE* has almost 400,000 atoms. *WNet* is a much smaller dataset, but has almost two thirds of the number of atoms. Last, *Tea* also has a large large number of atoms. In contrast, BC makes do with less than 200 new atoms. This is because atoms are used to specify discrete attributes, there is no free running text.

YAP uses a hash chain to store atoms. Collisions are resolved by keeping the atoms in a linked list. YAP uses an extra field to point at *properties*, which basically is a linked list anything associated the atom: procedures, internal database entries, global variables, operators, and so on. The total amount of space YAP needs per atom is thus:

$$2 * SIZE(CELL) + strlen(atom \rightarrow Name)$$

This representation seems close to what is used in other Prolog systems. Both XSB, SWI and ciao use hash tables to represent the atom table.

In most cases, the atom table has little impact on dataset memory usage. But there are significant exceptions. For YAP, costs can rise up to 23% of total space in *Tea*, and up to 20% of total usage in WNet. XSB reports even worse results for "string" plus "atom" usage, which together take up to almost half of the total data-base in *WNet*.

4.2   Indexing

Table 5 shows YAP performance after indexing. Because indices are generated on demand, we used a first call with all arguments unbound, and a second all with

Table 5. YAP Performance After Indexing

	YAP	YAP-2
BC	133	79
Cora	12	8
EachMovie	156	102
Gasch	45	52
IE	556	410
Tea	47	44
Thrombin	43	40
WNet	66	60

the first argument bound. The results show that, except for Gasch, memory usage actually decreases across datasets, and in several cases YAP now outperforms XSB Prolog (but not in all). This is due to the mega-clause optimisation, that we discuss in the next section.

5 Optimisations

Next, we focus on some optimisations included in the YAP Prolog system. The goal was to improve memory performance with least changes to the system. The two most obvious opportunities are improving the instruction set and in improving clause representation.

5.1 Instruction Merging

An effective approach to improve emulator performance is to combine often repeated sequences of instructions [30,12,22]. In these datasets, the most commonly used instruction is *get_constant*. We combined *get_constant* as follows:

- We combine contiguous sequences of up to 5 `get_constant` instructions.
- We assume the combined instruction is contiguous and starts from the first argument.

Therefore, the instruction format is very compact: we have an opcode and N operands. An example compressed instruction is shown in Figure 2. For longer sequences of constants, the space overhead per instruction gets close to just one cell. The impact of performing this optimisation is shown in Table 6: the column to the left show the optimised code and the column to the left shows the non-optimised results.

The results show significant benefits for a number of applications, but not for all of them. *EachMovie* benefits the most, this is because the `vote` table has a very large number of tuples of integers. Compressing them could be taken further: if we would also compress `proceed` then we would only need an opcode and four cells per clause, versus the original $4 * (OPCODE + OPERAND +$

Fig. 2. Get_NCONS

Table 6. YAP GetConstant compression

	merged	original
BC	133	176
Cora	12	16
EachMovie	156	245
Gasch	45	57
IE	556	600
Tea	47	49
Thrombin	43	49
WNet	66	66

$CELL) + OPCODE$. Assuming they all take the same space we reduce clause space from 13 to 5 cells. The current implementation does not optimise `proceed`, so the cost if of 6 cells per clause.

The optimisation fails on a number of benchmarks, including *IE*. There are two reasons for that:

- The first argument to *IE* is often a compound term, compound terms are also common in *Tea*;
- `Thrombin` includes floating-points, *WNet* includes very large numbers which are processed as blobs by YAP.

The results show a weakness of instruction merging: it is hard to adapt to every situation. It also shows that YAP's representation of blobs is clearly less efficient than other system', such as XSB.

5.2   MegaClauses

The second optimisation follows from the observation that if the compiled code for a clause only has 5 cells, than the overhead of compiling clauses separately can be significant. In the case of YAP, the overhead is at least 4 cells for the header, plus 1 cell for the tail. If one includes fragmentation and extra overheads from the memory collector, than more than half of total memory usage may be spent just in maintaining separate clauses.

XSB has a simple solution to this problem: clauses are compiled to a single structure (the `xwam` file). The compiled code is then loaded as a single block. This is very effective, and just by itself explains why XSB tends to use less memory than the other Prolog systems. It does impose restrictions on how to include clauses for a predicate: clauses must belong to a single module.

YAP uses an on-line approach in order not to impose such restrictions. The idea is to take advantage of the dynamic indexing mechanism: the compression algorithm is called just before the first time indexing is attempted. As a result, indexing often ends up being allocated in the code freed by the clause merging algorithm.

Clause merging is implemented by checking if all the clauses have the same size. If they do, they are copied into a new *mega-clause*, and their space is released. In order to achieve maximal compression, this optimisation is only performed if all clauses take the *same* space. This restriction makes it very easy to access individual clauses, which is necessary in order to generate indexing code and for other tasks, such as debugging. In fact, we have found it quite useful that this optimisation makes accessing individual clause extremely fast: we just need to add the clause number times clause size, so mega-clauses take constant time to access individual clauses, instead of the linear time one would have to take for the standard linked list of clauses.

Table 7. YAP MegaClauses

‖	‖Saved (MB)	Predicates	Av Size (KB)
BC	43	54	1072
Cora	4	26	199
EachMovie	44	2	38826
Gasch	0	0	0
IE	109	124	2734
Tea	4	25	334
Thrombin	5.3	9	4150
WNet	8	18	2164

Table 7 show the actual results. The leftmost column shows how much space is reclaimed, with a maximum of 109MB for *IE*. The two other columns show the number of predicates that benefit (often all of them), and the average size of a mega-clause per application, in KB.

The *BC* dataset is where we gain the most: about half of the space is recovered. *Thrombin* and *WNet* have significant benefits, even though clauses are larger. The results for *Gasch* were surprising, we would expect some benefit here. Mega-clauses do make an effort to deserve their name: average size is often over a Mega byte, in one case taking almost 40MB for a single clause.

6   Discussion

Our analysis show that Prolog systems can load files with sizes up to 10M lines in main memory, but that future work is still needed to improve performance. Unfortunately, there is very little published work on these issues. There is common knowledge that space usage is a problem with native code generation [31], but otherwise space considerations have most often been reserved for dynamic allocation, and namely for garbage collection [4,8,11]. We hope that the near future will see more work in this direction, and briefly discuss possible research directions.

Clause Representation. We have observed that clause representation overhead is dominant for current implementations. XSB performs better than other systems largely because it packs clauses together into a single structure. Alternatively, YAP uses "mega-clauses" to achieve much the same effect.

Assuming we have implemented this optimisation, the space spent on a simple clause with k constants would be, assuming one cell for opcode and operand:

$$ClSize = 3k + 1$$

In Yap, instruction merging can further reduce $ClSize$ to $k + 1$. For applications such as *EachMovie* the main table has arity 4 and size 2811662. This means that table space is reduced from $2811662 \times (4 + 3 * 4 + 1 + 1) \approx 50MB$ to $2811662 \times (2 + 4)) \approx 17MB$.

Further improvements can be achieved in a number of ways:

1. Items may have small domains, and it may be possible to compact the representation further by taking advantage of this.
2. YAP currently only optimises atoms and small numbers: it has difficulties for larger numbers and for floats. Further, several datasets store structured data. Unfortunately, having merged instructions for every case is cumbersome.

These two points suggest that it would be beneficial to first do compile-time analysis, before loading, in order to have the domains, and second, to generated instructions specialised for the dataset. There has been recent work on doing so, such as Java superinstructions [7] and Morales' emulator refinement work for Prolog [21].

Atom Table. We were surprised by the large size of the atom table on some applications. This seems to be typical of text processing applications (although *Tea* uses an object file, the original program is a text file). A more detailed analysis shows that strings tend to have similar prefixes: class names in *Tea*, structured reports in *WNet*.

We believe that the problem might be significant for applications such as text mining, and semantic web. It seems that the best idea would be to follow XSB: separate strings from atom data, and try to manipulate strings as efficiently as possible, possibly by using tries instead of an hash table to take advantage of similarity between prefixes.

Complex Data. A last point one should make is that users will take advantage of every Prolog feature. Namely, they will store compound terms, they will use very large integers, and they will use floats. Some observations:

1. If a dataset uses compound terms in a structured way, we can transform these terms into first normal form (1NF), which will always be more space effective. This again argues for a pre-compilation step.
2. Representing floats well is very important, but unfortunately it is not yet clear (to the author) how best to represent them in an Prolog environment.

We believe having the ability to represent complex data easily is a major advantage of Prolog: it is up to the implementers to make it as effective as possible.

7   Conclusions and Future Work

Recent progress in tabling and in indexing has made it be possible to process larger datasets effectively. But to do so one needs to be able to represent large datasets in Prolog. Our results show that relatively small transformations to the original WAM design, instruction merging and mega-clauses, can very significantly improve space efficiency. We also show that there is much open work to do. As discussed, incremental improvements are possible, and maybe it is time to consider alternative approaches to the traditional compilation style used in Prolog.

We have applied the optimisations we discuss here in the YAP system. We have obtained good performance in tasks related to several of these datasets. Indeed, these optimisations were originally motivated by even larger datasets.

Ultimately, the goal is to make logic programming an useful language for large datasets. We believe four tasks must be addressed for this to be true: data representation, discussed here; indexing, that we believe is key for data-base performance; reuse, where tabling has worked well; and query optimisation [29]. We believe all four tasks deserve further work, although we plan to focus on query optimisation and data representation in the near future.

Acknowledgements. This work was been partially supported by the CNPq and by funds granted to LIACC through the Programa de Financiamento Plurianual, Fundação para a Ciência e Tecnologia and Programa POSI.

References

1. H. Aït-Kaci. *Warren's Abstract Machine — A Tutorial Reconstruction.* MIT Press, 1991.
2. G. A.P., H. M., M. S., B. D., E. S.J., and B. P.O. Genomic expression responses to DNA-damaging agents and the regulatory role of the yeast ATR homolog Mec1p. *Mol Biol Cell.*, 12:2987–3003, 2001.
3. G. A.P., S. P.T., K. C.M., C.-H. O., E. M.B., S. G., B. D., and P. Brown. Genomic expression programs in the response of yeast cells to environmental changes. *Mol Biol Cell.*, 11:4241–57, 2000.
4. K. Appleby, M. Carlsson, S. Haridi, and D. Sahlin. Garbage collection for Prolog based on WAM. *Communications of the ACM*, 31(6):171–183, 1989.
5. J. R. Bell. Threaded code. *Communications of the ACM*, 16(6):370–372, 1973.

6. W. Benton. Personal communication, 2006.
7. K. Casey, D. Gregg, M. A. Ertl, and A. Nisbet. Towards superinstructions for java interpreters. In A. Krall, editor, *Software and Compilers for Embedded Systems, 7th International Workshop, SCOPES 2003, Vienna, Austria, September 24-26, 2003, Proceedings*, volume 2826 of *Lecture Notes in Computer Science*, pages 329–343. Springer, 2003.
8. L. F. Castro and V. Santos Costa. Understanding Memory Management in Prolog Systems. In *Proceedings of Logic Programming, 17th International Conference, ICLP 2001*, volume 2237 of *Lecture Notes in Computer Science*, pages 11–26, Paphos, Cyprus, November 2001.
9. W. Chen and D. S. Warren. Tabled Evaluation with Delaying for General Logic Programs. *Journal of the ACM*, 43(1):20–74, January 1996.
10. J. Davis, E. S. Burnside, I. Dutra, D. Page, R. Ramakrishnan, V. S. Costa, and J. W. Shavlik. View learning for statistical relational learning: With an application to mammography. In L. P. Kaelbling and A. Saffiotti, editors, *IJCAI-05, Proceedings of the Nineteenth International Joint Conference on Artificial Intelligence, Edinburgh, Scotland, UK, July 30-August 5, 2005*, pages 677–683. Professional Book Center, 2005.
11. B. Demoen. A different look at garbage collection for the wam. In P. J. Stuckey, editor, *Logic Programming, 18th International Conference, ICLP 2002, Copenhagen, Denmark, July 29 - August 1, 2002, Proceedings*, volume 2401 of *Lecture Notes in Computer Science*, pages 179–193. Springer, 2002.
12. B. Demoen and P.-L. Nguyen. So Many WAM Variations, So Little Time. In *LNAI 1861, Proceedings Computational Logic - CL 2000*, pages 1240–1254. Springer-Verlag, July 2000.
13. Fellbaum. *WordNet: An Electronic Lexical Database (Language, Speech, and Communication)*. The MIT Press, May 1998.
14. M. Ferreira and R. Rocha. Coupling optyap with a database system. In N. Guimarães and P. T. Isaías, editors, *AC 2005, Proceedings of the IADIS International Conference on Applied Computing, Algarve, Portugal, February 22-25, 2005, 2 Volumes*, pages 107–114. IADIS, 2005.
15. M. Goadrich, L. Oliphant, and J. Shavlik. Learning Ensembles of First-Order Clauses for Recall-Precision Curves: A Case Study in Biomedical Information Extraction. In *Proceedings of the 14th International Conference on Inductive Logic Programming*, Porto, Portugal, 2004.
16. H.-F. Guo and G. Gupta. A Simple Technique for Implementing Tabling based on Dynamic Reordering of Alternatives. In *Proceedings of ICLP'01*, November 2001.
17. S. Kok and P. Domingos. Learning the structure of markov logic networks. In *Proceedings of the Twenty-Second International Conference on Machine Learning*, pages 441–448. ACM Press, 2005.
18. T. G. Lindholm and R. A. O'Keefe. Efficient implementation of a defensible semantics for dynamic Prolog code. In J.-L. Lassez, editor, *Proceedings of the Fourth International Conference on Logic Programming*, MIT Press Series in Logic Programming, pages 21–39. University of Melbourne, "MIT Press", May 1987.
19. A. McCallum, K. Nigam, J. Rennie, and K. Seymore. Automating the construction of internet portals with machine learning. *Information Retrieval Journal*, 3:127–163, 2000. www.research.whizbang.com/data.
20. P. McJonese. Eachmovie collaborative filtering data set. Technical report, DEC Systems Research Center, 1997.

21. J. F. Morales, M. Carro, G. Puebla, and M. V. Hermenegildo. A generator of efficient abstract machine implementations and its application to emulator minimization. In M. Gabbrielli and G. Gupta, editors, *Logic Programming, 21st International Conference, ICLP 2005*, volume 3668 of *Lecture Notes in Computer Science*, pages 21–36. Springer, 2005.

22. H. Nässén, M. Carlsson, and K. F. Sagonas. Instruction merging and specialization in the sicstus prolog virtual machine. In *Proceedings of the 3rd international ACM SIGPLAN conference on Principles and practice of declarative programming, September 5-7, 2001, Florence, Italy*, pages 49–60. ACM, 2001.

23. H. Nilsson. The external database in sicstus prolog. In A. Voronkov, editor, *Logic Programming and Automated Reasoning: Proc. of the International Conference LPAR'92*, pages 493–495. Springer, Berlin, Heidelberg, 1992.

24. I. Ong, D. Page, and V. S. Costa. Inferring Regulatory Networks from Time Series Expression Data and Relational Data via Inductive Logic Programming. In *Inductive Logic Programming Meeting*, 2006.

25. S. Ray and M. Craven. Representing sentence structure in hidden markov models for information extraction. In B. Nebel, editor, *Proceedings of the Seventeenth International Joint Conference on Artificial Intelligence, IJCAI 2001, Seattle, Washington, USA, August 4-10, 2001*, pages 1273–1279. Morgan Kaufmann, 2001.

26. R. Rocha, F. Silva, and V. S. Costa. On Applying Or-Parallelism and Tabling to Logic Programs. *Theory and Practice of Logic Programming Systems*, 5(1-2):161–205, 2005.

27. K. F. Sagonas and T. Swift. An abstract machine for tabled execution of fixed-order stratified logic programs. *ACM Transactions on Programming Languages and Systems*, 20(3):586–634, May 1998.

28. V. Santos Costa. Performance Issues in Prolog Applications. In *Portuguese Conference on Artificial Intelligence (EPIA)*, volume 2902 of *Lecture Notes in Computer Science*, page 8, Beja, Portugal, December 2003. Springer.

29. V. Santos Costa, A. Srinivasan, R. Camacho, H. Blockeel, B. Demoen, G. Janssens, J. Struyf, H. Vandecasteele, and W. Van Laer. Query Transformations for Improving the Efficiency of ILP Systems. *Journal of Machine Learning Research*, 4:465–491, August 2003.

30. V. Santos Costa, D. H. D. Warren, and R. Yang. Andorra-I: A Parallel Prolog System that Transparently Exploits both And- and Or-Parallelism. In *Third ACM SIGPLAN Symposium on Principles & Practice of Parallel Programming PPOPP*, pages 83–93. ACM press, April 1991. SIGPLAN Notices vol 26(7), July 1991.

31. P. Van Roy. 1983-1993: The Wonder Years of Sequential Prolog Implementation. *The Journal of Logic Programming*, 19/20, May/July 1994.

32. D. H. D. Warren. Prolog Engine. Technical report, Artificial Intelligence Center, SRI International, 333 Ravenswood Ave, Menlo Park CA 94025, April 1983. Unpublished draft.

33. N.-F. Zhou. Implementation of a Linear Tabling Mechanism. In E. Pontelli and V. Santos Costa, editors, *Practical Aspects of Declarative Languages*, number 1753 in Lecture Notes in Computer Science, pages 109–123. Springer Verlag, January 2000.

34. N.-F. Zhou, T. Takagi, and U. Kazuo. A Matching Tree Oriented Abstract Machine for Prolog. In D. H. D. Warren and P. Szeredi, editors, *Proceedings of the Seventh International Conference on Logic Programming*, pages 158–173. MIT Press, 1990.

BAD, a Declarative Logic-Based Language for Brain Modeling

Alan H. Bond[1,2]

[1] Semel Institute for Neuroscience, Geffen Medical School,
University of California at Los Angeles, Los Angeles, California 90095
[2] National Institute of Standards and Technology,
MS 8263, Gaithersburg, Maryland 20899
alan.bond@exso.com
http://www.exso.com

Abstract. We describe a declarative language, called BAD (brain architecture description language), which we have developed for describing and then running brain models. Models are at the system-level of description, so that modules correspond to brain areas. Each module has a process and the set of modules runs in parallel and communicates via channels corresponding to observed brain connectivity. Processes are described using a parallel set of left-to-right first-order logical rules in clause form, but with additional activity in a rule body described by Prolog code. Data items are represented by logical literals. Both data and rules use certainty values. The overall system described by the user consists of more than one agent each controlled by a brain model, and behaving in a 3D virtual environment, which is described by logical literals. Interaction with this environment is described by Prolog code representing sensors and actuators. Brain models have been developed for social interaction, problem-solving, and episodic memory, routine memory and spatial working memory.

1 Introduction

We have developed BAD, Brain Architecture Description language, as a formal description language for specifying the anatomical structure and the information processing functionality of brains at the architectural level. This is the first published description of the detailed mechanisms of the BAD system. With BAD, the user can specify a particular set of processing modules corresponding to brain areas. For each module a parallel set of rules is given describing processing within that module, and the set of modules is organized as an architecture by defining communication channels among them.

2 Motivation from Neuroscience

We analyzed the neuroanatomy of the cortex, which is divided into neural areas with connections among areas [5]. We reviewed experiments which indicated the functions each neural area was involved in, and we construed these results as each

M. Hanus (Ed.): PADL 2007, LNCS 4354, pp. 200–214, 2007.
© Springer-Verlag Berlin Heidelberg 2007

neural area's action being to *construct* data items of data types characteristic of that area. We also defined neural *regions* made up of small numbers of contiguous neural areas. Our analysis is summarized in Figure 1.

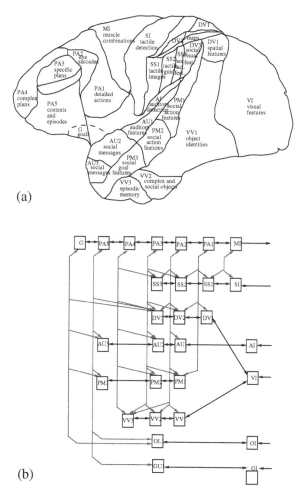

Fig. 1. (a) Lateral view of the cortex showing neural regions and their functional involvements, and (b) connectivity of regions showing perception-action hierarchy, note that the hierarchy is on its side with the top to the left

In order to design a model of the cortex, we abstracted from our review some biological information-processing principles:

1. Each neural area stores and processes data items of given types characteristic of that neural area; data items are of bounded size.
2. To form systems, neural areas are connected in a fixed network with dedicated point-to-point channels.

3. The set of neural areas is organized as a perception-action hierarchy.

4. Neural areas process data received and/or stored locally by them. There is no central manager or controller.

5. All neural areas have a common execution process, the "uniform process", which constructs data items.

6. All neural areas do similar amounts of processing and run at about the same speed.

7. There is data parallelism in communication, storage and processing. Processing within a neural area is highly parallel. Parallel coded data is transmitted, stored, and triggers processing. Processing acts on parallel data to produce parallel data.

8. The data items being transmitted, stored and processed can involve a lot of information; they can be complex.

9. The set of neural areas acts continuously and in parallel.

From these and other considerations which we will explain, we designed and implemented a simple abstract model of the cortex [1] [4]. Figure 2(a) diagrams our initial model, and Figure 2(b) shows an example scenario which determines the external input and output descriptions used by the model. This example has two modeled brains, one for each primate. The inputs to the brains are produced by sensor processes which sense the 3D environment, and outputs from the brains cause changes to the environment mainly by causing movements of the modeled primates.

In the last few years, we have conducted a series of studies and models concerning the human brain, including problem solving [3], episodic memory [7], natural language processing [6], routinization [10], spatial working memory [9], and social relationships [2]. Ours is the only work on a complete system level model of the brain and behavior; the closest other work uses collections of neural nets, without planning or complex behaviors. Detailed references justifying the neuroanatomical and neurophysiological basis of our model can be found in [5], as well as in each of our subsequent papers.

We used SICstus Prolog as a basic implementation language and added another layer which we called BAD, and which represented the parallel execution of modules and communication channels between modules. We used Prolog mainly for its powerful high level descriptive power, for unification matching, and for the ability to write a new language layer. We rarely used its nondeterminism.

3   Overview of Our Modeling Approach

A system-level brain model is a set of parallel modules with fixed interconnectivity similar to the cortex, and where each module corresponds to a brain area and processes only certain kinds of data specific to that module.

We represented each neural region by a module. A module has an associative store which is a Prolog store, and a set of left-to-right rules. The store can only store data of given data types, and these are made to correspond to the biological properties of the corresponding brain areas. In general the store is

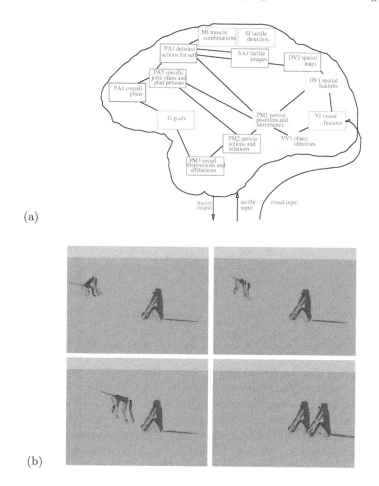

Fig. 2. (a) Outline diagram of an implemented brain model and (b) Snapshots from grooming sequence obtained by running this brain model

unbounded in size. Modules are connected by channels which again correspond to the connections observed for the brain.

Figure 3 shows the components and data flow within a module.

In a typical application, each primate or human is represented as a brain model, and in addition there is a 3D spatial environment within which they behave and interact. The environment includes the bodies of each primate or human. Each brain model is represented as a set of BAD files, one per module and also a connectivity information module. Each brain model is loaded into a separate Prolog session and the 3D environment into another session. A run command given to each session then causes the system to execute all the brain models for one cycle. During a cycle, each brain model requests sensory information from the environment, executes all of its modules, transmits all data among modules, and then sends motor commands to the environment.

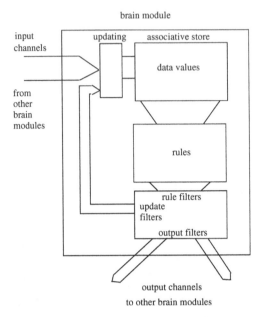

Fig. 3. The structure of a module, showing data flow and data storage

The model is executed in discrete temporal steps, which are fairly fine-grained. The intention is that a time step of one unit corresponds to 20 milliseconds of real time. This is the observed time taken for signals to be passed from one neural area to another in the primate cortex. During one time step, all the rules in all the modules are executed until data stability, without communication among modules, or with the environment. Thus the model is truly parallel and distributed.

Our approach is intended to be complementary to neural network approaches, and it should be possible, for a given abstract model, to construct corresponding neural network models.

4   Data Types and Storage Within Modules

Data items. Data items are represented by ground literals which we call *descriptions*. To indicate what data types can be stored in a given module, for each data type we give a *description pattern*, which defines the set of descriptions consisting of all of its instances. A description pattern is a literal of the form: `predicate(Weights,Context,[List_of_values])`
(using identifiers with initial capitals to indicate variables). The first argument of each description is a list of weights $[\mathtt{Ws}_i]$ which can be processed by the user as they wish. For the models we have developed, all our description patterns are of the form:

`predicate([C,W1,W2,Time_stamp,Rstate],Context,[List_of_values])`

Only C, W1 and W2 are weights, Time_stamp is used for housekeeping and is the last cycle that the item was updated, and Rstate is to keep track of the description's refractory state. The `Context` term is intended to be used for grouping descriptions into sets, i.e., all those descriptions with the same value of `Context` form a set. C is a certainty factor and W1 and W2 are weights; all of these are reals. In `List_of_values`, all values are ground terms, and preferably atomic. An example of a description pattern is `position(W,C,[Agent,X,Y,Z])`, which might be a data type whose instances represent the position X,Y,Z of a perceived `Agent`, with certain weights. An example of a description, i.e. data item, is a substitution instance of this data type:

`position([1.0,1.0,1.0,1,[]],any,[adam,300.0,200.0,0.000])`

At any one time, the module store has a set of stored descriptions of given types. A specification of a data type also includes its updating properties, its competition characteristics and its rates of update and attenuation, which will be explained below.

Storage of data, uniqueness, similarity and novelty. When we implemented and ran our model we soon realized that the store was updated from inputs every cycle and these updates were often very similar to those of the previous cycles. In order to update the store, we had to test if the input literal was the same as an existing stored literal. In fact there were four cases: (1) input literal identical to a stored one, including all the weights, (2) the input literal is the "same" as a stored one, i.e. only differing in the values of the weights, (3) "similar", which is given by equivalence expressions so that a data item may overwrite a "similar" one already in the store, for example if the action is walking and then the next input has it standing, we update the stored one, even though it is not the "same" as defined above, (4) the input literal is "novel" meaning it is not identical, same or similar, in which case it is simply stored. We also have sometimes used "corresponding", allowing overwriting based on X,Y,Z nearness.

In addition, we found we had to specify update characteristics for each data type; we used memory item update characteristic patterns, which we call *item types*. Items matching these patterns replace existing items, thus, for:

`item_type(Person,Module,Type,[Input_pattern,Stored_pattern])`.

an incoming description is matched to the `Input_pattern`, if it matches, then the `Stored_pattern` is matched to the store. If this matches then the incoming description updates the matching stored description. If no `Input_pattern` matches, or if the `Stored_pattern` does not match to the store then the description is simply stored, as it is a novel item.

So, e.g., `item_type(Person,Module,data,[goal(G),goal(G)])`.
any incoming goal description updates only an identical one. Thus there can be an indefinite number of goal descriptions, with different goals G.

And, e.g., `item_type(Person,Module,data,[action(M1,A1),action(M1,A2)])`.
an incoming action description for a given person M1 updates any other action

description for the same person. Thus, only one action description can exist for a given person, however there can be an indefinite number of different action descriptions each for a different person.

The updating of weights of memory items from incoming weights of matching item uses a multiplicative linear increment to the excitation of the item:

`update_weights_increment(Person,Module,Incw1,Incw2): −`

```
(((W1_input >= W1_old),W1_new is (W1_old*(1.0 + Incw1))) |
((W1_input < W1_old),W1_new is (W1_old*(1.0 - Incw2))))).
```

Attenuation. All stored data items are subject to an exponential attenuation process each cycle. Attenuation reduces the weight by a standard fraction each cycle. This fraction can be set to zero so there is no attenuation, and it can also be set to one, which erases the data item after one cycle (not before it contributes to rule matching in the cycle). Thus, attenuation factors are specified:

`attenuation_factor_input(Person,Module,Type,AF,Description pattern).`

AF is a list of real factors, one for each weight in the list of weights. e.g. for data to attenuate to noise level in about 20 cycles

`attenuation_factors(Person,Module,data,[0.1,0.1,0.1],C)`

Noise level can be set and is the value at which a description is removed from the store: `noise_level(Person,Module,Type,Noise_level)`.

As a result of continuous linear updating and exponential attenuation, with a constant input stream of data items, the stored value will settle to a steady value. Initially, there will be a build up of the weight taking a few cycles, starting from noise level, and when the input ceases or changes to some other data items, the weight will take a few cycles to attenuate to noise level, where it will then be deleted.

5 Processing Within Modules by Rules

The form of rules. Computation in modules is represented by a set of *description transformation rules* of the form:

```
rule(agent,rule_name,context,
  if((sequence of description patterns)),
  then ([list of description patterns]),
  provided((clause_body)),
  weights(weights)).
```

It is executed by matching the left hand side, the "if" term, to bind variables and then constructing and possibly storing the descriptions given by the right hand side, the "then" term.

For example:

```
rule(M,macroaction_2,context(all),
   if((position(W,C,[M,X,Y,Z]),
```

```
        position(W_p,C,[MP,XP,YP,ZP]))),
   then([near(W_1,any,[M,MP])],Wa),
   provided((MP \== M,
    distance(X,Y,Z,XP,YP,ZP,D),D<25.0)),
   weights(1.0,[1.0,1.0],[1.0])
   ).
```

The meaning of this rule is that if the primate perceives that another is near to it, then it notes this fact.

We prefer a style in which there is no branching in a rule, just conditionals, so for branching we use several different rules.

The set of rules in a module is executed in parallel, and the set of modules is executed in parallel.

The execution cycle first inputs all incoming data from other modules, then executes all rules and then outputs any output data to other modules.

In general, a rule is executed by matching all the left hand side description patterns to the store, executing all possible rule instances. The right hand side is executed, for a particular instance, by constructing from each description pattern on the right hand side a description obtained by substituting terms for variables. These constructed descriptions may then be stored in the module or output to other modules.

Processing of weights. Rules also have lists of weights: weights(Wo,[Wl_i],[Wr_j]), one for each of the left hand side patterns [Wl_i], one for each of the right hand side patterns [Wr_j] and also an overall rule weight, Wo, for the rule as a whole. These weights are usually fixed at the moment, but also can be variables and can be computed within the body of the rule.

We usually use just one weight, W1, in calculations, at the moment. When the rule is evoked, the weight for the rule instance is the bilinear combination of these weights: Wa = Wo * $\sum_i$ (Wl$_i$ * Ws$_i$). Ws$_i$ are of course the weights of the stored data items which matched to the left hand side patterns. It is Wa that is used in rule competition, the strongest rule activation usually being taken in preference.

The computed weight Wa of the rule instance is multiplied by the Wr$_j$ to give the weights for the right hand descriptions. These weights are used in update and output competition.

A brief discussion of the several uses of weights and uncertainty in this system can be found in [8].

Computation within rules. In addition, we can have computations in a rule. This is specified by the Landinesque *provided* part of the rule. Its argument is an arbitrary Prolog code "block", which can refer to any of the variables in the if and then parts of the rule. Computations are usually simple and used as filtering tests. However, for some purposes, it may be necessary to define complex predicates in Prolog and to use them in rules. The basic idea is that computations should be conceivably done by a neural area, and of course they can only use information present in the module. Ideally, all variable values should be obtained from the left hand side pattern match, but sometimes this ideal may need to be violated and a match made during the course of computation, for example, "not-exists" tests. For example:

`((position(W,C,[Agent,X,Y,Z]),Z > 100.0,!,fail) | true)`, which, if the variable `Agent` does not occur in the left hand side of the rule, means there does not exist any agent with `Z > 100.0`. If `Agent` does occur in the left hand side of the rule then this is equivalent to having a pattern `position(W,C,[Agent,X,Y,Z])` in the left hand side and a test `Z > 100.0` in the body of the rule.

Competition. All descriptions and all rule activations have a weight which is a number representing their strength. The simplest form of competition is just to compare the weights of all the rule instances and to select just the strongest one. The products of this one rule are then stored and/or transmitted.

However, we have found it useful, and necessary, to develop other forms of competition, as follows. First rule instances compete and then literals compete. This is necessary or else it would be possible for one literal from one rule and one from another to succeed, but other literals from the same rules to fail.

Rule instance competition is specified by the user in list_of_rule_number_sets:

`list_of_rule_number_sets(M,Mod,[list of lists of rule numbers]).`

Results from all the rule instances from rule numbers in each set compete against each other using the `Wa` values. For example,

`list_of_rule_number_sets(M,Mod,[[R1,R2],[R3,R5]]))).`

which defines a list of rule number sets e.g. `[R1,R2],[R3,R5]`. Then all the results from rules `R1` and `R2` have their `Wa` values compared and only the one with the largest `Wa` is used. The same for `R3` and `R5`. Results from any other rules all go through and are used.

After rule competition, all the surviving updates and outputs from the rule instances are made into two overall lists. These lists, of updates and outputs respectively, are then, if desired, subjected to individual competition among descriptions in the list. The user specifies *update_patterns* and *output_patterns*. For each pattern in a specified list of update patterns, all the generated descriptions which match to that pattern are compared and only the one with the largest `W1` weight is allowed to actually update the store. In addition, the winning `W1` weight must be greater than a specified threshold. Any generated updates which do not match any update pattern are allowed to update the store. The analogous method is used for outputs also.

In general, for rule competition, we are thinking of changing to using rule priority ordering, that is, each rule having a place in a, possibly partial, ordering which determines its dominance in competition, independently of computed strengths. Such an ordering could be dynamic. This would give a more stable method, with better expressive discrimination, than using rule instance weights.

Execution of rules until data coherence. The set of rules in a given module is executed repeatedly until data coherence, that is, until no more changes to the updates and outputs occur. The purpose of this is to ensure logical coherence of the store and coherence of the outputs to be sent to other modules. During these iterations, updates are performed but not outputs. Iteration continues until there are no more novel literals created. It does not continue until the weights have settled.

This process is very similar to finding the fixed point of the logic program defined by the set of rules, as in the treatment of logic programming semantics by VanEmden and Kowalski [11]. If there are no function letters involved, this process will be finite. Also, simple rule sets are similar to Datalog. At the moment, we are still using some recursion in rules and the computations within rule bodies are more general than allowed by Datalog.

6   Communication Among Modules and Updating Within a Module

Communication is specified by the user using *output_data_item* and *update_data_item* declarations. Connections will be given, for each module, by a set of statements each of which gives a description pattern and the name of a destination module.
output_data_item(Person,Mod_name,Descr_pattern, Target_module_name),
e.g.,
output_data_item(M,person_motion,action(Name,Action),person_action).

What a connection statement means is that all output descriptions matching the given description pattern will be transmitted to the given destination module. They will actually be located in the channel until stored by the module at the beginning of the next cycle.

Updates into the module's own store are specified and treated similarly.
update_data_item(Agent_name,Mod_name,Literal,Mod_name).
e.g., update_data_item(M,plan,working_goal(W,C,[WG])).

7   The Environment

Brain models operate in a 3D spatial environment which is defined by a set of logical literals which describe all the objects and agents and their spatial properties. A brain has a set of sensors for perceiving the environment and these create data items which are input to certain modules. A brain has a set of effectors, and certain modules send motor commands, represented as ground literals, to the effectors, which change the environment.

A complete model consists of a set of agents each controlled by a brain model. Agents interact via the environment, so their positions and movements are perceived, and gestures can also be explicitly used. Language communication uses a physical channel corresponding to acoustics. The environment resolves any conflicts among the set of motor commands it receives from the set of agents. The environment includes the agent's body, including muscles, blood, glands and so on.

8   Agent Architecture

As we indicated above, we have in our own work usually arranged the modules in a perception-action hierarchy. A schematic diagram of our concept of perception-action hierarchy is given in Figure 4.

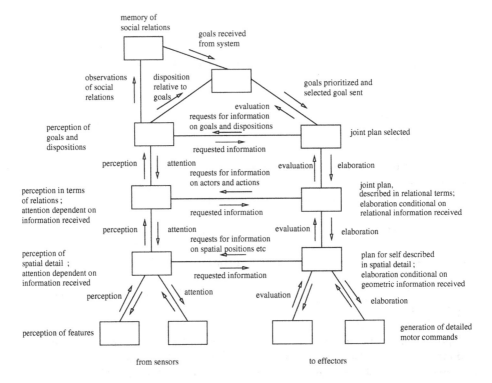

Fig. 4. The mechanisms of a perception-action hierarchy

Modules are arranged in a hierarchy of abstraction. The system elaborates a selected goal into a plan and then into a succession of more detailed plans until finally a concrete action for the next cycle is sent to effectors which act on the environment. We made the effector actually output a low-level motor goal which was renewed every cycle. We made the top level of plan description correspond to social plans, which specified, in each plan step, not only the action of the agent but also the expected perceived action(s) of the other interacting agent(s). In executing a social plan, the perceived behavior of the other interacting agents was first checked to ensure it was in agreement with the currently executed social plan, and also to extract matched variable values for use in constructing the agent's own actions. An example of a social plan is approaching and shaking the hand of another person.

At each level the currently selected plan element is computed, so all levels continuously compute in parallel every cycle. The interaction of the perception and action hierarchies results in conditional elaboration and attention mechanisms. By conditional elaboration, we mean that the current percept can modify the elaborated plan step, so for example the agent can track and act upon a changing environment. By attention, we mean that information from plan elaboration is passed to the perception hierarchy and can modify the use of perceptual resources to process in more detail the objects or other agents that the agent is interacting with.

9 Confirmation and Viable Dynamic States of Agents

In order to select rules which were successful in producing useful behavior, we developed a mechanism which we call *confirmation*. If a rule fires in one "source" module and sends a description to another "target" module, then if this causes some rule in the target module to fire then a confirmation message is sent back to the source module. This message is specific to the exact description originally sent. For this, there is no need for global evaluation, and the test is purely local to the target module. The rule instance in the source module then has its value boosted by the confirmatory message. This will tend to keep it in control and keep things stable, avoiding "jitter", i.e., rapid oscillations between two competing states. If on the other hand no rule in the target module is caused to fire, then the rule instance is disconfirmed which results in it being placed in a "refractory" state for a certain period of time. This allows other competing rule instances to be tried. The general idea is that the system will then try all the different rule instances until it finds one that makes something happen, so this is a little like backtracking but with a simpler mechanism. This is also our attempt to provide a simple form of logical completeness, i.e., that all rules will be tried at all levels, so a solution will be found if one exists.

The way this is actually implemented is to not send any message in the disconfirmation case, so the source module simply waits a certain number of cycles before timing out and disconfirming the currently active rule instance.

Thus, we keep time stamps stored in each literal which give its waiting state and its refractory state, and the attenuation mechanism updates these each cycle. Thus data items are actually time-dependent literals.

Confirm factors specify the impact of confirmation values on weights:

```
confirm_factors(Person,Module,Type,[CFNEG,CFPOS],
                      [Confirm_threshold,CSNEG,CSPOS])
```

where: (i) Confirm_threshold determines where the computed confirmation value is a positive or negative confirmation (ii) CFNEG is subtracted from W1 for negative, i.e. dis-, confirmation and (iii) CFPOS is used to multiply the confirmation value that is added to W1 for positive confirmation. Typical values are e.g. `confirm_factors(M,goal,data,[0.4,0.05],[0.2,1.0,1.0])`.

Viable states. A system will tend to transition into what we call a *viable state*, in which the perceived environment tends to support the selected plan and the plan is selected by and supports the currently selected goal. Thus, in a viable

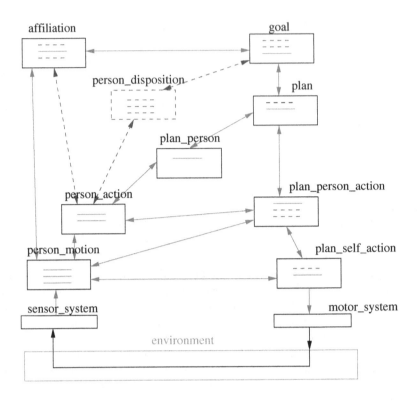

Fig. 5. The idea of a viable state

state, the agent carries out a planned action which is relevant to its current goals, and which can be successfully carried out in the current external environment. The idea of a viable state is depicted in Figure 5. In each module, there is a dominant rule, depicted as a solid line, which fires and wins the competition with other rule instances. The other rule instances, depicted as dashed lines, continue to be computed each cycle. This latter is necessary to provide for wellformed changes in the dynamic state.

Once in a viable state the system will tend to stay in it for several cycles, a few tens of cycles, up to thousands of cycles, before it has to select a new plan step at some level and to transition into another viable state. During a transition period, modules try different rules until they find one that is confirmed, and then until all the modules are selecting rules which are confirmed. It usually takes about 10 to 15 cycles to establish the next viable state, which corresponds to the experimentally observed time of 300 milliseconds to establish a conscious state.

Multiple interacting agents will also find mutually viable states, where the perceived behaviors of the other agents are compatible with the social plans being executed by each agent.

10 Using BAD

There is a BAD manual and also a document giving a complete BAD example of a working BAD program for a simple agent moving in a 3D world. A BAD system is actually set up as a set of directories, namely, (i) a directory for each agent type, (ii) world, which specifies the environment and visualization to be used, and (iii) exp, which has details of the experiment to be run. These are accessed by directory declarations in SICstus Prolog. An agent directory has a set of module specifications written in BAD, and in addition files giving the connectivity of modules. Sensors and effectors are specified in BAD and a Prolog file provided for each. An arrangement we have found most convenient and efficient is to have one agent, i.e., one complete brain model, per machine on a TCP/IP network and the world on another machine. The distribution of agents over machines is specified in Prolog. Socket communication between agents and the world is provided by BAD. The world receives sensing literals and motor commands from each agent in turn and replies to them in turn. There is at the moment no other support for managing the running of programs, so the user usually sits at the world machine and opens a window on each remote machine. Prolog sessions are started and the socket linkages started up, then calling a run(M) predicate in each session will run each agent and the world for M cycles. One can also use a file with a sequence of Prolog predicate calls to represent an experimental protocol. Consulting this file runs the experiment, it also helps clear garbage by taking the Prolog system back to the prompt each time. Typical cpu times for one cycle with an agent with 20 modules with 20 rules in each module are about 100 milliseconds on a 1 GHz Linux machine. The system provides support for VRML 2 graphical output for visualizations of the world and of agents' system states, as well as the terminal traces of the Prolog sessions. Geoffrey Irving, a Caltech undergraduate, managed to use BAD to program a predator-prey system with multiple predators and multiple prey, inspired by the arctic wolf and musk ox relationship. His project report is available from my website.

11 Summary and Conclusion

We have developed BAD, a declarative language in which to specify and execute agents inspired by the brain. The design is based on logic programming; data are literals, processes are parallel sets of rules and unification is the basic operation. Agents are modular and distributed based on distribution of storage and processing according to data type. The execution regime uses a discrete time step during which all rules are executed and all intermodule communication takes place before moving to the next time step. The time step is intended to be small relative to the rate of change of the external environment. Real-valued weights on data and rules can be used for many different purposes. BAD provides for updating and attenuation properties of data, and for defining modules by giving their data types and rules. Different connectivities among modules can be specified. A common agent architecture uses perception-action architecture, which has real time control properties. Rule execution proceeds until data coherence. BAD also provides a confirmation mechanism by which distributed processes over the architecture may be stabilized.

Acknowledgement. This work was carried out and funded by the author at Expert Software Inc., Santa Monica, California.

References

1. Alan H. Bond. Describing Behavioral States using a System Model of the Primate Brain. *American Journal of Primatology*, 49:315–388, 1999.
2. Alan H. Bond. Modeling social relationship: An agent architecture for voluntary mutual control. In Kerstin Dautenhahn, Alan H. Bond, Dolores Canamero, and Bruce Edmonds, editors, *Socially Intelligent Agents: Creating relationships with computers and robots*, pages 29–36. Kluwer Academic Publishers, Norwell, Massachusetts, 2002.
3. Alan H. Bond. Problem-solving behavior in a system model of the primate neocortex. *Neurocomputing*, 44-46C:735–742, 2002.
4. Alan H. Bond. A Computational Model for the Primate Neocortex based on its Functional Architecture. *Journal of Theoretical Biology*, 227:81–102, 2004.
5. Alan H. Bond. An Information-processing Analysis of the Functional Architecture of the Primate Neocortex. *Journal of Theoretical Biology*, 227:51–79, 2004.
6. Alan H. Bond. A psycholinguistically and neurolinguistically plausible system-level model of natural-language syntax processing. *Neurocomputing*, 65-66:833–841, 2005.
7. Alan H. Bond. Representing episodic memory in a system-level model of the brain. *Neurocomputing*, 65-66:261–273, 2005.
8. Alan H. Bond. A distributed modular logic programming model based on the cortex. In *Proceedings of the Workshop on Multivalued Programming Languages, Federated Logic Conference FloC-06, Seattle, August*, 2006.
9. Alan H. Bond. A System-level Brain Model of Spatial working Memory. In *Proceedings of the 28th Annual Conference of the Cognitive Science Society, Vancouver, August*, pages 1026–1031, 2006.
10. Alan H. Bond. Brain mechanisms for interleaving routine and creative action. *Neurocomputing*, 69:1348–1353, 2006.
11. Maarten H. VanEmden and Robert A. Kowalski. The Semantics of Predicate Logic as a Programming Language. *Journal of the Association for Computing Machinery*, 23:733–742, 1976.

From Zinc to Design Model

Reza Rafeh, Maria Garcia de la Banda, Kim Marriott, and Mark Wallace

Clayton School of IT, Monash University, Australia
{reza.rafeh,mbanda,marriott,wallace}@mail.csse.monash.edu.au

Abstract. We describe a preliminary implementation of the high-level modelling language Zinc. This language supports a modelling methodology in which the same Zinc model can be automatically mapped into different design models, thus allowing modellers to easily "plug and play" with different solving techniques and so choose the most appropriate for that problem. Currently, mappings to three very different design models based on constraint programming (CP), mixed integer programming (MIP) and local search are provided. Zinc is the first modelling language that we know of that supports such solver and technique-independent modelling. It does this by using an intermediate language called Flattened Zinc, and rewrite rules for transforming the Flattened Zinc model into one that is tailored to a particular solving technique.

1   Introduction

Solving combinatorial problems is a remarkably difficult task which requires the problem to be precisely formulated and efficiently solved. Even formulating the problem precisely is surprisingly difficult and typically requires many cycles of formulation and solving, while efficient solving often requires development of tailored algorithms which exploit the structure of the problem. Reflecting this discussion, recent approaches to solving combinatorial problems divide the task into two (hopefully simpler) steps. The first step is to develop the *conceptual model* of the problem which gives a declarative specification of the problem without consideration as to how to actually solve it. The second step is to *solve* the problem by mapping the conceptual model into an executable program called the *design model*. Ideally, the same conceptual model can be transformed into different design models, thus allowing modellers to easily "plug and play" with different solving techniques [8,6]. Here we describe the implementation of a new modelling language, Zinc [7], specifically designed to support this methodology.

We had three main aims when designing Zinc. First, we wanted the modelling language to be solver and technique independent, allowing the same conceptual model to be mapped to different solving techniques and solvers, i.e., be mapped to design models that use the most appropriate technique, be it local search, mathematical programming, constraint programming, or a combination of the above. Second, we wanted Zinc to provide high-level modelling features but still ensure that the models are executable. Thus, while Zinc provides sets, structured types, and user-defined predicates and functions, set domains must be finite and

M. Hanus (Ed.): PADL 2007, LNCS 4354, pp. 215–229, 2007.
© Springer-Verlag Berlin Heidelberg 2007

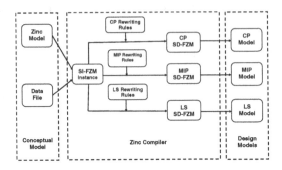

Fig. 1. Mapping a Zinc conceptual model to different decision models

recursion is restricted to iteration so as to ensure that evaluation terminates. And third, we wanted Zinc to have a simple, concise core that can be readily extended to different application areas by allowing Zinc users to define their own application specific library predicates, functions and types.

Of course there is considerable tension between these aims, since the higher-level the modeling language, the greater the gap between the conceptual model and the design model. The main contribution of this paper is to demonstrate that it is possible to map conceptual models written in a high-level modeling language, namely Zinc, into very different design models without introducing unnecessary overhead. This significantly extends our understanding of modeling language implementation since previous modelling languages and their implementations have been closely tied to specific underlying platforms and solving technologies. Note that, at this stage our objective is merely to minimise overhead, rather than competing with a directly encoded design model. In the future, we intend to build up a sufficiently broad range of transformations capable, under user control, of mapping a Zinc model to the best (known) possible design model.

Integral to the successful solver-independent implementation of Zinc is the use of an intermediate modelling language, called Flattened Zinc, to bridge the gap between conceptual and design model. Flattened Zinc is a subset of Zinc which is designed to be simple and low-level enough to be significantly closer to the decision model, yet sufficiently high-level to specify suitable intermediate models for all solvers. Therefore, it allows only simple constraints and data types.

The translation process from the conceptual model consisting of a Zinc model and instance specific data (optionally given in separate data files), to different design models is shown in Figure 1. The first step takes a Zinc model and performs syntax, semantics and type checking (which includes adding explicit coercions). The second step adds to the compiled Zinc model the information contained in the associated data file(s) (if any), and generates the Solver-Independent Flattened Zinc Model (SI-FZM) instance. This step is described more fully in Section 3. The advantage of first producing an SI-FZM model is that many common aspects of the mapping to the decision model can be performed during the Zinc to SI-FZM translation, thus reducing the burden when developing mappings to new solvers. In the third step rewrite rules are used to translate the SI-FZM into a Solver-Dependent Flattened Zinc Model (SD-FZM). As the name suggests, the rewrite rules used in this process depend on the target design model, and rewriting produces a Flattened Zinc model which is very close to the final design model. The mapping process is discussed in more detail in Section 4. The final step is to take the SD-FZM model and perform the minor syntactic rewriting required to generate the design model for a particular solving platform.

In our prototype implementation the Zinc model can be mapped into one of three design models, all of which are implemented in ECLiPSe. The first design model uses the standard constraint programming (CP) approach of a complete tree search with propagation based finite domain and set solvers. The second model is also complete but uses mathematical programming techniques, i.e. a Mixed Integer Programming (MIP) solver, while the third design model performs an incomplete search using local search methods. These are described and evaluated in Sections 5 and 6.

Modelling languages for specifying constrained optimization problems are one of the success stories of declarative programming. The first modelling languages, such as AMPL [4], provided little more than the ability to specify linear inequalities. More recent languages are considerably more expressive. Some are based on specification languages, e.g. ESRA [3] and ESSENCE [5], while others provide more programming language like features, e.g. OPL [13] and Localizer [10]. Zinc is somewhat similar to OPL but extends it by allowing constrained types and user-defined functions and predicates. The main innovation in Zinc is the ability to map a conceptual model to design models based on very different solving techniques. Other modelling languages have been designed for a particular underlying platform and solving technology. For example, AMPL is designed to interface to MIP solvers, ESSENCE is intended for propagation-based solvers, and Localizer was designed to map down to a local search engine. Although OPL models are automatically mapped to an underlying hybrid mathematical programming (MIP) and constraint programming library, the user cannot control the mapping to the same conceptual model of different design models. Also related is the mapping language Conjure [6], which uses rewrite rules to map ESSENCE models to an OPL-like language called ESSENCE'. The main difference is that while rewriting in Conjure produces alternative models for the same underlying solver, in Zinc it produces different models only for different solvers, tailoring the original model to the specific solver. Furthermore, to the best of our knowledge, a compiler for ESSENCE' has not been implemented yet.

2   Background: The Zinc Modelling Language

Zinc is a functional language with simple, declarative semantics. It provides: mathematical notation-like syntax (including automatic type coercions and operator overloading); expressive constraints (finite domain and integer, set and linear arithmetic); separation of data from model; high-level data structures and data encapsulation (including constrained types); user defined functions and

```
enum Customers ;
enum Products ;
array[Products] of set of Customers: Ordered ;

type Time = 1..card(Products) ;
array[Time] of var Products: Assign ;
array[Time] of var set of Customers: OpenStacks ;

constraint alldifferent([Assign[T] | T in Time]) ;

constraint forall(T in Time)
              (OpenStacks[T] ==
                  allunion (Ti in 1..T) Ordered[Assign[Ti]]
                  intersect
                  allunion ( Ti in T..card(Products) ) Ordered[Assign[Ti]]);

minimize max([ card(OpenStacks[T]) | T in Time]) ;
```

Fig. 2. Zinc model for the Minimisation of Open Stacks Problem (MOSP)

constraints. We illustrate some of these features by means of a simple example. For more details the interested reader is referred to our earlier paper [7] which discusses the modelling capabilities of Zinc more fully.

Example 1. A Zinc model for the Minimisation of Open Stacks Problem (MOSP) is shown in Figure 2. In MOSP, a factory can manufacture a number of products but only one at a time. Once a product in a customer's order starts being manufactured, a stack is opened for that customer to store their products. Once all products for a customer are manufactured, the order is sent and the stack closed. The MOSP [15] aims at determining the time sequence in which products should be manufactured in order to minimise the maximum number of open stacks.

The first three lines of the model define the parameters: two enumerations Customers and Products, and an array Ordered indexed by Product containing the set of Customers who ordered that Product. Next, the two arrays of decision variables are declared where the var keyword is used to distinguish decision variables from parameters. The array Assign which assigns to each Time in the sequence a given Product to be manufactured, and the array OpenStacks which is constrained so that OpenStacks[T] is the set of Customers whose stacks are open at time T. The two following constraints indicate that (1) all products in array Assign must be different (i.e., each product is manufactured only once), and (2) the number of open stacks at time T is the intersection of those customers who ordered products manufactured before or at T and those who ordered products manufactured after or at T.

Data for the model can be given in a separate data file as, for example:

```
enum Customers = {C1, C2, C3, C4, C5};
enum Products = {P1, P2, P3, P4};
Ordered = [P1:{C1,C3,C5}, P2:{C2,C4}, P3:{C2,C3,C4}, P4:{C1,C5}];
```

List, set and array comprehensions provide the standard iteration constructs in Zinc. Other iterations such as `forall`, `max`, `allunion` and `sum` are defined as Zinc library functions based on the built-in function `foldl(F,L,Z)`, which applies the binary function `F` to each element in list L (working left-to-right) with the initial accumulator value set to Z. For example, the definition of `allunion` is

`function var set of $T:allunion(list of var set of $T:L)=foldl(union(),L,{});`

where `$T` is a type variable. Any constraint or function `F` (including user-defined functions or predicates) that takes a single list comprehension as an argument, can be called using the mathematical-like syntax `F(G) E`, which is equivalent to `F([E | G])`. Thus, for instance, `allunion (Ti in 1..T) Ordered[Assign[Ti]]` is syntactic sugar for `allunion([Ordered[Assign[Ti]] | Ti in 1..T])`.

One of the novel features of Zinc not illustrated in the previous example is that types can have an associated constraint on elements of that type. This generalises the idea of constrained objects [9] and allows to the modeller to specify the common characteristics that a class of items are expected to have. Two examples are:

`type PosInt = (int:x where x>0);`
`record Activity = (var int: start, end, duration) where end=start+duration;`

Zinc provides the standard comparison and equality operators, including the `alldifferent` constraint. These are polymorphic since all base types are totally ordered and overloaded versions of the operators are generated automatically for each user-defined type (using a lexicographic ordering for compound types).

Zinc allows constraints and variables to be annotated by classes which can contain attributes. These do not change the semantics of the model but can be used to guide generation of a decision model for a particular solver or solving technique. For instance, the annotation `penalty(p)` on a constraint indicates that with local search that constraint will be treated as a "soft" constraint with penalty p for violation.

3   Solver-Independent Flattened Zinc Model (SI-FZM)

As we have seen, Zinc is a very high-level, expressive modeling language. While this makes it ideal for developing conceptual models, it also introduces a considerable gap between the conceptual Zinc model and an associated design model targeted to a specific solver and search technique. The first step in bridging this gap is to translate the conceptual Zinc model into the Solver-Independent Flattened Zinc Model (SI-FZM). This is an intermediate representation oriented towards computer implementation, but still as solver-independent as possible. The SI-FZM is written in a subset of the Zinc language called Flattened Zinc which omits features of the Zinc model that make it user friendly, while preserving any features that could be used to support solver or search heuristics.

The first step to generate the SI-FZM instance from a Zinc model and its associated data file(s) is to insert all assignment statements from the data file(s) into the model. From then on, one or more of the following steps are performed to every statement in the problem instance:

- Evaluate all parameters and check the associated integrity constraints are satisfied.
- Determine an initial domain or range for all decision variables.
- Simplify record types by (a): replacing all records by tuples, (b) flattening tuples of tuples into a single tuple, and (c) appropriately replacing field access in the constraints by the contents of the field addressed.
- Replace enumerated types by integer range types, and constraints over enumerated types by the appropriate integer constraints.
- Check that predicates and functions are sufficiently instantiated. For example, `foldl` requires its second argument to be a list of known length.
- Unfold the user-defined library and built-in predicates and functions such as `foldl`. Note that this may introduce new variables due to the formal parameters and to the existence of local variables in the definitions.
- Insert constraints arising from constrained objects, i.e., from the constraints associated with types. If these involve only parameters, check that they hold.
- Simplify arrays and lists by rewriting them to be one-dimensional arrays with an integer index set starting from 1, and appropriately updating computation of the array index in constraints.
- Translate variable sets of structured types into variable sets over integers and add a constraint mapping the structured type elements to integers. This is also used to flatten sets of sets into linked sets of integers. For instance:

```
var set of {{2,5},{1,3,6},{1,2}}: S1;
var set of {{2,5},{1,2},{3,4}}: S2;
constraint S1 intersect S2 == {1,2};
```

is translated to (assuming the encoding starts from 1):

```
var set of {1,2,3}: S1;          var set of {1,3,4}: S2;
constraint S1 intersect S2 == 3;
```

- Separate the logical combination of constraints from the constraints themselves, using reification, i.e., substituting c by $\text{reify}(c, T)$ which constrains Boolean variable T to be `true` iff c holds. For example, the constraint $c \equiv (x < y \vee x < z) \wedge (x > w)$ is substituted by:

```
constraint reify(x < y , T1);    constraint reify(x < z ,T2);
constraint reify(x > w , T3);    constraint T4 = T1 \/ T2 ;
constraint T4 /\ T3 ;
```

Note that reification is performed after unfolding predicates and functions, leaving only constraints defined by the underlying solvers. For constraints whose reification - and more specifically negation - is not supported by the solver, e.g. linear constraints in continuous variables, the reification is implemented using a specific transformation (in this case adding an ϵ so $\neg X \geq Y$ is transformed to $X \leq Y - \epsilon$)

Termination of the Zinc flattening is guaranteed as long as the unfolding of predicates, functions and iterators terminates, and only finitely many new variables are introduced. These conditions are guaranteed by the Zinc syntax.

We will illustrate some of these operations using the Zinc MOSP model given in Figure 2 with the data file of Example 1. The arrays `Assign` and `OpenStacks` which mapped `Time` to `Products` and to `set of Customers`, respectively, are translated into the FZM code:

```
array[{1, 2, 3, 4}] of var 1..4 : Assign ;
array[{1, 2, 3, 4}] of var set of 1..5 : OpenStacks ;
```

where the index type `Time` has been replaced by its range value 1..4 (represented using the more general set $\{1,2,3,4\}$), and the enumerated types `Products` and `Customers` have been replaced by ranges 1..4 and 1..5, respectively. Next, the `alldifferent([Assign[T] | T in Time])` constraint is translated as:

```
constraint alldifferent([Assign[1], Assign[2], Assign[3], Assign[4]]);
```

and the `forall` constraint is unfolded to give the four `OpenStacks` elements:

```
constraint
    OpenStacks[1]==(T_1) intersect (T_1 union T_2 union T_3 union T_4)
/\ OpenStacks[2]==(T_1 union T_2) intersect (T_2 union T_3 union T_4)
/\ OpenStacks[3]==(T_1 union T_2 union T_3) intersect (T_3 union T_4)
/\ OpenStacks[4]==(T_1 union T_2 union T_3 union T_4) intersect (T_4);
```

where each temporary variable `T_i` is equated to the result of the expression `Ordered[Assign[i]]`. Thus if `Assign[i]` $= 1$ then `T_i` $= \{1,3,5\}$, and if `Assign[i]` $= 2$ then `T_i` $= \{2,4\}$, etc. This is expressed using the standard constraint programming global constraint `element(I,L,X)` which holds if X is the Ith element in L, i.e. X = L[I]. The specific SI-FZM constraint is:

```
constraint element(Assign[i], [{1,3,5}, {2,4}, {2,3,4},{1,5}],T_i);
```

The flattened Zinc `element` constraint allows lists of complex types, rather than only the usual lists of integers.

Some of the optimisations used to improve the generated SI-FZM model are:

1. Substitution: If we can determine that a decision variable must take a unique value, then we can effectively treat it as a parameter and replace it by its value. For example, if we know that $X == 2$, constraint $X \times Y \geq 10$ can be simplified to $2 \times Y \geq 10$.
2. Omitting unnecessary `element` constraints: While Zinc supports arrays with arbitrary index sets, the `element` constraint supported by most solvers requires a range of the form $1..n$ as its index set. Thus, when we model an array access we use an extra `element` constraint to map the index set variable to a range of the required form. For example, the constraint in the Zinc code:

   ```
   array[{2,5,7,8}] of var int:A;
   var {2,5,7,8}:I;
   constraint A[I]==3;
   ```

   generates the Flattened Zinc code:

   ```
   var 1..4:T_1;          var int:T_2;
   constraint element(T_1,[2,5,7,8],I);
   constraint element(T_1,[A[2],A[5],A[7],A[8]],T_2);
   constraint T_2==3 ;
   ```

However, if the index set of the initial Zinc array is in fact a range, then we can replace the extra `element` constraint by an offset to the index variable. For instance, if we have `array[4,5,6,7] of var int:B` we can substitute `B[J]` by a new variable T which is constrained by a single `element` constraint:

```
constraint element(J-3,[B[4],B[5],B[6],B[7]],T);
```

3. Simplifying reifications and omitting unnecessary reification: While the naive translation of compound constraints of the form `constraint C1 ∧ C2` is

```
var bool: B1, B2;              constraint reify(C1,B1);
constraint reify(C2,B2);       constraint B1 /\ B2;
```

it is better to produce the simpler code

```
constraint C1;                 constraint C2;
```

which removes the potential overhead of reification and is more efficient, especially for MIP techniques.

One source of inefficiency in Zinc is the current lack of common sub-expression elimination for constraints which appear several times in our models. As a result, multiple `element` and/or `reify` constraints are created, instead of reusing the associated variables. We are currently resolving this issue.

4   Model to Model Transformation

Although the SI-FZM model is much closer to a design model than the original Zinc model, it may still contain constraints and data structures not supported by the intended solver. For example, Zinc supports variable sets of any type. Since current set solvers can support only sets over integer values, variable sets in a Zinc model are transformed to variable sets over integers in the generated SI-FZM. For the many solvers, including most MIP solvers, that do not support sets of integers, integer sets must in turn be converted to some other representation they can handle, such as Boolean arrays. To facilitate this kind of transformation the Zinc implementation supports solver specific rewrite rules that can be used to rewrite the SI-FZM model to a Flattened Zinc model that is much closer to the desired design model. Rewrite rules have the following syntax:

```
if A then substitute B with C in D where E;
```

where A is a conditional statement, B and C are two Zinc expressions, D is a subsection of a Zinc model (*declarations*, *constraints* or *model*) and E is a set of Zinc statements. Whenever A holds, all instances of B are substituted by C in scope D and the statements in E are added to the model. The *if* and *where* parts are optional.

The formal semantics of our rewrite rules is not yet fully worked out. A key issue is the specification of what can be tested in a conditional statement. In the rules used to date, the conditions have been restricted to tests on Zinc types.

Example 2. Consider the following four rules, which are among those used in our implementation to map a set S to an array of Boolean variables B, such that $B[x] \leftrightarrow x \in S$.

```
(1) substitute var set of $T:X with array[domain(X)] of var bool:X
       in declarations;

(2) if typeof(X)==array[$T] of var bool then
          substitute (I in X) with
          (if I in indexset(X,1) then X[I] else false)
          in constraints;

(3) if typeof(X)==set of $T then
        substitute X  with Z in constraints
        where
            array[$T] of bool:Z=[I:true| I in X];

(4) if typeof(L)==list of array[$T] of var bool then
        substitute element(I,L,X)
        with element(I, [extend(L[K],U)|K in 1..length(L)], extend(X,U))
        in constraints
        where U = unionall({indexset(L[H],1) | H in 1..length(L)})
                  union indexset(X,1);
```

and function extend is defined as:

```
function array[$T] of var bool: extend(array[$T] of var bool:B, set of $T:U)
        = [ if J in indexset(B,1) then B[J] else false | J in U]
```

Rule (1) substitutes in every declaration, any variable set X of some type $T by a Boolean array, assuming all set constraints can be mapped to equivalent constraints on Boolean arrays. Rule (2) rewrites the set membership expression (I in X) for any X known to be a Boolean array as a result from previous rule, into the expression X[I].[1] Zinc keeps track of which expressions have been newly introduced as a result of the mapping. Rule (3) maps the set of values X of some type $T into a Boolean array Z in which every element I in X is assigned value true. Rule (4) is used for an element(I,L,X) constraint in which L was a list of set values that has been transformed by Rule (3) into a Boolean array. It transforms the constraint into another element constraint whose second argument is a list of Boolean arrays, each defined over the same index set, U. Function extend extends an array of Booleans to a larger index set U, by adding the Boolean value false for each new index. It returns an array of Booleans over the extended index set U. The extend function has been used for readability reasons; in the implementation of Rule (4), the function is already unfolded. If we apply the above rules to the following code from the generated SI-FZM for the Open Stack Problem discussed in Section 3:

```
var set of {1,2,3,4,5} : T_3;
constraint element(Assign[1],[{1,3,5}, {2,4}, {2,3,4}, {1,5}], T_3);
```

the SD-FZM would be generated as follows (t stands for *true* and f for *false*):

```
array[{1,2,3,4,5}] of var bool : T_3;
constraint element(Assign[1],[[t,f,t,f,t],[f,t,f,t,f],
                             [f,t,t,t,f],[t,f,f,f,t],T_3);
```

---

[1] $indexset(A, I)$ returns the index set of the Ith dimension of array A.

First, Rule (1) changes the definition of T_3 in the declaration section. Then, Rule (3) maps all sets in the constraint into Boolean arrays. Finally, Rule (4) makes the length of all Boolean arrays equivalent by adding *false* for each missing member from set 1..5.

Our current implementation uses 20 rewriting rules of which 16 are used for transforming set constraints to constraints over Boolean arrays, and the remainder are used for implementing suitable versions of `max`, `min`, `maxlist` and `minlist` constraints in MIP techniques.

5   Mapping to Design Models

The primary focus of this paper is to investigate whether the high-level modelling language Zinc can provide solver and technique independent modelling. To do so, we must demonstrate that it is possible to map SI-FZM to design models using different solving techniques, and that the resulting design models do not suffer substantial overhead as compared to equivalent design models written by hand. To investigate this we have implemented mappings from SI-FZM to three very different design models.

For practical reasons all three design models were implemented using the ECLiPSe system [1]. We see no apparent reason why the choice of system should impact our experiments concerning the mapping overhead.

Mapping to CP: The SI-FZM constraints are mapped to finite domain propagation constraints. A simple complete tree search using variable *labeling* is added, and the CP system solves the problem using search and propagation. Standard CP propagation solvers typically support the SI-FZM constraints such as `reify`, `>=`, `=\=` etc. Specifically, we have used the ECLiPSe solvers `ic`, `ic_sets`, `ic_global` and, to support search and optimisation, the ECLiPSE `branch_and_bound` library.

We extended these libraries to provide comparison operators on compound data objects by generating a new constraint for each comparison operator and type. For example, the constraint `[a1,a2] =< [b1,b2]` effectively generates

```
(a1 < b1) \/  ((a1=b1) /\ (a2 =<  b2))
```

We also implemented a more general `element` constraint since, like most CP systems, ECLiPSe provides only a restricted form of `element` constraint which requires the list argument to be a ground list of integers. This more general version of `element` delays evaluation until two of its arguments are fixed.

Mapping to MIP: The SI-FZM constraints are mapped to integer and linear numeric constraints, and the problem is solved using standard MIP branch and bound search. This mapping is considerably more complex because the class of constraints handled by MIP is much more restricted.

Set constraints are mapped to Boolean constraints, which are in turn mapped to constraints over binary integer variables as detailed in Section 4. The remaining SI-FZM constraints are handled by specific translations.

Reified constraints are translated using the *Big M* technique [14]. For instance, if we assume X and Y are numeric variables and B is a binary integer variable, we model $reify(X \leq Y, B)$ by the inequalities

$$X + B \times M \leq Y + M \wedge X + M \geq Y + (1 - B) \times M + \epsilon$$

where M is a big number and ϵ a small number. If B becomes 0, the first constraint is relaxed while the second constraint forces X to be greater than Y. Otherwise, if B becomes 1, the first constraint forces X to be less than or equal to Y while the second constraint is relaxed.

Some global constraints, such as `alldifferent` have a standard mapping to MIP, as introduced in [11]. More novel and interesting is the mapping of the *element* constraint. For efficiency the translation depends on how the arguments of the constraint $element(I, L, X)$ are instantiated.

- I is instantiated to the value i: the translator impose an equality constraint between X and the ith element of L.
- L and X are ground: the translator finds the set of positions $S = \{i : L[i] = X\}$. The constraint is then translated as `var S : I`.
- Only L is ground: We associate a binary integer variable with each member of L. For each member Y, if $X = Y$, its associated binary variable becomes 1, otherwise 0. Assuming $L = [a_1, a_2, ..., a_n]$, the constraint `element(I,L,X)` is converted to the following constraints:
  $b_1, b_2, ..., b_n :: 0..1, integers([b_1, b_2, ..., b_n]), \sum_{i=1}^{n} b_i = 1$,
  $I = \sum_{i=1}^{n} i \times b_i, X = \sum_{i=1}^{n} a_i \times b_i$
  The first constraint restricts the range of each variable b_i to 0..1, the second enforces integrality, so $b_i \in 0, 1$, and the third checks that only one of the n binary variables is non-zero. On the next line, the fourth and fifth constraints establish the relationship between binary variables and I and X, respectively.
- Otherwise, in the case that L is not completely ground we use the above translation except that for each non-ground a_i, instead of generating the constraint $X = \sum_{i=1}^{n} a_i \times b_i$ we generate the two constraints: $X - M \leq a_i - M.b_i, X + M \geq a_i + M.b_i$, where M is a sufficiently large number. These behave like the *Big M* technique used for handling reification.

Mapping to local search solver: The final mapping uses a form of local search. Annotations on the constraints in the original Zinc model guide which constraints are enforced, i.e. hard, and which are handled by using a penalty in an automatically generated objective function, i.e. treated as soft.

The local search algorithm used for the experiments described in the next section is a hill-climber, with a tabu facility to prevent cycling on a plateau. The algorithm selects a variable in conflict, if there is one, and otherwise any variable. The value of the variable is changed and the algorithm then completes the move by changing any other variable values that are required by the hard constraints. The completion is greedy in the sense that each choice of variable and new value generates only one move. The neighbourhood search first considers integer variables generated from Zinc model variables, and then set variables, generated

Table 1. Zinc Mapping Statistics

Problem Name	Model Size		Generated Model Size			Mapping Time (sec)		
	Zinc	ECLiPSe	SI-FZM	SD-FZM	ECLiPSe	SI-FZM	SD-FZM	ECLiPSe
Golfers (sets)	273/5	–	1082	10706	65720/2492	20.119	31.262	34.143
Golfers (arrays)	269/5	1111/5	67451	43684	17178/485	0.1	0.475	0.55
Job-Shop	514/3	1021/5	9980	9980	16634/574	1.564	1.589	1.673
Knapsack	326/1	564/3	896	589	1181/2	0.2060	0.2220	0.2250
Stable-Marriage	527/4	955/4	16064	16064	24604/672	0.4770	2.3280	2.4330
Queens	88/3	308/3	81	81	245/3	0.047	0.047	0.047
Open-stacks	264/2	723/5	5240	29649	5104/981	0.1530	1.1070	1.4250
Perfect-squares	322/3	630/6	23446	23368	43289/231	1.578	1.644	1.933
Production	173/2	367/3	173	173	173/6	0.4190	0.4250	0.4480

from Zinc set variables. Auxiliary variables, introduced during the mapping, are automatically updated by the local search, via the introduced hard constraints that relate them to the original variables.

6 Evaluation

Our primary motivation for developing Zinc was to validate the idea of a high-level modelling language which is solver and technique independent. Therefore, our evaluation aims at demonstrating two things. First, that it is possible to map Zinc models to design models using different solving techniques. And second, that the resulting design model does not suffer substantial overhead when compared to an equivalent design model written by hand To achieve this, we used as benchmarks the Zinc model for the MOSP problem (9 customers, 7 products) given in Figure 1, and models for the following well known problems:

- Perfect Squares (7x7, 14 squares) - because of its use of disjunction
- Queens (18 queenss) - it spawns a large number of constraints.
- Knapsack (30 objects, 50%fit) - it has sets with multiple constraints on them.
- Stable Marriage (8 pairs) - it uses arrays with variable indices.
- Social Golfers (6 players, 3 groups, 3 weeks) - it uses sets of sets.
- Social Golfers (flat sets) - to reveal the cost of supporting sets of sets.
- Job Shop (4 jobs, 3 machines) - it uses many modelling features of Zinc.
- Production (3 products, 2 resources) - it involves continuous variables.

Our prototype implements the full syntax of Zinc. It is written in Mercury with a Yacc generated parser and flex generated lexical analyser. It is about twelve thousand lines of Mercury code, and five thousand lines of C. Experiments were performed on a 3GHz Pentium 4 with 1Gb memory on Fedora.

Table 1 gives statistics on the mapping using MIP techniques. The results for the other two mappings are similar, just a little bit smaller because MIP techniques cannot support high-level constraints and must be mapped to simpler ones. The first five columns give the size of the models as *number of "tokens" /*

number of constraints for the original Zinc model (in addition to the data file), the direct ECLiPSe program, and the generated SI-FZM, SD-FZM and ECLiPSe model, respectively. The last three give the time in seconds taken to generate the SI-FZM, SD-FZM and ECLiPSe model, respectively. Note that we do not give a model written directly in ECLiPSe for Golfers (sets), since it is not naturally expressible in ECLiPSe.

The Zinc model is consistently substantially smaller than the model written directly in ECLiPSe. The SI-FZM and generated ECLiPSe code is orders of magnitude larger than both the Zinc model and the direct ECLiPSe model. This is to be expected and reflects the flattening of high-level iteration constraints. Thus, the size is proportional to the number of constraints sent to the solver rather than to the number of constraints in the original model. The time to generate the ECLiPSe design model from the Zinc model is small, no more than a few seconds, for all mappings and examples, except for Golfers (sets), due to the number of set-related constraints generated, which grows exponentially. We are currently studying how to tackle this issue.

Our second experiment aimed at determining if the ECLiPSe code generated from the Zinc model had a substantial overhead as compared to an equivalent model written directly in ECLiPSe. Thus, we compared their execution times for all three design models: Constraint Programming (CP), Local Search (LS) and MIP. Table 2 shows the execution time in seconds for all programs when finding the first solution.

One possible confounding factor is the choice of search strategy. Clearly, this can greatly effect the performance of the design model. Since we are only interested on the relative performance of the two models, we ensured (as far as possible) that the direct ECLiPSe model used the same search strategy as that in the generated model. This is the reason behind the differences in the execution time for the two MIP models for Queens and Perfect Squares which, despite our efforts, perform different searches and return different solutions. Note that there were three problems whose structure was too complex to be solved with reasonable efficiency with our generic "blind" local search algorithm. These are indicated as "-" in the table.

Table 2. Comparing the execution times for the direct and mapped programs

Problem Name (cpu secs)	CP Model Direct	Generated	MIP Model Direct	Generated	LS Model Direct	Generated
Golfers (sets)	-	0.343	-	1.34	-	0.156
Golfers (arrays)	0.031	0.0	0.172	0.266	0.0	0.0
Job-Shop	0.094	0.109	4.125	3.218	0.375	0.39
Knapsack	22.828	22.675	0.00	0.00	0.797	0.828
Stable-Marriage	0.031	0.031	3.391	3.047	-	-
Queens	4.125	4.109	8.64	24.094	11.61	11.641
Open-stacks	1.547	1.843	1890.797	1971.688	0.94	0.95
Perfect-squares	0.031	0.031	3.469	1.5	-	-
Production	33.328	33.188	0.00	0.00	-	-

Table 2 shows no significant difference in execution time between the design model written directly in ECLiPSe and that generated from the Zinc model. This is true for all the design models: CP, LS and MIP. This preliminary evidence encourages our pursuit of a high level, solver independent modelling language.

7   Conclusion

We have presented the implementation of the first prototype of the modelling language Zinc. Unlike virtually all other modelling languages, a Zinc model can be mapped into design models that utilize different solving techniques such as local search, tree-search with propagation based solvers, or MIP techniques. A core feature of the Zinc implementation supporting such solver and technique-independent modelling is the use of an intermediate language called Flattened Zinc. Furthermore, the Zinc implementation provides a rewrite rule based model to model transformation facility to allow the implementers to map the Flattened Zinc model into one that is closer to the desired technique/solver.

We have compared a number of standard benchmarks written in Zinc and written in ECLiPSe. The Zinc models are considerably more concise and arguably more high-level and easier to understand. The ECLiPSe model automatically generated from Zinc (via FZM) has similar performance to an equivalent program written in ECLiPSe, assuming the same search method is used for all three mappings. This provides strong support for the hypothesis that it is possible to generate reasonably efficient design models from Zinc, and so allow Zinc modellers to readily experiment with different solving techniques. For instance, it is clear from our experiments that for the Knapsack and Production benchmarks MIP is the better technique, while for the others the CP propagation solver is the best. In the future, we plan to experiment with hybrid techniques.

Zinc has been developed as part of the G12 project and is intended to be its modelling language. Currently, mappings from Zinc to the three different design models have been crafted in Mercury with some transformations using rewrite rules. Besides the ECLiPSe platform, Zinc models will also be mapped down to Mercury itself [12]. In the longer term, we plan to use a specialised term rewriting language (Cadmium [2]) to implement the mappings from Zinc to Flattened Zinc along with model-transformations.

An important component of the mapping from conceptual to decision model is specification of the search. Currently, our implementation uses a naive search procedure, but user-controlled search is vital for scalable performance on real problems. Specification of search is deliberately not part of the Zinc language, since we believe this should not be part of the conceptual model. However, search is often naturally specified in terms of the variables and entities occurring in the decision model, so it seems sensible to allow the search component to be written in a Zinc-like language annotating the Zinc model. The inability to specify problem specific search is almost certainly the reason that the local search mapping was not competitive. We are currently exploring this.

Acknowledgements. We also like to thank members of the G12 team at National ICT Australia for helpful discussions, in particular Ralph Becket, Nick Nethercote and Peter Stuckey.

References

1. K. Apt and M. Wallace. *Constraint Logic Programming Using ECLiPSe*. Cambridge University Press, 2006.
2. G. Duck, P.J. Stuckey, and S. Brand. ACD term rewriting. In S. Etalle and M. Truszczynski, editors, *Proceedings of the International Conference on Logic Programming*, number 4079 in LNCS, pages 117–131. Springer-Verlag, August 2006.
3. P. Flener, J. Pearson, and M. Ågren. Introducing ESRA, a relational language for modelling combinatorial problems. In *LOPSTR*, pages 214–232, 2003.
4. R. Fourer, D. M. Gay, and B. W. Kernighan. *AMPL: A Modeling Language for Mathematical Programming*. Duxbury Press, 2002.
5. A.M. Frisch, M. Grum, C. Jefferson, B. Martinez-Hernandez, and I. Miguel. The essence of ESSENCE: A constraint language for specifying combinatorial problems. In *Fourth International Workshop on Modelling and Reformulating Constraint Satisfaction Problems*, pages 73–88, 2005.
6. A.M. Frisch, C. Jefferson, B. Martinez-Hernandez, and I. Miguel. The rules of constraint modelling. In *Proc 19th IJCAI*, pages 109–116, 2005.
7. M. Garcia de la Banda, K. Marriott, R. Rafeh, and M. Wallace. The modelling language Zinc. In *Proc. CP06*, pages 700–705. Springer-Verlag, 2006.
8. C. Gervet. *Large scale combinatorial optimization: A methodological viewpoint*, volume 57 of *Discrete Mathematics and Theoretical Computer Science*, page 151ff. DIMACS, 2001.
9. B. Jayaraman and P. Tambay. Modeling engineering structures with constrained objects. In *PADL*, pages 28–46, 2002.
10. L. Michel and P. Van Hentenryck. Localizer: A modeling language for local search. In *Proc. Principles and Practice of Constraint Programming - CP97*, pages 237–251, 1997.
11. P. Refalo. Linear formulation of constraint programming models and hybrid solvers. In *CP*, pages 369–383, 2000.
12. P. J. Stuckey, M. J. García de la Banda, M. J. Maher, K. Marriott, J. K. Slaney, Z. Somogyi, M. Wallace, and T. Walsh. The G12 project: Mapping solver independent models to efficient solutions. In *CP*, pages 13–16, 2005.
13. P. Van Hentenryck, I. Lustig, L.A. Michel, and J.-F. Puget. *The OPL Optimization Programming Language*. MIT Press, 1999.
14. H. P. Williams. *Model Building in Mathematical Programming*. John Wiley and Sons Ltd, 1999.
15. B. J. Yuen and K. V. Richardson. Establishing the optimality of sequencing heuristics for cutting stock problems. *European Journal of Operational Research*, 84:590–598, 1995.

Inductive Logic Programming by Instance Patterns

Chongbing Liu and Enrico Pontelli

Dept. Computer Science
New Mexico State University
{cliu,epontell}@cs.nmsu.edu

Abstract. Effectiveness and efficiency are two most important properties of ILP approaches. For both top-down and bottom-up search-based
approaches, greater efficiency is usually gained at the expense of effectiveness. In this paper, we propose a bottom-up approach, called *ILP by
instance patterns*, for the problem of concept learning in ILP. This approach is based on the observation that each example has its own pieces
of description in the background knowledge, and the example together
with these descriptions constitute a instance of the concept subject to
learn. Our approach first captures the instance structures by patterns,
then constructs the final theory purely from the patterns. On the effectiveness aspect, this approach does not assume determinacy of the
learned concept. On the efficiency aspect, this approach is more efficient
than existing ones due to its constructive nature, the fact that after the
patterns are obtained, both the background and examples are not needed
anymore, and the fact that it does not perform coverage test and needs
no theorem prover.

Keywords: Inductive Logic Programming, Concept Instance, Patterns.

1 Introduction

Inductive logic programming(ILP) [4,7,3,2,1,9] is a technology combining principles of inductive machine learning with the representation of logic programming.
The goal of ILP is the inductive construction of logic programs (called theories)
from (positive and negative) examples and some *incomplete* background knowledge. Effectiveness and efficiency are the two most important properties of any
ILP approaches [8]. Most of the existing ILP approaches are search-based, and
they are commonly classified as "top-down" and "bottom-up" methods. However, as pointed out in [8], "the problems related to search hamper both top-
down and bottom-up methods". Top-down systems, such as Shapiro's MIS [11]
and Quinlan's FOIL [10] search the hypothesis space of clauses from the most
general towards the most specific (MIS employs a (slow) breadth-first search
while FOIL makes use of a greedy search driven by an *information gain* measure). Both approaches sacrifice effectiveness of the solution to gain better performance. Bottom-up approaches based on *inverse resolution*, such as CIGOL [6],

M. Hanus (Ed.): PADL 2007, LNCS 4354, pp. 230–244, 2007.

also need to search a large clause space, since there may be many inverse resolvents at any stage. Greedy search strategies gain efficiency but degrade effectiveness, due to the existence of local maxima.

To avoid the problems incurred by searching through a predefined but large clause space, the bottom-up system GOLEM [8] *constructs* a unique clause as the generalization of a given set of examples, by computing the *relative least generalization (rlgg)* of them. We refer to this method as *non-search-based* because it just tries a very limited number of generalization candidates. To generate a single clause, GOLEM first randomly picks several pairs of positive examples, computes their consistent *rlgg*'s and chooses one with greatest coverage over the positive examples. The clause is further generalized by randomly choosing new positive examples and computing the *rlgg*'s of the clause and each of the examples. This step is repeated until the coverage of the best clause stops increasing. After one clause is learned, the positive examples covered by the clause are removed, and another clause is learned from the remaining positive examples and the negative examples. Although the efficiency of GOLEM is better than the search-based approaches, there is a loss of effectiveness due to the restriction placed on the hypothesis clauses—GOLEM requires them to be *determinate*.

The ILP approaches mentioned above are all based on θ-subsumption since the search space is ordered by θ-subsumption rather than by implication. Since θ-subsumption is incomplete (i.e., $C \leftarrow D$ does not mean C subsumes D necessarily), the Progol system [5] (and its Prolog version ALEPH [12]) are based on *inverse entailment*, and serves as a generalization and enhancement of the previous approaches. It is both bottom-up and top-down. For a given example, it first computes a most specific *bottom clause* from the example and the background knowledge in a bottom-up way. This clause bounds the search space from below. It then searches for a best clause in a top-down fashion, starting from the most general clause, i.e., the one without a body. Because the space is bounded from both above and below, the search is efficient. But we notice that the *bottom clause* is still too big and further efficiency may be gained by bounding the search space using a smaller one.

We also notice that the efficiency of existing ILP systems is hampered by the cost of the coverage tests for the hypotheses, that are performed very often during learning, even though they have only an auxiliary role in the induction process. In addition, the background knowledge and negative examples need to reside in memory, and the positive examples need to stay in memory as long as they are not covered by any learned clause (assuming a *covering* scheme [3]).

Various efforts have been devoted to improve effectiveness and efficiency of ILP systems. Nevertheless, we believe that there is room for further improvement. In this paper, we present a new approach, called *inductive logic programming by instance patterns (ILP-IP)*. This approach follows the general lines of *inductive concept learning* [3], and it is motivated by the following observations. Given a universe of objects $\mathcal{U}$, a concept $\mathcal{C}$ can be formalized as a subset of objects of $\mathcal{U}$. Learning a concept $\mathcal{C}$ means to learn a set of rules which answers the question of whether $x \in \mathcal{C}$ for each $x \in \mathcal{U}$.

In inductive concept learning, each example e is a ground atom of the target predicate p, and it represents a statement about an object obj. If the example is positive, then obj is in the concept, otherwise, it is not. Each example is supposed to have a corresponding set of ground facts in the background knowledge base, that directly or indirectly describes the object obj (or its sub-objects) in the example. For a given example, we also consider other examples as descriptions if they are related to the example under consideration. The example and the description facts, together, are called an *instance* of the concept. An instance can be naturally represented by a ground Horn clause. Each instance exhibits a certain structure, in terms of the description facts and the correspondence between obj (or its sub-objects) and the description facts. The structure of an instance is extremely important, because the rules for a concept are learned from the structural characteristics of the concrete instances. In order to represent the structure of an instance, general clauses with variables are quite appropriate. They can be obtained from the instances by consistently replacing the constants with variables. We call these rules *instance patterns*. Although both the *instance* and their *patterns* are entities that normally are present in the input of a learning problem, we have found no formal description of them or of their uses. Due to the fact that both instances and patterns have larger granularity than individual facts, making full use of the instances and patterns during learning may lead to temporal and spatial efficiency, and improve effectiveness.

The key idea of the approach we describe is to first capture the structural information of all the instances for positive and negative examples, by creating *instance patterns*, and then construct a correct theory for the target concept, by analyzing the differences and similarities between the *patterns*. Thus, the approach includes two stages—*pattern construction* and *theory construction*.

The advantages of our approach over existing ILP systems include both effectiveness and efficiency. This approach learns Horn programs allowing recursion and function symbols, but does not assume determinacy of the learned clauses. The efficiency of our approach stems from its constructive nature, from the fact that after the patterns are obtained, both the background and examples are not needed anymore, and the fact that it does not perform coverage test and needs no theorem prover.

Since this paper only represents our preliminary results, we assume a simple problem setting. We are given a target predicate p (to be learned), a background knowledge $\mathcal{B}$ of ground facts (not containing the target predicate), and a set of ground positive and negative examples $\mathcal{E}^+$ and $\mathcal{E}^-$ for p s.t.

$$\mathcal{B} \not\models e^+ \ for \ all \ e^+ \in \mathcal{E}^+ \tag{1}$$

$$\mathcal{B} \not\models e^- \ for \ all \ e^- \in \mathcal{E}^- \tag{2}$$

The objective is to find a Horn logic program Σ satisfying

$$\mathcal{B} \cup \Sigma \models e^+ \ for \ all \ e^+ \in \mathcal{E}^+ \tag{3}$$

$$\mathcal{B} \cup \Sigma \not\models e^- \ for \ all \ e^- \in \mathcal{E}^- \tag{4}$$

We assume *batch learning mode* in this article, i.e., all the examples are fed to our learner at one time before the learning process starts. A learned program Σ is said to *cover* example e, w.r.t. background knowledge $\mathcal{B}$, if $\Sigma \cup \mathcal{B} \models e$. Σ is said to be *complete* w.r.t. $\mathcal{E}^+$ if (3) is satisfied, and *consistent* w.r.t. $\mathcal{E}^-$ if (4) is satisfied. Σ is said to be *correct* if both (3) and (4) are satisfied.

2 Concept Instances

2.1 Connectedness and Constant Types

Definition 1 (Connectedness). *Let $constants(A)$ denote the set of distinct constants in ground atom A, and let $\phi(A, B) = constants(A) \cap constants(B)$. Distinct ground atoms A and C are connected $(A \frown C)$ if $\phi(A, C) \neq \emptyset$, or there exists a ground atom B such that $A \neq B$, $C \neq B$, $A \frown B$ and $B \frown C$. Ground atom A and itself are connected at depth 0 (denoted $A \frown^0 A$). Distinct ground atoms A and B are connected at depth 1 (denoted $A \frown^1 B$) if $\phi(A, B) \neq \emptyset$. For distinct ground atoms A and C, $A \frown^{d+1} C$ if there is a ground atom B s.t. $B \neq A$, $B \neq C$, $constant(B) \neq \emptyset$, $A \frown^d B$, $B \frown^1 C$ and $\phi(A, B) \cap \phi(C, B) = \emptyset$.*

If ground atoms A and B are connected (at depth d), we say that A connects to B (at depth d). The *connectedness* is not sufficient for determining which facts in our background knowledge describe the example in a way we intend.

Example 1 (Unintended Connectedness). Let us consider $\mathcal{E}=$ {daughter(mary, ann), daughter(eve,tom)}, and a background knowledge $\mathcal{B}$ as follows:

```
parent(ann,mary).                 parent(tom,eve).
female(ann).     female(mary).    female(eve).     male(tom).
age(mary,young). age(ann,old).    age(eve,young). age(tom,middle).
family_rank(ann,2).               family_rank(tom,2).
```

In $\mathcal{B}$, we intend to describe two pairs of people, i.e., ⟨mary, ann⟩ in the left half, and ⟨eve, tom⟩ in the right half. However, if the *connectedness* defined in Def. 1 is applied, then all the facts will be included for describing each example, since all the facts are *connected* to each example.

However, it is easy to observe that the constants "**young**" and "**2**" are the only constants that establish *connectedness* between the atoms in the left half and those in the right half. If these two constants are not considered as *connecting*, then the problem disappears. Thus, to use the *connectedness* for collecting the facts that describe a given example, we should predefine a set of constants that do not establish *connectedness* at all and a set of constants that do establish *connectedness*. We call these two sets of constants *non-object* type constants and *object* type constants, respectively. Informally, a constant is of *object* type if it is intentionally used to represent some object (e.g., mary, ann), and is of *non-object* type otherwise. *Non-object* constants include those used to represent quantitative properties, or categories to which an object belongs (e.g., young, middle and 2). Thus, *connectedness* is established only by *object* type constants.

Constants basically fall into two categories, non-numerical and numerical. By default, we consider non-numerical constants as of *object* type and consider numerical constants as of *non-object* type. Exceptions to the default rule (e.g., non-numerical constants to be treated as *non-object*) are expressed using declarations, based on two reserved predicates **non_object** and **object**. The declaration **object(c)** specifies that the constant c is of *object* type. The declaration **object(q,i)** specifies that all constants occurring at the argument position i of predicate q are of *object* type. Similarly, the declaration **non_object(c)** specifies that the constant c is of *non-object* type, and the declaration **non_object(q,i)** specifies that all the constants occurring in the argument position i of predicate q are of *non-object* type.

Example 2 (Constant Types). Suppose the following constant type declarations are with the background knowledge $\mathcal{B}$ in Example 1:

> **non_object(young).   non_object(middle).   non_object(old).**

The non-numerical constants **ann**, **mary**, **tom** and **eve** are, by default, of *object* type, while the non-numerical constants **young**, **middle** and **old** are of *non-object* type by declaration. The numerical constant 2, representing the family rank of a people, is of *non-object* type, by default.

2.2 Relative Connectedness and Instance

Let us define *connectedness* relative to a set of *constant type* declarations $\mathcal{D}$.

Definition 2 (Relative Connectedness). *Given a set of constant type declarations $\mathcal{D}$ and ground atom A, let $obj\_constants(A)$ be the set of distinct object constants in A according to $\mathcal{D}$. For ground atom A and B, we let $\phi'(A,B) = obj\_constants(A) \cap obj\_constants(B)$. Distinct ground atoms A and C are connected relative to $\mathcal{D}$ (denoted $A \frown_{\mathcal{D}} C$), if $\phi'(A,C) \neq \emptyset$, or there exists an ground atom B such that $A \neq B$, $C \neq B$, $A \frown_{\mathcal{D}} B$, and $B \frown_{\mathcal{D}} C$. The ground atoms A and B are connected at depth 1 relative to $\mathcal{D}$ ($A \frown_{\mathcal{D}}^{1} B$) if $\phi'(A,B) \neq \emptyset$. We have that $A \frown_{\mathcal{D}}^{d+1} C$ if there exists some ground atom B such that $A \neq B$, $C \neq B$, $obj\_constant(B) \neq \emptyset$, $A \frown_{\mathcal{D}}^{d} B$, $B \frown_{\mathcal{D}}^{1} C$ and $\phi'(A,B) \cap \phi'(C,B) = \emptyset$.*

If the atoms A and B are connected (at depth d) relative to $\mathcal{D}$, A is said to connect to B (at depth d) relative to $\mathcal{D}$.

Definition 3 (Description Facts). *Given an example $e \in \mathcal{E}$, a background knowledge $\mathcal{B}$, a set of constant type declaration $\mathcal{D}$, an atom $A \in \mathcal{B} \cup \mathcal{E}$ is called a description fact of e relative to $\mathcal{D}$ if $A \neq e$ and $e \frown_{\mathcal{D}} A$.*

However, even with the *unintended* facts eliminated, the number of collected *description facts* may still be large. We differentiate them by the depth at which they are connected to the example, and drop all the description facts connected to the example at a depth greater than some predefined threshold. Let us call this value *maximum connected depth* (*mcd*). We use the predicate *max_connected_depth/1* to declare *mcd*. The dropped description facts are considered as less important, as they less *directly* describe the example.

Example 3 (Maximum Connected Depth). Let us continue Example 1, but assume the constant type declarations of Example 2. Also, we assume that a new atom, `parent(eve,mary)`, is added to the background knowledge. The *connectedness* between example `daughter(mary,ann)` and the description facts is shown in Fig. 1. The root represents the example, each node represents a group of facts, and each edge stands for the connectedness established by the constants labeling the edge. The description facts of example `daughter(mary,ann)` are connected to the example at depth 1, 2, and 3, respectively. Note that the other example `daughter(eve,tom)` is connected to example `daughter(mary,ann)` at depth 2. If *mcd* is chosen as 1, then all the lower six facts are excluded.

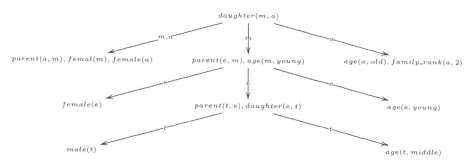

Fig. 1. Example of Connectedness (m=mary, e=eve, a=ann, t=tom)

We define the instance for an example as itself plus the set of description facts that connect to the example within some given depth and relative to some constant type declarations. We represent an instance as a ground Horn clause.

Definition 4 (Concept Instance). *Given a background knowledge $\mathcal{B}$, a set of examples $\mathcal{E} = \mathcal{E}^+ \cup \mathcal{E}^-$, a set of constant declarations $\mathcal{D}$, and a value for mcd, the* instance *of the target concept regarding example $e \in \mathcal{X}$ ($\mathcal{X} = \mathcal{E}^+$ or $\mathcal{E}^-$), denoted by $I = instance_{\mathcal{D}}^{mcd}(e, \mathcal{X}, \mathcal{B})$, is defined by a partially ordered ground definite program clause[1] $e \leftarrow b_1, \ldots, b_m$. where each b_i ($1 \leq i \leq m$) is a ground atom, $b_i \in \mathcal{B} \cup \mathcal{X}$, $b_i \frown_{\mathcal{D}}^{d_i} e$, $d_i \leq mcd$, and b_i is left of b_j if $d_i < d_j$. I is called positive if e is a positive example, and negative if e is a negative example. Concept instances are also called instances for short.*

The *object constant set* of a concept instance I, denoted by $object\_constant\_set(I)$, is defined as the set of *object constants* that occur in I. It is easy to see that $instance_{\mathcal{D}}^{mcd}(e, \mathcal{X}, \mathcal{B}) \models e$.

2.3   Data Localization

We call the process of creating instances *data localization*, because each of the resulting instances entails the corresponding example *locally*, without using any other data. Fig. 2 describes an algorithm for creating the instance for a given

---

[1] If $m = 0$, there is no description facts in $\mathcal{B} \cup \mathcal{X}$ for e and no instance is defined.

example e from a set of examples $\mathcal{X}$ ($\mathcal{X} = \mathcal{E}^+$ or $\mathcal{E}^-$) and a background knowledge $\mathcal{B}$, given the set of constant type declarations $\mathcal{D}$ and a value of mcd. After initializing the instance I as a bodyless rule $e \leftarrow$, this algorithm I grows I by adding to the body all the ground facts in $\mathcal{B} \cup \mathcal{X}$ connected to e at depth $depth$ relative to D in order, i.e., $depth = 1, 2, \ldots, mcd$. A set $\mathcal{F}$ keeps all the atoms to which e is connected at depth $depth - 1$, and a set $\mathcal{F}'$ stores all the atoms to which e is connected at depth $depth$. If no new fact is found to be connected to e at depth $depth$, i.e., $\mathcal{F}' = \emptyset$, then the process will stop.

Input : $e, \mathcal{X}, \mathcal{B}, \mathcal{D}$ and mcd
Output: $instance_\mathcal{D}^{mcd}(e, \mathcal{X}, \mathcal{B})$
Algorithm: $CreateInstance(e, \mathcal{X}, \mathcal{B}, \mathcal{D}, mcd)$

```
1     B' = B ∪ X
2     I = e ← .
3     F = {e}          // all atoms connected to e at depth 0
4     depth = 1        // start by atoms connected to e at depth 1
5     do
6        F' = ∅        // no atoms connected to e at depth depth+1 yet
7        for each A ∈ F              // A ⌢^depth_D e
8           for each B ∈ B' \ F' (in order) s.t. A ⌢^1_D B  // B ⌢^{depth+1}_D e
9              if B ∉ I
10                append B to the end of the body of I
11                F' = F' ∪ {B}
12                B' = B' \ {B}
13           if F' = ∅    // no atoms connected to e at depth depth+1
14              break
15        F = F'         // all atoms connected to e at depth depth+1
16        depth = depth + 1       // next depth
17     while depth ≤ mcd
18     output I
```

Fig. 2. Data Localization Algorithm

Example 4 (Data Localization). Consider learning predicate $daughter/2$ [3].

```
% positive examples:                    % negative examples:
  daughter(mary,ann).                     daughter(tom,ann).
  daughter(eve,tom).                      daughter(eve,ann).
% knowledge base    :
  max_connected_depth(1).
  parent(ann,mary).    female(ann).    parent(ann,tom).    female(mary).
  parent(tom,eve).     female(eve).    parent(tom,ian).
% positive instances
  daughter(mary,ann) :- parent(ann,mary), female(ann), parent(ann,tom), female(mary).
  daughter(eve,tom)  :- parent(ann,tom), parent(tom,eve), female(eve), parent(tom,ian).
% negative instances
  daughter(tom,ann) :- parent(ann,mary), female(ann), parent(ann,tom),
                       parent(tom,eve), parent(tom,ian), daughter(eve,ann).
  daughter(eve,ann) :- parent(ann,mary), female(ann), parent(ann,tom),
                       parent(tom,eve), female(eve), daughter(tom,ann).
```

For a given example e, a set of examples $\mathcal{X}$ with the same sign as e, a background knowledge base $\mathcal{B}$, a set of constant type declarations $\mathcal{D}$, and a value for mcd, the *data localization algorithm* in Fig. 2 collects in $instance_{\mathcal{D}}^{mcd}(e, \mathcal{X}, \mathcal{B})$ all the description facts $B \in \mathcal{X} \cup \mathcal{B}$ which satisfy $e \curvearrowright_{\mathcal{D}}^{depth} B$ for $depth = 1, 2, \ldots, mcd$.

There are some consequences that can be proved from the above definitions. Given an example e, the concept instance for e generated by the data localization algorithm is *unique*. Moreover, for a concept instance $I = instance_{\mathcal{D}}^{mcd}(e, \mathcal{X}, \mathcal{B})$ created by the algorithm, there is no ground atom $q(x_1, \ldots, x_k) \in \mathcal{B} \cup \mathcal{X}$ s.t.

1. $q(x_1, \ldots, x_k) \notin body(I)$,
2. $e \curvearrowright_{\mathcal{D}}^{depth} q(x_1, \ldots, x_k)$, $depth \leq mcd$, and
3. $\{x_1, \ldots, x_k\} \cap object\_constant\_set(I) \neq \emptyset$.

If $|\mathcal{B} \cup \mathcal{X}| = n$, all the predicates have arity less than k, and the output instance has m atoms in the body, then we can prove that the complexity of the algorithm in Fig. 2 is $O(n)$ if $m \ll n$ and $k \ll n$.

3 Instance Patterns

Instance patterns are devised to capture the structure of the concept instances. In this section we provide definitions regarding instance patterns, present an algorithm for constructing patterns for a given set of examples and a given background knowledge, and discuss their properties.

Definition 5 (Instance Pattern). *The instance pattern of I with respect to a set $\mathcal{D}$ of constant type declarations, denoted by $pattern(I, \mathcal{D})$, is defined as an ordered definite program clause, $pattern(I, \mathcal{D}) = I\theta_0$ where $\theta_0 = \{c_1/X_1, \ldots, c_n/X_n\}$ is an inverse substitution such that*

1. *$\{c_1, \ldots, c_n\} = object\_constant\_set(I)$ according to $\mathcal{D}$,*
2. *c_i always first occurs in I before c_j for all $i < j$, and*
3. *$X_1, \ldots, X_n$ are distinct variables.*

A pattern is a positive (negative) *pattern if it is obtained from a positive (negative) instance. Instance patterns are also called patterns for short.*

In the rest of the discussion, given an instance I, we say that I *matches* a pattern P if I and P have the same number of literals and there is a variable substitution θ such that $I = P\theta$. This leads us to the definition of a *super-pattern (sup-pattern)*. A sup-pattern S of pattern $P = A \leftarrow B_1, \ldots, B_n$ is defined as $S = A \leftarrow C_1, \ldots, C_m$ where $m > 0$, $\{C_1, \ldots, C_m\} \subset \{B_1, \ldots, B_n\}$, and S is an *allowed* clause[2] with a finite variable-depth (see Def. 7). S subsumes P and is thus *more general than* P.

A positive pattern P is consistent if there is no negative pattern N s.t. P is identical to or more general than N. Given a set $\mathcal{I}$ of concept instances and a pattern P obtained from an instance $I \in \mathcal{I}$, the *strength* of a positive (negative) pattern P is the number of positive (negative) instances in $\mathcal{I}$ that *match* P.

---

[2] A clause is *allowed* if all variables in the head appear also in the body.

Definition 6 (Local Knowledge Base and Cover Set). *Let us assume that the instance pattern P covers a set $\mathcal{I}$ of instance $I = instance_{\mathcal{D}}^{mcd}(e, \mathcal{X}, \mathcal{B})$. The local knowledge base of P, denoted by $\mathcal{KB}_{local}(P)$, is the set of all ground atoms in the bodies of $I \in \mathcal{I}$. The cover set of P, denoted by $cover\_set(P)$, is the set of all e in $I \in \mathcal{I}$.*

Definition 7 (Variable Depth [2]). *The variable-depth of a variable X in a pattern $A \leftarrow B_1, \ldots, B_n$ is defined as follows. If X occurs in A, then its variable-depth is 0. Suppose X first occurs in B_i. If none of the other variables in B_i occurs in $A \leftarrow B_1, \ldots, B_{i-1}$, then X has variable-depth ∞. Otherwise, the variable-depth of X is 1 plus the variable-depth of the variable in B_i with the greatest variable-depth occurring in $A \leftarrow B_1, \ldots, B_{i-1}$. The variable-depth of an ordered definite program clause is the largest variable-depth of its variables.*

Input : $\mathcal{X}$, $\mathcal{B}$, $\mathcal{D}$ and mcd
Output: a set of patterns $\mathcal{P}$
Algorithm: $PatternConstruction(\mathcal{X}, \mathcal{B}, \mathcal{D}, mcd)$
1      $\mathcal{P} = \emptyset$
2   for each $e \in \mathcal{X}$
3          $I = CreateInstance(e, \mathcal{X}, \mathcal{B}, \mathcal{D}, mcd)$
4          $P = pattern(I, \mathcal{D})$
5          $\mathcal{P} = \mathcal{P} \cup \{P\}$
6   increment $strength(P)$ by 1
7   output $\mathcal{P}$

Fig. 3. Algorithm for construction of instance patterns

An algorithm for obtaining instance patterns from a set of examples $\mathcal{X}$ and a background knowledge $\mathcal{B}$ is presented in Fig. 3. Note that none of the instances is stored, and if there are more than one instances that match a same pattern, only one pattern is stored for them. In other words, the set of facts in background knowledge $\mathcal{B}$ and the set of examples $\mathcal{X}$ are transformed to a potentially much smaller set of patterns. It is easy to see that the complexity of this algorithm is $O((|\mathcal{B}| + |\mathcal{X}|) \cdot |\mathcal{X}|)$.

Example 5 (Instance Pattern). The patterns obtained from the instances in Example 4 are as follows.

```
% positive patterns
daughter(A,B) :- parent(B,A), female(B), parent(B,C), female(A).
daughter(A,B) :- parent(C,B), parent(B,A), female(A), parent(B,D).

% negative patterns
daughter(A,B) :- parent(B,A), female(B), parent(B,C), parent(A,D),
                 parent(A,E), daughter(D,B).
daughter(A,B) :- parent(B,C), female(B), parent(B,D), parent(D,A),
                 female(A),   daughter(D,B).
```

It is possible to prove that instance patterns have the following properties.

1. A pattern obtained from instance $I = instance_{\mathcal{D}}^{mcd}(e, \mathcal{X}, \mathcal{B})$ is an *allowed* definite program clause which has variable-depth $d \leq mcd$.
2. For any pattern P, $P \cup \mathcal{KB}_{local}(P) \models cover\_set(P)$.
3. If pattern P is a sup-pattern of Q, then $P \cup \mathcal{KB}_{local}(Q) \models cover\_set(Q)$.
4. For a Horn clause C, if $\{C\} \cup \mathcal{B} \cup \mathcal{X} \models e$, $e \in cover\_set(P)$, then $C = P$ or there is a variable substitution θ s.t. $C\theta = P$ or $C\theta$ is a sup-pattern of P.

We can also prove that the set of all positive patterns $\mathcal{P}^+$ forms a correct theory.

Theorem 1 (Correctness of the Set of Positive Patterns). *For a given $\mathcal{B}$ and $\mathcal{E} = \mathcal{E}^+ \cup \mathcal{E}^-$, if there exists a Horn solution Σ for the learning problem such that $\Sigma \neq \mathcal{E}^+$, then a theory Σ_0 consisting of the set of positive patterns $\mathcal{P}^+$ generated by the algorithm in Figure 3 is correct.*

4   Theory Construction

We have already obtained a correct theory Σ_0 for the problem of concept learning, according to Theorem 1. This theory consists of all the positive patterns. However, Σ_0 may contain too many clauses, and the clauses may contain redundant literals. For example, there are two lengthy positive patterns in Example 5, while a much more efficient theory is one containing the single clause $daughter(A, B) \leftarrow parent(B, A), female(A)$. The second stage of our approach is to construct a satisfactory theory of the target concept by reducing the obtained positive patterns while preserving completeness and consistency. While the acquisition of patterns constitutes one step of generalization during the learning, this stage acts as a further generalization step.

The goal of this stage is to remove both the redundant patterns and redundant body atoms from $\mathcal{P}^+$, and thus obtain a smallest set of smallest consistent Horn clauses. Our algorithm for theory construction is presented in Figure 4. The construction is done by considering the set of positive patterns as a whole, rather than one at a time. As the first sub-step, we first eliminate the obvious redundant patterns. A pattern $P \in \mathcal{P}^+$ is obvious redundant if there exists a pattern $Q \in \mathcal{P}^+$ such that Q is more general than P.

In our second sub-step, we eliminate those not so obvious redundant patterns and redundant atoms in the bodies by making use of the notation of *sup-pattern* introduced earlier. We first construct a set $Super(P_i)$ of *best* valid and consistent sup-patterns for each $P_i \in \mathcal{P}^+$. Each sup-pattern in $Super(P_i)$ has the smallest number of body atoms. The set $Super(P_i)$ is determined by first trying the sup-patterns formed out from body atoms of P_i with smaller variable-depths. Once we find the set of smallest consistent sup-patterns formed from body atoms with variable-depth $\leq d$, there is no need to try sup-patterns with atoms whose variable-depths are greater than d. Then we start with the first pattern $P_i \in \mathcal{P}^+$ and compute the intersection of $Super(P_i)$ and each $Super(P_j)(i \neq j)$ in the following *iterative* way. If $Super(P_i) \cap Super(P_j) = \emptyset$, no reduction can be made between P_i and P_j. Otherwise, two patterns P_i and P_j are reduced to one pattern by updating $Super(P_i)$ with $Super(P_i) \cap Super(P_j)$ and dropping P_j from $\mathcal{P}^+$ (since at least one sup-pattern of P_j is already in $Super(P_i)$). We

Input : $\mathcal{P}^+, \mathcal{P}^-$
Output: a Horn theory Σ
Algorithm: TheoryConstruction($\mathcal{P}^+, \mathcal{P}^-$)
    // sub-step 1: remove obvious redundant patterns
1   remove from $\mathcal{P}^+$ all Q for which there exists $P \in \mathcal{P}^+$
      s.t. P is more general than Q
    // sub-step 2: remove not so obvious redundant patterns
    // and redundant body atoms
2   let $Super(P_i)$ = set of best valid and consistent
      sup-pattern of $P_i \in \mathcal{P}^+$
3    $\Sigma = \emptyset$
4   while $P^+ \neq \emptyset$
5   let P_i be the first pattern in $\mathcal{P}^+$
6   for each $P_j \in \mathcal{P}^+$ s.t. $P_j \neq P_j$
7   if $Super(P_i) \cap Super(P_j) \neq \emptyset$
8       $Super(P_i) = Super(P_i) \cap Super(P_j)$
9   remove P_j from $\mathcal{P}^+$
10    $\Sigma = \Sigma \cup \{Q\}$ where Q is any one in $Super(P_i)$
11   remove P_i from $\mathcal{P}^+$
    // sub-step 3: further simplification using non-ground clauses
12   for each $P \in \Sigma$
13   while there exists a non-ground clause $C \in \mathcal{B}$
      s.t. $body(C) \subseteq body(P)$ after variable renaming
      replace $body(C)$ in $body(P)$ with $head(C)$
14   return Σ

Fig. 4. Theory Construction Algorithm

iterate on another P_j using the updated $Super(P_i)$. When all P_j's are considered, $Super(P_i)$ contains the set of sup-patterns to which P_i and all P_j's satisfying $Super(P_i) \cap Super(P_j) \neq \emptyset$ are reduced. Since we are currently only interested in finding *one* correct theory but not *all* the correct theories, it suffices to take only one sup-pattern of P_i in $Super(P_i)$ and add it to the final theory Σ.

From the patterns in Example 5, a theory Σ containing only the following rule is constructed by the algorithm:

        `daughter(A,B) :- parent(B,A), female(A).`

The following example shows the capability of our approach for learning recursive programs, where predicate $g(A, B)$ means A is greater than B and $s(A, B)$ means that B is the *successor* of A.

Example 6 (Theory Construction).

```
%background knowledge      % E=E+      %constructed theory
max_connected_depth(2).    g(4,3).     % r1:  covers {g(2,1),g(3,2),g(4,3)}
object(s,1).               g(4,2).     g(A,B) :- s(B,A).
object(s,2).               g(4,1).
object(g,1).               g(3,2).     % r2:  covers {g(3,1),g(4,1),g(4,2)}
object(g,2).               g(3,1).     g(A,B) :- g(A,C), g(C,B).
s(3,4). s(2,3). s(1,2).    g(2,1).
```

It is easy to prove that the theory Σ constructed by the algorithm in Fig. 4 is correct. Assume all the predicates in the background knowledge $\mathcal{B}$ have arity less than k, and m be the maximum number of body atoms in the patterns. Let $\mathcal{P}^+$ and $\mathcal{P}^-$ be the set of positive and negative patterns respectively. Then the complexity of the algorithm in Fig. 4 is $O(\ |\mathcal{P}^+|\ m^2 k^2 (|\mathcal{P}^+| + |\mathcal{P}^-| \cdot 2^m)\ )$.

5   Discussion

5.1   General Characteristics

We outline our approach as a general algorithm (the *ILP-IP* algorithm) in Figure 5. Our approach has the following characteristics.

1. It is bottom-up, and learns a theory for the target concept in a purely constructive way—the instance patterns are constructed from *data localization* and the final theory is constructed directly from the fixed set of patterns.
2. It is not search-based. Although it performs a "search" for smallest consistent *sup-patterns*, it searches only through a definite set of possible sup-patterns of a given pattern, but not (part of) the large hypothesis space (e.g., formed by *variabilization*).
3. No coverage test of the sup-patterns against the examples is performed. The only test needed is whether a positive pattern is a *super-pattern* of some negative patterns or not.
4. After the patterns are obtained, we do not need the background knowledge and the examples anymore while constructing the theory.
5. It learns in *batch* mode, but does not use the *covering* technique.
6. No theorem prover is needed.

> **Input** : $\mathcal{B}, \mathcal{E}, \mathcal{D}, mcd$
> **Output:** a theory Σ
> **Algorithm:** $ILP\text{-}IP(\mathcal{E}, \mathcal{B}, \mathcal{D}, mcd)$
> 1: Let $\mathcal{E} = \mathcal{E}^+ \cup \mathcal{E}^-$
> 2: $\mathcal{P}^+ = PatternConstruction(\mathcal{E}^+, \mathcal{B}, \mathcal{D}, mcd)$
> 3: $\mathcal{P}^- = PatternConstruction(\mathcal{E}^-, \mathcal{B}, \mathcal{D}, mcd)$
> 4: $\Sigma = TheoryConstruction(\mathcal{P}^+, \mathcal{P}^-)$
> 5: output Σ

Fig. 5. ILP-IP Algorithm

5.2   Comparisons

We compare our approach with two existing most successful bottom-up approaches, GOLEM and Progol. GOLEM [8] is based on the notation of *rlgg*. This notation replaces search by the process of *cautiously* constructing a unique clause which covers a given set of examples. The *rlgg* of two example e_1 and e_2 w.r.t. background knowledge $\mathcal{B}^3$ is defined as

$$rlgg_{\mathcal{B}}(e_1, e_2) = lgg(e_1 \leftarrow \mathcal{B}, e_2 \leftarrow \mathcal{B}) \tag{5}$$

Since the generated *rlgg*'s are usually very long, the computation of *rlgg*'s is immediately followed by a post-processing phase, called *reduction*, where the *irrelevant* literals are removed. Our approach is similar to GOLEM, in that both GOLEM and our approach are constructive, start learning from ground clauses and basically go through two steps of generalization. But they differ as follows:

- The ground clauses in our approach are *concept instances*, where the body contains only a *subset* of $\mathcal{B}$, and the subset for one example is usually different from those for other examples. We achieve this by eliminating *unintended* descriptions. With *rlgg*, however, the body of each ground clause (e.g., $e_1 \leftarrow \mathcal{B}$ in (5)) *constantly* contains the *whole* set $\mathcal{B}$ for any example.

- GOLEM has to restrict the hypothesis clauses to be only *determinate*, to keep the *rlgg* length small. The *determinacy* is checked *semantically* during the post-processing. Our approach does not have this restriction.

- To construct a compressed theory, GOLEM randomly picks up more than one pair of (positive) examples and computes their *rlgg*'s, but only takes the one with the best coverage. This means that most of the computation of *rlgg*'s are discarded, and GOLEM relies on coverage test. The theory construction stage of our approach does not incur this waste and does not need coverage tests.

Our approach is also similar to Progol [5]. Progol first bottom-up computes the *bottom clause* for the first positive example. Then it searches top-down the bounded hypothesis space for a clause with the best coverage. The two stages of our approach roughly correspond to these two steps of Progol. However, significant differences exist:

- For each selected *positive* example, Progol computes *one* bottom clause and induces *one* best clause. Our approach first computes patterns of *all* examples, and then constructs the final theory as a whole.

- In general, the bottom clause can have arbitrarily large cardinality. Progol uses *mode declarations* to constrain the search for clauses which θ-subsume the bottom clause. Even with the help of mode declarations, the cardinality of the bottom clause is still much larger than that of the patterns generated by our approach. The obvious reason is that the computation of the bottom clause is based on *constant matching*, treating all the constants equally. In our approach, in contrast, we classify constants and treat them differently. Since the size of search space grows exponentially with the cardinality of the bottom clause, significant efficiency gains can be obtained if Progol adopts our constant declarations instead of *mode declarations*.

---

[3] GOLEM requires an extensional background knowledge base.

- The "search" occurring in the theory construction stage of our approach is totally different than the top-down search of Progol. Top-down search is essentially generate-and-test. We do not try any sup-patterns obtained by *variabilizing* the given pattern. We do not *test* any generated sup-patterns against the examples either. What we test is only the sup-pattern validity of the very limited set of possible clauses formed using the same set of body literals in the given pattern. In other words, the "search" degenerates to *construction* in our approach.

- If viewing our approach as "searching", the search space we need to go through is bounded simultaneously by as many clauses as the positive patterns rather than one single bottom clause.

5.3   Efficiency and Effectiveness

By combining the complexities of the two stages, and assuming that both m and k are constants, we obtain a total complexity of

$$Time(ILP\text{-}IP) = O((|\mathcal{B}| + |\mathcal{E}|) \cdot |\mathcal{E}|) + O(|\mathcal{P}^+| \cdot (|\mathcal{P}^+| + |\mathcal{P}^-|)). \quad (6)$$

It is reasonable, in practice, to assume that the number of patterns is much smaller than the number of instances. Thus, the second term in (6) can be neglected. We also assume $|\mathcal{E}| \leq |\mathcal{B}|$. The resulting complexity is $Time(ILP\text{-}IP) = O(|\mathcal{B}|^2)$.

As for GOLEM [8], its main algorithm uses a *covering* technique. The main loop terminates after $|\mathcal{E}|$ iterations. Within each iteration, a random sample of size s is taken from the positive examples. The number of *rlgg*'s computed is $|\mathcal{E}| \cdot s$ and the coverage test is performed for each *rlgg*. It takes $O(|\mathcal{B}|^2)$ to compute one *rlgg*, and it takes $|\mathcal{E}| \cdot |\mathcal{B}|$ to perform a coverage test. The resulting complexity is $Time(GOLEM) = O(s|\mathcal{E}| (|\mathcal{B}|^2 + |\mathcal{E}| \cdot |\mathcal{B}|)) = O(|\mathcal{B}|^3)$.

Progol [5] also uses the *covering* technique. The main loop is executed $|\mathcal{E}|$ iterations. Within each iteration, it first computes the most specific bottom clause $\perp$ for the first example, taking $d \cdot r \cdot |M| \cdot |\mathcal{B}|$, where r and d are the *recalling* and *depth* parameters of the algorithm, $|M|$ is the number of mode declarations, and $|\mathcal{B}|$ denotes the number of facts[4] in $\mathcal{B}$. Searching the bounded clause space of size $|\rho|$ for a best clause takes $|\rho| \cdot |\mathcal{E}| \cdot |\mathcal{B}|$. Note that $|\rho|$ is exponential in $|\perp|$ in general. The complexity of Progol is at least $Time(ALEPH) = O(|\mathcal{E}| (rd|\mathcal{B}| + |\rho| \cdot |\mathcal{E}| \cdot |\mathcal{B}|)) = O(|\mathcal{B}|^3)$.

As can be seen above, the complexity of our approach is one order lower than GOLEM and Progol. This is obtained by using the notation of instance patterns, but not at the sacrification of effectiveness as other approaches do. Potentially, this efficiency improvement can enable us to avoid any restrictions placed on the hypotheses due to the magnitude of the search space. In principle, our approach learns Horn programs allowing recursion and function symbols without restricting them to contain only determinate clauses.

---

[4] Progol and ALEPH do not require background knowledge to be only facts.

6   Conclusion

The ILP problem has long been thought of and solved as a search problem. GOLEM was the first attempt to avoid this by exploiting the notation of *rlgg*. Existing ILP systems are still searching an improved balance between learnability (effectiveness) in a large search space and efficiency. The approach presented in this paper represents a step towards a new solution to the ILP problem. Its novelty lies in the more direct use of *concept instance* and *instance pattern* during the learning process. These two entities are actually present in all the learning problems, but we propose a more formal and direct use. Our discovery that these entities might be very useful in ILP is based on the observation that the constants appearing in logic programs either represent some *objects* or some properties of the *objects*, and they can be distinguished by some declaration mechanism. A set of basic algorithms related to these entities have been developed, and used to establish a process to construct a theory, with significant advantages. Implementation of the approach is still in progress.

Future work includes handling classification errors if the consistency condition can not be strictly satisfied, incorporating non-extensional background information (including non-ground facts and non-ground program clauses), and comparing the performance of our approach with existing approaches. Because our approach is both *time* and *space* efficient, parallelization may also lead to excellent speedups for *very large problems*. New learning approaches can be also developed on top of what we presented here—e.g., a method for *non-monotonic inductive learning* can be designed on the proposed foundations.

References

1. Luc De Raedt (ed.), *Advances in Inductive Logic Programming*, IOS Press, 1996.
2. S. Hwei, N. Cheng and R. de Wolf. *Foundations of Inductive Logic Programming*. Springer, 1997.
3. N. Lavrac, S. Dzeroski. *Inductive Logic Programming, Techniques and Applications.* 1994.
4. S. Muggleton. Inductive Logic Programming. *New Generation Computing*, 8, 1991.
5. S. Muggleton. Inverse entailment and Progol. *New Gen. Computing*, 13:245-286, 1995.
6. S. Muggleton and W. Buntine. Machine invention of first-order predicates by inverting resolution. In *Int. Conf. on Machine Learning*, pages 339-352. 1988.
7. S. Muggleton, and L. De Raedt. Inductive Logic Programming: Theory and Methods. *Journal of Logic Programming*, 19,20:629-679, 1994.
8. S. Muggleton and C. Feng. Efficient induction in logic programs. In *Conf. on Algorithmic Learning Theory*, 1990.
9. D. Page and A. Srinivasan. ILP: a short look back and a longer look forward. *The Journal of Machine Learning Research*, Vol. 4, 2003.
10. J. R. Quinlan. Learning Logical Definitions from Relations. *Machine learning*, 5:239-266, 1990.
11. E.Y. Shapiro. Algorithmic program debugging. *Cambridge*, MA: MIT Press, 1983.
12. A. Srinivasan. The Aleph Manual. `web.comlab.ox.ac.uk/oucl/research/areas/machlearn/Aleph`.

ARMC: The Logical Choice for Software Model Checking with Abstraction Refinement

Andreas Podelski[1,3] and Andrey Rybalchenko[2,3]

[1] University of Freiburg
[2] Ecole Polytechnique Fédérale de Lausanne
[3] Max-Planck-Institut für Informatik Saarbrücken

Abstract. Software model checking with abstraction refinement is emerging as a practical approach to verify industrial software systems. Its distinguishing characteristics lie in the way it applies logical reasoning to deal with abstraction. It is therefore natural to investigate whether and how the use of a constraint-based programming language may lead to an elegant and concise implementation of a practical tool. In this paper we describe the outcome of our investigation. Using a Prolog system together with Constraint Logic Programming extensions as the implementation platform of our choice we have built such a tool, called ARMC (for Abstraction Refinement Model Checking), which has already been used for practical verification.

1 Introduction

Software model checking with (counterexample-guided) abstraction refinement is emerging as a practical approach to verify industrial software systems [2,4,5,13,16]. Its distinguishing characteristics lie in the way it applies logical reasoning to deal with abstraction. In particular, it implements the automatic construction of abstract domains based on logical formulas. This construction requires intricate operations on logical formulas, operations which involve both syntax-based manipulations and semantics-based logical operations such as entailment tests between constraints. It is therefore natural to investigate whether and how the use of a constraint-based logic programming language may lead to an elegant and concise implementation of a practical tool. In this paper we describe the outcome of our investigation.

Using a Prolog system together with extensions [15,17] as the implementation platform of our choice we have built such a tool, called ARMC (for Abstraction Refinement Model Checking). The tool has already been used for practical verification [20].

Our work builds upon, and also crucially differs from previous efforts to exploit constraint based programming languages for the implementation of model checkers (see e.g. [1,8,9,10,11,18,19,21]). Those efforts relate the fixpoint definitions of runtime properties of programs with the fixpoint semantics of

M. Hanus (Ed.): PADL 2007, LNCS 4354, pp. 245–259, 2007.

constraint logic programs. We also take advantage of this connection, but our
implementation may best be understood by its operational reading. We exploit
the logical reading of programming language constructs for the implementation
of operations that are specific to abstraction and abstraction refinement. As far
as we know, none of the existing CLP/logic-based implementations of model
checkers performs abstraction refinement.

We structure the paper as follows. First, we describe the representation of
the program to be verified by Prolog facts `trans(...)` that are stored in the
Prolog database. We then define the procedure `post` that implements the one-
step-reachability operator over sets of states, each set being represented by a
constraint. The abstraction procedure `abstract` takes a set of predicates (which
are atomic constraints stored in the Prolog database in a single fact `preds(...)`)
and maps a set of states to the corresponding over-approximation. We define
`abstract`, `concretize` and `abstract_post`. We are then ready to define the
abstract reachability procedure `abstract_fixpoint`.

If the abstraction is too coarse then the call to `abstract_fixpoint` may lead
to the call of a refinement procedure `refine`, which updates the Prolog fact
`preds(...)` stored in the Prolog database. The subsequent iteration calls the
abstract reachability procedure again, but now the procedure `abstract` refers
to the new set of predicates. The refinement procedure is based on the procedure `feasible` that performs an intricate analysis of counterexamples that
are possible in the abstract, but may be absent in the concrete. The insights
that are gained during this analysis guide the discovery of new predicates which
are added in order to refine abstraction (for a detailed account on the underlying algorithm we refer to [3]). We first define the procedure `feasible` and then
`refine`, and are then finally ready to define the 'main' procedure ARMC, which
is `abstract_check_refine`.

2   From Program Statements to Prolog Facts `trans(...)`

We illustrate the translation of the program to be verified into the representation
by Prolog facts in Figure 1. We translate each statement of the corresponding
goto program by a `trans(...)`-fact (all `trans(...)`-facts together represent the
transition relation of the program to be verified). In the next section, we will use
calls of the form `trans(FromState, ToState, Rho, StmtId)` where the first
two arguments represent the states (control location and data variables) before
and after the execution of the statement. The third argument will be bound to a
term that stands for a *transition constraint*, e.g. `Rho = (Xp=X+1, Yp=Y)`. Here
the logical variables `X` and `Xp` (read "x-prime") refer to the before- and after-
values of the C program variable `x`. Transition constraints relate the values of
program variables before and after the transition. We use the expression language
of the applied CLP system to form transition constraints. The fourth argument
will be bound to the label that identifies the statement. We encode the initial
and error conditions of the program with the help of the distinguished locations
`start(...)` and `error(...)`.

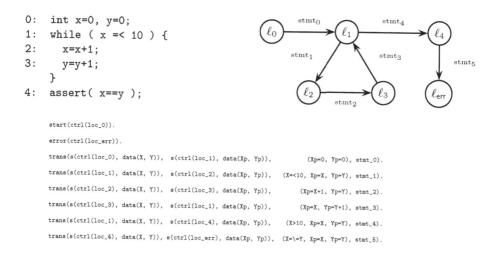

```
0:  int x=0, y=0;
1:  while ( x =< 10 ) {
2:      x=x+1;
3:      y=y+1;
    }
4:  assert( x==y );
```

```
start(ctrl(loc_0)).

error(ctrl(loc_err)).

trans(s(ctrl(loc_0), data(X, Y)),  s(ctrl(loc_1), data(Xp, Yp)),      (Xp=0, Yp=0), stmt_0).

trans(s(ctrl(loc_1), data(X, Y)),  s(ctrl(loc_2), data(Xp, Yp)),   (X=<10, Xp=X, Yp=Y), stmt_1).

trans(s(ctrl(loc_2), data(X, Y)),  s(ctrl(loc_3), data(Xp, Yp)),     (Xp=X+1, Yp=Y), stmt_2).

trans(s(ctrl(loc_3), data(X, Y)),  s(ctrl(loc_1), data(Xp, Yp)),     (Xp=X, Yp=Y+1), stmt_3).

trans(s(ctrl(loc_1), data(X, Y)),  s(ctrl(loc_4), data(Xp, Yp)),    (X>10, Xp=X, Yp=Y), stmt_4).

trans(s(ctrl(loc_4), data(X, Y)),  s(ctrl(loc_err), data(Xp, Yp)),  (X=\=Y, Xp=X, Yp=Y), stmt_5).
```

Fig. 1. Example program in C syntax and its representation by Prolog facts. The correctness of the program is defined by the validity of the assertion in line 4. In terms of the corresponding goto program depicted by the control-flow graph this means the non-reachability of the error location ℓ_{err} from the start location ℓ_0. It is always possible to encode the initial and the error condition of the program with the help of special locations ℓ_0 and ℓ_{err}.

3   One-Step-Reachability Operator post

Figure 2 shows the procedure post that implements the one-step-reachability operator over sets of states.

We "symbolically" represent a set of states by a constraint. For example, the constraint Y>=5, X=Y represents the set of all valuations of the program variables (see Figure 1) where the program variable y is not less than 5 and is equal to the value of the program variable x. A program state is determined by the valuation of the program variables and the control location. Assume the bindings Phi = (Y>=5, X=Y), and FromState = s(ctrl(loc_2), data(X, Y)). Then Phi and FromState together represent the set of program states at the location ℓ_2 with the valuations of the program variables constrained as described above. We explain the use of the data(...) term later.

We consider the set of successor states under the execution of a particular program statement in the goto program. The forth parameter of post is used to identify this statement. In our example, the identifiers of statements, i.e. the possible values of StmtId, range from stmt_0 to stmt_5.

We use our example to illustrate how post is executed. Assume the above bindings for Phi and FromState. The call {Phi} injects the constraint Y>=5, X=Y into the constraint store. The next call non-deterministically selects a trans(...) fact from the database, say the fact identified by stmt_2. This creates the bindings

```
ToState = s(ctrl(loc_3), data(Xp, Yp)),
Rho = (Xp=X+1, Yp=Y),
StmtId = stmt_2.
```

We observe that the variables in the term bound to FromState are unified with the from-variables of the transition. In the example, for legibility, we have already chosen the same variables, i.e., X and Y both for the variables in FromState and for the from-variables.

The call {Rho} injects the transition constraint Xp=X+1, Yp=Y into the constraint store. This means that the constraint store now contains the constraint Y>=5, X=Y, Xp=X+1, Yp=Y. The projection of this constraint on the variables Xp and Yp represents the set of valuations of the program variables after the application of the statement identified by StmtId. This projection yields Xp=1+Yp, Yp>=5. It is instructive to reflect that this constraints indeed represents the successor values of x and y after the increment operation for x.

The choice of the variables for the projection is determined by the term bound to ToState, which is s(ctrl(loc_3), data(Xp, Yp)) in our example. The projection is performed by the elimination of existentially quantified variables, in the example X and Y. We do not explicitly perform this elimination (neither the renaming of primed by unprimed variables, which is usually required by implementations of successor operators).

```
post(Phi, FromState, ToState, StmtId) :-
        {Phi},
        trans(FromState, ToState, Rho, StmtId),
        {Rho}.
```

Fig. 2. The procedure post

4   Abstract One-Step Reachability Operator abstract_post

The procedure abstract_post implements a function that is defined by the functional composition of three functions for which the notation α, *post* and γ is customary in the abstract interpretation framework [7]: the abstraction, the one-step-reachability operator, and the concretization. As we will show below, the procedure abstract_post is implemented in terms of the three procedures abstract, post and concretize.

Procedure abstract. We define the procedure abstract in Figure 3. This procedure computes a constraint that is an over-approximation of the current content of the constraint store. The first argument of abstract determines the approximation function. For example, Xp=1+Yp, Yp>=5 is approximated by the constraint Yp>=0, Xp>=Yp if the list of the four constraints Xp=<0, Yp>=0, Xp=<Yp, Xp>=Yp appears in the first parameter of abstract. It is customary to refer to the given set of constraints (which together determine

```
abstract([Pred-Id|PredIdPairs], Ids) :-
        ( entailed(Pred) ->
            abstract(PredIdPairs, TmpIds),
            Ids = [Id|TmpIds]
        ;
            abstract(PredIdPairs, Ids)
        ).
abstract([], []).
concretize([Id|Ids], [Pred-PId|PredIdPairs], Phi) :-
        ( Id = PId ->
            concretize(Ids, PredIdPairs, TmpPhi),
            Phi = (Pred, TmpPhi)
        ;
            concretize([Id|Ids], PredIdPairs, Phi)
        ).
concretize([], _, 1=1).
abstract_post(FromCtrl, FromIds, ToCtrl, ToIds, StmtId) :-
        FromState = s(FromCtrl, _),
        preds(FromState, FromPredIdPairs),
        concretize(FromIds, FromPredIdPairs, Phi),
        post(Phi, FromState, ToState, StmtId),
        ToState = s(ToCtrl, _),
        preds(ToState, ToPredIdPairs),
        abstract(ToPredIdPairs, ToIds).
```

Fig. 3. The procedures `abstract`, `concretize`, and `abstract_post`

the approximation function) as *predicates*. In our running example, we refer to the four predicates given above.

We give each predicate a unique identifier. This is its position in a given list of predicates. The call `abstract(PredIdPairs, Ids)` computes a list of identifiers that is bound to `Ids`. This list consists of the identifiers of the predicates that appear in the approximation of the constraint in the constraint store. For technical reasons, the first parameter of `abstract` is not a list of predicates, but a list of pairs containing a predicate and its identifier (which we write using - in Prolog).

We continue our example. If `PredIdPairs` is bound to `[(Xp=<0)-1, (Yp>=0)-2, (Xp=<Yp)-3, (Xp>=Yp)-4]` and the constraint store contains `Xp=1+Yp, Yp>=5` then `abstract` creates the binding `Ids = [2,4]`.

Note that we have used an implicit assumption. Namely, the variables that appear in the constraint to be approximated are literally the variables that appear in the list of predicates (from predicate-identifier pairs). This assumption is justified by the context in which `abstract` is called. Namely, the call `abstract(PredIdPairs, Ids)` is preceded by the call `preds(State, PredIdPairs)` and `State` is bound to a term of the form `s(..., data(Xp,Yp))`.

We assume that the Prolog database contains a fact of the form `preds(...)`. In our example, this fact is

```
preds(s(ctrl(_), data(X, Y)), [(X=<0)-1, (Y>=0)-2, (X=<Y)-3, (X>=Y)-4]).
```

The call `preds(State, PredIdPairs)` now succeeds and realizes the appropriate α-renaming in the predicates, namely by unifying the variable X and Y with Xp and Yp respectively. Therefore it computes the binding of `PredIdPairs` shown above.

Procedure `concretize`. The procedure `concretize` is defined in Figure 3. It takes a list of identifiers and computes a constraint that is the conjunction of predicates whose identifiers are in the input list. As `abstract`, the procedure `concretize` takes a list of predicate-identifier pairs as a parameter. Continuing our example, we call `concretize(Ids, PredIdPairs, Phi)` given the binding of `Ids` to the list of predicate identifiers [2, 4] and the above binding of `PredIdPairs`. The resulting binding to `Phi` is `Yp>=0, Xp>=Yp, 1=1`.

Procedure `abstract_post`. The procedure `abstract_post` is given in Figure 3. It is the composition of the procedures `concretize`, `post`, and `abstract`.

We may view the procedure `abstract_post` as a function that maps an abstract state to a successor abstract state (for a fixed statement). We define an abstract state as the pair given by a control location and a list of identifiers of predicates. For example, under the binding of `FromCtrl` to `ctrl(loc_2)` and the binding of `FromIds` to the list of identifiers [2, 4], an abstract state is given by `FromCtrl` and `FromIds`.

The application of `abstract_post` on `FromCtrl` and `FromIds` under the above binding computes a successor abstract state as follows. The execution of the first line binds `FromState` to the term `s(ctrl(loc_2), FromData)` where `FromData` is a fresh variable. The call `preds(FromState, FromPredIdPairs)` binds the list of predicate-identifier pairs that is stored in the Prolog database to `FromPredIdPairs`. These predicates are over fresh variables, say X and Y. The variable `FromData` gets bound to the term `data(X, Y)`.

Now, the call to `concretize` translates the list of predicate identifiers [2, 4] to the constraint `Y>=0, X>=Y, 1=1`, which is bound to `Phi` (and represents the set of states whose successors will be computed and abstracted).

The call of the procedure `post` proceeds as described in Section 3. We assume that the statement `stmt_2` is selected for application. This statement goes from location ℓ_2 to location ℓ_3. The call to `post` binds `ToState` to the term `s(ctrl(loc_3), data(Xp, Yp))`, where Xp and Yp are fresh variables. Now, the constraint store contains the constraint `Y>=0, X>=Y, 1=1, Xp=X+1, Yp=Y`. Its projection to the variables Xp and Yp that are referenced by `ToState` is a new constraint, namely, `Xp>=1+Yp, Yp>=0`. It represents the set of states that are reachable by applying the statement `stmt_2` to the set of states denoted by the constraint `Y>=0, X>=Y, 1=1` (which is the previously computed concretization of the abstract state given by `FromState` and `FromIds`).

```
assert_abst_reach_state(_, Ctrl, Ids, _, _, _) :-
        abst_reach_state(_, Ctrl, ReachedIds, _),
        ord_subset(ReachedIds, Ids),
        !.
assert_abst_reach_state(Iter, Ctrl, Ids,
                        AbstStateId, StmtId, NextAbstStateId) :-
        bb_get(abst_reach_state_count, LastAbstStateId),
        NextAbstStateId is LastAbstStateId+1,
        bb_put(abst_reach_state_count, NextAbstStateId),
        assert(abst_reach_state(iter(Iter),Ctrl,Ids,NextAbstStateId)),
        assert(abst_parent(NextAbstStateId, from(state(AbstStateId),
                                               trans(StmtId)))).
abstract_fixpoint_step(Iter, NextIter) :-
        abst_reach_state(iter(Iter), FromCtrl, FromIds, AbstStateId),
        abstract_post(FromCtrl, FromIds, ToCtrl, ToIds, StmtId),
        assert_abst_reach_state(NextIter, ToCtrl, ToIds,
                        AbstStateId, StmtId, NextAbstStateId),
        ( error(ToCtrl) ->
            throw(abst_error_state(NextAbstStateId))
        ;
            true
        ).
abstract_fixpoint(Iter) :-
        NextIter is Iter+1,
        ( bagof(_, abstract_fixpoint_step(Iter, NextIter), _) ->
            abstract_fixpoint(NextIter)
        ;
            true
        ).
```

Fig. 4. The procedures assert_abst_reach_state, abstract_fixpoint_step, and abstract_fixpoint. bb_get/bb_put store/read facts from the mutable repository.

The execution of ToState = s(ToCtrl, _) binds ToCtrl to the term ctrl(loc_3), which represents the to-location. The call to abstract assumes that it is applied to the predicates over the variables Xp and Yp. We create such predicates by calling preds with the first parameter bound to s(ctrl(loc_3), data(Xp, Yp)). Finally, the outcome of the call to abstract is a list of predicate identifiers [2, 4] that is bound to ToIds.

5   Abstract Reachability Procedure abstract_fixpoint

We define the procedure abstract_fixpoint together with the auxiliary procedures assert_abst_reach_state, abstract_fixpoint_step in Figure 4.

Figure 8 (shown in the appendix) presents the execution of `abstract_fixpoint` on our example program, which is shown in Figure 1. The procedure `abstract_fixpoint` computes an approximation of the set of reachable states of the program to be verified. It also checks whether the error location is contained in the approximation, i.e., if an abstract state at location `loc_err` is created. If this check succeeds then the iteration halts and throws an exception. We discuss the exception handling in Section 6.

The procedure `abstract_fixpoint` implements a fixpoint computation that iteratively builds up a set of facts `abst_reach_state(...)` stored in the Prolog database. Each such fact represents an abstract state that is determined to be reachable by the abstract fixpoint computation. For example, the fact `abst_reach_state(iter(2), ctrl(loc_2), [2,3], 3)` represents an abstract state at the control location `ctrl(loc_2)` and the list of predicate identifiers `[2, 3]`. The first argument of `abst_reach_state(...)`, here `iter(2)`, shows at which iteration the abstract state is created and inserted into the database. The last argument shows the identifier of the abstract state, which is 3 in our example. Since the list `[2, 3]` refers to the predicates `X-Y=<0`, `X-Y>=0` (from the list of predicates as fixed by the fact `preds(...)` currently in the Prolog database, see Figure 8), the abstract state represents the set of program state at the location ℓ_3 with equal values of the variables `x` and `y`. Figure 8 also shows facts `abst_parent(...)`. We do not discuss them in this section. They will play a role in Section 6.

The procedure `assert_abst_reach_state` first checks whether a given abstract state, which is represented by `Ctrl` and `Ids`, is already present in the database. This is the case if there exists a reachable abstract state whose list of identifiers `ReachedIds` is contained in the list `Ids`. In this case the given abstract state represents a smaller set of program states at the same control location. For example, an abstract state with predicate identifiers `[2, 3, 4]` represents a smaller set of program states than an abstract state with predicate identifiers `[3, 4]`. A longer list of identifiers corresponds to a larger conjunction of predicates, i.e. to a stronger constraint. We implement the comparison between lists of identifiers by a call to the library procedure `ord_subset` because our implementation guarantees that these lists are ordered.

The procedure `assert_abst_reach_state` inserts the given abstract state into the database if it is not already present. It computes the value for `NextAbstStateId`, which is used to label the given abstract state.

The procedure `abstract_fixpoint` calls `abstract_fixpoint_step` by using the bagof procedure of Prolog. It iterates over all abstract states that are created at the iteration with number `Iter` (and stored as `abst_reach_state(...)` facts in the Prolog database) and over all program statements (which are stored as `trans(...)` facts). The call to `abstract_fixpoint_step` fails if no new abstract state is created (and hence a fixpoint is reached).

6 Abstraction Refinement Procedure
abstract_check_refine

Given a set of predicates, the procedure abstract_fixpoint computes an over-approximation of the reachable state space of the program, as we described in the previous section. If this over-approximation does not contain the error location then the program is proven correct. Otherwise, there exists a sequence of abstract states that begins at the start location and ends at the error location. Each step in this sequence corresponds to the application of a program statement to an abstract state. We call this sequence of statements a *counterexample path*, or *counterexample* for short. Now, the procedure feasible determines which of the following two cases applies.

In the first case, the error location is indeed reachable (from the initial location) by executing the sequence of statements. We say that the counterexample is *feasible*. We report that the program is not correct and return the counterexample. In the second case, the sequence is not feasible. We say that the counterexample is *spurious*. The abstraction was too coarse. This means that the set of predicates does not yet contain the "right" predicates. The procedure refine discovers new predicates and adds them to the set of existing ones.

The procedure abstract_check_refine repeatedly executes abstract_fixpoint, feasible, and refine. It terminates in one of two cases. Either a feasible counterexample is computed, or it discovers the right set of predicates. The latter case means that the procedure abstract_fixpoint computes a sufficiently precise over-approximation of the set of reachable states of the program, one which does not contain the error location. In this section, we define the procedures feasible, refine, and abstract_check_refine.

Counterexample checking procedure feasible. We check the feasibility of the path between the initial and error location in the abstract reachability tree by applying the procedure feasible. It is defined in Figure 5. If the procedure succeeds for the abstract state identifier SId that is given in the exception abst_error_state(ErrorStateId), see Figure 4, then we report that the program is incorrect and print the error path.

```
feasible(AbstStateId, ToState, AccPath, ErrorPath) :-
      ( abst_parent(AbstStateId, from(state(PrevAbstStateId),
                                      trans(StmtId))) ->
            trans(FromState, ToState, Rho, StmtId),
            {Rho},
            feasible(PrevAbstStateId,FromState,[StmtId|AccPath],ErrorPath)
      ;
            ErrorPath = AccPath
      ).
```

Fig. 5. The procedure feasible

Continuing our example, we will follow the execution of the call `feasible(9, _, [], ErrorPath)`. We assume the context of Figure 8. That is, the call of `abstract_fixpoint` has inserted the shown `abst_parent(...)` facts. These facts form a tree whose root is the start abstract state 0. Each path in the tree corresponds to a sequence of statements, according to the `abst_parent(...)` facts. The call `feasible(9, _, [], ErrorPath)` determines whether the path is feasible or whether it is a spurious counterexample.

The first execution step of the call `feasible(9, _, [], ErrorPath)` retrieves the fact `abst_parent(9, from(state(8), trans(stmt_5)))` and binds `StmtId` to `stmt_5`. Then, it retrieves the fact

```
trans(s(ctrl(loc_4), data(X1, Y1)), s(ctrl(loc_err), data(X0, Y0)),
      (X1=\=Y1, X0=X1, Y0=Y1), stmt_5)
```

and binds `Rho` to the transition constraint `X1=\=Y1, X0=X1, Y0=Y1`. The next line injects this constraint into the constraint store.

The effect of the recursive call to `feasible` is that the line `{Rho}` in that recursive call injects the transition constraint `X2>10, X1=X2, Y1=Y2`, which belongs to the statement `stmt_4`. This statement precedes the statement `stmt_5` on the path that ends in the abstract state 9.

The recursion in the procedure `feasible` terminates, and upon termination we distinguish two cases. In the first case, the conjunction of transition constraints that are injected into the constraint store is not satisfiable. This means that the corresponding sequence of statements is not feasible. In the second case, we have explored the path from the given abstract state to the start abstract state. Since the start abstract state does not have a corresponding `abst_parent` fact, the call `abst_parent(1, ...)` fails. Hence, `feasible` terminates and binds `ErrorTrace` to the list of identifiers of the statements along the path.

In our example, the call `feasible(9, ...)` fails. The transition constraint for the statement `stmt_0` is inconsistent with the conjunction of the transition constraints for other statements on the path leading to the error abstract state 9. This means that the call `{Rho}` fails in the recursive call `feasible(2, ...)`.

We have already discussed the handling of fresh variables in terms `FromState` and `ToState` in Section 3. The situation here is analogous. We need to create instances of constraints over the appropriate variables. We observe that the term bound to `FromState` gets passed to the formal parameter `ToState` in the recursive call to `feasible`. Hence, we obtain the sequence of transition constraints such that the from-variables of each constraint are equal to the to-variables of its successor constraint. In our example, the constraint store contains `X1=\=Y1, X0=X1, Y0=Y1, X2>10, X1=X2, Y1=Y2` after the first recursive call to `feasible`.

Predicate discovery procedure `refine`. The procedure `refine` is defined in Figure 6. We assume that each transition constraint can be partitioned into two lists. The first list consists of constraints over from-variables, and is called list of guards. The second list consists of a list of update expressions of the form `Xp = Exp` where `Xp` is a to-variable and `Exp` is an expression over the from-variables.

```
wp(Updates, Guards, Formula, WP) :-
       ( Updates = [U|Us] ->
             U,
             wp(Us, Guards, Formula, WP)
         ;
             append(Guards, Formula, WP)
       ).
refine(AbstStateId, ToState, Formula) :-
       ( abstract_parent(AbstStateId, from(state(PrevAbstStateId),
                                              trans(StmtId))) ->
             stmt(FromState, ToState, Guards, Updates, StmtId),
             wp(Updates, Guards, Formula, WP),
             insert_preds(FromState, WP),
             refine(PrevAbstStateId, FromState, WP)
       ;
             true
       ).
```

Fig. 6. The procedures `wp` and `refine`

```
abstract_check_refine :-
       start(StartCtrl),
       bb_put(abst_reach_state_count, 1),
       assert(abst_reach_state(iter(0), StartCtrl, [], 1)),
       catch( abstract_fixpoint(0),
             abst_error_state(AbstErrorStateId),
             ( feasible(AbstErrorStateId, _, [], Path) ->
                 format('counterexample ~p\n', [Path]),
                 fail
             ;
                 refine(AbstErrorStateId, _, []),
                 retractall(abst_reach_state(_, _, _, _)),
                 retractall(abst_parent(_, _)),
                 abstract_check_refine
             )
       ).
```

Fig. 7. The procedure `abstract_check_refine`

For each fact `trans(FromState, ToState, Rho, StmtId)` we assume that the Prolog database contains a fact `stmt(...)` of the form

```
       stmt(FromState, ToState, Guards, Updates, StmtId)
```

where `Guards` and `Updates` form a partition of `Rho`. For example, given the bindings `FromState = s(ctrl(loc_4), data(X, Y))`, `ToState = s(ctrl(loc_err), data(Xp, Yp))`, and `StmtId = stmt_5` we obtain the list of guards `[X=\=Y]` and the list of updates `[Xp=X, Yp=Y]`.

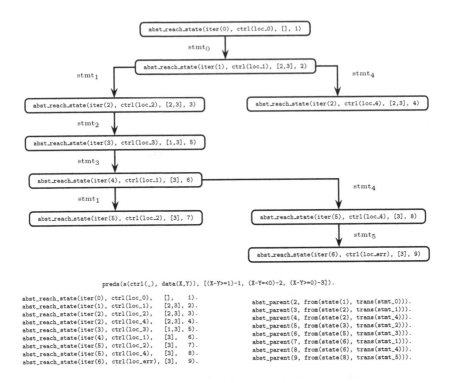

preds(s(ctrl(_)), data(X,Y)), [(X-Y>=1)-1, (X-Y=<0)-2, (X-Y>=0)-3]).

```
abst_reach_state(iter(0), ctrl(loc_0),    [],     1).
abst_reach_state(iter(1), ctrl(loc_1),    [2,3],  2).
abst_reach_state(iter(2), ctrl(loc_2),    [2,3],  3).
abst_reach_state(iter(2), ctrl(loc_4),    [2,3],  4).
abst_reach_state(iter(3), ctrl(loc_3),    [1,3],  5).
abst_reach_state(iter(4), ctrl(loc_1),    [3],    6).
abst_reach_state(iter(5), ctrl(loc_2),    [3],    7).
abst_reach_state(iter(5), ctrl(loc_4),    [3],    8).
abst_reach_state(iter(6), ctrl(loc_err),  [3],    9).
```

```
abst_parent(2, from(state(1), trans(stmt_0))).
abst_parent(3, from(state(2), trans(stmt_1))).
abst_parent(4, from(state(2), trans(stmt_4))).
abst_parent(5, from(state(3), trans(stmt_2))).
abst_parent(6, from(state(5), trans(stmt_3))).
abst_parent(7, from(state(6), trans(stmt_1))).
abst_parent(8, from(state(6), trans(stmt_4))).
abst_parent(9, from(state(8), trans(stmt_5))).
```

Fig. 8. The facts abst_reach_state(...) and abst_parent(...) computed and asserted by the call of abstract_fixpoint. We assume the context of the Prolog database with the given fact preds(...) (fixing the set of predicates) and the trans(...)-facts given in Figure 1 (representing the program to be verified). The pictorial representation relates the facts abst_reach_state(...) by edges according to the facts abst_parent(...).

We continue our example. We follow the execution of the call refine(9, _, []). This call is performed after the call feasible(9, ...) fails. The call to abstract_parent binds PrevAbstStateId to 8 and StmtId to stmt_5. The next line retrieves the guards and updates for stmt_5. These are passed to the procedure wp, which computes the weakest precondition of Formula with respect to the guards and updates.

The call wp([Xp=X, Yp=Y], [X=\=Y], [], WP) binds WP to [X=\=Y]. The call to insert_preds(s(ctrl(loc_4), data(X, Y)), [X=\=Y]) adds the predicates to the list of predicates that is stored in the Prolog database as preds(...). The recursive call to refine continues the discovery of predicates, which is guided by the remaining statements from the counterexample.

We continue to follow the execution of refine and show the execution of the call to wp after the second recursive step. For simplicity of presentation

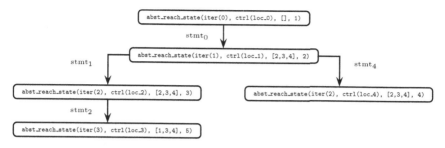

Fig. 9. Sufficiently precise reachable abstract states computed by `abstract_check_refine` for the program in Figure 1. None of abstract states visits the error location `ctrl(loc_err)`.

we assume the from-variables X and Y together with to-variables Xp and Yp. Then, the call `wp([Xp=X, Yp=Y+1], [], [Xp=\=Yp], WP)` binds WP to the list `[X=\=Y+1]`.

The presented implementation of WP exploits the particular syntactic form of update expressions, and can be generalized to arbitrary updates by resorting to the projection of the constraint store, e.g. using techniques from [12].

Abstraction refinement procedure `abstract_check_refine`. The procedure `abstract_check_refine` is defined in Figure 7. It calls the procedures `abstract_fixpoint`, `feasible`, and `refine` as described above.

We continue the illustration based on the example in Figure 1. See Figure 8. First, `abstract_check_refine` creates the root of the tree. It binds `StartCtrl` to the start location. For our program it is `loc_0`. Then, it initializes the counter for reachable abstract states. The creation of the start abstract state completes the setup required to compute the reachable abstract states. Now, the abstract reachability tree is computed by `abstract_fixpoint`. The control location of the abstract state 9 is the error location. Hence, after this abstract is created the procedure `abstract_fixpoint` throws an exception given by the term `abst_error_state(9)`. This exception triggers the analysis of the corresponding counterexample by the procedure `feasible`. The analysis is described above in this section. Its outcome is negative, i.e., `feasible` fails. The call to `refine` refines the abstraction. Now, the previously created facts `abst_reach_state` and `abst_parent` are pruned from the Prolog database. This finishes the current iteration of `abstract_check_refine`.

We continue with the recursive call to `abstract_check_refine`. See Figure 9. It shows the new set of predicates computed by the refinement procedure. Again, the root of the tree is created and the tree is computed by a call to `abstract_fixpoint`. Observe that the error location `loc_err` is not reached. ARMC proves the program correct.

7   Conclusion and Future Work

By presenting the procedures above, we have demonstrated how the use of a constraint-based logic programming language may lead to an elegant and concise implementation of a practical tool for software model checking with abstraction refinement.

We believe that our work may trigger further activities of research in two directions, corresponding to two groups of researchers. The first group consists of expert logic programmers who can optimize the presented implementation by using the programming constructs we have found suitable, but doing so in more sophisticated ways than we have been able to. The second group consists of expert developers of software verification tools who want to evaluate new algorithms (e.g. for abstraction refinement) and use the implementation techniques that we present in this paper.

Acknowledgements. We thank Jan-Georg Smaus for his comments on the paper.

References

1. E. Albert, P. Arenas-Sánchez, G. Puebla, and M. V. Hermenegildo. Reduced certificates for abstraction-carrying code. In *ICLP*. 2006.
2. T. Ball, R. Majumdar, T. Millstein, and S. Rajamani. Automatic predicate abstraction of C programs. In *PLDI*. 2001.
3. T. Ball, A. Podelski, and S. K. Rajamani. Relative completeness of abstraction refinement for software model checking. In *TACAS*. 2002.
4. B. Blanchet, P. Cousot, R. Cousot, J. Feret, L. Mauborgne, A. Miné, D. Monniaux, and X. Rival. A static analyzer for large safety-critical software. In *PLDI*. 2003.
5. S. Chaki, E. Clarke, A. Groce, S. Jha, and H. Veith. Modular verification of software components in C. In *ICSE*. 2003.
6. E. M. Clarke, O. Grumberg, S. Jha, Y. Lu, and H. Veith. Counterexample-guided abstraction refinement. In *CAV*. 2000.
7. P. Cousot and R. Cousot. Abstract interpretation: a unified lattice model for static analysis of programs by construction or approximation of fixpoints. In *POPL*. 1977.
8. B. Cui, Y. Dong, X. Du, K. N. Kumar, C. R. Ramakrishnan, I. V. Ramakrishnan, A. Roychoudhury, S. A. Smolka, and D. S. Warren. Logic programming and model checking. In *PLILP*. 1998.
9. G. Delzanno and A. Podelski. Model checking in CLP. In *TACAS*. 1999.
10. C. Flanagan. Automatic software model checking via constraint logic. *Sci. Comput. Program.*, 50(1-3), 2004.
11. L. Fribourg. Constraint logic programming applied to model checking. Invited tutorial. In *LOPSTR*. 2000.
12. N. Heintze, S. Michaylov, P. Stuckey, and R. Yap. Meta-programming in CLP(R). *J. of Logic Programming*, 33(3), 1997.
13. T. Henzinger, R. Jhala, R. Majumdar, G. Sutre. Lazy abstraction. In *POPL*. 2002.
14. T. A. Henzinger, R. Jhala, R. Majumdar, and K. L. McMillan. Abstractions from proofs. In *POPL*. 2004.
15. C. Holzbaur. *OFAI clp(q,r) Manual, Edition 1.3.3.* Austrian Research Institute for Artificial Intelligence, Vienna, 1995. TR-95-09.

16. F. Ivancic, H. Jain, A. Gupta, and M. K. Ganai. Localization and register sharing for predicate abstraction. In *TACAS*. 2005.
17. J. Jaffar and J. Lassez. Constraint logic programming. In *POPL*. 1987.
18. J. Jaffar, A. E. Santosa, and R. Voicu. A CLP method for compositional and intermittent predicate abstraction. In *VMCAI*. 2006.
19. M. Leuschel and M. Butler. Combining CSP and B for specification and property verification. In *FM*. 2005.
20. R. Meyer, J. Faber, and A. Rybalchenko. Model checking data-expensive real-time systems. To appear in *ICTAC*, 2006.
21. U. Nilsson and J. Lübcke. Constraint logic programming for local and symbolic model-checking. In *CL*. 2000.
22. A. Rybalchenko and V. Sofronie-Stokkermans. Constraint solving for interpolation. Submitted, 2006.

The Joins Concurrency Library

Claudio Russo

Microsoft Research Ltd, 7JJ Thomson Ave, Cambridge, United Kingdom
crusso@microsoft.com

Abstract. Cω extended C$^\#$ 1.x with a simple, declarative and powerful model of concurrency - join patterns - applicable both to multithreaded applications and to the orchestration of asynchronous, event-based distributed applications. With Generics available in C$^\#$ 2.0, we can now provide join patterns as a library rather than a language feature. The Joins library extends its clients with an embedded, type-safe and mostly declarative language for expressing synchronization patterns. The library has some advantages over Cω: it is language neutral, supporting other languages like Visual Basic; its join patterns are more dynamic, allowing solutions difficult to express with Cω; its code is easy to modify, fostering experimentation. Although presenting fewer optimization opportunities, the implementation is efficient and its interface makes it trivial to translate Cω programs to C$^\#$. We describe the interface and implementation of Joins which (ab)uses almost every feature of Generics.

1 Introduction

Cω [1] promised C$^\#$ 1.x users a more pleasant world of concurrent programming. Cω presents a simple, declarative and powerful model of concurrency - *join patterns* - applicable both to multithreaded applications and to the orchestration of asynchronous, event-based distributed applications. Using Generics in C$^\#$ 2.0 (and the .NET runtime in general), we can now provide join patterns as a .NET library – called Joins – rather than a language extension. Encoding language features in a library has some obvious drawbacks, restricting the scope for both optimization and static checking – but it also has some advantages. The Joins library is language neutral; it can be used by C$^\#$ but also by Visual Basic and other .NET languages. A library can be more dynamic: the Joins library already supports solutions that are more difficult to express with the declarative join patterns of Cω (Section 3.1). A library is easier to modify than a compiler, promoting experimentation. The Joins implementation is reasonably efficient and takes advantage of the same basic optimizations performed by the Cω compiler. Its interface makes it particularly easy to translate Cω programs to C$^\#$, but it can also be used to write concurrent code from scratch.

Section 2 presents join patterns as found in Cω. Section 3 introduces the Joins library by example, showing how to re-express the Cω programs of Section 2 as C$^\#$ 2.0 code that references the library. Section 4 provides a concise, yet precise, description of the Joins library as it appears to the user. Section 5 gives

M. Hanus (Ed.): PADL 2007, LNCS 4354, pp. 260–274, 2007.

an overview of the implementation which exercises most features of Generics. Section 6 concludes, discussing related work. The Joins download and tutorial [2] presents many more examples including encodings of active objects or actors, bounded buffers, reader/writer locks, futures, dining philosophers, a lift controller and simple, distributed applications using web services and Remoting.

2   Background: Cω's Concurrency Constructs

Cω extends the $C^\#$ 1.2 programming language with new asynchronous concurrency abstractions. The new constructs are a mild syntactic variant of those previously described under the name 'Polyphonic $C^\#$' [3]. Similar extensions to Java were independently proposed by von Itzstein and Kearney [4].

In Cω, methods can be defined as either *synchronous* or *asynchronous*. When a synchronous method is called, the caller is blocked until the method returns, as is normal in $C^\#$. However, when an asynchronous method is called, there is no result and the caller proceeds immediately without being blocked. Thus from the caller's point of view, an asynchronous method is like a void one, but with the useful extra guarantee of returning immediately. We often refer to asynchronous methods as *messages*, as they are one-way communications.

By themselves, asynchronous method declarations are not particularly novel: the innovation of Cω is the way method bodies are defined. In most languages, including $C^\#$, methods in the signature of a class are in bijective correspondence with the code of their implementations. In Cω, however, a body may be associated with a *set* of synchronous and/or asynchronous methods, including at most one synchronous method. Such definitions are called *chords* and a particular method may appear in the header of several chords. The body of a chord can only execute once *all* the methods in its header have been called. Calling a chorded method may thus enable zero, one or more chords:

- If no chord is enabled then the method invocation is queued up. If the method is asynchronous, then this simply involves adding the arguments (the contents of the message) to a queue. If the method is synchronous, then the calling thread is blocked.
- If there is a single enabled chord, then the arguments of the calls involved in the match are de-queued, and any blocked thread involved in the match is awakened to run the chord's body in that thread. The body of a chord involving only asynchronous methods runs in a new thread.
- If several chords are enabled, an unspecified one is selected to run.
- If multiple calls to one method are queued up, which call will be de-queued by a match is left unspecified.

Here is the simplest interesting example of a Cω class:

```
public class Buffer {
  public async Put(string s);
  public string Get() & Put(string s) { return s; }
}
```

This class contains two methods: a synchronous one, `Get()`, which takes no arguments and returns a string, and an asynchronous one, `Put(s)`, which takes a string argument and (like all asynchronous methods) returns no result. The class definition contains two things: a declaration (with no body) for the asynchronous method, and a chord. The chord declares the synchronous method and defines a body (the return statement) which can run when *both* the `Get()` and `Put(s)` methods have been called.

Now assume that producer and consumer threads wish to communicate via an instance b of the class `Buffer`. Producers make calls to b.`Put(s)`, which, since the method is asynchronous, never block. Consumers make calls to b.`Get()`, which, since the method is synchronous, will block until or unless there is a matching call to `Put(s)`. Once b has received both a `Put(s)` and a `Get()`, the body runs and the actual argument to `Put(s)` is returned as the result of the call to `Get()`. Multiple calls to `Get()` may be pending before a `Put(s)` is received to reawaken one of them, and multiple calls to `Put(s)` may be made before their arguments are consumed by subsequent `Get()`s. Note that:

1. The body of the chord runs in the (reawakened) thread corresponding to the matched call to `Get()`. Hence no new threads are spawned in this example.
2. The code which is generated by the class definition above is completely thread safe. The compiler generates the necessary locking. Furthermore, the locking is fine-grained and brief - chorded methods do not lock the whole object and are not executed with "monitor semantics".
3. The return value of a chord is returned to its synchronous method, of which there can be at most one.

In general, the definition of a synchronous method in Cω consists of more than one chord, each of which defines a body that can run when the method has been called *and* a particular set of asynchronous messages are present. For example, we could modify the example above to allow `Get()` to synchronize with calls to either of two different `Put1(s)` and `Put2(n)` methods:

```
public class BufferTwo {
  public async Put1(string s); public async Put2(int n);
  public string Get() & Put1(string s) { return s;}
                  & Put2(int n) { return n;} // ie. n.ToString()
}
```

Now we have two asynchronous methods and a synchronous method which can synchronize with either one, with a different body in each case.

A chord may involve more than one message; this synchronous chord waits for messages on both `Put1` and `Put2`:

```
public string Both() & Put1(string s) & Put2(int n) { return s + n;}
```

In Cω, a purely asynchronous chord is written as a class member, like this:

```
when Put1(string s) & Put2(int n) { Console.WriteLine(s + n);}
```

This chord spawns a new thread when messages arrive on Put1 and Put2.

The previous Buffer class is unbounded: any number of calls to Put(s) could be queued up before matching a Get(). We now define a variant in which only a single data value may be held in the buffer at any one time:

```
public class OnePlaceBuffer {
    private async Empty();
    private async Contains(string s);
    public void Put(string s) & Empty() { Contains(s); }
    public string Get() & Contains(string s) { Empty(); return s;}
    public OnePlaceBuffer() { Empty(); }
}
```

The public interface of OnePlaceBuffer is similar to that of Buffer, but the Put(s) method is now synchronous and will block if there is already an unconsumed value in the buffer.

The implementation of OnePlaceBuffer makes use of two *private* asynchronous messages: Empty() and Contains(s). These are used to carry the state of the buffer and illustrate a very common programming pattern in Cω. The class is best understood by reading its code declaratively:

- When a new buffer is created, it is initially Empty().
- If you call Put(s) on an Empty() buffer then it subsequently Contains(s) and the call to Put(s) returns.
- If you call Get() on a buffer which Contains(s) then the buffer is subsequently Empty() and s is returned to the caller of Get().
- Implicitly, in all other cases, calls to Put(s) and Get() block.

The constructor establishes and the chords maintain the invariant that there is always exactly one Empty() or Contains(s) message pending on the buffer. The chords can easily be read as the specification of a finite state machine.

3   The Joins Library

In Cω, classes that declare (a)synchronous methods joined in chords implicitly declare a set of communication channels. An asynchronous method has a backing queue of pending method calls. A synchronous method has a backing queue of waiting threads. The state of the queues is protected by a hidden lock. Invoking an (a)synchronous method executes some specialized scheduling code that decides, given the current queues and the declared chords, which, if any, chord gets to fire, either on the current or any waiting thread. Thus each object (or, for purely static methods, class) includes its own scheduling logic. Instead of relying on a central scheduling thread, threads that invoke chorded methods each spend a little time helping to schedule each other. To optimize the detection of enabled chords, the implementation maintains some additional state: a bit vector representing the set of non-empty queues. Pattern matching is compiled to subset tests against this state, implemented using one bitmask operation per chord.

In the Joins library, the scheduling logic that would be compiled into the corresponding Cω class receives a separate, first-class representation as an object of the special Join class. The Join class provides a mostly declarative, type-safe mechanism for defining thread-safe synchronous and asynchronous communication channels and patterns. Instead of (a)synchronous methods, as in Cω, the communication channels are special delegate values (first-class methods) obtained from a common Join object. Communication and/or synchronization takes place by invoking these delegates, passing arguments and optionally waiting for return values. The allowable communication patterns as well as their effects are defined using *join patterns*: bodies of code whose execution is guarded by linear combinations of channels. The body, or *continuation*, of a join pattern is provided by the user as a (typically anonymous) delegate that can manipulate external resources protected by the Join object.

Using the Joins library, we can implement the Cω Buffer in C# as follows:

```
using Microsoft.Research.Joins;
public class Buffer {
  // Declare the (a)synchronous channels
  public readonly Asynchronous.Channel<string> Put;
  public readonly Synchronous<string>.Channel Get;
  public Buffer() {
    // Create a Join object
    Join join = Join.Create();
    // Use it to initialize the channels
    join.Initialize(out Put); join.Initialize(out Get);
    // Finally, declare the patterns(s)
    join.When(Get).And(Put).Do(delegate(string s) { return s;});
}}
```

The code declares a buffer class with two fields of special delegate types. The Put field contains an asynchronous channel that, when invoked, returns void (immediately) and *takes* one string argument. The Get field contains a synchronous channel that, when invoked, *returns* a string but takes no argument. Both fields are initially null. The constructor allocates a new Join object, join, using the factory method Join.Create. The join object is a private scheduler for the buffer. The constructor then calls Initialize on join, passing the locations of each of the channels: this assigns two new delegate values into the fields, each obtained from and owned by join. Finally we declare the Cω chord by constructing a pattern on the join object, passing the synchronous channel Get to When and Anding it with the asynchronous channel Put. The pattern is completed by invoking Do, passing the continuation for this pattern, expressed here as an anonymous delegate. The continuation expects exactly one argument (the argument to Put); the continuation's return value is returned to the caller of Get. Notice that the bodies of the continuation and Cω chord are identical.

If we ignore the boilerplate calls to Initialize then what remains retains the declarative flavour of the original Cω code. Moreover, client code of the Cω and C# buffers is syntactically identical. Given a buffer b, clients invoke b.Put(s);

to send a string s and b.Get() to receive one. Of course, these calls are compiled slightly differently, just invoking a method in the Cω client, but reading a field and then invoking its delegate value in the C# client.

A synchronous method with several chords translates to several patterns constructed on the same initial channel. In general, calls to And may be iterated, and a continuation may bind zero or more parameters and return zero or one values, depending on the pattern. An asynchronous chord translates to a pattern with an initial asynchronous channel whose continuation returns void.

Here is Cω's OnePlaceBuffer, made generic in C# for good measure:

```
public class OnePlaceBuffer<S> {
  private readonly Asynchronous.Channel Empty;
  private readonly Asynchronous.Channel<S> Contains;
  public readonly Synchronous.Channel<S> Put;
  public readonly Synchronous<S>.Channel Get;
  public OnePlaceBuffer() {
    Join j = Join.Create();
    j.Initialize(out Empty); j.Initialize(out Contains);
    j.Initialize(out Put); j.Initialize(out Get);
    j.When(Put).And(Empty).Do(delegate(S s) { Contains(s);});
    j.When(Get).And(Contains).Do(delegate(S s) { Empty(); return s;});
    Empty();
}}
```

Empty and Put introduce two more channel types. An Asynchronous.Channel delegate takes zero arguments and returns void. As in Cω, nullary channels use a more efficient counter instead of a queue of argument values to record pending invocations. A Synchronous.Channel<S> delegate returns void and takes one argument of type S. To protect the buffer's invariant, we translate the private Cω Empty and Contains messages to private fields, accessible from the continuations but not externally. The constructor establishes the invariant by calling Empty(), after initializing the channels and constructing the patterns.

3.1   Beyond Cω: Dynamic Joins

What if we need to declare, and synchronize, a dynamic set of channels? A Cω class can only declare a static set of channels and chords so a dynamic set has to be encoded by resorting to multiplexing. Although possible, this is inconvenient. Inspired by a similar feature in the CCR [5], the Joins library lets you initialize, and join *arrays* of asynchronous channels. Since the size of an array is determined at runtime, this supports *dynamic* synchronization patterns.

For example, the JoinMany<R> class below declares and supports waiting on n channels of type R, which is awkward to express in Cω. The class declares an array, Responses, of response channels, each carrying a value of type R. An object o = new JoinMany<R>(n) requires $n + 1$ channels: n asynchronous response channels, o.Responses[i] ($0 \leq i < n$), and one synchronous channel, o.Wait. The constructor Creates a Join object supporting $n + 1$ channels; it then `Initializes` the response channels field with an array of n distinct channels and declares a pattern that waits on all the channels in this array. The continuation of the pattern receives all of the responses as a separate array (also of size n) of correlated values of type R. The consumer calls o.`Wait`(), blocking until/unless all responses have arrived; producer i just posts her response r on o.`Response`(i)(r), asynchronously. Here, we have taken the precaution of hiding the array in a private field to prevent external updates – we could avoid this if C$^\#$ supported immutable arrays or we bothered to roll our own.

```
public class JoinMany<R> {
 private readonly Asynchronous.Channel<R>[] Responses;
 public readonly Synchronous<R[]>.Channel Wait;
 public Asynchronous.Channel<R> Response(int i) { return Responses[i]; }
 public JoinMany(int n) {
   Join j = Join.Create(n + 1);
   j.Initialize(out Responses, n); j.Initialize(out Wait);
   j.When(Wait).And(Responses).Do(delegate(R[] r) { return r; });
 }}
```

4   Joins **Library Reference**

Users of `Joins` reference the assembly `Microsoft.Research.Joins.dll` and import the namespace `Microsoft.Research.Joins`.

A new `Join` instance j is allocated by calling an overload of factory method `Join.Create`([*size*]). The optional integer *size* bounds the number of channels supported by j and defaults to 32; it also sets the constant property j.`Size`.

A `Join` object notionally owns a set of asynchronous and synchronous *channels*, each obtained by calling an overload of method `Initialize`, passing the location of a *channel* or array of *channels* using an **out** argument:

j.`Initialize`(**out** *channel*); or j.`Initialize`(**out** *channels, length*);

The second form assigns to location *channels* an *array* of *length* distinct, asynchronous channels. It is possible to initialize the same location twice.

Channels are instances of the following delegate types, summarized by a simple grammar of type expressions:

(`Asynchronous` | `Synchronous`[$\langle R \rangle$]).`Channel`[$\langle A \rangle$]

The outer class of a channel, `Asynchronous`, `Synchronous` or `Synchronous<R>`, should be read as a modifier that specifies its blocking behaviour and optional return type R. Type A, if present, determines the channel's optional argument type. The six channel flavours support zero or one arguments of type A and zero or one results of type R. Multiple arguments or results must be passed in tuples, either using the provided generic `Pair<A, B>` struct or by other means.

Apart from its channels, a `Join` object notionally owns a set of *join patterns*. A join pattern is constructed by invoking an overload of the instance method

When followed by zero or more invocations of instance method And (or AndPair), followed by a final invocation of instance method Do. A constructed join pattern typically takes the form:

$$j.\texttt{When}(a_1).\texttt{And}(a_2)\cdots.\texttt{And}(a_n).\texttt{Do}(d);$$

Alternatively, using an anonymous delegate for d:

$$j.\texttt{When}(a_1).\texttt{And}(a_2)\cdots.\texttt{And}(a_n).\texttt{Do}(\texttt{delegate}(P_1\ p_1,\ldots,P_m\ p_m)\{\ldots\});$$

Argument a_1 of When(a_1) may be a synchronous or asynchronous channel or an array of asynchronous channels. Each subsequent argument a_i to And(a_i) (for $i > 1$) must be an asynchronous channel or an array of asynchronous channels; it cannot be a synchronous channel. The argument d to Do(d) is a *continuation* delegate that defines the body of the pattern. Although its precise type varies with the pattern, the continuation always has a delegate type of the form:

$$\texttt{delegate [void | R] Continuation}(P_1\ p_1,\ldots,P_m\ p_m);$$

The precise type of the continuation d, including its arity or number of arguments m, is determined by the sequence of channels guarding it. If the first argument a_1 in the pattern is a synchronous channel with return type R, then the continuation's return type is R; otherwise the return type is void.

The continuation receives the arguments of the joined channel invocations as delegate parameters $P_1\ p_1,\ldots,P_m\ p_m$, for $m \leq n$. The presence and types of any additional parameters $P_1\ p_1,\ldots,P_m\ p_m$ varies according to the type of each argument a_i joined with invocation When(a_i)/And(a_i) (for $1 \leq i \leq n$):

- If a_i is of type Channel or Channel[], then When(a_i)/And(a_i) adds no parameter to delegate d.
- If a_i is of type Channel<P> or Channel<P>[] then When(a_i)/And(a_i) adds one parameter p_j of type $P_j = P$ or $Pj = P[]$ (respectively) to delegate d.

Parameters are added to d from left to right, in increasing order of i. A continuation can receive at most $m \leq max$ parameters ($max = 8$ in the current implementation). If necessary, it is possible to join more than max generic channels by calling method AndPair(a_i) instead of And(a_i). AndPair(a_i) modifies the last argument of the new continuation to be a pair consisting of the last argument of the previous continuation and the new argument contributed by ai.

Readonly property j.Count is the current number of channels initialized on j; it is bounded by j.Size. Any invocation of j.Initialize that would cause j.Count to exceed j.Size throws JoinException. Join patterns must be well-formed, both individually and collectively. Executing Do(d) to complete a join pattern will throw JoinException if d is null, the pattern repeats an asynchronous channel (i.e. is non-linear), an (a)synchronous channel is null or *foreign* to this pattern's Join instance, the join pattern is *redundant*, or the join pattern is *empty*. A channel is foreign to a Join instance j if it was not allocated by some call to j.Initialize. A pattern is redundant when the set of channels joined by the pattern subsets or supersets the channels joined by another pattern on this Join instance. A pattern is empty when its set of channels is empty.

5   Implementation

The implementation avoids using Reflection and only uses checked casts to extract the underlying queue from a channel when constructing a pattern. These casts could have been avoided by defining the channel delegates to contain queue fields (possible in bytecode, but not $C^{\#}$), or by representing channels as *classes*. We preferred to retain the convenient delegate invocation syntax for sending messages and to provide a pure $C^{\#}$ implementation. To be useful in practice, we provide 6 flavours of channel rather than two basic ones (Asynchronous.Channel<A> and Synchronous<R>.Channel<A>) because passing or returning ML-like unit values is just unnatural in $C^{\#}$ and VB. We favour n-ary continuations, despite the (soft) limit on n, because uniform currying is awkward in $C^{\#}$ and unsupported in VB; similarly, without pattern matching, using uniformly nested pairs to bind continuation arguments requires unwieldy projections. Compare the first void-returning, 3-argument continuation with its uglier, but more "uniform" alternatives:

```
1. delegate(int i,bool b,float f){ Console.Write("{0},{1},{2}",i,b,f);}
2. delegate(int i){return delegate(bool b){return delegate(float f){
     Console.Write("{0},{1},{2}", i, b, f); return new Unit();};};}
3. delegate(Pair<Pair<int, bool>,float> p){
     Console.Write("{0},{1},{2}", p.Fst.Fst, p.Fst.Snd, p.Snd); }
```

5.1   Join and Channel Object Representations

The Join class is abstract. Each Join object j has runtime type Join<IntSet>, a specific instantiation of a private, overloaded generic class Join<S> that subclasses Join. IntSet is a *struct* type that implements a set of j.Size-bounded integers as a packed sequence of bits. A Join<IntSet> object looks like this:

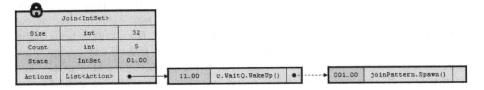

It contains the following fields:

Size: an immutable bound on the number of channels that may be owned.
Count: the mutable, current number of channels owned by the instance and the ID of the next channel, incremented by calls to Initialize.
State: a mutable IntSet with a capacity of at least Size elements. State encodes the current set of non-empty channels as a set of channel IDs. Since IntSet is a struct, State is inlined in the object, not stored on the heap.
Actions: a mutable, IntSet-indexed list of pattern match *actions*: each action either wakes up one thread waiting on a synchronous channel's WaitQ or spawns the continuation of an asynchronous pattern on a new thread.

The regular object lock on a `Join` instance protects both its own state and the states of its channels. `Actions` is extended (under the `Join`'s lock) whenever a legal pattern is completed by calling a `Do` method. Registering a pattern pre-computes its `IntSet` for faster matching and early error detection.

Channels are delegates and thus contain a target object and a target method, comparable to the environment and code pointer of a closure in functional languages. All channel target objects contain the following immutable fields.

`Owner`: a reference to the `Join<IntSet>` instance that initialized the channel.
`ID`: an identifier for the channel, unique for the channels of `Owner`.
`SetID`: a pre-computed `IntSet` corresponding to the singleton set {`ID`}.

A `Synchronous<R>` channel, for example, looks like this:

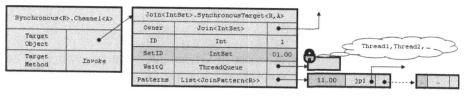

Its target object additionally contains these fields:

`WaitQ`: a notional queue of waiting threads, itself implemented using the implicit waitset of a privately allocated lock as in [3]. The `ThreadQ.WakeUp` method efficiently targets at most one waiting thread, avoiding `Monitor.PulseAll()`.
`Patterns`: an `IntSet`-indexed list of all R-returning patterns containing `ID`.

When invoked, the channel's target method acquires the `Owner`'s lock, scans `Patterns` for matches with the `Owner`'s `State` and either:

If there is no matching pattern: enqueues its thread, updates `State`, releases the `Owner` lock and blocks awaiting notification on the `WaitQ` lock.

If there is some matching pattern: dequeues the asynchronous channels involved in the pattern, updating `State`, scans for any enabled actions[1], releases the `Owner`'s lock and returns the value of invoking the pattern's continuation with the dequeued values in the current thread. Since the channel and continuation both return a value of type `R`, this involves no casting.

When it wakes up, the waiting thread re-acquires the `Owner`'s lock, and re-attempts to find a match amongst its patterns. If it fails, because some intervening thread has consumed some channel values available when the thread was awoken, the thread blocks, resuming its wait for a match.

The target object of a `Asynchronous` channel contains just one additional field, a queue `Q` of pending calls, so a `Channel[<A>]` looks like this:

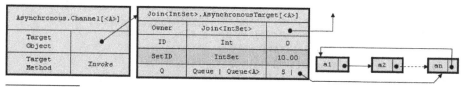

---

[1] The additional scan is used to avoid deadlock – see [3] for a discussion.

The representation of Q depends on the channel's arity. A `Channel<A>` contains a proper FIFO queue of type `Queue<A>`, implemented as a circular list of A-values with constant time access to both ends of the queue. A nullary and thus data-less `Channel` contains an optimized `Queue` struct, implemented in constant space by just recording the current *count* of notional queue entries.

When invoked, the channel's target method acquires its `Owner`'s lock and enqueues its argument or bumps its counter; if Q was empty, it updates `Owner`'s `State` and performs some action enabled by its new `State` (if any); finally, the method releases its `Owner`'s lock and returns. Assuming no malicious third party has grabbed the `Owner`'s lock, which is easily prevented by keeping all `Join` objects private, executing the action and the channel invocation is guaranteed to return since the lock is only held briefly by other channels.

5.2   Exploiting Generics

The `Joins` library makes extensive use of $C^\#$ language features to present an API that we hope is relatively simple to use: a user only has to know a handful of identifiers and understand a simple grammar of channel types and join patterns. We rely on overloading and type argument inference to implicitly resolve method calls, that, were they explicit, would obscure the user's intentions.

The various channel flavours of Section 3 are implemented as (generic) delegate types, nested within (generic) static classes:

```
static class Asynchronous    { delegate void Channel();
                               delegate void Channel<A>(A a);}
static class Synchronous      { delegate void Channel();
                               delegate void Channel<A>(A a);}
static class Synchronous<R> { delegate R Channel();
                               delegate R Channel<A>(A a);}
```

Using both nesting and generic arity to overload the `Channel` identifier makes it easy for a user to independently change the blocking behaviour, argument and return type a channel.

The `Join` class provides essentially three methods: `Create`, `Initialize` and `When` and two integer properties `Count` and `Size` which are rarely needed:

```
abstract class Join {
  static Join Create([int size]);
  void Initialize[<A>](out Asynchronous.Channel[<A>] c);
  void Initialize[<A>](out Synchronous.Channel[<A>] c);
  void Initialize<R[, A]>(out Synchronous<R>.Channel[<A>] c);
  void Initialize[<A>](out Asynchronous.Channel[<A>][] cs, int length);
  JoinPattern.OpenPattern[<P>] When[<P>](Asynchronous.Channel[<P>] c);
  JoinPattern.OpenPattern[<A>] When[<A>](Synchronous.Channel[<A>] c);
  JoinPattern<R>.OpenPattern[<A>] When<R[,A]>(
     Synchronous<R>.Channel[<A>] c);
  JoinPattern.OpenPattern[<P[]>] When[<P>](
     Asynchronous.Channel[<P>][] cs);
  int Count { get; } int Size { get; }}
```

Create(int size) is a factory method that, internally, uses polymorphic recursion to construct, at runtime, an IntSet struct with a capacity of size (or more) elements. The library defines primitive 32- and 64-element sets, IntSet32 and IntSet64, represented as one field structs of unsigned integers or longs. Each implements a simple interface IIntSet<S> providing imperative operations on the integer set type S: i.e. IntSet32 implements IIntSet<IntSet32>, IntSet64 implements IIntSet<IntSet64>. A generic struct PairSet<S> with type parameter constraint where S:IIntSet<S> is used to construct a double-capacity set from a smaller set representation. Notice that PairSet<S> uses a recursive type constraint (a.k.a F-bounded polymorphism) to parameterize over a representation S supporting a set of operations on S. The concrete, generic class Join<S> also declares this constraint on S so it can access set operations to manipulate its otherwise parametric State field. In C#, calls to an interface method on a struct actually pass the *this* pointer by reference, not value, and can therefore mutate the original value. We exploit this feature, updating State fields in-place.

The Initialize method assigns the location of a channel or array of channels with a new (set of) channel(s) allocated and owned by this Join instance. The method has eight overloads (summarized above), some generic, some not, with one overload per channel flavour and two additional overloads for arrays of asynchronous channels. We resort to an out parameter simply to simulate overloading on return type, which is, unfortunately, illegal in C#. Although distasteful, overloading in this way means that boilerplate calls to Initialize(out channel) do not have to be altered when changing the flavour of channel.

The When method begins the construction of a new join pattern and like Initialize, has eight overloads, one per channel flavour and two more for arrays of asynchronous channels. The return type of When is invariably some instance of the class scheme:

$$\text{JoinPattern}[\langle R \rangle].\text{OpenPattern}[\langle A \,|\, A[] \rangle]$$

Here R is the optional return type of a synchronous pattern and A is the optional argument type of the channel or channel array.

There are two flavours of JoinPattern. The non-generic JoinPattern class contains nested OpenPattern classes whose continuations all return void. The generic JoinPattern<R> family of classes contains nested OpenPattern classes whose continuations all return R. More precisely, each JoinPattern family contains $max + 1$ nested subclasses, OpenPattern$\langle P_1, \ldots, P_n \rangle$ $(0 \leq n \leq max)$, each overloaded on generic arity n:

```
abstract class JoinPattern[<R>] {
  class OpenPattern: JoinPattern[<R>] { ...}
  class OpenPattern<P₁>: JoinPattern[<R>] { ...}
  ⋮
  class OpenPattern<P₁, ..., Pₘₐₓ>: JoinPattern[<R>] { ...} }
```

In turn, each $\texttt{OpenPattern}\langle P_1,\ldots,P_n\rangle$ class has the schematic form:

```
class OpenPattern<P₁,...,Pₙ> : JoinPattern[<R>] {
  delegate [void | R] Continuation(P₁ p1,...,Pₙ pₙ);
  void Do(Continuation continuation);
  OpenPattern<P₁,...,Pₙ> And(Asynchronous.Channel c);
  OpenPattern<P₁,...,Pₙ> And(Asynchronous.Channel[] cs);
  OpenPattern<P₁,...,Pₙ,Pₙ₊₁> And<Pₙ₊₁>(
    Asynchronous.Channel<Pₙ₊₁> c);       (n < max)
  OpenPattern<P₁,...,Pₙ,Pₙ₊₁[]> And<Pₙ₊₁>(
    Asynchronous.Channel<Pₙ₊₁>[] cs);    (n < max)
  OpenPattern<P₁,...,Pair<Pₙ, Pₙ₊₁>> AndPair<Pₙ₊₁>(
    Asynchronous.Channel<Pₙ₊₁> c);       (n > 0)
  OpenPattern<P₁,...,Pair<Pₙ,Pₙ₊₁[]>> AndPair<Pₙ₊₁>(
    Asynchronous.Channel<Pₙ₊₁>[] cs);    (n > 0)
}
```

Class $\texttt{OpenPattern}\langle P_1,\ldots,P_n\rangle$ declares its own nested $\texttt{Continuation}$ delegate type taking invocation arguments $p_1,\ldots,p_n$ of types $P_1,\ldots,P_n$ and returning $\texttt{void}$ or R, as appropriate. The $\texttt{And}$ and $\texttt{AndPair}$ methods with side conditions on n are only included for satisfying n. The class declares up to four overloads of method $\texttt{And}$, two generic, two non-generic, one for each flavour of asynchronous channel and one for each array thereof. A non-generic $\texttt{And}$ method constructs a new open pattern of the same type (and thus expecting the same type of $\texttt{Continuation}$) as $\texttt{this}$, that synchronizes with an additional (data-less) channel or set thereof. A generic $\texttt{And<}P_{n+1}\texttt{>}$ method on $\texttt{OpenPattern}\langle P_1,\ldots,P_n\rangle$ constructs a new successor pattern of type $\texttt{OpenPattern}\langle P_1,\ldots,P_n,P\rangle$, thus binding one additional continuation type and argument. Type P is P_{n+1} or $P_{n+1}[]$, if the argument is a single channel, $\texttt{c}$, or array of channels, $\texttt{cs}$. The $\texttt{AndPair<}P_{n+1}\texttt{>}$ methods use pairing to avoid introducing another continuation argument: in particular, for $n = \texttt{max}$, calling $\texttt{AndPair}$ is the only way to extend the pattern to wait for additional data-carrying channels.

Every $\texttt{JoinPattern}$ contains an instance of an internal class $\texttt{Pattern}$, which represents a conjunction of atomic patterns (channels or channel arrays), as a tree. $\texttt{Pattern}$'s $\texttt{GetIntSet}$ method computes the summary $\texttt{IntSet}$ used for scheduling which is all the $\texttt{Join}$ scheduler needs to know to select a pattern for execution; it also does some error checking. $\texttt{Pattern}$ has these subclasses (omitting similar ones for synchronous channels and channel arrays):

```
abstract class Pattern { S GetIntSet<S>(...) where S: IIntSet<S>; }
abstract class Pattern<P> : Pattern { abstract P Get(); }
class Atom: Pattern<Unit> { Atom(Asynchronous.Channel c); ... }
class Atom<A>: Pattern<A> { Atom(Asynchronous.Channel<A> c); ... }
class And<Q,R>: Pattern<Pair<Q,R>>
  { And(Pattern<Q> fst, Pattern<R> snd); ... }
class And<Q>: Pattern<Q> { And(Pattern<Q> fst, Pattern<Unit> snd); ... }
```

Subclass $\texttt{Pattern<P>}$ of $\texttt{Pattern}$ hides an existential type P, the return type of its abstract method P $\texttt{Get()}$. Method $\texttt{Get}$ is used to dequeue all of a

pattern's channels, returning a single, composite value of their queue heads. Get
is interesting because, due to base class specialization, its return type actually
varies with each concrete subclass: new Atom(c).Get() returns P=Unit (Unit
is an empty struct with one value); new Atom<A>(c).Get() returns P=A; new
And<Q,R>(fst,snd).Get() returns P=Pair<Q,R> (a struct with two fields) and
new And<Q>(fst,snd).Get() returns P=Q, absorbing the data-less Unit-pattern
snd. Technically, the hierarchy rooted at Pattern is a simple instance of a *Generalized Algebraic Datatype (GADT)* [6]. When a JoinPattern is selected for
execution, a virtual method Fire() or Spawn(), declared on JoinPattern, but
overridden in each OpenPattern$\langle P_1, \ldots, P_n \rangle$ subclass, calls pattern.Get() on
a private field, pattern, of specialized type And$\langle$Pair$\langle \ldots$Pair$\langle P_1, \ldots \rangle, \ldots \rangle, P_n \rangle$.
This yields a nested pair of n-components of the appropriate type to pass on,
component-wise, to its n-ary Continuation. This is quite elegant since no box-
ing, heap allocation or casting is required to implement the dequeuing and transfer of multiple values. The And method of an OpenPattern extends its current
pattern by conjoining it with a new atomic pattern; AndPair extends its current
pattern - a conjunction - by conjoining its first component with the conjunction
of its second component and a new atomic pattern.

Calling When allocates a new OpenPattern with an atomic pattern field
and null continuation. The OpenPattern contains another field storing a callback to invoke with a JoinPattern when the OpenPattern is supplied with
a continuation. Calling And/AndPair returns a new OpenPattern with an extended pattern, same callback and null continuation. Calling Do creates a new
OpenPattern with the same pattern, null callback and non-null continuation
and passes it, as a JoinPattern, to the original callback. The callback finally
grabs the Join lock, calls GetIntSet and either detects an illegal pattern or
inserts an entry into the appropriate lists (Actions and perhaps Patterns).

6   Conclusion and Related Work

Compared with Joins, Cω offers more static checking, e.g. rejecting non-linear
patterns, and much better error messages. It also has more opportunities for optimization: Cω could use static analysis to determine whether an asynchronous
continuation can safely be run in the enabling thread, rather than a new one.
Cω knows the methods and patterns belonging to a class and can thus compile pattern matching as a cascading test of the state against pre-computed
bitmask constants, with the scheduling code shared between all instances of
the class; Joins must instead perform a linear search through a heap-allocated,
unshared list of patterns, (re-)constructed for each Join instance. Cω can also
inline all the continuations of a synchronous method into its compiled body, instead of indirecting through delegates. On one micro-benchmark, pitting a Cω
OnePlaceBuffer against a Joins implementation, we found that allocating 1000
buffers in a tight loop is roughly 60x slower with Joins, due to the overhead of
reconstructing the patterns for each buffer; executing 1000 Put then Get calls in
the same thread is 2x slower, reflecting the cost of indirecting through a channel delegate and consulting the heap-allocated patterns; but the time needed

to run a producer and consumer thread exchanging 1000 messages is roughly comparable, with any differences dominated by the cost of context switching.

The join calculus [7] provides the foundation for join patterns. JoCaml [8] and Funnel [9] are functional languages supporting declarative join patterns. The CCR [5] is an asynchronous concurrency library for $C^\#$ that uses custom scheduling rather than integrating with the host's thread API as Joins does. The CCR supports join patterns, but not synchronous ones; programs must be written in an awkward continuation passing style, alleviated sometimes by the use of $C^\#$ iterators. Singh [10] builds an experimental combinator library for joins patterns using software transactional memory in STM Haskell but the implementation is more expository than practical due to performance issues.

Future avenues to explore include supporting Ada-style synchronous rendezvous, allowing more than one synchronous channel to occur in a pattern. Executing asynchronous patterns in a new thread is expensive and not always required: if the continuation is non-blocking and guaranteed to return quickly, it can be executed immediately in the thread that enabled the pattern. Adapting Joins to support such user-controlled scheduling of asynchronous patterns is straightforward and has other applications, for instance to queue continuations in a thread pool or in the event loop of a GUI thread. A library makes such experimentation much easier.

References

1. Microsoft Research: Cω, http://research.microsoft.com/Comega (2004)
2. Russo, C.: Joins: A Concurrency Library (2006) Binaries with tutorial and samples: http://research.microsoft.com/research/downloads.
3. Benton, N., Cardelli, L., Fournet, C.: Modern concurrency abstractions for $C^\#$. ACM Transactions on Programming Languages and Systems **26** (2004)
4. Itzstein, G.S., Kearney, D.: Join Java: An alternative concurrency semantics for Java. Technical Report ACRC-01-001, University of South Australia (2001)
5. Chrysanthakopoulos, G., Singh, S.: An asynchronous messaging library for $C^\#$. In: Synchronization and Concurrency in Object-Oriented Languages (SCOOL), OOPSLA 2005 Workshop, UR Research (2005)
6. Kennedy, A.J., Russo, C.V.: Generalized algebraic data types and object-oriented programming. In: Object-Oriented Programming: Systems, Languages, Applications (OOPSLA), San Diego, ACM (2005)
7. Fournet, C., Gonthier, G.: The join calculus: a language for distributed mobile programming. In: APPSEM Summer School, Caminha, Portugal, September 2000. Volume 2395 of LNCS., Springer-Verlag (2002)
8. Fournet, C., Le Fessant, F., Maranget, L., Schmitt, A.: JoCaml: a language for concurrent distributed and mobile programming. In: Advanced Functional Programming, 4th International School, Oxford, August 2002. Volume 2638 of LNCS., Springer-Verlag (2003)
9. Odersky, M.: An overview of functional nets. In: APPSEM Summer School, Caminha, Portugal, September 2000. Volume 2395 of LNCS., Springer-Verlag (2002)
10. Singh, S.: Higher-order combinators for join patterns using STM. TRANSACT ACM Workshop on Languages, Compilers and Hardware Support for Transactional Computing (2006)

HPorter: Using Arrows
to Compose Parallel Processes

Liwen Huang[1], Paul Hudak[2], and John Peterson[3]

[1] Yale University, Dept. of Computer Science
liwen.huang@yale.edu
[2] Yale University, Dept. of Computer Science
paul.hudak@yale.edu
[3] Western State College, Computer Information Science
jpeterson@western.edu

Abstract. *HPorter* is a DSL embedded in Haskell for composing processes running on a parallel computer. Using arrows (a generalization of monads), one can "wire together" processes in a manner analogous to a signal-processing application. The processes themselves are typically existing C or C++ programs, but may also be programs written in a first-order sub-language in Haskell that supports basic arithmetic, trigonometric functions, and other related operations. In both cases, once the processes are wired together, the supporting Haskell implementation is out of the loop – imported C programs run unimpeded, the Haskell sub-language is compiled into C code, and all data paths run directly between C processes. But in addition, HPorter's event-driven reactivity permits reconfiguration of these tightly-coupled processes at any time, thus providing a degree of dynamism that is critical in many applications.

The advantages of our approach over conventional scripting languages include a higher degree of type safety, a declarative style, dynamic reconfiguration of processes, having the full power of Haskell, and portability across operating systems. We have implemented HPorter both on the QNX operating system and using conventional TCP/IP sockets, and are using it in a practical application in Yale's Humanoid Robotics Laboratory, where the processes correspond to soft-real-time tasks such as computer vision, motor control, planning, and limb kinematics.

1 Introduction

A humanoid robot has many time-critical tasks, including vision processing, motor control, limb kinematics, high-level planning, and so on. State-of-the-art applications place heavy demands on these tasks, and require parallel computers to deal with them effectively. In addition, the "modes" of a robot vary – if it is moving, it might need to focus on its kinematics, but if it is trying to pick up an object, it might need to focus on vision processing and planning. Scripting these processes efficiently and in the correct manner is thus an important task for the robotics programmer.

M. Hanus (Ed.): PADL 2007, LNCS 4354, pp. 275–289, 2007.

In this paper we describe *HPorter*,[1] a DSL embedded in Haskell for composing processes running on a parallel computer. HPorter is based on *arrows*, a generalization of monads. One way to think of the generalization afforded by arrows is that they permit functions (processes) to be composed "in parallel," rather than in the linear, sequential style dictated by monads. This makes arrows a good choice for composing parallel processes in a rigorous, robust, and type-safe manner.

Although the processes themselves could in the abstract be any arbitrary computations, including ordinary Haskell programs, our primary interest is in scripting existing processes written in C (or compiled into C), for the sake of efficiency. On the other hand, any extra processing needed to glue a couple of processes together (for example, incrementing each value in a stream, or taking the sine of each value) is something easily expressed in Haskell, and it would be inconvenient to insist that the user write a new C program for each new piece of glue code. Therefore, we also have designed a small first-order Haskell sub-language called GLUE, based on previous work on Pan and Pan# [2,14], that is easily compiled into C.

Once the C processes are wired together, the supporting Haskell implementation is completely out of the loop – the imported C programs run unimpeded, the Haskell sub-language is compiled into C code, and all data paths run directly between C processes.

But in addition, a key aspect of HPorter is that it is *reactive*, since, as mentioned earlier, there are times when the process configuration needs to change, often in drastic ways. We achieve this by using *switch* combinators borrowed from our work on FRP and Yampa [16,12]. This provides event-driven reactivity that permits dynamic reconfiguration of the otherwise tightly-coupled processes.

In contrast to existing approaches to scripting parallel processes, our approach offers the following advantages:

1. HPorter is type-safe. All input and output ports are strongly typed, thus providing a robust interface not typically found in the C world.
2. HPorter is declarative, resulting in more concise and easier to understand code. Rather than saying "how" things are wired together as in a conventional approach, HPorter describe "what" the process interconnections are in an arrow-based style.
3. HPorter is reactive, permitting reconfiguration of the processes in an event-driven manner.
4. HPorter is embedded in Haskell, thus affording the user the full expressive power of a modern functional language. Process-wiring code can be reused, recursion can replicate networks, higher-order functions can capture repeating patterns, and so on.

In our robotics application these advantages are even greater because some of the processes are actually *Dance* [6,5] programs that have been compiled into

---

[1] The name "HPorter" comes from the name of the QNX scripting language *Porter*, and our use of *H*askell.

C. Dance is a DSL embedded in Haskell for controlling humanoid robots, and uses principles similar to those in HPorter and Yampa – this similarity is an advantage to the user.

We originally implemented HPorter two years ago on the QNX real-time operating system running on a tightly-coupled network of four multiprocessors, each of which has four processors (thus 16 processors in all).[2] Recently, however, the hardware was upgraded to more powerful nodes (although only 8 instead of 16), and we decided to explore the use of conventional TCP/IP sockets to interconnect processes, rather than using the specialized QNX machinery. We felt that this would result in a more robust design and would allow the system to be more portable, since TCP/IP sockets are ubiquitous in Unix-based systems. In porting HPorter to this new platform, all we had to do was change the back-end interface and process-specific code – none of the arrow-based source code had to be changed. Thus we point out the final advantage of our approach:

5. HPorter is portable.

We are currently using HPorter to program a real humanoid robot in the Yale Robotics Laboratory. Our robot consists of a torso, two arms, a head, and shoulders (which move). It has twenty-one degrees of freedom, each corresponding to a separate motor, and each of those in turn requiring a separate motor controller. In addition, the robot's two eyes provide stereo vision, with two cameras for each eye – one for wide-angle viewing, and the other to simulate foveal vision. The vision processing is in fact the most demanding computational task.

The performance of HPorter is excellent. Once the processes are running, no performance degradation is apparent. Although reactive processing (for event processing and process reconfiguration) requires Haskell intervention, for our applications the response time of the reactive component is more than acceptable. Just as important, users of HPorter find the system easier to use than a conventional scripting approach.

The remainder of this paper is organized as follows. We start with a brief introduction to arrows in Section 2, following by an example of HPorter in Section 3. In Section 4 we discuss the notions of processes, ports, and connections in HPorter, as well as other implementation details. In Section 5 we discuss performance, and related work is summarized in Section 6.

2   A Brief Introduction to Arrows

We assume that the reader is familiar with Haskell. In this section we give a brief introduction to arrows; more detail can be found in [8,7].

Arrows are a generalization of monads that relax the stringent linearity imposed by monads, while retaining a disciplined style of composition. This discipline is enforced by requiring that composition be done in a "point-free"

---

[2] On the other hamd, hard real-time constraints are not something we address in this work, nor is it a requirement of our robotics application.

style – i.e. combinators are used to compose functions without making direct reference to the functions' values. These combinators are captured in the Arrow type class:

```
> class Arrow a where
>    arr   :: (b -> c) -> a b c
>    (>>>) :: a b c -> a c d -> a b d
>    first :: a b c -> a (b,d) (c,d)
```

arr lifts a function to a "pure" arrow computation; i.e., the output entirely depends on the input (it is analogous to return in the Monad class). (>>>) composes two arrow computations by connecting the output of the first to the input of the second (and is analogous to bind ((>>=)) in the Monad class). But in addition to composing arrows linearly, it is desirable to compose them in parallel – i.e. to allow "branching" and "merging" of inputs and outputs. There are several ways to do this, but by simply defining the first combinator in the Arrow class, all other combinators can be defined. first converts an arrow computation taking one input and one result, into an arrow computation taking two inputs and two results. The original arrow is applied to the first part of the input, and the result becomes the first part of the output. The second part of the input is fed directly to the second part of the output.

Other combinators can be defined using these three primitives. For example, the dual of first can be defined as:

```
>    second :: (Arrow a) => a b c -> a (d,b) (d,c)
>    second f = let swapA = arr (\(a,b) -> (b,a))
>               in swapA >>> first f >>> swapA
```

Finally, it is sometimes desirable to write arrows that "loop", such as in a signal processing application with feedback. For this purpose, an extra combinator (not derivable from the three base combinators) is needed, and is captured in the ArrowLoop class:

```
> class ArrowLoop a where
>    loop :: a (b,d) (c,d) -> a b c
```

We find that arrows are best viewed pictorially, especially for the application at hand: composing parallel processes. Figure 1 shows the basic combinators in this manner, including loop.

3   HPorter by Example

In this section we present some examples that highlight the three key features of HPorter: the use of arrows to wire together parallel processes, the ability to reconfigure processes dynamically, and the ability to write glue code without leaving Haskell.

```
arr     :: Arrow a => (b -> c) -> a b c
(>>>)   :: Arrow a => a b c -> a c d -> a b d
(<<<)   :: Arrow a => a c d -> a b c -> a b d
first   :: Arrow a => a b c -> a (b,d) (c,d)
second  :: Arrow a => a b c -> a (d,b) (d,c)
(***)   :: Arrow a => a b c -> a b' c' -> a (b,b') (c,c')
(&&&)   :: Arrow a => a b c -> a b c' -> a b (c,c')
loop    :: Arrow a => a (b,d) (c,d) -> a b c
```

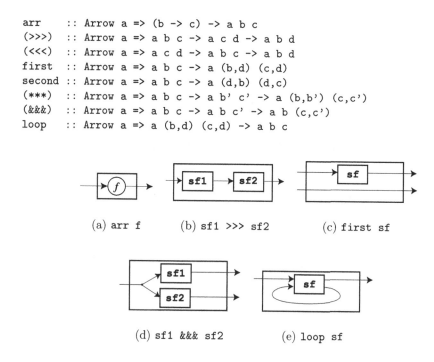

(a) arr f   (b) sf1 >>> sf2   (c) first sf

(d) sf1 &&& sf2   (e) loop sf

Fig. 1. Commonly Used Arrow Combinators

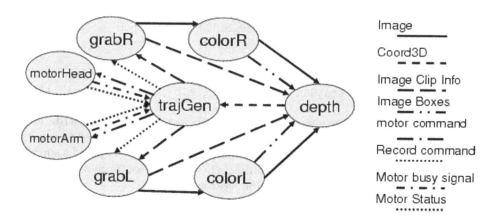

Fig. 2. Structure of a Robot System

3.1 Processes as Arrows

In HPorter, a process is represented as an arrow of type `Proc T1 T2`. In other words, a process takes as input a stream of values of type `T1`, and yields as output a stream of values of type `T2`. If a stream of values were represented as an infinite list, we would have the following correspondence:

```
Proc T1 T2 = [T1] -> [T2]
```

In fact it is easy to make this representation an instance of class `Arrow`, and an (overly) abstract semantics for HPorter can be devised. In practice, the representation is much more involved, since these processes are actually imperative C programs running as QNX processes. We defer discussion of these implementation details until a later section.

As a realistic example, suppose we want our robot to perform a vision-guided reaching task, for which we need eight processes: two video image grabbers, two color processors, a scene depth calculator, two motor controllers, and a reaching trajectory planner.[3] Our only concern here is how to wire them together: the streams of images captured from the grabbers are processed by the color filters to generate "boxes" that identify objects of interest. Then the boxes along with the images from the color filters are passed to the depth calculator to generate the 3D coordinates of the objects. These coordinates are sent to the reaching trajectory planner, which computes the arm trajectory and passes that to the motor controller to move the arm. Besides this main information flow, there is inter-process communication for auxiliary functionality, like recording requests for the image grabber. Figure 2 shows the detailed information flow graphically for the overall system – note that the graph is circular.

This information flow can be captured in HPorter as follows:

```
> vision :: Proc ((Rec,CClip),(Rec,CClip)) ((Image,Image),Coord3D)
> vision = (grabR >>> (first colorR)) *** (grabL >>> (first colorL))
>          >>> (arr (\ (((imR,bR),cR),((imL,bL),cL))->
>              (((imR,imL),(bR,bL)),(cR,cL)))) >>> ndepth
>
> reach :: Proc () ()
> reach = loop ((motorHead *** motorArm) *** (vision >>> (arr snd))
>               >>> trajGen >>> (arr (\ ((a,b),c) -> (a,(b,c)))))
```

From this example the reader can see how cumbersome it can be to write in a point-free style – in particular, the pairing and merging of inputs and outputs becomes quite tedious. To alleviate this problem, Paterson has proposed a special syntax for arrows [13], much in the spirit of the "do" syntax for monads. Using arrow syntax, the above program can be written:

```
> reach :: Proc () ()
> reach = proc x -> do
>             rec
>               (cGR,imgR)   <- grabR     -< (cpR,rcR)
>               (cGL,imgL)   <- grabL     -< (cpL,rcL)
>               (imgCR,boxR) <- colorR    -< imgR
>               (imgCL,boxL) <- colorL    -< imgL
```

---

[3] The trajectory planner is actually a Dance (i.e. Haskell) program compiled into C using GHC.

```
>                  ((imgDR,imgDL), depD)
>                            <- ndepth     -<
>                       (((imgCR,imgCL),(boxR,boxL)),(cGR,cGL))
>              (((cmd0,cmd1),(cpR,rcR)),(cpL,rcL))
>                            <- headarm'  -<
>                                (((bz0,hm),(bz1,am)),depD)
>                  (bz0,hm)    <- motorHead -< cmd0
>                  (bz1,am)    <- motorArm  -< cmd1
>              returnA -< ()
```

Unlike the "do" syntax for monads, the arrow syntax requires both an input and an output for each process. As with monad syntax, the inputs and outputs "strip off" the arrow constructor. For example, in the above, `colorR` has type `Proc Image (Image, Boxes)`, and thus imgR has type `Image` and `(imgCR,boxR)` has type `(Image,Boxes)`.

Although more verbose than the original point-free style, this is arguably a very natural and easy to understand way of wiring processes together. Indeed, it is isomorphic to the diagram in Figure 2. Its constrained style permits us to guarantee, eventually, that the processes run stand-alone, without the help of the Haskell subsystem.

Continuing with this example, the processes we use are generated from existing C programs in the following way. Suppose the C program for the color filter is located at `"/home/user/bin/color"`. Suppose further that the TCP/IP ports for this process have identifiers `"inputa"` and `"inputb"` for input, and `"outputc"` for output. Suppose finally that we wish to map this process to processor id 5. We can do this as follows:

```
> colorR :: Proc Image (Image, Boxes)
> colorR = makeProc progColor "-b -N 1 -s 0 -o /colorR" 5 5
```

where `progColor` is defined as:

```
> progColor = defProg { procName = "/color",
>                       progName = "/home/user/bin/color",
>                       input = image "inputa"
>                       output = lift2 (image "inputa") (box "inputb"),
>                       param = colorP}
```

The details of `image` and `box`, and of the string argument to `makeProc`, are not important. Each of the other processes can be defined in a similar way.

3.2   Reactivity

In order to add reactivity to HPorter, we adopt the ideas of *functional reactive programming* [16,12,1,3], in particular as they are embodied in *Yampa*, which also uses arrows [7].

One key idea in Yampa is a *signal function*, whose type is `SF a b`, and is analogous to HPorter's `Proc a b`. Another fundamental concept is that of an *event*, which occurs at discrete points in time. This idea is captured in Yampa through an option type called `Event`:

```
> data Event a = NoEvent | Event a
```

`Event` is isomorphic to `Maybe`, but it is an abstract type whose constructors are not exposed. Yampa provides a rich set of functions for generating event sources and for operating point-wise on events.

In HPorter we treat a reactive process as a signal function that generates non-reactive processes. In other words:

```
> type (HasPort a, HasPort b) =>
>       ReactProc a b c = SF a (Proc b c)
```

Here, type `a` represents the signal type that our process reacts to. Now Yampa's facilities for reactivity – i.e. its "switching" combinators – can be used to switch to a new signal function when an event occurs. The most commonly used switching combinator is:

```
>    switch :: SF (a, (b,Event c)) -> (c -> SF a b) -> SF a b
```

For example, the expression `(sf1 &&& es) 'switch' \e -> sf2` behaves as `sf1` until the first event in the event stream `es` occurs, at which point the event's value is bound to `e` and the behavior switches over to `sf2`.

With this background we can now give an example of reactivity that highlights our application domain. The robot's vision system has a variety of image processing capabilities, such as a color filter and a motion detector:

```
> color  :: Proc Image Image
> motion :: Proc Image Image
```

For input and output, suppose we also have an image grabber and a video player:

```
> grabber :: Proc () Image
> video   :: Proc Image ()
```

Now suppose we want the vision system to switch between looking for objects of a certain color (signaled by `Event 1`), objects that are moving (`Event 2`), or no objects at all (`Event 0`). This behavior can be achieved as follows:

```
> colorOrMotion :: ReactProc (Event Int) () ()
> colorOrMotion = filterSelect noFilter
>
> colorFilter  = grabber >>> color >>> video
> motionFilter = grabber >>> motion >>> video
> noFilter     = grabber >>> video
>
> filterSelect :: Proc () () -> ReactProc (Event Int) () ()
> filterSelect p = switch (proc e do
>                             returnA -< (p,e))
```

```
>                         (\a -> case a of
>                             0 -> filterSelect noFilter
>                             1 -> filterSelect colorFilter
>                             2 -> filterSelect motionFilter
```

`filterSelect` is a recursive switch function that starts with a process of type `Proc () ()`, and watches the input signal for an event. When an event happens, `filterSelect` is called recursively, but possibly with a new process, depending on the value of the integer event. It is important to understand that the switching process is not the same as a conditional – a switch may imply the reconfiguration of parallel processes.

3.3 GLUE'ing Processes Together

In this section we give an example of the third and final key feature of HPorter, namely the ability to write simple glue code without resorting to C or C++.

As mentioned in the introduction, sometimes simple glue code is needed to interconnect processes – for example, we might want to increment each value in a stream, or take the sine of each value. It would be inconvenient to insist that the user write a new C or C++ program for each new piece of glue code. Our solution is to introduce a small first-order imperative language called GLUE that allows the user to write the glue code directly within her HPorter program, but which is simple enough that it can be compiled into efficient C++ code.

In our original design we simply defined an AST data type in Haskell and wrote our glue code using values of that type. With the overloading afforded by Haskell's type classes, this was a reasonable approach, and it worked quite well. More recently, however, we have defined a simple lexical syntax for this language, which makes writing GLUE code even easier. As an example, here is a program that takes two streams of integers and adds them pairwise:

```
name glueplus
input Int a;
      Int b;
output Int c;
c := a + b
```

This program is compiled into our AST data type, where it is type-checked and compiled into C++, borrowing ideas from **Pan** and **Pan#**, which are DSLs for graphics that are embedded in Haskell. Since that compilation process is well-documented elsewhere (see [2,14]), we omit a detailed discussion in this paper.

Since GLUE is an imperative language, one might ask why we don't just write the glue code in C or C++. But in addition to the small piece of straight-line code that, in the example above, adds two numbers together, there is a plethora of additional "boilerplate code" that needs to be written as well, such as the inclusion of header files, and establishing the linkages between this process and the ones that we are scripting. Indeed, our compilation process turns the above five-line program into a ninety-five line C++ program.

4   Processes, Ports, and Connections

In this section we describe in detail how the underlying processes, ports, and connections are implemented in HPorter. All of this is hidden from the user.

Running Processes. As mentioned in Section 3.1, a process can abstractly be thought of as a stream transformer. But concretely, it is a C or C++ process running stand-alone on an individual *node* of a parallel computer with a unique TCP/IP *address*. Each process has a *pathname*, a unique *id*, and both an input and output *port*. Finally, processes are wired together via *connections* between pairs of ports.

In order to achieve this in Haskell, we need to represent all of these gory details within the abstraction for processes in HPorter. We begin with the simple notion of a *running process*, or RProc:

```
> type RProc    = (ID, ProgPath, Parameter, Address, Node)

> type ProgPath = String;  type Parameter = String;
> type Address  = String;  type ID        = Int;
> type Node     = Int;      type PIDMap    = [(ID,Address)]
```

An RProc thus contains a unique ID, a program pathname, a parameter (i.e. an argument), the number of the node on which it is running, and the TCP/IP address of the node. We also introduce the concept of PID map, which maps the ID of each process to the TCP/IP address of the node on which it is running.

Ports and Connections. Next, we define the types needed for process communication. The connection of a server/client pair is built upon the notion of a *port*:

```
> type Port     = (ID, PortName)
> type PortName = String
```

which contains the ID of the process that it is defined within and a unique local name. Then a *server port*:

```
> type ServerPort = (Port, PortNum)
> type PortNum = Int
```

is a pair of port and port number, and a *connection*:

```
> type Connection = (Port,Port)
```

is a pair of ports, whose order matters: data flows from the first to the second.

Process State and Arrow Instances. Finally, as we compose processes together (using the arrow framework), we need to generate a new ID for each composite process and a free port number for each pair of communication ports, and we need to keep track of all live socket port servers, the internal connections, and the internal process ids. This information is contained in the `PState` data type, which is then used to define the `Proc` data type as follows:[4]

```
> data Proc a b = Proc ((PState, a) -> (PState, b))
>
> data PState = PState { nextID     :: ID,
>                        nextPort   :: PortNum,
>                        serverPort :: [ServerPort],
>                        conns      :: [Connection],
>                        procs      :: [RProc],
>                        pidMap     :: PIDMap}
> emptyPState = PState { nextID = 0, nextPort = 5000, serverPort = [],
>                        conns = [], procs = []}
```

Now we can declare `Proc` to be an instance of `Arrow` and `ArrowLoop`:

```
> instance Arrow Proc where
>    arr f = Proc (\(s, x) -> (s, f x))
>    Proc f1 >>> Proc f2 = Proc (f2 . f1)
>    first (Proc f) = Proc (\ (s, (a,c)) ->
>          let (s', b) = f (s, a) in (s', (b, c)))
>
> instance ArrowLoop Proc where
>    loop (Proc f) = Proc (\ (s, a) ->
>                      let (s', (b, c)) = f (s, (a, c)) in (s', b))
```

Running a Composite Process. At the outermost level of an HPorter program, there is one value of type `Proc () ()` that needs to be executed, just as in monadic IO there is one value of type `IO ()` to be executed. Indeed, to execute the `Proc () ()` value in Haskell, it must be converted into a value of type `IO ()`. The function `runProc` achieves this for us:

```
> runProc :: Proc () () -> IO ()
> runProc (Proc p) =
>    let (s, output) = p (emptyPState, ())
>        obs         = procs s
>        cs          = conns s
>        sv          = serverPort s
>        adList      = pidMap s
>    in do sequence_ (map (run sv cs adList) obs)
```

(`sequence_` is a standard Haskell library functions that takes a list of monadic actions and "runs" them in sequence.)

---

[4] Note that if `Proc` could be defined as `Proc (a -> (PState, b))` then it would be a *Kleisli arrow*, and thus a monad. But it cannot, and thus the more general arrow class must be used.

The initial PState, emptyPState, contains no server port, no connections, no process, an initial id value and an initial port number (which is set to 5000 to avoid possible conflict with the system processes). By applying p to the initPState, we get a final PState named s that contains all of the connections, processes, PID-IP address mapping and server port number assignment for the whole program. run generates the appropriate QNX commands to begin execution of each process with the proper port number initialization parameters for each.

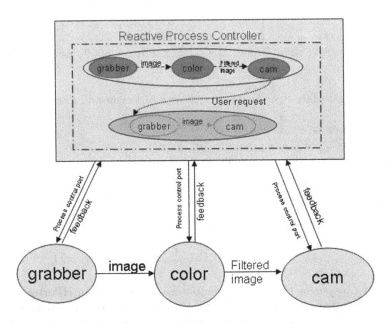

Fig. 3. Process Controller and Processes

Adding Reactivity. The presentation we have given so far has actually been oversimplified. In particular, we have not taken into account how HPorter dynamically reconfigures processes, including stopping them and restarting them if necessary. We need a new execution model to enable dynamic process re-wiring, in which we:

– Add an input port in all the source programs for process control command.
– Add an output port in all the source programs for control command feedback.
– Adjust the programs to allow process control interruption during execution.
– Add a command line option for switching between online and offline process control.

These new ports are exclusively for process control purposes, and connect only to what we call the *process controller*. They are not user-controllable and do not appear in the program or process abstractions. Through these new ports the process controller acts as a central controller for all of them.

The relationship between the process controller and each process is that of a standard client/server model, as shown pictorially in Figure 3. The controller (server) sends commands to each process (client) through a "control" port, and receives responses through a "feedback" port. The process control commands are captured in:

```
> data ProcCmd = StartServer ID PortName PortNum
>                | ConnectTo ID PortName Address PortNum
>                | Stop ID PortName
>                | Quit ID
>                | Suspend PID
>                | Continue PID
```

The command `StartServer pid pn i` asks process `pid` to start a TCP/IP socket server `pn` at port `i`. Command `ConnectTo pid1 pn addr i` asks process `pid1` to connect port `pn` to the port number `i` at address `addr`. `Stop pid pn` tells the process `pid` to close the port named `pn`, and `Quit pid` is used to kill process `pid`. The `Suspend` and `Continue` commands allow interrupting and resuming a process, for situations where a batch of commands needs to be addressed before the process can proceed safely.

Although the details are too numerous to include in this paper, reactivity works as follows: The state that is accumulated by the running system includes all of the running processes and how they are interconnected. When an event occurs that triggers a switch, a computation is performed to determine the best way to achieve the reconfiguration (some processes may need to be killed; others suspended, rewired, and restarted; and others created from scratch). The above commands are then issued to the processes to effect this reconfiguration, and the computation continues. All of this stateful computation is "hidden" within the arrow and the switching combinators.

5   Performance

We have implemented HPorter on two different networks of parallel processors running under the QNX real-time operating system, one having 8 processors, and the other having 16. The current system is running under QNX Version 6.3, and we use TCP/IP sockets for inter-process communication.

GHC Version 6.4 is used to compile any Haskell processes that are being scripted (for example the Dance program for the trajectory planner discussed in Section 3.1), as well as the GLUE code and the process controller.

We have compared our implementation of HPorter to the QNX *Porter* scripting language, and find them to be comparable in performance for our application.

- For non-reactive processes, Haskell is only needed for starting and interconnecting the processes. The extra overhead at start-up time is not noticeable, because the start-up time for most processes is much longer.
- For processes that contain GLUE code, some overhead is incurred to compile the glue code. Once compiled and interconnected, however, Haskell once

again is out of the loop. And because the glue code is usually very small, the overhead of compilation is not significant. Also, our implementation works hard to ensure that GLUE code is not recompiled every time it is invoked – thus the overhead is only incurred the first time around.

– For processes with reactivity, we have found that for our applications, where the mode switches do not happen frequently, the response time is more than adequate. In vision-based robotics, vision processing is the computationally limiting factor, and rates of 10-20 hertz are considered good. At that rate HPorter's impact on the system is negligible. For applications requiring more rapid response, we expect that pre-compilation of the glue code may be necessary. This would be straightforward using our approach, but thus far we have not needed to do so.

6   Related Work

There are many "architectural description languages," or ADLs, such as Darwin/regis [11], ACME [4], and Rapide [10], designed for specifying the architectures of a software system. HPorter shares with these language the ability to specify a software architecture, but there are several important differences:

– Most ADLs represent the architecture as a collection of components and connections, whereas we treat it as a *transition function* and cast it into an arrow framework.
– ADLs are meant primarily for the design of software systems, whereas HPorter is targeted at composing and executing a real distributed application.
– HPorter supports reactivity – i.e., the expression of dynamic, reconfigurable architectures – which is seldom found in ADLs.
– New processes can be defined and created dynamically in HPorter.
– Programs in HPorter are more concise than ADLs, which express components and their interconnections separately.

Our work is probably most similar to Ptolemy [9], which serves both as an ADL and as a language for composing real-time processes. Ptolemy is much richer than HPorter, although its notion of process interconnection is more complex than that of HPorter.

HaskellScript [15] is a scripting language embedded in Haskell that interconnects COM objects dynamically. Like HPorter, it also has strong typing. However, the focus is on uniprocessor applications, whereas HPorter allows true parallelism. Furthermore, HaskellScript uses monads to structure programs, and thus does not have the generality afforded by arrows.

7   Conclusion

In this paper we present an embedded DSL, HPorter, for composing parallel processes. HPorter has a concise and declarative syntax, via the employment of the arrow framework. The host language Haskell makes it more robust in the sense of type safety, compared to conventional scripting techniques. Reactivity in HPorter allows system reconfiguration through the use of switching combinators derived from Yampa. We have also presented a sub-language, GLUE, for specifying the glue code that is sometimes needed when interconnecting processes. An efficient implantation of HPorter is achieved by compiling glue code into C, and by interpreting process interconnections as QNX system calls.

References

1. C. Elliott. Modeling interactive 3D and multimedia animation with an embedded language. In *Proceedings of the first conference on Domain-Specific Languages*, pages 285–296. USENIX, Oct. 1997.
2. C. Elliott, S. Finne, and O. de Moor. Compiling embedded languages. In *SAIG*, pages 9–27, 2000.
3. C. Elliott and P. Hudak. Functional reactive animation. In *International Conference on Functional Programming*, pages 263–273, June 1997.
4. D. Garlan, R. Monroe, and D. Wile. ACME: An architecture description interchange language. In *Proceedings of CASCON'97*, pages 169–183, Toronto, Ontario, November 1997.
5. L. Huang. *Robot Dance with Functional Reactive Programming*. PhD thesis, Department of Computer Science, Yale University, December 2006.
6. L. Huang and P. Hudak. Dance: A declarative language for the control of humanoid robots. Technical Report YALEU/DCS/RR-1253, Yale University, Department of Computer Science, July 2003.
7. P. Hudak, A. Courtney, H. Nilsson, and J. Peterson. Arrows, robots, and functional reactive programming. In *Summer School on Advanced Functional Programming, Oxford University*. Springer Verlag, to appear, 2003.
8. J. Hughes. Generalising monads to arrows. *Science of Computer Programming*, 37:67–111, May 2000.
9. E. A. Lee. Overview of the ptolemy project. Technical Report Technical Memorandum UCB/ERL M03/25, Univerisity of California, Berkeley, CA, 94720, USA, July 2003.
10. D. C. Luckham, J. L. Kenney, L. M. Augustin, J. Vera, D. Bryan, and W. Mann. Specification and analysis of system architecture using rapide. *IEEE Transactions on Software Engineering*, 21(4):336–355, 1995.
11. J. Magee, N. Dulay, and J. Kramer. Regis: A constructive development environment for distributed programs, 1994.
12. H. Nilsson, A. Courtney, and J. Peterson. Functional reactive programming, continued. In *Proceedings of the 2002 ACM SIGPLAN Haskell Workshop (Haskell'02)*, pages 51–64, Pittsburgh, Pennsylvania, USA, Oct. 2002. ACM Press.
13. R. Paterson. A new notation for arrows. In *International Conference on Functional Programming*, pages 229–240. ACM Press, Sept. 2001.
14. J. Peterson. A language for mathematical visualization. In *Proceedings of FPDE'02: Functional and Declarative Languages in Education*, October 2002.
15. S. Peyton Jones, E. Meijer, and D. Leijen. Scripting COM components from Haskell. In *Fifth International Conference on Software Reuse (ICSR'98)*, Victoria, B.C., Canada, June 1998. IEEE Computer Society Press.
16. Z. Wan and P. Hudak. Functional reactive programming from first principles. In *Proceedings of PLDI'01: Symposium on Programming Language Design and Implementation*, pages 242–252, June 2000. http://haskell.org/frp/publication.html#frp-1st

Coupled Schema Transformation and Data Conversion for XML and SQL

Pablo Berdaguer, Alcino Cunha*, Hugo Pacheco, and Joost Visser*

DI-CCTC, Universidade do Minho, Portugal
joost.visser@di.uminho.pt

Abstract. A two-level data transformation consists of a type-level transformation of a data format coupled with value-level transformations of
data instances corresponding to that format. We have implemented a system for performing two-level transformations on XML schemas and their
corresponding documents, and on SQL schemas and the databases that
they describe. The core of the system consists of a combinator library for
composing type-changing rewrite rules that preserve structural information and referential constraints. We discuss the implementation of the system's core library, and of its SQL and XML front-ends in the functional
language Haskell. We show how the system can be used to tackle various
two-level transformation scenarios, such as XML schema evolution coupled with document migration, and hierarchical-relational data mappings
that convert between XML documents and SQL databases.

Keywords: Haskell, Transformation, SQL, XML.

1 Introduction

Coupled software transformation involves the modification of multiple software
artifacts such that they remain consistent with each other [12,8]. Two-level data
transformation is a particular instance of coupled transformation, where the
coupled artifacts are a data format on the one hand, and the data instances
that conform to that format on the other hand [7]. In this paper we will focus
on the transformation of data formats described in the XML Schema or in the
SQL language, coupled with the conversion of the corresponding data captured
in XML documents or stored in SQL databases.

The phenomenon of two-level data transformation occurs in a variety of contexts. For example, software maintenance commonly involves enhancement of
the data formats employed for storing or exporting an application's data. Typically such enhancements are fairly conservative, such as adding new fields to the
format. When the enhanced format only serves internal data storage, a one-off
conversion of old data into new data may be sufficient to restore conformance.
When the format concerns data exported to other applications, or shared with
older versions of the same application, old-to-new as well as new-to-old data
conversions may be needed on a repetitive or continuous basis.

---

* Work funded by Fundação para a Ciência e a Tecnologia, POSI/ICHS/44304/2002.

M. Hanus (Ed.): PADL 2007, LNCS 4354, pp. 290–304, 2007.

Two-level data transformation also encompasses less conservative format changes, such as data mappings between programming paradigms. For example, the logic of an application may be programmed against an XML schema, while for efficient storage of its persistent data a relational database is employed. The required data mapping involves a format transformation from an XML schema to an SQL schema, as well as forward and backward data conversions between XML documents and an SQL database. Unlike format enhancements in the maintenance context, data mappings typically involve profound structural modifications.

Other contexts in which two-level data transformations may play a role include: system integration, where data needs to be exchanged between independently developed applications; evolution of programming languages, where grammar modifications between versions spark the need for migration of source programs; and model-driven engineering where high-level (meta-)model transformations give rise to conversion of their instances.

Previously, we have shown how data refinement theory can be employed to formalize two-level data transformation, and how the functional programming language Haskell can be employed to capture this formalization in a type-safe manner [7]. We also provided suites of rule combinators as well as basic rules for format evolution and hierarchical-relational data mappings from which two-level data transformation pipelines are built in compositional fashion.

In the present paper, we discuss practical application of our Haskell-based two-level transformation support. In particular, we make these contributions:

1. We elaborate the rule combinators and basic rules to take into account not only structural information, but also *constraint information*, such as primary keys and foreign keys (Section 4).
2. We embed the general transformation kernel into a language-specific transformation framework, including front-ends for SQL (schemas and data) and for XML Schema and XML documents (Section 5).
3. We illustrate by example how the XML/SQL transformation framework is used to handle various two-level transformation scenarios, including XML-to-SQL data mappings, XML schema evolution, and SQL database migration (Section 6).

Before discussing these contributions, we will present a motivating example (Section 2) and briefly recapitulate our previous work on two-level data transformation (Section 3). We end with a discussion of related work (Section 7) and concluding remarks (Section 8).

2 Motivating Example

The tree in Figure 1 represents an XML movie database schema, before and after evolution. Before evolution, the database holds information for movies and actors only. The evolution steps aims to add information for TV series to the database. This is done through the following changes:

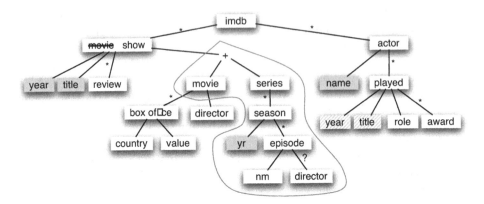

Fig. 1. Evolution of a movie database schema, inspired by IMDb (`http://www.imdb.com/`). The circled area points out the introduced structure.

1. The `movie` element is renamed to `show`.
2. Some information specific to movies is factored out into a new `movie` element.
3. An element `series` with information specific to TV series is introduced as an alternative to the `movie` element.

In the original schema, the following constraints should hold:

1. A `movie` is identified by its `year` and `title`.
2. An `actor` is identified by his/her `name`.
3. The `year` and `title` of a `played` element refers to the `year` and `title` of a `movie`.

The evolution step introduces the following additional constraint:

4. A `season` is identified by its `yr`.

When an XML-to-SQL data mapping is applied to the original and the evolved schema, different SQL databases with different constraints will result. For example, the original schema is mapped to the following database (this example will be revisted and continued in Section 6):

```
movies(year,title,director)
reviews(id,year,title,review)
   foreign key (year,title) references movies(year,title)
boxoffices(id,year,title,country,value)
   foreign key (year,title) references movies(year,title)
actors(name)
playeds(id,name,year,title,role)
   foreign key (year,title) references movies(year,title)
   foreign key (name) references actors(name)
awards(id,name,playedid,award)
   foreign key (playedid,name) references playeds(id,name)
```

In the sequel we will show how both evolution and mapping can be specified by composing library combinators. The backward and forward data conversions induced by these schema transformations will come for free. The properties of the combinators guarantee that the conversions are invertible, i.e. that no data gets lost. The propagation and generation of constraints support the preservation of not only structural, but also semantic information.

3   Two-Level Data Transformation

Two-level data transformation can be formalized in terms of data refinement theory, and can be modeled in Haskell as systems of type-changing rewrite rules [7]. These rewrite rules operate on Haskell types. In Section 5, we will discuss how XML and SQL schemas are represented by such types.

Data Refinements. A datatype A can be refined to a datatype B, usually denoted by the inequation $A \leqslant B$, if there is an injective, total function $to : A \rightarrow B$ (the *representation function*) and a surjective, possibly partial function $from : B \rightarrow A$ (the *abstraction function*) such that $from \cdot to = id_A$, where id_A is the identity function on datatype A.

The inequations of data refinement theory can be used as rewrite rules that replace one datatype by another. When applied left-to-right, an inequation $A \leqslant B$ will preserve or enrich information content, while applied right-to-left it will preserve or restrict information content. The (potential) partiality of the *from* function implies that left-to-right application is only valid if the invariant $to \cdot from = id_B$ can be shown to hold.

In fact, when used as a left-to-right rewrite rule, a data refinement inequation $A \leqslant B$, witnessed by functions to and $from$, can be interpreted as a two-level data transformation step that takes its input datatype A into the triple $(B, to, from)$.

Representation of Types and Rules. The core of the model of two-level data transformations in Haskell are the following declarations:

> **type** *Rule* = $\forall a$. *Type a* $\rightarrow$ *Maybe* (*View* (*Type a*))
> **data** *Type a* **where**
>   *Int* :: *Type Int*
>   *Prod* :: *Type a* $\rightarrow$ *Type b* $\rightarrow$ *Type* (a, b)
>   *Either* :: *Type a* $\rightarrow$ *Type b* $\rightarrow$ *Type* (*Either a b*)
>   *Map* :: *Type a* $\rightarrow$ *Type b* $\rightarrow$ *Type* (*Map a b*)
>   ...
> **data** *View a* **where** *View* :: *Rep a b* $\rightarrow$ *Type b* $\rightarrow$ *View* (*Type a*)
> **data** *Rep a b* = *Rep*{ *to* :: $a \rightarrow b$, *from* :: $b \rightarrow a$}

Note that *Type* and *View* are *generalized* algebraic data types (GADTs) [19], an extension to the Haskell type system that allows (partially) instantiated type parameters in the result type of data constructors.

The *Rule* type expresses that a two-level transformation step is a partial function that takes a type into a view of that type. Here we use a value-level representation of datatypes [11], where a value of *Type a* is the representation of type *a*. For instance, the value *Prod Int Int* represents type (Int, Int).

The *View* constructor expresses that a type *a* can be transformed into a type *b*, if there are functions *to* :: $a \rightarrow b$ and *from* :: $b \rightarrow a$, bundled in the *Rep* constructor, that allow data conversion between *a* and *b*. Note that only the source type *a* escapes from the *View* constructor, while the target type *b* remains encapsulated — it is implicitly existentially quantified.

Two-Level Transformation Combinators. To construct complex two-level transformations from basic ones, combinators are defined for identity, sequential composition, left-biased choice, repetition, and generic traversal:

> *nop* :: *Rule*
> *nop x* = *Just* (*View* (*Rep id id*) *x*)
>
> $(\triangleright)$ :: *Rule* $\rightarrow$ *Rule* $\rightarrow$ *Rule*
> $(f \triangleright g)\ a$ = **do** *View* (*Rep t1 f1*) *b* $\leftarrow$ *f a*
> $\qquad\qquad\quad$ *View* (*Rep t2 f2*) *c* $\leftarrow$ *g b*
> $\qquad\qquad\quad$ *return* (*View* (*Rep* (*t2* · *t1*) (*f1* · *f2*)) *c*)
>
> $(\oslash)$ :: *Rule* $\rightarrow$ *Rule* $\rightarrow$ *Rule* $\qquad$ *everywhere* :: *Rule* $\rightarrow$ *Rule*
> *many* :: *Rule* $\rightarrow$ *Rule* $\qquad\qquad\quad$ *somewhere* :: *Rule* $\rightarrow$ *Rule*

These combinators are common for typed strategic rewriting libraries [16,15]. For conciseness, we show definitions of the first two only. These combinators allow us to combine local, single-step transformations into a single global transformation.

Several local, single-step transformation rules are shown in Figure 2. These rules are implemented in Haskell in a straightforward way. For example, the rule for adding alternatives is implemented as follows:

> *addalt* :: *Type b* $\rightarrow$ *Rule*
> *addalt b a* = *Just* (*View* (*Rep Left* (λ(*Left x*) $\rightarrow$ *x*)) (*Either a b*))

Using these basic rules and the rule combinators, we can compose sophisticated strategies for two-level transformation. For example, a hierarchical-relational mapping can be defined along the following lines (details in [7]):

> *toRDB* :: *Rule*
> *toRDB* = *many* (*somewhere* (*listelim* $\oslash$ *setelim* $\oslash$ ... $\oslash$ *flatmap*))

Such compositions are guaranteed to be refinements again, i.e. they induce invertible data conversion function. The combinators give full control over the order and conditions under which rules are applied.

4   Constraint Preserving Transformation

The type representation and the two-level transformation rules from [7], recapitulated above, fail to take into account constraint information. In particular, foreign key relationships play an important role in relational database modeling and querying. A similar concept is present in XML Schema, though its usage is limited [13]. In this section we discuss how the type representation and transformation rules can be augmented to take constraint information into account.

Hierarchical-to-relational data mapping	
$[A] \leqslant I\!N \to A$	List elimination
$2^A \cong A \to 1$	Set elimination
$A? \cong 1 \to A$	Optional elimination
$A + B \leqslant A? \times B?$	Sum elimination
$A \times (B + C) \cong (A \times B) + (A \times C)$	Distribute product over sum
$A \to (B + C) \leqslant (A \to B) \times (A \to C)$	Distribute map over sum (range)
$(B + C) \to A \cong (B \to A) \times (C \to A)$	Distribute map over sum (domain)
$A \to (B \times (C \to D)) \leqslant (A \to B) \times (A \times C \to D)$	Flatten nested map
Format evolution	

$A \leqslant A \times B$	Add field		$A^+ \leqslant [A]$	Allow empty list
$A \leqslant A + B$	Add alternative		$A? \leqslant [A]$	Allow repetition
$A \leqslant A?$	Make optional		$A \leqslant A^+$	Allow non-empty repetition

Fig. 2. One-step rules for two-level transformation systems. More details can be found elsewhere [7].

Representation of Field Names and Referential Constraints. To represent field names and references, we introduce an annotation mechanism on data types. We will write ${}_k A_r^n$ to denote a datatype A with name n, key k, and key references r.

- The name annotation n is either empty, or contains a single name.
- The key annotation k is either empty, or contains a globally unique identifier.
- The key references annotation r is a list of zero or more identifiers.

With such annotations, we can represent the first two tables of our example as:

$$
({}_1(Int^{\texttt{year}} \times Str^{\texttt{title}}) \to Str^{\texttt{director}})^{\texttt{movies}} \times
$$
$$
((Int^{\texttt{id}} \times (Int^{\texttt{year}} \times Str^{\texttt{title}})_1) \to Str^{\texttt{review}})^{\texttt{reviews}}
$$

Note that we represent tables with finite maps, where the map's domain is the primary key of the table. The compound foreign key relationship is represented by the annotation **1** on the year-title pair inside each map.

Constraint-Preserving Transformation Rules. Using our datatype annotation mechanism, we can enhance some of our two-level transformation rules to manipulate constraint and name information in addition to structural information. Concatenation of reference lists is denoted by juxtaposition.

For example, the introduction of a new key reference when flattening nested maps is captured by the following:

$$
({}_k A_r \to (B \times (C \to D)^o))^m \quad \cong \quad ({}_k A_r \to B)^m \times ({}_\emptyset A_{kr} \times C \to D)^o
$$

Here we use $\emptyset$ to denote absence of keys. Where annotations on types are omitted, we assume that the annotations get copied over from left to right without modifications. The first map on the right-hand side inherits its key k from the outer map on the left-hand side. If no key is present on A, a new key is generated. The second map on the right-hand side contains a datatype A that is annotated with a reference to that key k. Note also that the rule is no longer an

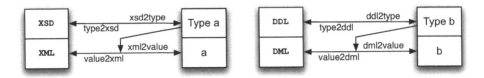

Fig. 3. Overview of the XML and SQL front ends

inequation, but an isomorphism, because the referential constraint ensures that the flat maps can always be nested again.

The presence of annotations may also *invalidate* the applicability of a rule. For example, the distribution of a map over a sum may only be performed when the domain of the map is not a key (name annotations omitted for brevity):

$$_{\emptyset}A \rightharpoonup B + C \quad \leqslant \quad _{\emptyset}A \rightharpoonup B \times {}_{\emptyset}A \rightharpoonup C$$

The $\emptyset$ indicates that the key annotation of A is required to be empty. This prevents that the target of a reference gets distributed over two different tables, which would break referential integrity. Our system of rules handles types of the form $_{k}A \rightharpoonup B + C$, where k is *not* empty by first applying the sum elimination rule, followed by the optional elimination rule (name annotations omitted again):

$$_{k}A \rightharpoonup B + C \quad \leqslant \quad _{k}A \rightharpoonup B? \times C? \quad \cong \quad _{k}A \rightharpoonup (1 \rightharpoonup B) \times (1 \rightharpoonup C)$$

After this, the rule for flattening nested maps, given above, can be applied twice to obtain a relational representation.

We have adapted the datatype *Type* to accomodate annotations on type representations, and we have augmented all implementations of two-level rewrite rules with appropriate annotation handling.

5   XML and SQL Front-Ends

In order to embed the general transformation kernel presented above into a language-specific transformation framework, we developed front ends for the relational database language SQL, and the document markup language XML. The essential operations offered by these front ends are shown in Figure 3.

Both front-ends perform their work in two phases (first schema conversion, then value conversion) and in two directions (from external to internal representation and *vice versa*). In the case of XML, schema information and values are stored separately, using separate languages (XML Schema and XML itself), while in the case of SQL type and value information are stored together (**CREATE** and **INSERT** statements).

The functions for the first phase of the XML front end have the following type signatures:

> *type2xsd* :: *Type a* → *Maybe XSD*
> *xsd2type* :: *XSD* → *Maybe DynType*
>
> **data** *DynType* **where** *DynType* :: *Type a* → *DynType*

The *type2xsd* function converts a type representation into the abstract syntax of an XML Schema file, if possible. The *xsd2type* function performs the opposite conversion, but it returns the computed type representation wrapped in the *DynType* constructor. Note that the type variable *a* does not escape from the *DynType*, which means that it is implicitly existentially quantified. This is essential since the *xsd2type* function is to be applied without knowing the type it will produce. The *Maybe* monad indicates the partiality of the conversions.

The second-phase functions of the XML front end have the following type signatures:

$$xml2value :: Type \; a \rightarrow XML \rightarrow Maybe \; a$$
$$value2xml :: Type \; a \rightarrow a \rightarrow Maybe \; XML$$

The first argument of both functions is the type representation from the first phase. Using this type representation, a string representation of an XML document gets converted into a value of the represented type, or *vice versa*. These functions are partial, since parsing may fail (*xml2value*) or the type may not have the appropriate form (*value2xml*).

These four XML front-end functions are combined with parsers and pretty-printers for the *XSD* and *XML* abstract syntax trees. For *XML* we use the HaXml parser and printer [22]. For *XSD* we use XML Schema support from the XsdMetz tool [21] which in turn again uses HaXml (schemas in XML Schema are themselves XML files).

The functions of the SQL front end have very similar signatures:

$$create2type :: DDL \rightarrow Maybe \; DynType$$
$$type2create :: Type \; a \rightarrow Maybe \; DDL$$

$$insert2value :: Type \; a \rightarrow DML \rightarrow Maybe \; a$$
$$value2insert :: Type \; a \rightarrow a \rightarrow Maybe \; DML$$

Here, *DDL* is an abstract syntax for the data definition sublanguage of SQL (**CREATE** statements), and *DML* is an abstract syntax for the data manipulation sublanguage (**INSERT** statments). These functions are combined with an SQL parser that we generated with the Happy parser generator [17], and a hand-crafted pretty-printer.

The pattern shared by the two front ends is captured in the following class and corresponding instances:

class *FrontEnd t v | t → v, v → t* **where**
   parsetype :: t → Maybe DynType
   printtype :: Type a → Maybe t
   parsevalue :: Type a → v → Maybe a
   printvalue :: Type a → a → Maybe v
instance *FrontEnd XSD XML* **where** ...
instance *FrontEnd DDL DML* **where** ...

For brevity, the straightforward instance bodies are not shown. Against the interface of the *FrontEnd* class, we can program an overloaded function that lifts

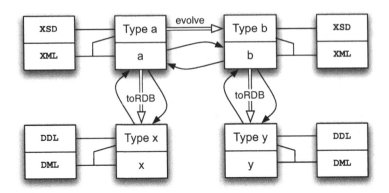

Fig. 4. Overview of the application scenarios

a *Rule* on our internal type representation to a two-level transformation on external abstract syntaxes:

$transform :: (FrontEnd\ t\ v, FrontEnd\ t'\ v')$
$\qquad\qquad \Rightarrow Rule \rightarrow t \rightarrow Maybe\ (t', v \rightarrow Maybe\ v', v' \rightarrow Maybe\ v)$
$transform\ r\ t = \mathbf{do}$
$\quad DynT\ a \leftarrow parsetype\ t$
$\quad View\ (Rep\ to\ from)\ a' \leftarrow r\ a$
$\quad t' \leftarrow printtype\ a'$
$\quad \mathbf{let}\ to'\ v = \mathbf{do}\ \{\,x \leftarrow parsevalue\ a\ v; printvalue\ a'\ (to\ x)\,\}$
$\quad \mathbf{let}\ from'\ v' = \mathbf{do}\ \{\,x \leftarrow parsevalue\ a'\ v'; printvalue\ a\ (from\ x)\,\}$
$\quad return\ (t', to', from')$

Note that the result type is a triple, where t' is the transformed type, and the partial functions convert v to v' and *vice versa*. In the upcoming sections, we resolve the overloading of the *transform* function in different ways to obtain various concrete two-level transformations for XML and SQL.

6   Application Scenarios

We now illustrate by example how the two-level transformation rules can be combined with the XML and SQL front ends to handle various two-level transformation scenarios. See Figure 4 for an overview.

XML Evolution. The evolution of Section 2, where TV series are added as an alternative to movies, can be encoded as follows:

$evolve :: Rule$
$evolve = somewhere\ (changeName\ \texttt{"movie"}\ \texttt{"show"}) \triangleright$
$\qquad\quad somewhere\ (when\ isMovie\ (putName\ \texttt{"movie"} \triangleright addalt\ series))$
$\quad \mathbf{where}$
$\qquad isMovie :: Type\ a \rightarrow Bool$
$\qquad isMovie\ (Prod\ (List\ a)\ b) = getName\ a \equiv Just\ \texttt{"boxoffice"} \wedge$
$\qquad\qquad\qquad\qquad\qquad\qquad\quad getName\ b \equiv Just\ \texttt{"director"}$

$$isMovie \_ = False$$
$$series = setName \text{ "series"} (Map \; year \; episodes)$$
$$year = setName \text{ "yr"} Int$$
$$episodes = ...$$

$$when :: (\forall a \; . \; Type \; a \to Bool) \to Rule \to Rule$$
$$getName :: Type \; a \to Maybe \; String \quad changeName :: String \to String \to Rule$$
$$putName :: String \to Rule \qquad\qquad setName :: String \to Type \; a \to Type \; a$$

Thus, the movie name is changed into show in a single traversal, using *somewhere*. Then, in a second traversal, the schema fragment to be factored out is located with the *isMovie* predicate. This predicate tests for the presence of boxoffice and director. If the predicate is satisfied, at that point in the schema the movie name is reintroduced, and the *addalt* rule is triggered to insert the series fragment. Note that this latter fragment is defined by a *Map*, which encodes that a season is uniquely identified by its year.

We can now feed the *evolve* rule to our *transform* function to perform a data mapping:

```
> xsd ← parseXsdFile "imdb.xsd"
> let Just (xsd′, to, from) = transform evolve xsd
> xml ← parseXmlFile "imdb.xml"
> let Just xml′ = to xml
> show xml′
<imdb>
  <show><title>Pulp Fiction</title><year>1994</year>
    <movie><director>Quentin Tarantino</director></movie>
  </show>
  <actor><name>John Travolta</name>
    <played><title>Pulp Fiction</title><year>1994</year>
      <character>Vincent Vega</character>
    </played>
  </actor>
</imdb>
```

Thus, we use the resulting *to* function and apply it to an input document, to obtain a converted document. Note that the show tag appears in the original place of the movie tag, which now tags nested information specific to movies.

XML to SQL Data Mapping. We map the original schema to SQL as follows:

```
> xsd ← parseXsdFile "imdb.xsd"
> let Just (ddl, tosql, fromsql) = transform toRDB xsd
> xml ← parseXmlFile "imdb.xml"
> let Just dml = tosql xml
> show dml
insert into movies (year,title,director)
  values (1994,'Pulp Fiction','Quentin Tarantino');
insert into actors (name)
  values ('John Travolta');
```

```
insert into playeds (id,name,year,title,role)
   values (0,'John Travolta',1994,'Pulp Fiction','Vincent Vega');
```

Here we have supplied the *toRDB* strategy to the *transform* function. The resulting *ddl* corresponds to the pseudo-SQL that we showed in Section 2. Note that the *tosql* function would return *Nothing* if this document does not conform to the original XML schema. Multiple documents can be converted into SQL insert statements and loaded into a relational database:

> *createDB* "imdb" *ddl*
> *loadDB* "imdb" *dml*
> *xml* ← *parseXmlFile* "imdb2.xml"
> **let** *Just dml* = *tosql xml*
> *loadDB* "imdb" *dml*

With *createDB* and *loadDB* we connect to an external DBMS. If the combination of documents violates the propagated constraints, the DBMS will refuse to load the data. An XML view of the complete database can be obtained as follows:

> (*ddl*, *dml*) ← *dumpDB* "imdb"
> **let** (*Just xml*) = *fromsql dml*
> *show xml*

```
<imdb>
  <movie><title>Pulp Fiction</title><year>1994</year>
    <director>Quentin Tarantino</director>
  </movie>
  <movie><title>Videodrome</title><year>1983</year>
    <director>David Cronenberg</director>
  </movie>
  <actor><name>John Travolta</name>
    ...
  </actor>
  ...
</imdb>
```

Note that we use the *fromsql* function to do backward conversion.

Data Mapping After Evolution. Like the original XML schema, the evolved schema can be mapped to a relational database:

> **let** *Just* (*ddl'*, *tosql'*, *fromsql'*) = *transform toRDB xsd'*

In the pseudo-SQL notation, the relational schema *ddl'* looks as follows:

```
shows(year,title)
reviews(id,year,title,review)
   foreign key (year,title) references shows(year,title)
movies(year,title,director)
   foreign key (year,title) references shows(year,title)
boxoffices(id,year,title,country,value)
   foreign key (year,title) references movies(year,title)
seriess(year,title)
   foreign key (year,title) references shows(year,title)
```

```
seasons(year,title,yr)
  foreign key (year,title) references seriess(year,title)
episodes(id,year,title,yr,nm,director?)
  foreign key (year,title,yr) references seasons(year,title,yr)
actors(name)
playeds(id,name,year,title,role)
  foreign key (year,title) references shows(year,title)
  foreign key (name) references actors(name)
awards(id,name,playedid,award)
  foreign key (playedid,name) references playeds(id,name)
```

Note that the **shows** table was called **movies** before, and that the **director** field has moved to the new **movies** table. New tables for series, seasons, and episodes have appeared. The generated referential constraints enforce that all movies and series also appear in the **shows** table.

Database Migration. With the composition $tosql' \cdot to \cdot fromsql$ of various conversion functions, we can migrate the relational database **imdb** to an evolved relational database. However, this pipeline performs various superflous pretty-print and parse steps, since the intermediate types are XML ASTs. To avoid this, we can use a dedicated function for migrations:

$$migrate :: Rule \rightarrow XSD \rightarrow Maybe\ (DML \rightarrow Maybe\ DML, DML \rightarrow Maybe\ DML)$$
$$migrate\ r\ t = \textbf{do}$$
$$DynT\ a \leftarrow parsetype\ t$$
$$View\ (Rep\ to\ from)\ b \leftarrow toRDB\ a$$
$$View\ (Rep\ to'\ from')\ b' \leftarrow (r \triangleright toRDB)\ a$$
$$\textbf{let}\ to'\ v = \textbf{do}\ \{\,x \leftarrow parsevalue\ b\ v; printvalue\ b'\ (to'\ (from\ x))\,\}$$
$$\textbf{let}\ from'\ v' = \textbf{do}\ \{\,x \leftarrow parsevalue\ b'\ v'; printvalue\ b\ (to\ (from'\ x))\,\}$$
$$return\ (to', from')$$

The *migrate* function takes an evolution rule and an initial XML schema, and produces forward and backward conversion functions between the relational databases corresponding to the initial and the evolved schema. For example:

$$> \textbf{let}\ Just\ (migrateto, migratefrom) = migrate\ evolve\ xsd$$
$$> \textbf{let}\ Just\ dml' = migrateto\ dml$$
$$> createDB\ \texttt{"evolvedimdb"}\ ddl'$$
$$> loadDB\ \texttt{"evolvedimdb"}\ dml'$$

After this, a second movie database has been created and filled with the data from the old database.

7   Related Work

XML-to-Relational Mappings. A large number of approaches has been proposed for mapping XML to relational databases [1]. Most approaches offer a fixed mapping strategy, but some allow manual intervention [3] or automatic cost-based selection of an optimal target schema [4]. Many approaches only offer forward data conversion, though some offer backward conversion as well [2]. Our approach is fully compositional, and allows various mappings known from the literature to be recomposed in a purely declarative way from basic rules.

XML-to-relational mappings are expected to be information-preserving in some sense, but few approaches come with a precise definition or formal guarantees of such preservation properties. An exception is the use of the notion of *invertibility* by Barbosa *et al* [2], which in turn is based on the classic notion of relative information capacity in the database context. The same property of invertibility is satisfied by our two-level data transformation rules, as expressed by the law $from \cdot to = id_A$. Data refinement theory shows that structural and sequential composition of our rules maintain invertibility.

Constraint Preservation. Few XML-to-relational mapping approaches take constraint information into account. A notion of *XML Functional Dependency* (XFD) is introduced by Chen *et al* [5,6], based on path expression, and mapping algorithms are provided that propagate XFDs to the target relational schema, and exploit XFDs to arrive at a schema with less redundancy. Davidson *et al* [9] and Barbosa *et al* [2] present alternative constraint-preserving approaches, also involving constraints based on path expressions.

Our approach, by contrast, employs a type annotation mechanism to capture constraints, rather than path expressions. As a result, we capture a smaller class of possible XML constraints. The advantage, however, is that our annotation mechanism allows a compositional treatment of constraints, which fits better with our rule-based mapping approach.

XML Format Evolution. Lämmel *et al* [14] propose a systematic approach to evolution of XML-based formats, where DTDs are transformed in a well-defined, step-wise fashion, and migration of corresponding documents can largely be induced from the DTD-level transformations. They discuss properties of transformations and identify categories of transformation steps, such as renaming, introduction and elimination, folding and unfolding, generalization and restriction, enrichment and removal, taking into account many XML-specific issues, but they stop short of formalization and implementation of two-level transformations. In fact, they identify the following 'challenge': "We have examined typeful functional XML transformation languages, term rewriting systems, combinator libraries, and logic programming. However, the coupled treatment of DTD transformations and induced XML transformations in a typeful and generic manner, poses a challenge for formal reasoning, type systems, and language design." We have now met this challenge, albeit for XML Schema rather than DTDs.

Bi-directional Programming. Foster *et al* tackle the classical *view-update problem* for databases with *lenses*: combinators for bi-directional programming [10]. Each lens connects a concrete representation C with an abstract view A on it by means of two functions $get : C \rightarrow A$ and $put : A \times C \rightarrow C$. Thus, get and put are similar to our *from* and *to*, except for put's additional argument of type C. Also, an additional law on these functions guarantees that put can be used to reconstruct an updated C from an updated A. Hu *et al* take a smilar approach [20].

We believe that our techniques for coupled transformations can equally be beneficial for bi-directional programming with lenses. In particular, we are currently designing an embedding of bi-directional programs in Haskell that provides strong, inferable types, as well as strategic rewrite systems for lens composition.

8   Concluding Remarks

We have shown how XML format evolution, XML-to-SQL mappings, and SQL migrations can be given a unified declarative treatment as instances of two-level data transformations. Schema-level transformations produce new schemas, as well as bi-directional conversion functions between old and new. Name information and constraint information can be preserved through transformation steps. The approach is compositional, in the sense that full transformations are composed from basic transformation rules and rule combinators, and properties such as invertibility are preserved under composition. The approach can be extended to cover other hierarchical and relational data languages, by providing more implementations of the *FrontEnd* class. Source code and examples are available from the homepages of the authors under the name 2LT.

Future Work. Though already useful in practise, our approach suffers from various limitations that we intend to overcome.

In [8] we have shown that two-level data transformation systems can be supplemented with type-directed program transformation systems to perform optimization of the induced conversion functions. Moreover, such combined rewriting systems can be used to perform migration of queries through evolution. We would like to extend our XML and SQL front-ends to leverage such program transformations for corresponding query languages.

So far, all our transformations *on the type level* are performed in the refinement direction, i.e. from abstract to more concrete types. Constraint handling opens the door to performing these steps in the opposite direction, i.e. to perform reverse engineering from low-level data schemas to higher-level ones [18].

Our annotation mechanism is sufficient to capture a large class of common XML and SQL constraints. We would like to enlarge this class further.

Acknowledgements. We thank Flávio Ferreira and Diogo Lapa for their work on the front ends, and José Nuno Oliveira for inspiring discussions.

References

1. S. Amer-Yahia, F. Du, and J. Freire. A comprehensive solution to the XML-to-relational mapping problem. In *WIDM '04: Proc. 6th annual ACM Int workshop on Web Information and Data Management*, pages 31–38. ACM Press, 2004.
2. D. Barbosa, J. Freire, and A.O. Mendelzon. Designing information-preserving mapping schemes for XML. In *VLDB'05: Proc. 31st Int. Conf. Very Large Data Bases*, pages 109–120. VLDB Endowment, 2005.

3. P. Bohannon et al. LegoDB: Customizing relational storage for XML documents. In *Proc. 28th Int. Conf. on Very Large Data Bases*, pages 1091–1094, 2002.

4. P. Bohannon, J. Freire, P. Roy, and J. Siméon. From XML schema to relations: A cost-based approach to XML storage. In *ICDE '02: Proc. 18th Int. Conf. on Data Engineering*, pages 64–. IEEE Computer Society, 2002.

5. Y. Chen, S.B. Davidson, C.S. Hara, and Y. Zheng. RRXS: Redundancy reducing XML storage in relations. In *Proc. 29th VLDB Conference*, pages 189–200, 2003.

6. Y. Chen et al. Constraints preserving schema mapping from XML to relations. In *Proc. 5th Int. Workshop Web and Databases (WebDB)*, pages 7–12, 2002.

7. A. Cunha, J.N. Oliveira, and J. Visser. Type-safe two-level data transformation. In J. Misra et al., editors, *Proc. Int. Symp. of Formal Methods Europe*, volume 4085 of *LNCS*. Springer, 2006.

8. A. Cunha and J. Visser. Strongly typed rewriting for coupled software transformation. In M. Fernandez and R Lämmel, editors, *Proc. 7th Int. Workshop on Rule-Based Programming (RULE 2006)*, ENTCS. Elsevier, 2006. To appear.

9. S.B. Davidson et al. Propagating XML constraints to relations. In *Proc. 19th Int. Conf. on Data Engineering*, pages 543–. IEEE Computer Society, 2003.

10. J.N. Foster et al. Combinators for bi-directional tree transformations: a linguistic approach to the view update problem. In *Proc. 32nd ACM SIGPLAN-SIGACT Symp. on Principles of Programming Languages*, pages 233–246. ACM Press, 2005.

11. R. Hinze, A. Löh, and B.C.d.S. Oliveira. "Scrap your boilerplate" reloaded. In *Proc. 8th Int. Symp. on Functional and Logic Programming*, volume 3945 of *Lecture Notes in Computer Science*, pages 13–29. Springer, 2006.

12. R. Lämmel. Coupled Software Transformations (Extended Abstract). In *First International Workshop on Software Evolution Transformations*, November 2004.

13. R. Lämmel, S. Kitsis, and D. Remy. Analysis of XML schema usage. In *Conference Proceedings XML 2005*, November 2005.

14. R. Lämmel and W. Lohmann. Format Evolution. In *Proc. 7th Int. Conf. on Reverse Engineering for Information Systems*, volume 155 of *books@ocg.at*, pages 113–134. OCG, 2001.

15. R. Lämmel and S. Peyton Jones. Scrap your boilerplate: a practical design pattern for generic programming. *ACM SIGPLAN Notices*, 38(3):26–37, March 2003.

16. R. Lämmel and J. Visser. Typed Combinators for Generic Traversal. In *Proc. Practical Aspects of Declarative Programming PADL 2002*, volume 2257 of *LNCS*, pages 137–154. Springer, January 2002.

17. S. Marlow. *Happy User Guide*. Glasgow University, December 1997.

18. F.L. Neves, J.C. Silva, and J.N. Oliveira. Converting informal meta-data to VDM-SL: A reverse calculation approach. In *VDM in Practice!*, September 1999.

19. S. Peyton Jones, G. Washburn, and S. Weirich. Wobbly types: type inference for generalised algebraic data types. Technical Report MS-CIS-05-26, Univ. of Pennsylvania, July 2004.

20. M. Takeichi S.-C. Mu, Z. Hu. Bidirectionalizing tree transformation languages: A case study. *JSSST Computer Software*, 23(2):129–141, 2006.

21. J. Visser. Structure metrics for XML Schema. In J.C. Ramalho et al., editors, *XATA2006, XML: Aplicações e Tecnologias Associadas*. Univ. of Minho, 2006.

22. M. Wallace and C. Runciman. Haskell and XML: generic combinators or type-based translation? In *Proc. 4th ACM SIGPLAN Int. Conf. on Functional Programming*, pages 148–159. ACM Press, 1999.

Aspect-Oriented Programming in Higher-Order and Linear Logic

Chuck C. Liang

Department of Computer Science, Hofstra University
Hempstead, NY 11550
chuck.liang@hofstra.edu

Abstract. Essential elements of aspect-oriented programming can be formulated as forms of logic programming. Extensions of Horn Clause Prolog provide richer abstraction and control mechanisms. Definite clauses that pertain to a common aspect, and which *crosscut* other program components, can be encapsulated using the connectives of higher-order intuitionistic logic. The integration or *weaving* of program fragments can be formulated using normalized forms of proof search in linear logic.

1 Introduction

Aspect-oriented programming [7] is emerging as an important advancement in software development. Its attraction lies in a new approach to modularity in the structuring of programs. Multiple concerns in the construction of software, such as security and optimization, *crosscut* each other and cannot be easily separated by traditional approaches to modular programming. AOP concerns program specifications as well as programming language characteristics. This paper focuses on the realization of AOP in a class of logic programming languages.

There is currently no widely accepted formal theory for AOP, unlike with the case of functional programming. However, much work already exist on the paradigm, including several formal specifications [2,15,16]. Logic programming has also been used [14] as a meta-programming device for AOP, generating code for conventional target languages (Java). Although the languages discussed here can also be used for this purpose, we are interested in writing aspect-oriented logic programs directly. One possible approach to this effect would be to extend Prolog by imitating the constructs of existing AOP languages such as AspectJ [6]. We offer a different approach here. We show the extent to which AOP concepts are already embodied in logics that are sufficiently expressive.

Using the terminology of AOP, one can consider a definite clause of a logic program as a piece of *advice* on how to proceed when certain conditions are encountered. These advice clauses are triggered at what are called *join points* in a program. The organization of a logic program also does not need to mimic the style of functionally or procedurally oriented programs. They can be grouped according to the aspect that they aim to address. For example, one may wish to consider all clauses concerned with error checking as a separate unit, regardless of

M. Hanus (Ed.): PADL 2007, LNCS 4354, pp. 305–319, 2007.

what predicate is at the head of a clause. In general, we can envision the following style of programming. Let $p_1 \ldots p_n$ be the predicates of a logic program. Let aspects (such as error checking) be represented by the symbols $t_1 \ldots t_m$. Instead of a singleton atom at the head of each definite clause we can qualify the atom using a new operator @, to indicate the aspect that the clause pertains to. The program will have the general form:

$$p_1(\ldots) @ t_1 \; :- \; \mathcal{A}_1^1$$
$$\vdots$$
$$p_n(\ldots) @ t_1 \; :- \; \mathcal{A}_n^1$$
$$\vdots$$
$$p_1(\ldots) @ t_m \; :- \; \mathcal{A}_1^m$$
$$\vdots$$
$$p_n(\ldots) @ t_m \; :- \; \mathcal{A}_n^m$$

Formula $\mathcal{A}_i^j$ represents the "advice code" for predicate p_i *pertaining to* aspect t_j. Goal formulas indicate the aspects it should be solved *with respect to*, and have the form

$$G @ t_j @ \ldots @ t_k.$$

Any subset of $t_1 \ldots t_m$ can be used in a query. It will be shown in Section 3 that the operator @ can be modeled with multiplicative disjunction in linear logic. Each set of clauses pertaining to the same aspect constitute an aspect-oriented program fragment. Each such fragment may include clauses for any of the predicates $p_1 \ldots p_n$, thus *crosscutting* the organization of the base predicates.

To fully realize this form of *separation of concern* in programming, however, at least two important issues must be addressed. First, we wish to construct each aspect-oriented fragment not just as a loose collection of clauses but as a modular unit of abstraction, with the desired characteristics of locality and information hiding. Secondly and most delicately, mechanisms must be available to integrate or *weave* the various fragments into a coherent program. These issues are the focus of this paper and are addressed respectively in the following sections. Because of the lack of formal definitions for AOP concepts, our presentation relies significantly on examples. The paper culminates in the formulation of AOP as linear logic programming in Section 3.

2 Abstractions in Logic Programming

The first-order theory of Horn clauses that traditionally forms the foundation of logic programming is limited in its ability to provide mechanisms for abstraction. A formulation and classification of logic programming as deterministic proof search was given in [11]. Under such a generalized context, logics richer than Horn clauses can be considered as basis for logic programming. Higher-order, intuitionistic and linear logics offer more complex mechanisms for expressing abstraction.

To provide a framework for discussion, we consider the Java language extension AspectJ [6], which seeks to support AOP in a general-purpose programming language. It is now the most popular manifestation of the paradigm. Several languages based on AspectJ have also been developed, including Aspectual CAML [13]. In AspectJ, program fragments that address a common concern can be encapsulated in modules called *aspects*. Such a structure may contain declarations or modifications of data structures that are specific to the aspect in question. For example, if the aspect concerns security, then a new field such as *encryption_key* may be added to an existing class. Join points are identified using a language (*pointcuts*) of regular expression-like patterns as well as primitives for determining more meaningful computational context. Aspects define *advice* code fragments that are executed at specified join points.

2.1   AOP in λProlog

λProlog, based on the theory of higher-order intuitionistic logic, extends traditional Prolog. Simply typed lambda terms and the associated unification algorithm are used in place of first-order terms and unification. Universal quantification, including quantification over predicates, can be used in goal clauses. The operational meaning of a goal of the form $\forall x.G$ is to prove G using a fresh constant for x. The intuitionistic connective for implication, unlike its classical counterpart, provides a stronger notion of scope, and can be used without restriction in λProlog. A goal $A \Rightarrow B$ is provable if and only if B is provable under the local assumption of A. These extensions provide a basis for expressing abstraction in programming. There is now a high-performance, compiler-based implementation [12] of λProlog.

Intuitionistic implication augments an existing program with a temporary clause, and can also be thought of as *adding a piece of advice to the existing program*. Likewise, higher-order universal quantification introduces a new constant, which can be a predicate or function symbol, to the existing signature. As early as in [9], it was demonstrated how these capabilities can be used to dynamically define new data structures in a program.

To demonstrate how AOP can be manifested in this setting, we use a predicate of the form

$$advice \ \ Aspect\_name \ \ Goal$$

as the head of λProlog clauses. Here, *Aspect_name* identifies the aspect or concern that the body of the clause gives advice to. *Goal* is a λProlog goal to which the advice is to be applied. We present in Figures 1 and 2 a simplified example to provide a comparison between a λProlog program and the corresponding AspectJ program. The purpose of this comparison is not to argue about the superiority of this or that language. We only wish to show how aspect-oriented concepts can be realized in entirely different contexts.

The syntax of λProlog follows Prolog conventions except that applications are written in Curried form $((f \ x)$ instead of $f(x))$. For readability we use the

```
class aopbase
{
    static boolean divisible(int A, int B)
    { return (A % B == 0); }

    static int factorial(int N, int Accum)
    { if (N==0) return Accum; else return factorial(N-1,N*Accum); }
} // class aopbase

aspect parameters
{
    // advice to check that B is non-zero:
    boolean around(int B) :
        call(static boolean aopbase.divisible(..)) && args(..,B)
    {
        if (B==0)
        {
            System.out.println("warning: B is zero, returning false");
            return false;
        }
        else return proceed(B);
    }

    // advice to check that x is non-negative
    before(int x) : call(int aopbase.factorial(..)) && args(x,int)
    {
        if (x<0) throw new Error("invalid parameter");
    }

    // enforce that the initial value of the accumulator is 1
    int around(int N, int A) :
        call(int aopbase.factorial(..)) &&
            !withincode(int aopbase.factorial(..)) && args(N,A)
    {
        return proceed(N,1);
    }
} // aspect to check parameters

aspect trace
{
    before() : call(int aopbase.*(..))
    { System.out.println(thisJoinPoint); }

    declare precedence : trace, parameters; // trace has higher precedence
} // aspect to trace calls
```

Fig. 1. Sample AspectJ Program

module aopexample.

%% type declarations

type divisible int → int → o.
type fact int → int → int → o.
type advice string → o → o.
type useaspects (list string) → o → o.

%% base program

divisible A B :- 0 is (A mod B).
fact 0 A A.
fact N A B :- N1 is (N - 1), A1 is (N * A), fact N1 A1 B.

%% aspects

% clauses pertaining to aspect "parameters"
advice "parameters" G :-
*   (∀A∀B (divisible A 0 :- print "warning...", !, fail))*
*   ⇒*
*   ∀ withinfact (*
*   (∀A∀B∀C (fact A B C :- A < 0, print "warning...", stop))*
*   ⇒*
*   (∀A∀B∀C (fact A B C :- not (withinfact), !,*
*   withinfact ⇒ fact A 1 C))*
*   ⇒ G).*

% clauses pertaining to aspect "trace"
advice "trace" G :-
*   (∀A∀B (divisible A B :- printterm std_out (divisible A B), fail))*
*   ⇒*
*   (∀A∀B∀C (fact A B C :- printterm std_out (fact A B C), fail))*
*   ⇒ G.*

%% integrating multiple aspects:

useaspects [] G :- G.
useaspects [A|As] G :- useaspects As (advice A G).

Fig. 2. Separation of Concerns in λProlog

symbol ∀ for explicit universal quantification in goals. Other upper-case letters are implicitly quantified over the entire clause, as usual.

The *"base program"* for our example consists of two simple operations: that of checking for divisibility and the familiar tail-recursive factorial relation. We have deliberately left out the checking for invalid parameters in the base program. In the case of the factorial predicate, we have also not constrained that the initial value of the second parameter should be 1. We leave these separate concerns to an aspect module called "parameters". The second, "trace" aspect, which traces procedure calls, is perhaps the most popular example of AOP. These small programs may not be best-suited to illustrate the advantages of AOP over conventional methods, but it suffices to demonstrate the principle of separation-of-concerns and the kind of programming devices that can realize the aspect-oriented paradigm.

The use of the control primitive *!* is required in these examples. Also required is that in solving a goal of the form $A \Rightarrow B$ the new clause A is consulted first. These extra-logical characteristics are required to ensure that the advice clauses *must* be applied, as well as to specify the precedence ordering among advice. In other words, they control the *weaving* of the aspect-oriented fragments into the program. We shall use linear logic in Section 3 to achieve this purpose declaratively. However, λProlog currently provides a more practical implementation. The *withinfact* predicate, being quantified inside the body of the first clause, is local to the clause and represents another instrument for weaving. It serves to identify recursive calls to *fact,* for which the advice should not be applied, and is comparable to the *cflowbelow* pointcuts of AspectJ. Integration of multiple aspects is achieved with the *useaspects* clauses. The order of the aspect names in the list argument determines the precedence of the aspects. For example, calling

?- useaspects ["trace","parameters"] G

will apply the *trace* aspect first while solving G. Critically, however, the use of either aspect with the base program is optional.

Since λProlog was not implemented with AOP in mind, one cannot reasonably expect features such as *thisJoinPoint,* even as extra-logical additions. However, the essential aim of the separation of concerns is achieved. The advice clauses clearly *crosscut* the base program procedures.

In addition to declaring advice, we can use second-order quantification to introduce a new construct to a program. The purpose of the following clause is to implement a password-checking aspect for some arbitrary predicate $q\ A$:

advice "password protection" G :- ∀ pw ∀ passed (
(∀A∀X (q A :- not(passed), !, print "enter password:",
read X, pw X, passed ⇒ q A))
⇒
(print "set password:", read W, pw W ⇒ G)).

The predicate *pw* is introduced to assert the password, and *passed* is used to signify that a valid password has been given. The scoping rules of the logical connectives are crucial to the validity of this clause. In particular, *pw* is a predicate symbol that is unique and local to the advice clause. It cannot appear free in G, and thus cannot be circumvented. Likewise, the *passed* predicate cannot be asserted arbitrarily except by the advice clause. The scope of $\Rightarrow$ restricts its assertion to individual goals. That is, multiple calls to *q,* excluding recursive calls, which are within the scope of $\Rightarrow$, will all require password checks.

Using logical abstraction mechanisms to reflect the aspect-oriented approach to program organization has obvious benefits. One of the criticisms of the AspectJ manifestation of AOP has been that it conflicts with the conventional notions of abstraction and information hiding found in Java-like languages. By formulating advice in light of lambda abstraction, universal quantification and implication, we can reconcile aspect orientation with well-understood notions of abstraction. This observation suggests that the perceived conflict between AOP and traditional abstraction principles are due to ad-hoc characteristics of non-declarative systems such as Java and AspectJ.

2.2   Join Points in the Continuation Passing Style

There are certainly features of Java and AspectJ that cannot be emulated easily in a logic programming language. On the other hand, there are also examples where an enriched logic programming language can offer AOP-related capabilities that are not found in conventional settings. Higher-order languages of both the functional and logic-programming varieties support the *continuation passing style* of programming. CPS introduces the sequential ordering of execution to a logic program. CPS in λProlog, given its ability to inspect the structure of λ-terms via higher-order unification, gives rise to interesting possibilities.

The following example is partially motivated by the image processing example described in [7]. Compared to the examples of the previous section, it better illustrates why one may wish to consider the AOP approach to program organization. The λProlog clauses of Figure 3 implement the typical higher order predicates, *map, fold* and *filter,* using a form of CPS. The last parameter of each predicate is a λ-term that relates the result of the current computation to a continuation goal.

The base program clauses are relatively elegant but lack refinement. When boolean operators are folded over lists, short-circuiting can be applied. Similarly, when an operation such as *filter* is immediately followed by one such as *map*, it is often possible to combine the operations, avoiding the generation of an intermediate list and improving efficiency. Adding such special-case clauses to the base program directly would compromise its elegance. The conventional, procedurally oriented approach would be to declare new procedures that encapsulate these cases for special treatment. Problems occur, however, when multiple features are required in combination. That is, combining the *short circuit* and *merge traversals* features would require yet another procedure. There are also situations, such as when no lists of booleans are present, when some refinements are not desired. For n distinct refinements, it is unlikely that one can foresee which of the 2^n possible subsets should be encapsulated. These problems are avoided by encapsulating the refinements not as ordinary procedures but as *aspects of separate concern*. They can be decoupled from a program as the situation demands.

Critical to this program is the use of higher-order unification, which identifies the join points where the advice clauses are applicable. We note that the pointcut language of AspectJ has no facility to identify situations when one function is called immediately after another, (such as in *f(); g();* or even just *g(f())*). The

%% base program

type map $(A \to B) \to (list\ A) \to ((list\ B) \to o) \to o.$
type fold $(A \to A \to A) \to A \to (list\ A) \to (A \to o) \to o.$
type filter $(A \to o) \to (list\ A) \to ((list\ A) \to o) \to o.$

map M [] G :- (G []).
map M [H|T] G :- map M T λx(G [(M H) | x]).

fold Op Id [] G :- (G Id).
fold Op Id [A|T] G :- fold Op Id T λx(G (Op A x)).

filter P [] G :- (G []).
filter P [H|T] G :- (P H), !, filter P T λx(G [H|x]).
filter P [H|T] G :- filter P T G.

%% aspects

advice "short circuit" G :-
       ($\forall L \forall C$ (fold and true [false|L] C :- !, (C false)))
       $\Rightarrow$
       ($\forall L \forall C$ (fold or false [true|L] C :- !, (C true)))
       $\Rightarrow$ G.

advice "merge traversals" G :-
       ($\forall P \forall L \forall Op \forall Id \forall Cg$ (
             map P L λx(fold Op Id x Cg) :- !, fold $\lambda a \lambda b$(Op (P a) (P b)) Id L Cg))
       $\Rightarrow$
       ($\forall P \forall L \forall M \forall Cg$ (
             filter P L λx(map M x Cg) :- !,
                  ($\forall H \forall T$ (map M [H|T] Cg :- not (P H), !, map M T Cg))
                  $\Rightarrow$ map M L Cg))
       $\Rightarrow$ G.

Fig. 3. Optimization Aspects in Continuation Passing Style

higher-order patterns of the *merge traversals* aspect not only identify such cases but also the condition that the result of the first operation is not used elsewhere in the continuation goal (i.e, x is not free in Cg).

    A further implication of CPS is that it becomes possible to logically distinguish between advice that should be applied *before* and *after* a join point.

3   Weaving in Linear Logic

Logic programming languages have also been devised for linear logic [3], among them Forum [10], Lolli [5] (an executable fragment of Forum), LinLog [1] and Lygon [4]. Linear logic have been used to declaratively express computational properties such as side effects and concurrency. Forum in particular is complete with respect to linear logic, although formulas must be converted to a certain form. We have seen how the primitives of λProlog can provide a basis for aspect-oriented abstraction, although extra-logical features were needed to precisely control the *weaving* of aspects. Linear logic encompasses intuitionistic logic and the abstraction mechanisms described in the forgoing. In this section we describe how weaving can be formulated as proof search in linear logic. We shall write abstract program clauses in the form *Head* ∘– *Body* where ∘– is the reverse linear implication symbol. For sake of illustrations we assume the availability of arithmetic operations and the IO primitives *read* and *print*. That is, we assume that goals such as *read W* are provable from the empty linear context.

Linear logic requires the *accounting of resources* during proofs. This sensitivity can be used to formulate mechanisms for controlling the synthesis or weaving of program fragments.

We formulate AOP in linear logic as follows. Every aspect is associated with a unique predicate symbol or *token*, such as *trace*. Intuitively, each token identifies an aspect and represents an obligation to apply some advice. An advice clause that pertains to an aspect token t_k will have the general form

$$Head \,\,⅋\,\, t_k \,\,⅋\,\, \ldots \,\,∘\text{–} \,\, Body$$

and goals will have the general form

$$G \,\,⅋\,\, t_1 \,\,⅋\,\, t_2 \,\,⅋\,\, \ldots \,\,⅋\,\, t_n$$

where $t_1 \ldots t_n$ represent *aspects that must be weaved into the solution of G*. Since all such tokens must be accounted for in solving G, their assertion entails the application of the corresponding advice clauses. In other words, it is possible to associate with any goal a multiset of aspects, and we shall refer to $t_1 \ldots t_n$ as an *aspect multiset*. An equivalent scheme would be to have advice clauses of the form $H \,∘\text{–}\, t_k \,⊗\, \ldots \,⊗\, Body$ and goals of the form $t_1 \,–∘\, \ldots \,–∘\, t_n \,–∘\, G$. We prefer the form using ⅋ since it names the aspect at the head of the clause.

For the aspect tokens to be distributed to the subgoals of G, G should be composed from connectives such as & and ⊕, which copy the linear context upon right-introduction (applied bottom-up). For goals formed from multiplicative connectives, multiple occurrences of the tokens may be required.

At first glance, the mechanism used here may seem little different from adding parameters to predicates. The role of aspect tokens, however, is to specify synchronization points during proof search. The tokens are associated not just with predicates but also with goal formulas.

As a simplified example, an advice to trace calls to the *divisible* predicate of Section 2 can be written as

$$!\forall A \forall B. \; divisible \; A \; B \,\,⅋\,\, trace \,\,∘\text{–}\, print \; "calling \ldots" \,⊗\, divisible \; A \; B.$$

The modal operator ! is intended to scope over the entire ∀-quantified clause [1].

---

[1] The examples suggest that goals separated by ⊗ are called from left to right. The ordering of goals technically requires the continuation passing style. However, we forgo this refinement for sake of clarity.

The need for finer means for controlling weaving are illustrated by recursive predicates. We may wish some advice to be applied to each recursive call, and others to be applied only once and "as soon as possible." Specific to the *fact* example, one advice checks for an invariance on the first parameter and should be applied for each recursive call. In contrast, the other advice ensures that the initial value of the accumulator is one, and must be used only at the outset. For *recursive advice*, we employ predicate tokens that are parameterized by the same inductive measure as the base predicate. This ensures synchronization with the corresponding advice clause each time the inductive measure is decreased:

$$!\forall A \forall B \forall C.\ fact\ A\ B\ C \,\text{⅋}\, check\ A \,\circ\!\!-\, A > 0 \otimes (fact\ A\ B\ C \,\text{⅋}\, check\ A\text{--}1)$$
$$!\forall B \forall C.\ fact\ 0\ B\ C \,\text{⅋}\, check\ 0 \,\circ\!\!-\, fact\ 0\ B\ C$$

In goal clauses, we complement this device by allowing for existential quantification over parameterized aspect tokens. Solving goals of the form $G \,\text{⅋}\, \exists x.t_k$, where G is composed from additive connectives, may use multiple instantiations for x should they be required.

The problem of ensuring that an advice is only applied at the outset is handled in AspectJ by specially designed pointcuts such as *!withincode(...)*. Such fine-grained control over weaving can also be achieved by imposing a precedence ordering on advice clauses. We first observe that the "base" program fragment can be considered as just another aspect. We therefore introduce a *base* token and uniformly write all program clauses as advice clauses[2]. Precedence relations among advice can then determine the exact manner of weaving.

3.1   Proof Search, Modalities and Advice Precedence

Much of the non-determinism in linear logic proof search can be brought under control using normalized forms of proofs, such as the focused proofs of Andreoli [1] and the uniform proofs of Forum and Lolli. In such systems, the manner of proof search can be finely controlled. It is important to point out the following. Let Γ represent the multiset $\{A \,\text{⅋}\, C \,\circ\!\!-1,\ B \,\circ\!\!-C\}$. Consider:

$$
\cfrac{
\vdash 1 \quad \cfrac{
A \vdash A \quad \cfrac{
\cfrac{C \vdash C \quad B \vdash B}{B \,\circ\!\!-C, C \vdash B}\ \text{⅋}L
}{B \,\circ\!\!-C, A \,\text{⅋}\, C \vdash A, B}\ \circ\!\!-L
}{}
}{\Gamma \vdash A, B}\ \circ\!\!-L
\qquad
\cfrac{
B \vdash B \quad \cfrac{
\vdash 1 \quad \cfrac{
\cfrac{A \vdash A \quad C \vdash C}{A \,\text{⅋}\, C \vdash A, C}\ \text{⅋}L
}{A \,\text{⅋}\, C \,\circ\!\!-1 \vdash A, C}\ \circ\!\!-L
}{}
}{\Gamma \vdash A, B}\ \circ\!\!-L
$$

While both proofs are valid, only the right-hand one represents a *focused* proof (assuming atoms of negative polarity). all atoms at the head of the clause is found in the goal multiset. Thus the second clause in Γ must be applied first (from the bottom). Andreoli used the focusing property to define backchaining for clauses with multiple atoms at the head, thus providing a basis for linear logic

---

[2] Implicitly there is a base token for each predicate, although it should also be possible for multiple predicates to form a common base aspect.

programming. Uniform proofs behave similarly. The characteristic of ordered backchaining is the basis of our general scheme for weaving.

We define for each token t_k a unique predicate symbol $\widehat{t_k}$. If aspect t_j is to have lower precedence than $t_k \ldots t_l$ with respect to H, then their respective advice clauses will have the forms

$$H \,\text{⅋}\, t_j \,\text{⅋}\, \widehat{t_k} \ldots \text{⅋}\, \widehat{t_l} \;\circ\!\!-\; [\textit{advice code} \ldots], \text{ and}$$

$$H \,\text{⅋}\, t_k \ldots \;\circ\!\!-\; [\textit{advice code} \ldots] \otimes (H \,\text{⅋}\, ?\widehat{t_k}).$$

That is, the head of a t_j clause should contain $\widehat{t_k} \ldots \widehat{t_l}$ and the body of each clause for t_k asserts $?\widehat{t_k}$. The modal operator allows for the use of partial orderings, since multiple clauses may require the token. In the context of focused or uniform proofs, the assertion of $?\widehat{t_k}$ grants permission to advice with lower precedence than t_k to become applicable. The presence of $?\widehat{t_k}$ in a goal multiset also signifies that the goal is *no longer dependent* on aspect t_k.

Given aspects $t_1 \ldots t_n$, a goal of the form

$$G \,\text{⅋}\, t_1 \,\text{⅋}\, \ldots \text{⅋}\, t_m \,\text{⅋}\, ?\widehat{t_{m+1}} \,\text{⅋}\, \ldots \text{⅋}\, ?\widehat{t_n}$$

thus represents a computation that is dependent on aspects $t_1 \ldots t_m$ and independent of aspects $t_{m+1} \ldots t_n$.

To allow maximum flexibility in combining aspects with goals, we also use clauses of the form $H \,\text{⅋}\, t_k \;\circ\!\!-\; H$, to explicitly declare that aspect t_k is independent of goals H.

To illustrate the usage of this paradigm, we present in Figure 4 a full set of clauses based on the examples of Section 2. Assume it is desired that no advice should be executed before those of the *param* aspect and that *trace* is to have precedence over *check*.

Note that tokens such as $?\widehat{param}$ need not be re-asserted by the clauses that depend on it, since the ?-formulas are reusable The last clause of Figure 4 specifies that *divisible* goals are independent of *check*. It is possible to generate such independence clauses between known atoms and aspects automatically.

Given the above logic program, a goal such as

$$\exists M (\textit{divisible } 6 \; 2 \;\&\; \textit{fact } 5 \; 3 \; M) \,\text{⅋}\, \textit{param} \,\text{⅋}\, \exists N.(\textit{check } N) \,\text{⅋}\, \textit{trace} \,\text{⅋}\, \textit{base}$$

would be solved as follows by a uniform-proof interpreter. The aspect multiset of the goal would be copied for both atomic subgoals upon $\&Right$. The independence clause for *divisible* eliminates the *check* obligation for the left subgoal. Since no precedence relation was defined between the *param* and *trace* clauses for *divisible*, either is applicable first. However, *base* is only applicable after $?\widehat{param}$ is asserted. For the *fact* subgoal, the order of advice execution is necessarily *param*, *trace* and *check*. Each advice rewrites the aspect multiset to a new state. For example, after *trace*, the multiset becomes

$$\exists N.(\textit{check } N) \,\text{⅋}\, ?\widehat{param} \,\text{⅋}\, ?\widehat{trace} \,\text{⅋}\, \textit{base}$$

!∀A∀B. divisible A B ⅋ base ⅋ $\widehat{param}$ ∘− A mod B = 0
!∀A∀B∀C. (fact A B C) ⅋ base ⅋ $\widehat{param}$ ∘− fact (A−1) (A∗B) C ⅋ base
!∀B. fact 0 B B ⅋ base ⅋ $\widehat{param}$

!∀A∀B∀C. fact A B C ⅋ param ∘− (fact A 1 C) ⅋ $?\widehat{param}$
!∀A∀B. divisible A B ⅋ param ∘− B ≠ 0 ⊗ (divisible A B ⅋ $?\widehat{param}$)

!∀A∀B∀C. fact A B C ⅋ trace ⅋ $\widehat{param}$ ∘−
        print " ..." ⊗ (fact A B C ⅋ $?\widehat{trace}$)
!∀A∀B divisible A B ⅋ trace ∘− print " ..." ⊗ divisible A B

!∀A∀B∀C. (fact A B C) ⅋ check A ⅋ $\widehat{trace}$⅋ $\widehat{param}$ ∘−
        A > 0 ⊗ (fact A B C ⅋ check A−1).
!∀B∀C. (fact 0 B C) ⅋ check 0 ⅋ $\widehat{trace}$⅋ $\widehat{param}$ ∘− fact 0 B C
!∀A∀B∀N. divisible A B ⅋ check N ∘− divisible A B

Fig. 4. Weaving of Aspects in Linear Logic

The parameter of *check* can only be instantiated with 5. Every recursive call to *fact* will invoke the *check* advice.

As a variation, suppose we desired that tracing is not to be included in the computation. In that case *trace* should be replaced by $?\widehat{trace}$ in the initial goal.

The above scheme is not the only means for specifying precedence among advice. To enforce that t_k has precedence over $t_m \ldots t_n$, the advice clauses for t_k can also be of the form

$$Goal ⅋ t_k ⅋ t_m ⅋ \ldots ⅋ t_n ∘− Body ⅋ t_m ⅋ \ldots ⅋ t_n$$

That is, the head of the t_k advice clause should include the tokens for all aspects that t_k is to have precedence over. Backchaining over such a clause would be necessary *before* the tokens $t_m \ldots t_n$ are consumed. In this scheme, the body of advice clauses for aspect t_k must reassert the tokens $t_m \ldots t_n$. Suppose we wish to add an advice that takes user input for *divisible* goals. This advice should have precedence over *param*. Suppose further that we wish to add the advice without modifying the existing clauses (a desirable, though not always possible benefit of AOP). This *io* advice can be written as:

!∀A∀B. divisible A B ⅋ io ⅋ param ∘−
        read A ⊗ read B ⊗ (divisible A B ⅋ param).

The new clause is consistent with those of Figure 4: no modification of the existing program was necessary. However, here the *io* aspect must always be used together with *param*. The scheme described above, using $?\widehat{t_k}$ formulas, will allow arbitrary aspects to be coupled with goals.

Additional control mechanisms for weaving can also be encoded. For example, control flow information, which in the context of proof search amounts to the subproof relation, can be captured using a pair of special tokens in_q and out_q for each predicate q. An advice that is only applicable outside of the flow control of q will include out_q at the head and assert in_q. An advice that is only applicable under the flow control of q can then check for the presence of the in_q token.

As a final example, we reformulate the password-protection aspect of Section 2 as a linear logic specification. Taking advantage of linear logic, we also add the ability to change passwords. The formulation again critically relies on second-order quantification:

$$\exists\, pw\ \forall\, W\ \forall\, W'\ [$$
$$(read\ W)\ \multimap$$
$$(\ pw\ W\ \otimes\ (pw\ W'\multimap 1)\ \otimes$$
$$!\forall X \forall Y \forall G(changepasswd\ G\ \circ\!-$$
$$read\ X\ \otimes\ pw\ X\ \otimes\ read\ Y\ \otimes\ (pw\ Y\ \multimap\ G))\ \otimes$$
$$!\forall X(checkpasswd\ \circ\!-\ read\ X\ \otimes\ pw\ X\ \otimes\ (pw\ X\ \multimap\ \bot))\ )\ ]$$

The specification can be used alongside any set of clauses as a *password-pro-tection aspect*. Since the specification is to be kept on the left side of sequents, the existential quantification of pw ensures its locality (see [8] for thorough discussion on such uses of $\exists$-quantification). The *read W* clause sets the initial password. Since each clause rewrites the pw clause, the inclusion of $(pw\ W'\multimap 1)$ prevents the clause from becoming an unaccounted-for resource at the completion of proofs, as can be seen from the following derivation:

$$\cfrac{\cfrac{\cfrac{A \vdash A}{A, 1 \vdash A}\ 1L \quad P \vdash P}{A, P, (P\multimap 1) \vdash A}\ \multimap\! L}{}$$

Existing linear logic programs commonly use $\top$ to abort programs, even in the presence of unclaimed resources. Such a usage could neutralize the obligations imposed by the aspect tokens. In particular, an advice could even be activated *after* the completion of the base program. Finer means are therefore preferable for the maintenance of resources.

Unlike previous examples, we have chosen not to synchronize the *checkpasswd* advice with any specific predicate. This allows the advice to be weaved into any goal of the form $G\ \mathbin{\rotatebox[origin=c]{180}{\&}}\ checkpasswd$. Furthermore, the solution of G can potentially proceed in parallel to the reading and checking of the password[3].

In terms of usage, several existing linear logic programming languages, such as LO and LinLog, allow for clauses whose heads are multisets of atomic formulas. However, these languages lack the abstraction mechanisms described in Section 2. Forum can of course be used for these specifications, but is too general

---

[3] A subtle point here is the use of $pwX\multimap\bot$ (equivalently $pwX^{\perp}\,\mathbin{\rotatebox[origin=c]{180}{\&}}\,\bot$) instead of simply $pwX^{\perp}$ or using $checkpasswd\ \mathbin{\rotatebox[origin=c]{180}{\&}}\ pwX$ at the head of the clause. By hiding the atom pwX under a right-asynchronous connective, we cause proof search to "loose focus" on the atom, delaying its use until needed. Without this device, the *checkpasswd* clause cannot be applied before solving G.

to be interpreted efficiently. The simplified language Lolli also provides λProlog-style abstraction, and can be implemented effectively. However, clauses and goals must be rewritten with —○ and ! in place of $\otimes$ and ?. All but the last of our examples can be converted to Lolli. With Lolli, clauses and constructs pertaining to a common aspect can again be encapsulated with intuitionistic implication and quantification. The abstraction scheme for the separation of concerns can thus be merged with the weaving mechanisms of linear logic.

4   Future Work

Another approach to weaving logic program fragments is through meta program-ming. We can use a specification language that allows us to declare aspects and weaving relations in a more natural manner, such as:

> *aspect trace, param o.*
> *aspect check int → o.*
> *precedence trace check.*
> *precedence param trace.   etc ...*

A meta-program can be devised to check for circularity among the precedence declarations, then transform a given logic program by adding the required $\widehat{t_k}$ and $?\widehat{t_k}$ tokens. The meta-program can also automatically generate the independence clauses for unrelated aspects and goals (such as between *check* and *divisible* in Figure 4). The task of writing advice clauses would become more intuitive. Such a device also improves the ability to incorporate new aspects and advice while minimally altering existing code. Furthermore, as Miller has noted, linear logic programs behave like ordinary Prolog programs most of the time. We can envision extending ordinary Prolog in a minimal way, by adding the *"@"* operator alluded to in the introduction. Together with a specification such as above, a meta program can then compile a Prolog program into a linear logic program. Thus the mechanisms described here can also be used as a basis for adopting AOP to Prolog.

Acknowledgments

The author wishes to acknowledge Dale Miller for valuable advice and discussion.

References

1. Jean-Marc Andreoli. Logic programming with focusing proofs in linear logic. *Journal of Logic and Computation*, 2(3), 1992.
2. G. Bruns, R. Jagadeesan, A. Jeffrey, and J. Riely. muABC: A minimal aspect calculus. In *Fifteenth International Conference on Concurrency Theory (CONCUR 2004)*, LNCS vol. 3170, pages 209–224. Springer-Verlag, 2004.
3. Jean-Yves Girard. Linear logic. *Theoretical Computer Science*, 50:1–102, 1987.

4. James Harland, David J. Pym, and Michael Winikoff. Programming in lygon: An overview. In *AMAST*, pages 391–405, 1996.
5. Joshua Hodas and Dale Miller. Logic programming in a fragment of intuitionistic linear logic. *Information and Computation*, 110(2):327–365, 1994.
6. G. Kiczales, E. Hilsdale, J. Hugunin, M. Kersen, J. Palm, and W. G. Griswold. An overview of AspectJ. In *European Conference on Object-oriented Programming*, LNCS vol. 2072, pages 327–353. Springer-Verlag, 2001.
7. G. Kiczales, J. Lamping, A. Menhdekar, C. Maeda, C. Lopes, J. Loingties, and J. Irwin. Aspect-oriented programming. In *European Conference on Object-oriented Programming*, LNCS vol. 1241, pages 220–242. Springer-Verlag, 1997.
8. D. Miller. Lexical scoping as universal quantification. In *Sixth International Logic Programming Conference*, pages 268–283. MIT Press, June 1989.
9. D. Miller. Abstractions in logic programming. In Piergiorgio Odifreddi, editor, *Logic and Computer Science*, pages 329–359. Academic Press, 1990.
10. D. Miller. Forum: A multiple-conclusion specification language. *Theoretical Computer Science*, 165(1):201–232, 1996.
11. D. Miller, G. Nadathur, F. Pfenning, and A. Scedrov. Uniform proofs as a foundation for logic programming. *Annals of Pure and Applied Logic*, 51:125–157, 1991.
12. G. Nadathur and D. J. Mitchell. System description: Teyjus—a compiler and abstract machine based implementation of λProlog. In *Automated Deduction–CADE-16*, number 1632 in LNCS, pages 287–291. Springer-Verlag, 1999.
13. Hideaki Tatsuzawa, Hidehiko Masuhara, and Akinori Yonezawa. Aspectual Caml: An aspect-oriented functional language. In *10th ACM SIGLAN International Conference on Functional Programming*, 2005.
14. K. De Volder and T. D'Hondt. Aspect-oriented logic meta programming. In *2nd International Conference on Meta-Level Architectures and Reflection*, LNCS vol. 1616, pages 250–272. Springer-Verlag, 1999.
15. D. Walker, S. Zdancewic, and J. Ligatti. A theory of aspects. In *International Conference on Functional Programming*, pages 127–139, 2003.
16. M. Wand, G. Kiczales, and C. Dutchyn. A semantics for advice and dynamic join points in aspect-oriented programming. *ACM Transactions on Programming Languages and Systems*, 26(5):890–910, 2004.

Partial Evaluation of Pointcuts

Karl Klose[1], Klaus Ostermann[1], and Michael Leuschel[2]

[1] Darmstadt University of Technology, Germany
{klose,ostermann}@st.informatik.tu-darmstadt.de
[2] University of Düsseldorf, Germany
leuschel@cs.uni-duesseldorf.de

Abstract. In aspect-oriented programming, pointcuts are usually compiled by identifying a set of shadows — that is, places in the code whose execution is potentially relevant for a pointcut — and inserting dynamic checks at these places for those parts of the pointcut that cannot be evaluated statically. Today, the algorithms for shadow and check computation are specific for every pointcut designator. This makes it very tedious to extend the pointcut language.

We propose the use of declarative languages, together with associated analysis and specialisation tools, to implement powerful and extensible pointcut languages. More specifically, we propose to *synthesize* (rather than program manually) the shadow and dynamic check algorithms. With this approach, it becomes easier to implement powerful pointcut languages efficiently and to keep pointcut languages open for extension.

1 Introduction

Aspect-oriented programming (AOP) eases the modularization of crosscutting concerns in a single module called an *aspect*. *Pointcuts* are used to describe at which point in the execution an aspect affects the execution of the basic program. The points that can be selected by a pointcut are called *joinpoints*. Pointcuts can be thought of as defining a set of joinpoints and a pointcut is said to be *triggered* at a joinpoint, if the joinpoint is in that set. Pointcuts are often used to control the execution of *advice*. An advice is executed at every point in the execution which triggers the associated pointcut. Although this is currently the primary usage of pointcuts, they can be used for a wide range of purposes, such as reverse engineering [6], detection of application errors [14], or flexible instrumentation of applications [7].

The first pointcut languages such as those in early versions of AspectJ [10] were static in that pointcuts could be mapped directly to locations in the source code of the underlying program. Recently, there is a trend towards more dynamic pointcut languages which can quantify over dynamic information such as the callstack [20,17], dynamic argument values [8], the full execution trace of the application [1,16], the structure of the dynamic heap [16], or even the future of the execution [11]. Such complex dynamic pointcuts cannot easily be mapped to places in the source code.

M. Hanus (Ed.): PADL 2007, LNCS 4354, pp. 320–334, 2007.

The most common approach to implement dynamic pointcuts is to identify a set of pointcut *shadows* - places in the code, where the pointcut is *potentially* triggered - and to insert dynamic checks at these places. However, the algorithms for computing the set of shadows and computing the right dynamic checks are highly non-trivial. Worse yet, these algorithms are specific to the constructs of a particular pointcut language. Hence, if the pointcut language is to be extended, the algorithm has to be revisited and extended as well. This is not only very elaborate. It is also a major obstacle to keeping the pointcut language extensible. Extensible pointcut languages have been recognized as a way to make pointcuts more robust, precise, and high-level, to enable domain-specific libraries of pointcuts, and to put the pointcut language design into the hand of the programmers [8,4,16,5].

The contributions of this paper are as follows: We propose a *generic* approach to finding shadows and generating dynamic checks, where the algorithms for finding shadows and computing dynamic checks are synthesized from the pointcut specification rather than programmed manually. To this end, we propose the use of declarative languages, together with associated analysis and specialisation tools—in particular partial evaluation—to implement powerful and extensible pointcut languages. This is the first work to embed the shadow search and dynamic check generation problem into the framework of partial evaluation. Our measurements show that our approach scales to reasonably large programs and we describe different options to weave the remaining dynamic checks into the program.

The remainder of this paper is structured as follows: Sec. 2 gives an overview of our approach by means of small examples and describes the encoding of source code in Prolog and the design of the pointcut language. The use of partial evaluation and the approximation of runtime entities in our framework is explained in Sec. 3. Different possibilities to weave residual pointcuts into a program are described in Sec. 4. Sec. 5 discusses related work and Sec. 6 concludes.

2   Overview

In this section we give a quick overview of our approach without going into the details of the partial evaluation process itself. We limit our elaborations to pointcut queries over Java programs in this work, but other languages can be handled in a similar manner, with appropriate changes to the encoding of the program and the type system related predicates.

2.1   Prolog Representation of the Bytecode

Pointcut queries in our language are Prolog predicates. To enable these Prolog predicates to reason about the program's static structure and execution, these must be represented in the Prolog database.

We have built a converter which transforms Java bytecode into a Prolog representation of the bytecode. Fig. 2 illustrates how the converted example from Fig. 1 looks like.

```
1  package shapes;
2
3  interface Shape {
4    public void moveBy(int dx, int dy);
5  }
6  class Point implements Shape {
7    private int x, y;
8    public int getX() { return x; }
9    public int getY() { return y; }
10   public void setX(int x) { this.x = x; }
11   public void setY(int y) { this.y = y; }
12   public void moveBy(int dx, int dy) {
13     x += dx; y += dy;
14   }
15 }
16 class Line implements Shape {
17   private Point p1, p2;
18   public Point getP1() { return p1; }
19   public Point getP2() { return p2; }
20   public void moveBy(int dx, int dy) {
21     p1.setX(p1.getX()+dx);
22     p1.setY(p1.getY()+dy);
23     p2.setX(p2.getX()+dx);
24     p2.setY(p2.getY()+dy);
25   }
26 }
27 class GraphicApp {
28   public void test(Shape s, Line l,
29       int dx, int dy){
30     s.moveBy(dx,dy)
31     l.moveBy(dx,dy);
32     l.getP1().setX(42);
33   }
34 }
```

```
1  class('shapes',ref('shapes.Line'),
2    default,false,false,false,
3    ref('java.lang.Object')).
4  interfaces(ref('shapes.Line'),
5    ref('shapes.Shape')).
6  field(ref('shapes.Line'),'p1',
7    private,false,false,
8    false,false, false,
9    ref('shapes.Point')).
10 field(ref('shapes.Line'),'p2',
11   private,false,false,false,false,
12   false,ref('shapes.Point')).
13 method(6,ref('shapes.Line'),
14   'moveBy',public,false,
15   false,false,false,false,false,
16   [prim(int),prim(int)],void).
17 ...
18 def(6,2,21,ref('shapes.Point'),p4,
19   get(ref('shapes.Point'),'p1',
20   ref('shapes.Line'),thisValue)).
21 def(6,3,21,ref('shapes.Point'),p6,
22   get(ref('shapes.Point'),'p1',
23   ref('shapes.Line'),thisValue)).
24 def(6,4,21,prim(int),p7,
25   invokeFunc('getX',ref('shapes.Point'),
26   p6,[],[],prim(int))).
27 def(6,5,21,prim(int),p9,
28   add(p7,param(1))).
29 invokeProc(6,6,21,'setX',
30   ref('shapes.Point'),p4,
31   [prim(int)],[p9]).
32 ...
33 return(6,22,25).
```

Fig. 1. The shape example   **Fig. 2.** Prolog encoding

The Prolog representation contains the declarations and definitions of all classes in one database file. There a two kinds of facts in this database: information about classes, interfaces, methods and fields and their relationships and facts describing the bytecode instructions which form the body of the methods.

For each class there is a fact called **class**, which includes (in the order of appearance) the package and class name, the modifiers (**public**, **abstract**, etc.), the super class and the implemented interfaces. The class name is wrapped in a **ref** term to indicate that it denotes a reference type (in contrast to a primitive type) and can be used to access the methods defined in that class.

Methods are represented by **method** facts. Each method is identified by a unique number (as its first argument) and the name of its enclosing class. The remaining arguments are the method name, flags for the method modifiers, the return type and the list of argument types, in that order.

The remaining facts in the representation encode the different types of bytecode instructions: **get** and **put** for field access instructions, **returns**, and **invoke** for method returns and calls, respectively. Assignments to local variables (which are used to represent intermediate results) are encoded as **def** facts. A local variable declaration includes an initializing instruction, which may be either method calls which return a value (**invokeFunc**), reading field access (**get**) or object creation via **new**. Each bytecode instruction starts with a number identifying the method which contains the instruction and a number denoting the position of this instruction in the method body. The third argument identifies the line number in the source code[1].

2.2   Programming Model

Pointcut queries in our language can refer to the static structure of the program and a well-defined subset of the dynamic runtime properties. Based on this information, arbitrary calculations can be used to decide whether or not the pointcut matches the current state of execution (and thus decide whether an aspect is applicable or not).

The runtime information that can be used in pointcut queries is not limited to the current joinpoint (or event), but comprises the whole callstack. The callstack is represented as a list containing all calls to methods that are currently in execution, i.e. have not yet finished.

In order to describe the matched joinpoints, pointcuts need to refer to the context in which they are evaluated. This context comprises — in our model — the current callstack, the current lexical position and the program. This context information can be kept implicitly available, as it is the case in AspectJ's pointcut language, or given as parameters to the pointcut query. In our case, we decided to make the callstack and the lexical position explicit parameters of the pointcut queries, whereas the program is implicitly available as a global set of facts in the Prolog database.

We use the variable names **Stack** for callstacks and **Loc** for lexical positions. A location is a pair **loc(MethodNumber,InstrNumber)** which represents the method- and instruction number as given in the bytecode. A callstack is represented by a list of stack frames, where each but the top frame must be a method call, represented by terms using the functor **calls**. The current instruction is at the top of the stack.

The following listing gives an example callstack as it may look like when modifying the field x in the method **Point.setX**, which was called by **Line.moveBy**:

```
[set(loc(10,2), value(ref('shapes.Point'),ι2), x, 42),
 calls(loc(6,6), value(ref('shapes.Point'),ι2), setX, [value(prim(int),42)]),
 calls(loc(2,2), value(ref('shapes.Line'),ι1), moveBy, [value(prim(int),1),
 value(prim(int),1)]) ]
```

The location **loc(6,6)** in the call to **Point.setX** corresponds to source code line 21 (Figure 1) and to the bytecode instruction at line 29 in Figure 2.

The first parameter in each stack frame denotes the location of the corresponding instruction in the program - it is hence a pointer into the Prolog representation of the bytecode. Values are encoded as pairs which consists of a type and an address or primitive value like boolean or integer. The ι_n expressions are object references in the runtime environment. The representation of values is hidden from the pointcut programmer, however; the static type, dynamic type and the value (address for reference values like objects, otherwise the

---

[1] Please note that there can be multiple bytecode instructions for a line of sourcecode.

int, bool etc.) must instead be retrieved with the getter predicates stype(V,T), dtype(V,T) and value(V,A), respectively. The reason is that the static representation of values during specialisation is different from the representation of runtime values, and hiding the representation by means of getters is an easy way to hide details of the specialisation process from the pointcut programmer (as well as leading to cleaner code).

Depending on the weaving strategy, such callstacks may never be explicitly reified as physical data, but should mainly be seen as the data model upon which pointcuts are expressed.

2.3   The Pointcut Library

looseness 1So far, we have seen how pointcuts can be formulated using the representation of the bytecode and of the callstack directly. The real power of the approach lies in the fact that we can easily extend the pointcut language by means of Prolog predicates on top of the raw representation of the callstack and the byte code.

```
calls( Stack, Location, Receiver, MethodName, Arguments ) :-
  Stack = [calls( Location, Receiver, MethodName, Arguments ) | _ ].
% cflow/2: succeeds if the callstack contains a given event
cflow(Stack, Ev) :- member(Ev,Stack), !.
% cflowbelow/2: Like cflow/2, but excludes the current jointpoint(event)
cflowbelow([_|Cs], Ev) :- cflow(Cs, Ev).
% directSubtype/2: A is a direct subtype of B
directSubtype( A, B ) :- class(_, A, _, _, _, _, B) ; interfaces(A,B).
% subtype/2: transitive closure of directSubtype/2
subtype(A,B):-directSubtype(A,B) ; (directSubtype(A,C),subtype(C,B)).
% subtypeeq/2: reflexive closure of subtype/2
subtypeeq(A,B) :- A=B ; subtype(A,B).
% instanceof relations use subtype relation
instance_of(Val, Type) :- dtype(Val,T), subtypeeq(T,Type).
withinMethod( Location, MethID ) :- Location = loc(MethID,_),
  method(MethID,_,_,_,_,_,_,_,_,_),
  methodInvokation(Location,_,_,_,_,_,_).
```

Fig. 3. Excerpt from the pointcut library

The predicates which form the pointcut language are defined as Prolog predicates themselves, which use the Prolog encoding of the program. The implementation of these predicates defines the connection between the semantics of the pointcut language and that of the bytecode language. An excerpt is given in Fig. 3. For instance, in the definition of instance_of the subtype relation is used, which is directly extracted from the inheritance relation exposed by the bytecode representation. Similar to the corresponding AspectJ pointcut designators, the cflow predicate checks whether a particular entry can be found in the callstack; cflowbelow checks all but the first stack frame.

The pointcut library is the extension point of the pointcut language: new pointcut predicates can be introduced by defining them in the pointcut library in terms of existing predicates and the bytecode representation. Furthermore it can be of interest to add new descriptions of the program – for example, the complete trace of the application or profiling information – and to use these descriptions in the definition of new pointcut predicates, thus providing the programmer with access to the new model. If the added descriptions are static (e.g., representations of configuration files), the specialiser will automatically compile all references to the static data away. If the added descriptions are dynamic, a corresponding static approximation of the dynamic data has to be provided. We will discuss this point later.

2.4   Example Pointcuts

Fig. 4 shows an aspect in the language AspectJ for keeping a display showing graphical shapes up to date. The base program defining the shapes hierarchy is given in Fig. 1. The pointcut **change** in line 1 describes the points in the execution, where the display should be updated and the advice in line 8 specifies that a call to **display.update** should be executed *after* such a modification (specified by **change**).

```
1   pointcut change():
2   (call(void Point.setX(int))
3    || call(void Point.setY(int))
4    || call(void Shape+.moveBy(int, int)) )
5   && !cflowbelow(
6      call(void Shape+.moveBy(int, int)));
7
8   after() returning: change() {
9      display.update();
10  }
```

```
1   (calls(Stack,Loc,Target,setX,_),
2    stype(Target,'shapes.Point') );
3   (calls(Stack,Loc,Target,setY,_),
4    stype(Target,'shapes.Point') );
5   (calls(Stack,Loc,Target,moveBy,_),
6    instance_of(Target,'shapes.Shape') ),
7   \+ cflowbelow(Stack,calls(_,_,moveBy,_))
```

Fig. 4. Display updating in AspectJ   **Fig. 5.** Pointcut in Prolog

The first two conditions (Lines 2 and 3) of the pointcut select calls to a method called **setX** resp. **setY** of an object of static type **Point** with exactly one parameter of type **int**. The condition in line 4 selects calls to the **moveBy** method with two integer arguments defined in the type **Shape** or any of its subtypes. This is expressed by the + sign appended to **Shape**. These conditions are combined by || meaning **or**, which selects any point that satisfies one of these conditions.

The last condition excludes (this is expressed by the negation operator ! in front of the pointcut) any joinpoint which is *in the control flow* of a call to **Shape+.moveBy(int,int)** but not such a call itself. The control flow of a call (expressed by **cflow**) comprises all joinpoints which appear while executing this call, including the call joinpoint itself. The pointcut **cflowbelow** excludes this call joinpoint from the set, selecting only joinpoints below the **call** joinpoint in the control flow. This pointcut is combined with the other three by the && operator meaning *and* (or intersection). Fig. 5 shows how the same pointcut can be expressed in our pointcut language.

In order to illustrate the effect of specialisation, we will now consider a few pointcuts and the result of their specialisation, without talking yet about how the specialisation actually works.

- `calls(Stack,Loc,_,setX,_),withinMethod(Loc,MethID),method(MethID,_,_,public,_,_,_,_,_)`
  Shadows: (21,true), (23, true)
- `calls(Stack,Loc,R,moveBy,_), instance_of(R, 'shapes.Line')`
  Shadows: (30, dtype(R,T), subtypeeq(T,'shapes.Line')), (31 true)
- `calls(Stack,Loc,_, setX, _), cflow(Stack, calls(_,_,moveBy,_))`
  Shadows: (21, true), (23, true), (32, cflow(Stack,calls(_,_,moveBy,_)))

Fig. 6. Example pointcuts and their shadows and dynamic checks

Fig. 6 shows a few sample pointcuts and the result of specialising them with the example program from Fig. 1. Shadows are given as pairs (line number from Fig. 1[2], residual check).

The first pointcut selects all calls of a `setX` method within a public method. The relation between the method and the call is expressed in terms of the location (`Loc`) of the instruction and the identifier of the method (`MethID`). The predicate `withinMethod` binds `Loc` to all locations in the code which are lexically contained in the method identified by `MethID`.

The second pointcut (all calls of `moveBy` where the receiver object is an instance of class `Line` at runtime) illustrates how static type information is incorporated into the specialisation. At the first shadow, the static type of the receiver is `Shape`, hence a dynamic check is required whether the receiver is actually a `Line`. At the second shadow, however, the statically known receiver type is already `Line`, hence no dynamic check is necessary.

The third pointcut (all calls of a `setX` method in the control flow of a `moveBy` method) illustrates the effectiveness of the static approximation of the callstack during specialisation. Whereas the first shadow requires a dynamic check, the second (and third) shadow has no dynamic check because it is known statically that the `setX` calls in lines 21 and 23 are in the control flow of a `moveBy` call. We will see that the design of the static approximation of the callstack is an important parameter for the specialisation in computing residual pointcuts.

3   The Specialisation Framework

Our specialisation framework performs the task of computing shadows and the respective residual programs for pointcut queries. This is achieved by partially evaluating the pointcut query w.r.t. the static part of the input. This static part is given by the representation of the program, which determines the possible static contexts in which the pointcut may be evaluated. Specialisation is then

---

[2] In the actual implementation, the method/instruction indexes from the bytecode are used for this purpose.

performed by a partial evaluator for Prolog. The behavior of this tool is controlled by a description of the pointcut primitives and predicates in the pointcut library which marks certain parts of the pointcut program as *callable*, i.e. they can be (safely) evaluated at specialisation time.

In this section we present the partial evaluation of pointcut queries with respect to the program source.

3.1 The Specialiser

Program specialisation is a technique to specialise a given general purpose program for certain specific application area. Partial evaluation [9] is a well-established technique that obtains a specialised program by pre-computing parts of the original source program that only depend on some given part of the input (called the static data) and leaving a residual program that only contains the dynamic checks. The partial evaluation (or *specialiser*) tool used throughout this work is based on the core of the offline specialiser presented in [12] and is thus similar to the core of LOGEN [13][3]. To control the behavior of the specialiser, an annotated form of the program has to be provided. We use the following three annotations of those described in [12]: `call` evaluates the goal using the prolog interpreter, `rescall` leaves the goal in the residual program and `unfold` replaces the goal by the residual program obtained from specialising the (annotated) body of the predicate.

There are basically two alternatives to obtain the annotations for a clause: *online specialisers* generate the annotations on the fly while *offline specialisers* use annotations provided by the user or a generator.

Although being based on an offline specialiser, our system does not require the programmer to annotate most of her pointcuts manually, but we rather use a set of rules for the standard predicates of the pointcut library. These rules are used to perform the annotation automatically before specialisation. For predicates that do not have a corresponding rule in the database the `rescall` annotation is used by default. Only in the case where these annotations are not optimal from the programmer's view, should he annotate the program himself, for example, when introducing user-defined predicates.

3.2 Approximation of Runtime Entities

In the scenario of pointcut specialisation, only the static part of the program is available, i.e., the class, interface and field declarations and a set of bytecode instructions. However, our pointcut language allows to quantify over runtime conditions. The easiest way to handle runtime values like the actual types of values is to generate all possible instantiations and explore them by backtracking. Because this approach does not scale well for large programs, we use approximations of dynamic entities instead. We will now describe the approximation of the actual type of a value and the elements of the callstack and how they are used in the specialisation process.

---

[3] Albeit being an offline partial evaluator rather than a compiler generator.

The values of variables are not accessible at specialisation time. Nevertheless specialisation should be able to benefit from the *static information* about the variables that can be retrieved from the programs bytecode. We use an approach based on the idea to associate with each variable the set of all classes whose instances the variable can possibly hold. In the context of Java single inheritance, we can describe the set of all possible types of a variable by the most general (class) type of this set. To make this abstraction compatible with unification, we encode this most general type of the variable as an *open list* containing all its super classes[4]. In this form, two encodings can be unified if one is the prefix of the other list, which means that it encodes a super type of the other list.

For example, the list presentation of the class `shapes.Line` from our example is `['java.lang.Object','shapes.Line'|_]`. A class `shapes.Arrow` which is a subtype of `shapes.Line` would be encoded as `['java.lang.Object','shapes.Line','shapes.Arrow'|_]` and the unification of both would yield the latter list as required.

To associate the abstract type with the variable for the dynamic type and argument, type variables are bound to a term `value(AbsType,DynType,DynValue)`, where `AbsType` is the encoding of the possible types of this variable and `DynType` and `DynValue` denote the dynamic type and value and are variables in the specialisation phase. The predicate `abstractValue(V,Class)` is used to bind a variable `V` to an abstract value of type `Class`.

For the approximation of the callstack, we use the notion of *static events* for approximations of the real runtime events which have the same structure as dynamic events, but contain variables or approximations for the runtime information. Using the static event, we approximate the callstack at a given location by a list containing the static event as first element. Furthermore, the second element of the callstack must be a call to the method containing that location. For the example callstack in the last section we can thus give the following approximation:

```
[set(loc(10,5),value(['java.lang.Object','shapes.Point'|_],_,_),x,value([prim(int)],_,_)),
  calls(_,value(['java.lang.Object','shapes.Point'|_],_,_),setX,[value([prim(int)],_,_)]),
  _ ]
```

Better approximations that contain more elements or more precise type information can be generated by using the call and control flow graph of the program. As the construction of the application's callgraph can be very costly, it is desirable to be able to control the amount of approximation. In our framework this can easily be accomplished by modifying the predicate which produces the stack approximation.

3.3   Description of Pointcut Predicates

To take advantage from the approximation of runtime values and the callstack, we provide *descriptions* of the pointcut predicates defined in the pointcut library:

---

[4] The approximation of interfaces is simply a variable as they lack a common base interface.

a description of a pointcut library predicate does not only provide the necessary annotations for the partial evaluator, but also includes additional calls to handle the approximations of dynamic entities.

The following code listing shows the description of the `instance_of` and the `cflow` predicate:

```
instance_of(Var,Cls) :- abstractValue(Var,Cls),dtype(Var,DT),subtypeeq(DT,Cls).
                        _____/ _____/ _____/
                             call          call     rescall

cflow(S,Ev) :- S = [Ev|Cs], (\+ var(Ev), Ev = calls(L,R,M,A),calls(S,L,R,M,A),! ;cflow(Cs,Ev)).
               _____/    _____/  _____/ _____/    _____/
                  call          call            call              call             rescall
```

The first subgoal of `instance_of` is evaluated at specialisation time and checks if the variable can be unified with the abstract type of `Cls`; otherwise the instance check can be refuted at specialisation time. The second subgoal binds `DT` to the variable for the dynamic type of `Var` to be used in the subtype check which is left as residual program by the third subgoal.

The first clause of the `cflow` description checks (at specialisation), if the event `Ev` is at the top of the stack. In this case, no residual program is necessary. Otherwise, for example, if the head of the list is a variable, a call to the `cflow` predicate is left as residual program by the second clause.

3.4   Example Specialisations

After introducing the specialisation and approximation techniques, we demonstrate the specialisation process using example pointcuts. We use the program given in Fig. 1 in Sec. 2.

We will discuss three pointcuts (`pc1-pc3`), accessible via `pointcut/2` and the result of their specialisation. These examples show a statically determinable shadow, a pointcut leaving a residual type check and an example for the results of specialising the `cflow` predicate.

The first pointcut we want to discuss is `pc1 = calls(S,L,Rec,moveBy,_)`, selecting all method call joinpoints to a method called `moveBy`. The following two interpreter invocations show the access to the pointcut predicates and the result of specialisation:

```
3 ?- specialisePointcut(pc1,Result).
Result = pointcut([ [calls(loc(2, 2), _G394, moveBy, [prim(int), prim(int)]),
   calls(loc(_G608, _G609), _G604, test, _G606)|_G529],  loc(2, 2) ],  true )  ;
Result = pointcut([ [calls(loc(2, 3),
   value([ref('java.lang.Object'), ref('shapes.Line')|_G644], _G620, _G621),
   moveBy, [prim(int), prim(int)]), calls(loc(_G608, _G609), _G604, test, _G606)|_G529],
    loc(2, 3) ],  true )
```

The lengthy output is a result of the partial instantiation of the callstack parameter and the binding of values to type abstractions. The shadows location and the residual pointcut are marked with a frame in both results. Both residual pointcuts are `true`, meaning that there is no dynamic check required at the shadow. The locations (2,2) and (2,3) refer to lines 29 and 30 in Fig. 1, respectively.

In the next example we show the effect of constraining the set of possible types of a variable. In the pointcut pc2, only calls to a moveBy method are selected that go to an instance of 'shapes.Point' at runtime. Calculating the shadows gives

```
5 ?- pointcut(pc2,P).
P = pointcut([_G338, _G341], (calls(_G338, _G341, _G349, moveBy, _G351),
                          instance_of(_G349, 'shapes.Point')))
6 ?- shadows(pc2,S).
S = [ (loc(2, 2), subtypeeq(_G383, ref('shapes.Point')))]
```

The call at location (2,2) requires a runtime check (via subtypeeq) to determine, if the receiver is an instance of shapes.Point.

The location (2,3) is not a shadow of this modified pointcut, as the static type of the receiver is shapes.Line and its abstract type thus cannot be unified with the abstract type of shapes.Point used in the pointcut.

In our last example, calls to setX in the control flow of a call to the method test are selected.

```
7 ?- pointcut(pc3,P).
P = pointcut([_G335, _G338], (calls(_G335, _G338, _G346, setX, _G348),
                          cflow(_G335, calls(_G353, _G354, test, _G356)))) ;
8 ?- shadows(pc3,S).
S = [ (loc(2, 5), true),
  (loc(6, 6), cflow([calls(loc(_G427, _G428), _G423, moveBy, _G425)|_G420],
                calls(_G430, _G431, test, _G433))),
  (loc(6, 16), cflow([calls(loc(_G396, _G397), _G392, moveBy, _G394)|_G389],
                calls(_G399, _G400, test, _G402))) ]
```

The location (2,5) corresponds to line 31 of Fig. 1, (6,6) and (6,16) to line 21 and 22, respectively.

The specialisation of the three example pointcuts is quite fast (about 0.1 ms), which is no surprise given the size of the program. To demonstrate the feasibility of our approach for larger programs, we tested specialisation of pointcuts on a bytecode toolkit project called *BAT* with about 800 types (classes+interfaces) and a bytecode size of about 2,25 MB. We used some quite general pointcuts which return a large number of shadows to test the performance of our specialisation tool: callStringMethod matches each call to a method of the class java.lang.String, ctor matches all invocations of a constructor, ctorRec matches all invocations of a constructor inside another constructor, and ctorNotRec matches all invocations of a constructor *not* inside another constructor. Fig. 7 shows the results of specialising these pointcuts[5].

Pointcut	Shadows	Time
callStringMethod	6,655	0.30 sec
ctor	3,187	0.32 sec
ctorRec	1,313	0.55 sec
ctorNotRec	1,874	0.50 sec

Fig. 7. Specialisation runtime

---

[5] Tests performed with SWI-Prolog on a 2.8GHz Windows XP machine.

3.5 Language Extension

An important feature of our framework is the extensibility of the pointcut language. This is a necessary property to write aspects on an abstract level, as stated in [16]. Extensions to the language can be written by the programmer to adapt the language to a single program or implemented as domain-specific pointcut library to be used within a whole class of applications.

Extending the pointcut language requires the follow steps: 1) its implementation must be added to the pointcut library to make it available to predicates that call it at runtime, 2) the annotation of its body has to be provided as a rule for unfolding and 3) an unfold-annotation for the predicate has to be added to the annotation database, which is used by the rule generator.

As an example, we extend our pointcut language with a predicate to detect loops in the callstack. A loop is the re-occurence of a method call to the same method on the same object and with the same argument values. Below is the annotated implementation of this predicate.

```
loop_detect(S,L) :- calls(S,L,Rec,Method,Args), cflowbelow(S,calls(_,Rec,Method,Args)).
                    _____/  _____/
                              call                                unfold
```

To integrate this predicate, the predicate definition without the annotations has to be added to the pointcut library and the annotated form has to be stored into the annotation database (we omit the technical details for brevity).

4 Weaving Residual Programs

Hitherto we have only tackled the problems of finding shadows and computing efficient residual pointcut programs. However, this is only one part of the weaving process. What remains is to insert the residual pointcut checks into the bytecode. We identified the following possibilities to process the residual Prolog programs:

Under the assumption that a Prolog interpreter is part of the runtime environment, Java code can be inserted which calls this interpreter for the residual pointcut query, checks the solutions and possibly calls the advice. Although this approach is quite simple, the overhead of keeping a Prolog interpreter and the libraries available for the virtual machine may not be tolerable in practice. Still, there are many tools for embedding Prolog within Java (e.g., [3], [22]), so this is a definitely a feasible solution. In order to produce efficient Java code, there are in principle several possible avenues. A first approach is to produce code in a special subset of Prolog that can be efficiently translated to Java. For example, one could try and ensure that all the residual code is in a form similar to Mercury [18] which can be compiled into efficient imperative code. Another solution is to ensure that the specialized code is close to *abstract machine code* or assembly code. This can be achieved by threading the environment of the interpreter via definite clause grammars; see [21] for more details and a worked out case study.

Certain parts of the residual program, for example predicates that refer to entities which are present in the Java virtual machine, like the callstack, or argument values, could be treated in a special way. It is a promising idea to include a way to make this information *directly* accessible from the Java virtual machine. Calls to those predicates could then be translated directly into special bytecode instructions for an augmented virtual machine. The analysis of such techniques and their efficient implementation is part of ongoing research.

5   Related Work

Masuhara et al. have proposed a model where an aspect-oriented compiler is generated from a Scheme interpreter of the AO language using partial evaluation of Scheme programs [15]. Hence this work assumes that an interpreter for the whole base language is available. Also, the execution speed of a partially evaluated interpreter cannot keep up with today's optimizing compilers and virtual machines. Our work takes a different approach which does not require an interpreter for the language and with which programs can still be executed on optimizing virtual machines.

Ostermann, Mezini and Bockisch [16] present ALPHA, a prototype language with a very expressive logic-based pointcut language. ALPHA's pointcut language served as the base of our pointcut language. An implementation approach based on abstract interpretation of pointcut queries is presented, which aims primarily at the reduction of space usage. Our work goes beyond [16] in that we give a realistic approach to implement (a subset) of such an expressive pointcut language in the context of Java, a non-toy programming language.

Walker and Viggers [19] discuss *temporal pointcuts*, called *tracecuts*, to enrich the AspectJ [2] pointcut language with the ability to reason about former calls and their temporal relations. Moreover, data that has been passed as an argument can be accessed by the advice as it could be done via variable binding in our language. Although more information about the computation history is available, the expressiveness of the pointcut language is very limited in comparison to our approach.

In [1], Allan et al. discuss the extension of the AspectJ language to be able to express sequences of "classic" AspectJ pointcuts. The extended language allows a sequencing pattern of ordinary AspectJ pointcuts to be considered as a pointcut and to bind values to variables which are unified on later occurrence. The implementation of shadow computation and optimization remains hand-coded, which is the main difference to the approach we presented.

Goldsmith et al. [7] present *PARTIQLE*, a framework to automatize the instrumentation of source code to find static and dynamic pattern in programs. The language *PQTL* they introduce is basically a subset of SQL which operates on a database representing the program trace. In the database, each type of event is represented as a table, include timing information for each event. The relations between events are expressed using *JOIN*s and SQL logical connectives. The difference between PARTIQLE and our approach lies in the expressiveness and extensibility of the pointcut language: PQTL can recognize patterns formulated in a very limited and fixed language, whereas in our language arbitrary predicates over the callstack can be expressed and user-defined pointcuts can be added to the pointcut language.

Another work targeting at detection of statically or dynamically wrong behavior, is discussed in [14] by Martin et al. The PQL language has a Java-like syntax which allows to define named queries and to use them to build more complex and even recursive queries. PQL queries are composed of the primitives method call, field access, object creation and the end of the program as well as negation, matching another query and partial-order matching of events. Although the language can match context-sensitive patterns over the execution trace, the pattern language is fixed and is - in comparison to our language - limited in its expressiveness.

6   Conclusions

We have presented a generic and extensible framework for finding pointcut shadows in Java programs using logic programming together with associated analysis and specialisation tools.

The framework is extensible at different points: the joinpoint model can be extended by adding new events or modifying existing ones, new program models and pointcut predicates can be added to provide the programmer with a more domain specific language and the level of abstraction used in the approximation of the runtime behavior can be varied to switch between fast compile-test cycles and more accurate — but slower — compilation. Furthermore, as we have demonstrated, the performance of our framework scales reasonable with program size.

Acknowledgements. This work was partly supported by the feasiPLe project financed by the German Ministry of Education and Research (BMBF).

References

1. C. Allan, P. Avgustinov, A. S. Christensen, L. Hendren, S. Kuzins, J. Lhotak, O. Lhotak, O. de Moor, D. Sereni, G. Sittampalam, and J. Tibble. Adding trace matching with free variables to aspectj. In *Proceedings of OOPSLA 2005*, pages 345–364, New York, NY, USA, 2005. ACM Press.
2. AspectJ Home Page. http://www.eclipse.org/aspectj/.
3. M. Calejo. Interprolog: Towards a declarative embedding of logic programming in java. In *Proceedings of JELIA 2004*, pages 714–717, 2004.
4. S. Chiba and K. Nakagawa. Josh: an open aspectj-like language. In *Proceedings of AOSD 2004*, pages 102–111, New York, NY, USA, 2004. ACM Press.
5. M. Eichberg, M. Mezini, and K. Ostermann. Pointcuts as functional queries. In *Proceedings of APLAS 2004*. Springer LNCS, 2004.
6. M. Eichberg, M. Mezini, K. Ostermann, and T. Schäfer.   Xirc: A kernel for cross-artifact information engineering in software development environments. In B. Werner, editor, *Eleventh Working Conference on Reverse Engineering*, pages 182–191, Delft, Netherlands, November 2004. IEEE Computer Society.

7. S. Goldsmith, R. O'Callahan, and A. Aiken. Relational queries over program traces. In *Proceedings of OOPSLA 2005*, pages 385–402. ACM Press, 2005.
8. K. Gybels and J. Brichau. Arranging Language Features for More Robust Pattern-Based Crosscuts. In *AOSD 2003 Proceedings*, pages 60–69. ACM Press, 2003.
9. N. D. Jones, C. K. Gomard, and P. Sestoft. *Partial Evaluation and Automatic Program Generation*. Prentice Hall, 1993.
10. G. Kiczales, E. Hilsdale, J. Hugunin, M. Kersten, J. Palm, and W. G. Griswold. An overview of AspectJ. In *Proceedings of ECOOP 2001*, pages 327–353. Springer-Verlag, 2001.
11. K. Klose and K. Ostermann. Back to the future: Pointcuts as predicates over traces. In *Foundations of Aspect-Oriented Languages workshop (FOAL'05), Chicago, USA, 2005.*, 2005.
12. M. Leuschel, S. Craig, M. Bruynooghe, and W. Vanhoof. Specializing interpreters using offline partial deduction. In K.-K. L. Maurice Bruynooghe, editor, *Program Development in Computational Logic*. Springer Verlag, 2004.
13. M. Leuschel, J. Jørgensen, W. Vanhoof, and M. Bruynooghe. Offline specialisation in Prolog using a hand-written compiler generator. *Theory and Practice of Logic Programming*, 4(1):139–191, 2004.
14. M. Martin, B. Livshits, and M. S. Lam. Finding application errors and security flaws using PQL: a program query language. In *Proceedings of OOPSLA 2005*, pages 365–383, New York, NY, USA, 2005. ACM Press.
15. H. Masuhara, G. Kiczales, and C. Dutchyn. A compilation and optimization model for aspect-oriented programs. In *Proceedings of CC 2003*. Springer, 2003.
16. K. Ostermann, M. Mezini, and C. Bockisch. Expressive pointcuts for increased modularity. In *Proceedings of ECOOP 2005*. Springer LNCS, 2005.
17. D. Sereni and O. de Moor. Static analysis of aspects. In *Proceedings of AOSD'03*. ACM, 2003.
18. Z. Somogyi, F. Henderson, and T. Conway. The execution algorithm of Mercury: An efficient purely declarative logic programming language. *Journal of Logic Programming*, 29(1–3):17–64, 1996.
19. R. J. Walker and K. Viggers. Communication history patterns: Direct implementations of protocol specifications. Technical report, University of Calgary, 2004.
20. M. Wand, G. Kiczales, and C. Dutchyn. A semantics for advice and dynamic join points in aspect-oriented programming. *TOPLAS 2004*, 26(5):890–910, 2004.
21. Q. Wang, G. Gupta, and M. Leuschel. Towards provably correct code generation via Horn logical continuation semantics. In *Proceedings of PADL 2005*, pages 98–112, 2005.
22. Q. Zhou and P. Tarau. Garbage Collection Algorithms for Java-Based Prolog Engines. In *Proceedings of PADL 2003*, pages 304–320, New Orleans, USA, 2003. Springer, LNCS 2562.

Author Index

Printing: Mercedes-Druck, Berlin
Binding: Stein + Lehmann, Berlin

Lecture Notes in Computer Science

For information about Vols. 1–4271

please contact your bookseller or Springer